MW00824242

Syntax

Syntax: Basic Concepts and Applications provides a systematic introduction to core topics in syntax, focusing on how the basic concepts
apply in the analysis of sentences. Assuming no background in linguistic
analysis, the book gives students a working knowledge of syntactic analysis from a minimalist perspective. Step by step it explains the fundamentals of phrase structure, movement, and deletion. Well-placed exercises
throughout reinforce and extend the concepts and analyses presented in
the text, allowing readers to gain understanding of progressively complex
issues at a comfortable pace. Much of the data comes from English, but
crucial examples are also drawn from a range of other languages, including
Russian, Chinese, Japanese, French, Italian, Spanish, Irish, Welsh, and
Greek.

ROBERT FREIDIN is Professor of Linguistics in the Council of the
Humanities at Princeton University.

Syntax
Basic Concepts and Applications

ROBERT FREIDIN

Princeton University

CAMBRIDGE UNIVERSITY PRESS
Cambridge, New York, Melbourne, Madrid, Cape Town,
Singapore, São Paulo, Delhi, Mexico City

Cambridge University Press
The Edinburgh Building, Cambridge CB2 8RU, UK

Published in the United States of America by Cambridge University Press, New York

www.cambridge.org
Information on this title: www.cambridge.org/9780521605786

© Robert A. Freidin 2012

This publication is in copyright. Subject to statutory exception
and to the provisions of relevant collective licensing agreements,
no reproduction of any part may take place without the written
permission of Cambridge University Press.

First published 2012

Printed and bound in the United Kingdom by the MPG Books Group

A catalog record for this publication is available from the British Library

Library of Congress Cataloging in Publication data
Freidin, Robert.
    Syntax : basic concepts and applications / Robert Freidin.
        p.   cm.
    Includes bibliographical references and index.
    ISBN 978-0-521-84427-7 (hardback) – ISBN 978-0-521-60578-6 (pbk.)
    1. Grammar, Comparative and general–Syntax. 2. Generative grammar.   I. Title.
    P291.F746 2012
    415–dc23
    2011052725

ISBN 978-0-521-84427-7 Hardback
ISBN 978-0-521-60578-6 Paperback

Additional resources for this publication at www.cambridge.org/freidin

Cambridge University Press has no responsibility for the persistence or
accuracy of URLs for external or third-party internet websites referred to in
this publication, and does not guarantee that any content on such websites is,
or will remain, accurate or appropriate.

"There is nothing more deceptive than an obvious fact."
Sherlock Holmes in "The Boscombe Valley Mystery"

Contents

Preface

This book is an introduction to syntactic analysis that is concerned with basic concepts of sentence structure and how they apply in the analysis of sentences and their constituent parts. It covers the standard core phenomena: the internal structure of phrases headed by nouns, verbs, prepositions, adjectives, etc.; the structure of coordinate and subordinate clauses; word order variation across languages; displacement (movement) involving interrogative phrases (wh-movement), verbal heads (head movement), non-interrogative nominal phrases (NP-movement), and clauses; and ellipsis. In addition, a significant part of the discussion deals with the morphosyntactic topics of Case and agreement, and the lexical semantic topic of argument structure. These topics demonstrate the centrality of the lexicon for any theory of syntax. Thus one of the fundamental questions for syntactic analysis is how the lexicon interfaces with a syntactic computational system that constructs linguistic expressions out of individual lexical items. This book is based on the answer that emerged over fifteen years ago under the Minimalist Program. It involves a single minimal operation Merge that combines two syntactic objects into a single new syntactic object.

Much of the data comes from English, but crucial examples from a range of other languages are utilized, including French, Italian, Spanish, Portuguese, German, Greek, Norwegian, Russian, Japanese, Chinese, Irish, and Welsh. To a large extent these data are fortuitous, so it should be possible for the reader (and especially the instructor who is using this book) to provide additional evidence from a wide range of additional languages.

This text assumes no background in linguistic analysis. Ideally, a reader can start on page one of Chapter 1 and by reading through to the end of Chapter 9 acquire a working knowledge of syntactic analysis and the theory on which it is based. Each chapter contains about a dozen exercises (Chapters 6, 8, and 9 each contain over two dozen) that will reinforce and extend the analyses presented in the text. Most exercises are broken into a series of successive steps to guide the reader.

Chapter 1 begins with a nontechnical discussion of the computational complexity of English syntax, using the orthographic form *fish*, which is itself multiply ambiguous. It demonstrates how any multiple of this form yields a syntactically well-formed sentence, even though speakers of English can only process a maximum of seven naturally (excluding six). The discussion lays the groundwork for a system of analysis that distinguishes between overt and covert elements and also between phonetic and "semantic" representations – what is called Phonetic vs. Logical Form (PF vs. LF). Chapter 2 lays out a general framework for syntactic analysis that studies language as a form of human knowledge, part of human biology. From this biolinguistic perspective, knowledge of a language consists of a lexicon and a computational system that combines lexical items into linguistic expressions that have a pronunciation and an interpretation (sound and meaning). These two components form what is called a grammar. Such a grammar exists in the mind of the speaker and is therefore finite, but capable of infinite output. The grammar is thus internal and individual, what is called an I-language. From this perspective, I-language is the primary focus of inquiry, not the data we use to construct a formal model of a speaker's knowledge of language. The internalist perspective that underlies the concept of I-language leads to five fundamental questions about human language concerning its nature, acquisition, use, material basis, and evolution within the species. These questions are discussed in the latter part of the second chapter.

Chapter 3 begins the discussion of how the lexicon is crucially involved in determining syntactic analysis – specifically, the relation between the syntactic categories of lexical items and the notion of a phrasal constituent. It contrasts the top-down approach of phrase structure rules with the bottom-up approach developed in the mid 1960s (see Chomsky 1970) and which is finally replaced by Merge (a transformational operation) in the mid 1990s (see Chomsky 1995a). The first section of this chapter explicates the terminology for describing hierarchical structure. The following two sections discuss how displacement phenomena and coordinate constructions can be used diagnostically to identify phrasal constituents. Chapter 4 presents a theory of phrase structure based on Merge, which constitutes the one recursive structure-building operation of the computational system, and several constraints that limit its operation (including a No Tampering Condition, which enforces minimal computation). The first section lays the groundwork. The second section develops an analysis of the indefinite pronoun *one* to demonstrate binary constituent structure in NPs. This leads to a three-way distinction among constituents of a phrase that are functionally related to the head of that phrase (i.e. complement, adjunct, and specifier) and a constraint on the order of Merge as applied to these constituents. The last section of the chapter considers reasons for concluding that the phrase structure of coordinate structures might not be binary.

Chapter 5 presents a phrase structure analysis of clauses. It begins with the phrase structure of VP, developing the standard head-complement relations of subcategorization and selection. This leads naturally to a discussion of the linear order of a head and its complements, which varies across languages (the Head Parameter) and which provides an explanation for some of the Greenberg Universals (Greenberg 1966) concerning word order correlations that occur crosslinguistically. The remainder of this section applies the selection relation to account for some of the basic properties of English verbal morphology. The next section extends the selectional analysis to clausal complements, in which the CP/TP analysis of subordinate clauses follows as a natural consequence.

Chapter 6 is the first of three chapters that develop an extensive analysis of displacement phenomena. This chapter is devoted to displacement in which the "landing site" is generally a "subject" position (Spec-TP). The first section covers the fundamental concepts involved in such analyses, using inter-clausal subject raising as a paradigm case. This includes a version of what is called the copy theory of movement – i.e. the application of Merge that creates nontrivial chains. This also connects with a notion a Spell-Out, a point (or points) in a derivation where phonetic features are separated from semantic features onto distinct derivational paths. The second section discusses how displacement relates to interpretation. This is mediated via an analysis of argument functions vs. grammatical functions, what goes under the heading of θ-theory – essentially, the θ-Criterion of Chomsky 1981b. With respect to displacement, a NP only moves to a position that is not independently assigned its own argument function. However in the case of a subject position that is not assigned an independent argument function but nonetheless has to contain an overt expletive (hence semantically null) element, another principle, the EPP (Extended Projection Principle, Chomsky 1982), is required. The third section develops a theory of Case, which places further constraints on displacement involving Spec-TP. Such a theory crucially involves a notion of context in which Case is licensed (abstract Case). Case theory involves two basic principles: (1) the Case Filter, which requires that NP chains with phonetic content be licensed for Case, and (2) a Case Uniqueness Principle, which prohibits a NP chain from having multiple members that are independently licensed for Case. The final section of the chapter deals with the local nature of displacement/movement, demonstrating that a constraint on local movement is required in addition to constraints on argument structure and Case. This constraint, formulated as the Subjacency Condition, will play a role in the next three chapters, a central role in Chapter 8 and the last section of Chapter 9.

Chapter 7 continues the discussion of displacement by developing an analysis of head movement that is involved prominently in the syntax of interrogatives, both direct yes/no questions and direct wh-questions. The chapter begins with the analysis of direct yes/no questions in English as a way to extend the CP/TP analysis of clauses to root clauses. Direct yes/no questions in English implicate a movement from T-to-C. This is analyzed as a morphological operation required in order to avoid a violation of the No Free Affix Condition (Lasnik 1981), an analysis that receives some empirical support from corresponding constructions in Russian. However, Russian unlike English allows a main verb to raise to C. This raises the question of whether such movements are one-step (V-to-C) or two-step (V-to-T and T-to-C). A comparison of French, which provides evidence of an independent movement of V-to-T, with Russian demonstrates that Russian must have a one-step derivation, thus arguing against a Head Movement Constraint, which imposes a two-step derivation generally. The second section turns to an analysis of the auxiliary *do* in English, based on the assumption that main verbs are not inflected for finite tense in the lexicon and therefore a finite tense affix enters a derivation as an independent syntactic object that has to be connected to a stem during the course of a derivation (essentially the analysis of Chomsky 1957). The two options affecting this, Affix-hopping and *do*-Support, are both driven by the No Free Affix Condition. The last section looks briefly at VSO languages as illustrated by Welsh. The fact that in subordinate clauses the V can occur between an overt complementizer and a subject indicates that V is moving to some intermediate head position between C and T, suggesting a Split Inflection analysis along the lines of Pollock 1989.

The first section of Chapter 8 begins with the analysis of wh-questions in English, considering both direct and indirect question constructions. Unlike head movement in direct yes/no questions, wh-movement affects LF representation. The analysis of LF representations of wh-questions in English raises a question about the analysis of corresponding questions in a language like Chinese where no displacement (i.e. overt movement) of wh-phrases occurs. This section explores the assumption that the LF representations in English and Chinese are in fact the same (see Huang 1982). It develops an analysis in which the mismatch between PF and LF representations is handled solely in the PF component. Instead of post Spell-Out wh-movement, the section explores a form of chain reduction where tail of the chain remains at PF rather than the head. The section goes on to examine other cases of PF/LF mismatch in English involving pied piping and reconstruction. And finally, it generalizes the wh-movement analysis to relative clauses.

The second section addresses the locality of wh-movements, starting with the fact that an interrogative wh-phrase cannot be moved out of a relative clause. Such constructions can be characterized as syntactic islands – barriers to movement – in two ways: as a complex NP construction or as a wh-construction. In the example examined, the movement of the wh-interrogative violates the Subjacency Condition. Subjacency then imposes successive cyclic derivations on wh-movement as well as NP-movement. Spanish and Irish provide different sorts of empirical evidence that support this successive cyclic movement analysis. However, the successive cyclic analysis raises a problem for Subjacency with respect to some complex NP constructions, indicating that Subjacency formulated solely in terms of TP does not yield a complete theory of syntactic islands. Nonetheless, Subjacency can be parameterized in a way that accounts for variation across languages with respect to wh-islands – e.g. Italian. The final section considers some wh-movement phenomena that cannot be explained with Subjacency, the so-called complementizer-trace construction and superiority constructions where a wh-phrase that is lower in a structure is moved over one that is higher. The latter can be subsumed under the Minimal Link Condition (MLC, Chomsky 1995a), using the concept of "attract" rather than "move." The MLC analysis seems to unite Superiority and Subjacency, although empirical problems remain (e.g. exceptions to Superiority and the facts that motivated the parametric analysis of Subjacency).

Chapter 9 is concerned with the analysis of ellipsis phenomena, mostly in English. The chapter is based on the assumption that ellipsis results from a deletion operation that applies on the PF side of a derivation and that this operation is governed by some condition on recoverability. Recoverability results from a matching constraint between the ellipsis site and an antecedent in the sentence in which the ellipsis occurs. There is also a configurational property that determines whether the antecedent is in a proper structural relationship with the ellipsis site, which would allow the deletion. The first section deals with VP ellipsis, including antecedent contained deletion (ACD) constructions where the ellipsis site is apparently a constituent of its antecedent. To avoid the problems inherent in the ACD analysis, the matching property is formulated as phonetic nondistinctness. This formulation of the matching property generalizes to gapping, pseudogapping, and sluicing constructions. In the case of the latter two, chain reduction must apply before deletion. In sluicing constructions island violations via wh-movement appear to be "repaired" by the deletion. This does not occur with VP ellipsis. This repair phenomenon creates a puzzle about how, where, and when Subjacency is implemented by the computational system. It also suggests that ellipsis and chain reduction are distinct kinds of deletion.

Many issues and questions raised in these chapters are left open. This is first and foremost a book about syntactic analysis – that is, how the basic concepts of analysis apply to some of the core phenomena in a way that, hopefully, provides some significant insight into the nature of human language. It does not attempt to give definitive analyses, or respond to every question that arises; nor does it attempt to present the latest results from the frontiers of research. Unlike Freidin 1992, it is not an exercise in rationally reconstructing a theory of syntax from what might be considered the current perspective (then, some version of GB theory).

What then is left out? In terms of phenomena, there is no discussion of the syntax of existential constructions, very little about the analysis of double object constructions, nothing about small clauses, comparatives, or the syntax of clitics – all substantial topics to be sure. Perhaps the most glaring omission is binding theory, which had two full chapters in Freidin 1992. Examples of anaphora (bound and pronominal) are mentioned in Chapters 3 through 6, but aside from the c-command condition on bound anaphors discussed in note 2 of Chapter 3, there is no discussion of the major principles that govern the distribution and interpretation of bound anaphors, pronouns, and R-expressions. In this regard, note also that the discussion of VP ellipsis in Chapter 9 does not discuss the strict vs. sloppy reading conundrum that arises when the antecedent contains a pronoun. It seemed a better strategy for the purposes of this text to put aside the analysis of such complex and subtle issues of interpretation and thus leave open the question of how LF representations might have to be expanded and what additional technical machinery added to account for the interpretation of these constructions.

And although the book pursues a minimalist approach to basic concepts, certain technology that regularly appears in minimalist analyses won't be found in these pages: the strong/weak feature distinction or the interpretable/uninterpretable feature distinction, VP shells (including light v), the Linear Correspondence Axiom and remnant movement, Multiple Spell-Out and cyclic linearization, the operation Agree. The VP internal subject hypothesis is mentioned in reference to the analysis of VSO languages but not pursued, as is the Split Infl analysis. The operation Attract along with the concepts of probe and goal is mentioned once in Chapter 7 but not pursued. Attract makes another appearance at the end of Chapter 8 in reference to the Minimal Link Condition. The DP hypothesis is not discussed. It is not that I have definitive arguments against such technology and analyses; rather I found that they were unnecessary for the analyses being explicated. What I hope is that the analysis presented here can be easily extended to incorporate these proposals if needed. The book is intended as a foundation for discussion and building on – including swapping out some parts for others.

Nonetheless, the approach in this book is minimalist to the core. It assumes that the computational system for human language is optimal, in answer to the first minimalist question that Chomsky first posed in 1992. It rejects what turned out to be a false dichotomy between phrase structure rules and transformations by fully embracing Merge and thus rejecting D-structure and S-structure as levels of syntactic representation. It assumes a version of Full Interpretation, which leads to derivations involving Spell-Out, and it utilizes the No Tampering Condition, which in effect guarantees that derivations obey strict cyclicity. Moreover, it tries to account for the syntactic phenomena under analysis with as little machinery as possible. It also operates on the assumption that human language is a "perfect" system, in response to Chomsky's second minimalist question – to the extent that we can give substance to the adjective *perfect*. In this regard, it tries to adhere to the constraint imposed by the Inclusiveness Condition, not always successfully.

Like Freidin 1992, this book is concerned with formal grammatical analysis as a way of thinking about human language. The term "formal" is used here as a synonym for "explicit" and therefore could also be replaced by the term "generative" which is also used in the same way. In science, there is no viable alternative to being explicit about the analysis of phenomena and the claims being made on the basis of that analysis.

Acknowledgements

In writing this book, conversations with colleagues over the years have been invaluable. I am especially indebted to Len Babby, Noam Chomsky, Joshua Katz, Jay Keyser, Howard Lasnik, Jim McCloskey, Carlos Otero, Carlos Quicoli, Ian Roberts, Alain Rouveret, Larry Solan, Jon Sprouse, Chris Tancredi, Tarald Taraldsen, and Jean-Roger Vergnaud. I have profited from comments on various versions of the manuscript from Terje Lohndal, Carlos Otero, Carol Puckette, and Chris Tancredi. Thanks to my students at Princeton over the past several years for their comments and reactions to various parts and versions. For assistance with some of the foreign language examples I thank Len Babby, Jim Lavine, and Asya Pereltsvaig for Russian, David Willis and Wayne Harbert for Welsh, and Jim Huang for Chinese. I am indebted to Sarah Green and Andrew Winnard, my editors at Cambridge University Press, for their advice and assistance with this project and to their anonymous reviewer of the penultimate draft whose comments led to significant improvements. Thanks also to Jon Billam, whose copy-editing improved the quality of this book. And thank you, Barbie, for your constant support over the long haul.

1   The computational nature of human language

Whenever we hear (or see) a word or string of words of the language that we speak, our minds perform a special kind of computation on the expression, assigning it a syntactic structure that corresponds to a particular meaning. Consider the deceptively simple example of the orthographic form *fish*. We can use this orthographic form by itself to represent a sentence, defined at this preliminary point as a linguistic expression that begins with a capital letter and ends with a terminal punctuation mark (period, question mark, or exclamation point):

(1)   Fish!

(1) can be assigned more than one interpretation because *fish* can designate either a verb or a noun. Under both interpretations the expression has the same pronunciation (whose representation is called **Phonetic Form** (PF)). Syntactically, however, there are two distinct linguistic representations for (1), one as a verb and the other as a noun. These representations correlate with the different interpretations of (1). In this way, the syntax provides a structural basis for the representation of meaning. This aspect of meaning is called **Logical Form** (LF). Ambiguity arises when a single PF corresponds to more than one LF. In this case, (1) is **structurally ambiguous** because its ambiguity derives from a difference in syntactic structure – i.e. whether the PF of (1) is construed as a verb (labeled V) or a noun (labeled N).

Taking *fish* in (1) to be a verb, we understand the linguistic expression that (1) represents to be an **imperative** sentence, which expresses a command, consisting of an understood subject *you* (the second person pronoun) and a predicate (the imperative verb *fish*). The LF of this imperative sentence must therefore contain the covert – because unpronounced and unwritten – subject *you*, hence "you fish." In this way the LF representation differs significantly from its corresponding PF representation. LF representations may contain covert elements that play a role in interpretation, whereas PF representations never do.

This analysis of the imperative sentence gives us a second way to define a sentence. Following traditional grammar, a sentence is a linguistic expression that consists of a subject and a predicate. More precise definitions of the terms "subject" and "predicate" will be developed in subsequent chapters.

What about the LF of (1) when *fish* is interpreted as a noun? The answer is less straightforward because there are a number of different ways one might construe (1) where *fish* is interpreted as a noun. For example, (1) might be construed as a command "look at the fish over there!" or as a statement "there are fish over there."

The noun *fish* could be used to refer to biological entities in the real world or it could just as well be used to refer to the word *fish* written on a sign, or even to a graphic representation of a fish (anywhere between a photograph and a cartoon). In contrast to the construal of the verb *fish* in (1), the interpretation of (1) as a noun is somewhat indeterminate. Moreover, the orthographic representation of *fish* as a noun involves yet another ambiguity, a **lexical ambiguity**, where the noun *fish* represents both the singular form (one fish) and the plural form (more than one fish). The syntactic identity of the expression (as a noun) remains the same under both interpretations. Note the contrast with structural ambiguity as discussed above. The difference between the noun *fish* and the imperative verb *fish* constitutes a structural ambiguity because they involve different syntactic categories.

EXERCISE 1.1

It is in part because of this lexical ambiguity that the title of the famous book by Dr. Seuss *One fish, two fish, red fish, blue fish* is multiply ambiguous.

a. How many fish does Dr. Seuss intend with this title? (See the cover of the book.)
b. How could this title be used to designate one fish less than is on the cover?
c. Could it be used to designate one fish more?
e. What is the smallest number of fish this title could be used to describe?
f. There is another source of lexical ambiguity in the title involving the interpretation of the numbers. What is it?

Just as one *fish* yields a structurally ambiguous sentence, so do two *fish*.

(2)   Fish fish!

Given that *fish* could represent either a noun or a verb, (2) has potentially four distinct analyses. However, let's ignore for the time being the interpretations where both instances of *fish* are taken to be either nouns or verbs. The remaining two interpretations are structurally represented in (3a) and (3b), where the whole expression (2) is also designated as a **clause**, a structural unit containing a subject and, crucially, a predicate.[1]

(3)   a.   [$_\text{Clause}$ Fish-N fish-V]
       b.   [$_\text{Clause}$ Fish-V fish-N]

The syntactic representation (3a) corresponds to an emphatic statement (hence the exclamation point) that fish attempt to catch (other) fish, where the first instance of *fish*, a noun, is the subject and the second, a verb, is the predicate. The verb *fish* is used here intransitively in that it does not require an overt object. It is interpreted as **indicative** (making a statement) rather than imperative (giving a command). The syntactic representation (3b) corresponds to a command to make fish the object of the activity of fishing (e.g. not eels or other creatures that one might fish). The verb *fish* is used transitively here, taking an overt object, the noun *fish*. The LF representation of (3a) would be essentially identical to (3a), whereas the LF of (3b) would contain the subject 'you' as given in (4).

(4)   [$_{Clause}$ [$_N$ *you*] [$_{Predicate}$ Fish-V fish-N]]

Furthermore, the phrase *fish fish* constitutes a predicate, as identified in (4). Since the pronoun *you* does not occur in the PF representation of this sentence, it is covert (identified here with italics in the syntactic representation).

Following traditional grammatical analysis, the verb and its object constitute a structural unit, the predicate, which excludes the subject of the clause. Thus in the syntactic representation of clauses, the subject is external to the predicate. Note too that the LF of (3b) given in (4) must also distinguish the verb as imperative as opposed to indicative because otherwise it won't properly distinguish the command from the statement *you fish fish*, where the subject *you* is overt rather than covert. Since the PF representations of the two verb forms are identical, they are distinguished in terms of covert syntactic and/or semantic features, which account for the LF distinction between a command and a statement.

Although English does not phonetically distinguish the imperative form of the verb from other indicative forms (e.g. **Read the book!** vs. **They *read* many books** – *read* in the present tense), some languages do (e.g. German, with strong verbs in the singular familiar form, **Lies das Buch!** vs. **Du das Buch *liest*** 'you read the book'). The imperative form *lies* uniquely designates the imperative familiar singular form. The distinction in English is therefore covert – necessary for LF representation, but not expressed in PF.

Given that the verb *fish* can be transitive – i.e., occur with an object, there is at least one sentence of English composed of three *fish*.

(5)   Fish fish fish.

The straightforward interpretation of (5) is as a statement with an overt subject *fish* and a predicate consisting of a verb *fish* followed by an object *fish*, a predicate with the same structure as the predicate in (4), but with an indicative verb not an imperative. The interpretation corresponds to the structure (6), which is essentially the structure of (3b), except that the covert subject *you* of the command is replaced by the overt noun *fish*, and the two verb forms differ semantically (indicative vs. imperative).

(6)   [$_{Clause}$ [$_{Subject}$ fish$_a$] [$_{Predicate}$ [$_V$ fish, +indicative] [$_{Object}$ fish$_b$]]]

(6) gives us the structure of a simple sentence – simple in that it contains a single subject and a single predicate, thus a single clause.

The interpretation of (5) requires that the group of fish designated by the subject must be disjoint (i.e. have no member in common) from the group of fish designated by the object. (5) cannot be interpreted as 'fish fish themselves' or 'fish fish each other.' That is, the set of hunter fish identified as *fish$_a$* does not contain any members of the set of prey fish identified as *fish$_b$*. Thus the two sets are disjoint, not just nonequivalent. This interpretation is represented by assigning different indices to the two occurrences of the noun *fish* in LF under the assumption that a ≠ b and further that the set designated by the index a is disjoint from the set designated by the index b.

With four *fish*, as in (7), the syntactic structure takes on a new dimension of complexity.

(7)   Fish fish fish fish.

In fact, the first impression of many English speakers to (7) is that it is gibberish, not a sentence of English. One problem is that if you try to interpret (7) as a simple sentence, you will wind up with an extra *fish* that doesn't fit – unless you resort to the vocative interpretation where the last (or first) *fish* is interpreted as the addressee, in which case (7) is simply (5) with a vocative instance of *fish* appended to the beginning or end of the sentence. Let us set such interpretations aside.

If (7) constitutes a viable English sentence with normal clause structure, then the string of four *fish* must divide into a subject and a predicate. The main verb of that clause can be either transitive or intransitive. If it's intransitive, then the predicate of the clause consists of a single verb *fish* and the string containing the other three instances of *fish* must be interpretable as the subject of the clause. As the subject, one of the three instances of *fish* must be a noun and furthermore, all three instances cannot be nouns. Therefore, the subject phrase must contain at least one instance of a noun and one of a verb. The presence of a verb in the subject phrase indicates a predicate of some kind, in this case one that contains at least a finite indicative verb. Moreover, the predicate embedded as a subpart of the subject phrase of the main clause must bear some relation to the noun *fish* that constitutes the principal part of the subject. Normally, such predicates do not modify nouns; however, a clause can modify a noun – what is called a **relative clause**, as in the nominal expression *the fish that you caught*, where the relative clause appears in italics. If in the subject phrase *fish fish fish* a noun *fish* is modified by a clause, then of the remaining two instances of *fish,* one must be a verb (for reasons discussed above) and the other must be another noun.

To see how this works, let's eliminate the repetitions of *fish* in (7), as in (8).

(8)   Fish sharks chase flee.

In (8), *sharks chase* constitutes a relative clause modifying the noun *fish*. The phrase *fish sharks chase* constitutes the subject of the clause (8). In terms of nouns and verbs, (8) consists of N + N + V + V. Substituting the noun *fish* for the noun *sharks* and the verb *fish* for the verbs *chase* and *flee*, we come back to (7). So if (8) is a viable English sentence, then so is (7) where the first two instances of *fish* are interpreted as Ns and the latter two instances are interpreted as Vs.

The structural analysis for the subject phrase (8) at PF is given in (9).

(9)   [Subject fish-N [Clause [Subject sharks-N] [Predicate chase-V]]]

The relative clause *sharks chase* is embedded as a part of the larger nominal phrase *fish sharks chase*, where the relative clause modifies the noun *fish*. However, (9) does not properly represent the interpretation of the relative clause that modifies the noun (i.e. the LF of the clause) because the representation (9) does not explicitly capture the relation between the relative clause and the noun it modifies.

The interpretation of the relative clause must obviously involve in some way the noun that it modifies. Notice also that the verb of the relative clause, *chase*, is only a transitive verb – that is, it must be construed as having an object. The expression *sharks chase*, where the verb appears to be intransitive, does not constitute a viable English sentence in its own right. In fact, the interpretation of the relative clause in (8) corresponds to the simple sentence (10).

(10)   Sharks chase fish.

Thus the noun *fish* in (9) is also interpreted as the object of the verb *chase* in the relative clause. This object of *chase* constitutes another instance of a covert element that must occur in LF to satisfy the requirements of semantic interpretation. Because it is not pronounced, it is therefore absent from PF.

Furthermore, the two instances of *fish* in LF that correspond to (9) must be interpreted as referring to the same set of fish. This is indicated by assigning them the same index. Thus the LF of the subject phrase in (8) will be (11).

(11)   [$_{Subject}$ [$_N$ fish$_a$] [$_{Clause}$ [$_{Subject}$ sharks] [$_{Predicate}$ chase [$_{Object}$ *fish$_a$*]]]

The LF of (8) will thus be (12).

(12)   [$_{Clause}$ [$_{Subject}$ fish$_a$ [$_{Clause}$ [$_{Subject}$ sharks] [$_{Predicate}$ chase [$_{Object}$ *fish$_a$*]]]][$_{Predicate}$ flee]]

To convert (12) into the LF for (7) simply substitute the N *fish* for the N *sharks* and the V *fish* for the Vs *chase* and *flee*.

The relative clause under consideration here lacks a relative pronoun (e.g. *who* or *which*), which can occur in a relative clause. Thus alongside expressions like (9), we also have (13a), which contains the relative pronoun *which*, or (13b), which contains a relative particle *that* (see Chapter 5 for analysis and discussion).

(13)   a.   fish which sharks chase
            b.   fish that sharks chase

Thus the relative clause that lacks both the relative pronoun and *that* can be distinguished as a **reduced relative clause**, the phrase *sharks chase* in (8).

EXERCISE 1.2

A reduced relative clause consisting of an overt noun *fish* and an overt verb *fish* has a single interpretation. In contrast, a non-reduced relative clause consisting of the same two overt lexical items is in fact ambiguous. It has two distinct interpretations and hence two distinct LF representations. Consider the following example.

   (i) Squid which fish fish flee.

a.   Give an unambiguous paraphrase for each of the two interpretations.
b.   Match these two interpretations to distinct syntactic representations that capture the difference in interpretation.
c.   Identify what aspect of the syntactic representations captures the difference in interpretation.

The reduced relative clause in (8) identifies a subset of the set of all fish – i.e. those that sharks chase, as opposed to those that sharks do not chase. It restricts the interpretation of the noun it modifies and is therefore a **restrictive** relative clause. All reduced relative clauses are restrictive. So are all relative clauses that begin with the particle *that*. The relative clause in (13a) has a restrictive interpretation but it also has a **nonrestrictive** interpretation under which all fish are chased by sharks. The nonrestrictive interpretation of the relative clause in (13a) can be distinguished orthographically, using commas as in (14).

(14)   Fish, which sharks chase, flee.

The same ambiguity occurs with *who*, as illustrated in (15).

(15)   Martians who live in glass houses are sunburned.

On the nonrestrictive reading, all Martians live in glass houses and all Martians are also sunburned; whereas the restrictive reading only asserts that those Martians (not all) living in glass houses are sunburned and entails that there are other Martians who do not live in glass houses.

In (13a) the relative pronoun *which* is interpreted as the object of the verb *chase*. In (16), *which* is interpreted as the subject of *chase*.

(16)   fish which chase sharks

The relative clause with the overt relative pronoun in (16) can be interpreted as either restrictive or nonrestrictive in the same way that (13a) has a dual interpretation. The corresponding form of relative clause (17) with *that* instead of the relative pronoun has only the restrictive interpretation.

(17)   fish that chase sharks

Note further that when the noun modified by a relative clause is interpretively linked to the subject position of that clause, the reduced relative clause option is not viable (for standard English, but cf. Example (1a) in the following chapter), as illustrated by the deviance of (18).

(18)   a.   *[NP fish chase sharks] flee
          b.   *Fred admires [NP fish chase sharks]

Thus a reduced relative clause can never have a verb as its first overt element. This has important consequences for the analysis of the *fish* examples.

EXERCISE 1.3

The 4-*fish* example is ambiguous (minus the terminal punctuation). The interpretation under which it constitutes an indicative clause requires that the verb of the main clause be intransitive. However, if the verb of the main clause is construed as transitive, then it must occur with an overt object phrase.

a. Under this interpretation why can't the sentence also be construed as indicative?

b. What is the syntactic representation of this alternative interpretation of the 4-*fish* example?
c. What kind of ambiguity is involved?

Remember that there are actually two representations to consider: the PF and the LF, which will be different.

Purely in terms of syntactic structure, a sentence containing a relative clause is itself a clause and thus a clause that contains another instance of a clause embedded within it. This kind of embedding gives us **recursive** structures. Recursion in syntactic structure is perhaps the fundamental property of human languages (see Hauser, Chomsky, and Fitch (2002)). In the syntax of human languages we find over and over again instances of syntactic constructions that contain other instances of the same construction as a constituent subpart.

EXERCISE 1.4

Consider for example the following sentence.

(i) They gave no credence to the appraisal of that painting by Klee.

It contains a prepositional phrase (PP) *to the appraisal of that painting by Klee*, which consists of a preposition *to* and its object, the noun phrase (NP) *the appraisal of that painting by Klee*. The object itself contains two PPs, thus there is recursion of PP.

a. Identify the two PPs and show how the recursive embedding works.

Notice that this structure also involves recursion of NP structures.

b. Identify them and show how this works.
c. Note that the NP can be interpreted in two ways. Discuss how this might be related to the syntactic structure of the NP.

Given that a phrase containing three instances of *fish* can be interpreted as a noun modified by a reduced relative clause, and that a phrase containing four instances of *fish* can be analyzed as an indicative clause whose subject contains a relative clause, the analysis of five instances of *fish* becomes almost trivial. The fifth instance of *fish* can be interpreted as the object of the main clause verb, now construing the verb of the main clause as transitive rather than intransitive. Thus the syntactic structure of five *fish* will be as in (19), where Cl = clause and Pred = predicate.

(19) $[_{Cl} [_{Subject}$ fish-N $[_{Cl}$ fish-N $[_{Pred}$ fish-V $]]] [_{Pred}$ fish-V fish-N$]]$

Note however that this is the syntactic structure for the PF representation where only the overt elements of the sentence are expressed. The LF representation requires an additional instance of *fish* to indicate how the noun modified by the relative clause is related to that clause, as in (20).

(20) $[_{Cl} [_{Subject}$ fish-N_a $[_{Cl}$ fish-N_b $[_{Pred}$ fish-V *fish*-N_a]]] $[_{Pred}$ fish-V fish-N_c]]

The second occurrence of *fish*$_a$ is a covert copy of the first occurrence that accounts for the interpretation of the relative clause. The indices *a*, *b*, and *c* distinguish disjoint groups of fish, as discussed above in reference to the interpretation of (5).

The example just analyzed involves a relative clause that modifies the object noun. Since the subject noun may also be modified by a relative clause, the sentence (21) is structurally ambiguous.

(21)   Fish fish fish fish fish.

EXERCISE 1.5

a. Construct the relevant structural descriptions of the PF and LF representations for this second interpretation.

Now examine the following two illustrations (courtesy of Tudor Dimofte '04).

(a)

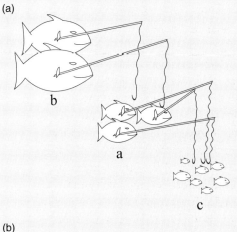

(b)

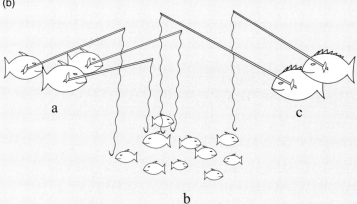

Each drawing depicts the interpretation of one analysis of the 5-*fish* example.

b. Identify which drawing goes with which analysis and explain how this works.

Consider the following phrase (i) where the first instance of *fish* is a noun and what follows is a relative clause modifying that noun.

   (i) fish that fish fish

(i) has two possible interpretations depending on whether the second instance of *fish* is interpreted as a N or a V.

c. Give the two distinct LF representations that correspond to (i).

These LF representations pick out different groups of fish.

d. For the second figure, match each group of fish to the LF that identifies it.
e. There is one group of fish in the first figure that is not identified by either LF representation. Explain.

In this case the resulting structural ambiguity is basically an artifact of the graphic representation of the sentence because the intonational contour assigned to the structure with the relative clause as part of the subject will be distinct from the intonational contour of the sentence where the relative clause is part of the object of the verb.

LF representations are never ambiguous (i.e. can be interpreted in more than one way), a standard assumption in linguistics. Whether a single PF representation can be ambiguous (i.e. mapped onto two distinct LF representations) depends on what information is contained in such representations. Consider again for example the analysis of the linguistic expression containing just one instance of *fish*. If lexical categories (e.g. noun and verb) are part of the PF representation, then there will be no ambiguity at PF. If not, then unless the two PF representations are distinguished by some feature beyond their phonetic parts (e.g. intonation), there will only be a single PF representation that maps onto two distinct LF representations. However, with larger linguistic expressions containing many words, differences in intonational contour can in some instances suffice to distinguish between PF representations, as the five *fish* example demonstrates.[2]

Given that either the subject *fish* or the object *fish* may be modified by a reduced relative clause, it is also possible that both could be so modified, giving a grammatical and in this case apparently unambiguous (but see the discussion below) sentence of 7 *fish*.

(22)   Fish fish fish fish fish fish fish.

In (22) the first two *fish* are nouns, the next two are verbs, the following two are nouns and the last is a verb. It will be easier to process this construction if the nouns and verbs used have distinct PFs, as in (23).

(23)   Professors students admire praise students professors admire.

Nonetheless, (23) still involves considerable computational complexity. In addition to the complex computation involved in organizing the string of nouns and verbs into constituent groupings, there are also the computations that relate the two relative clauses to the noun each modifies, computations which involve covert elements. Furthermore, given that the sentence contains two instances of the lexical item *professors* and the two instances of *students*, the issue of coreference also arises. Can the two instances of *professors* be construed as designating a single group of professors, or must each be construed as designating a different (i.e. disjoint) group? The same question arises for the two instances of *students*. The disjoint interpretations, which are always available, are easier to get.

EXERCISE 1.6

a. For (23) identify the two relative clauses and the noun each modifies.
b. What would the main clause be if the two relative clauses were eliminated?
c. Identify the verb of the main clause, its object, and the subject of the clause.
d. Specify the LF representation of (23).
e. Compare this representation to the LF representation of (22).

Returning to our *fish* sentences, you may be wondering whether six *fish* yields a grammatical sentence of English given that five *fish* and seven *fish* do. At first it may seem obvious that it doesn't because a grammatical sentence of six instances of *fish* cannot be obtained by adding either the noun *fish* or the verb *fish* to the beginning or end of the two possible analyses of five *fish*. The extra *fish* just doesn't fit with those structures. Nor is it possible to take the structure for seven *fish* and drop one instance of *fish*.

EXERCISE 1.7

a. Give the structural representation for the 7-*fish* example.
b. Now discuss why is it not possible to turn this structure into a representation for 6-*fish* simply by dropping one of the overt instances of *fish*.

However there is a way to analyze six *fish* that appears to accord with the grammatical processes of English – although the result is a structure that speakers normally cannot process.

To see how this works, let's start with a different set of sentences that will avoid the perceptual difficulties that result from using a noun and verb that have the same PF representation and interpretive complexity that results from using the same noun several times in a single sentence. Consider the following scenario. A boy is walking a dog. The dog bites a girl, who then curses the boy – at which point the boy flees. This can be described in the following three sentences.

(24)   a. The dog bit the girl.
        b. The girl cursed the boy.
        c. The boy fled.

The three independent sentences can be converted into a single compound sentence by conjoining them with *and*: a *and* b *and* c. (24a) and (24b) can also combine by turning one into a relative clause that modifies the noun both contain, as in (25).

(25)   The girl who the dog bit cursed the boy.

The relative pronoun *who* is optional in this context, so the reduced relative clause in (26) is also possible.

(26)   The girl the dog bit cursed the boy.

In both (25) and (26) the relative clause is a clause structure that has been embedded inside another clause structure. Since there is phonetic material on either side of the embedded relative clause it can be called **center embedded** in these structures.

In both (25) and (26) the clause in (24a) is subordinated as a relative clause within the clause in (24b). Thus relative clauses constitute one form of grammatical subordination where one clause is subordinated with respect to another by being embedded as part of a superordinate (or matrix) clause.

EXERCISE 1.8

Note that there is another way in which two clauses can be combined so that subordinate clause in (25–26) becomes the matrix clause. This yields two variants rather than three (i.e. excluding the reduced relative clause).

a. Give the two sentences that result.
b. What is the structural difference between the relative clause constructions in (25–26) and your answer to (a) above?

Subordination can also apply with the pair (24b and 24c). The sentence that results is unexceptional and easy to understand.

EXERCISE 1.9

a. Give the sentence that results from combining the clauses (24b) and (24c) to create a reduced relative clause.
b. How can (24b) and (24c) be combined to produce a relative clause configuration that doesn't allow a reduced relative clause construction?
c. Discuss whether this construction can be construed in the same way as the coordination of (24a–c) in that order.

Yet if the relative clause formation process applies to (25) and (24c), the result is virtually impossible to process in a natural way.

(27)   The boy (who) the girl (who) the dog bit cursed fled.

EXERCISE 1.10

a. Give the syntactic structure for (27) omitting the relative pronouns *who*.

On the simplest account, (27) conforms to the grammatical processes of English, which allow a clause to be embedded in a nominal phrase as a modifier of a noun. Therefore, sentences like (27) can be designated as **grammatical** even though native speakers of English will find them **unacceptable**. What seems to be at issue is a limitation on the kind of linguistic structures humans can process naturally.

This distinction between grammatical (i.e. conforms to the grammatical processes of the language and therefore is structurally well-formed) and acceptable (i.e. is recognized by a speaker as a viable sentence of her language) is worth keeping in mind. As the multiply center embedded examples suggest, just because a speaker finds a linguistic expression to be unacceptable, does not guarantee that it must therefore be ungrammatical in the technical sense. An example can be designated ungrammatical only if it can be established that it violates some process or principle of grammatical structure. That is, a grammatical analysis is required to support the claim that the example is in fact ungrammatical. A speaker's intuition of unacceptability by itself does not establish that the linguistic expression under consideration is unacceptable because it is ungrammatical. Linguistic expressions that are ungrammatical are usually considered unacceptable, for example *John thinks that himself is clever*. Following standard practice, ungrammatical examples are preceded by an asterisk. In general, a reflexive pronoun like *himself* cannot occur as the subject of a finite clause – even though the interpretation would be clear and unambiguous (compared to the ambiguous grammatical counterpart where a personal pronoun *he* replaces the reflexive pronoun). For further discussion of the grammatical vs. acceptable distinction see Chomsky (1965, Chapter 1).

This can't be a matter of the number of times the relative clause formation process occurs within a single nominal expression, because of sentences like (28) where relative clauses may be embedded one inside another indefinitely.

(28)   This is the cat who ate the rat who ate the cheese that Mary made in the
            kitchen that Jack built.

(27) differs structurally from (28) in that (27) but not (28) involves multiple center embedding. The relative clause *(who) the dog bit* is center-embedded inside the relative clause *(who) the girl cursed* and that relative is center-embedded inside the clause *the boy fled*. Thus multiple center-embedded constructions like (27) are unusable parts of English that the grammatical processes of English would appear to allow.

Getting from (27) to the 6-*fish* example is easy. Notice that the last three words in (27) are all verbs. They can be replaced with the verb *fish*. (27) begins with *the boy*, *the girl*, and *the dog*, all nominal phrases containing a determiner *the* followed by a noun. If these singular nouns are converted into plurals, the determiner is no longer required, yielding the sentence (29).

(29)   Boys girls dogs bite curse flee.

(29) has the pattern N + N + N + V + V + V. Having replaced all the verbs with the verb *fish*, we can now replace all the nouns with the noun *fish*, yielding the 6-*fish* sentence.

You may have noticed that the nouns and verbs are paired as given in (30), using numerical indices.

(30) $N_1 + N_2 + N_3 + V_3 + V_2 + V_1$

Thus N_3 and V_3 form a clause, a relative clause modifying N_2, and in turn N_2 plus the relative clause that modifies it and V_2 form a relative clause that modifies N_1. And finally N_1 plus the relative clause that modifies it and V_1 form the main clause. N_3 in (30) is not modified by a relative clause, but it could be. This would yield another N + V structure embedded between the adjacent N and V – in this case N_4 + V_4. Thus every subsequent embedding of a relative clause will yield an adjacent pair N + V. The number of overt Ns will always match the number of overt Vs.

EXERCISE 1.11

a. Give the PF and LF analysis of a 6-*fish* construction in the indicative.
b. What is the other way that the 6-*fish* example can be constructed?

With this analysis, any sentence containing an even number of *fish* from four onwards will have at least one grammatical representation. Is that true for sentences containing an odd number of *fish* from nine onwards? If so, then any number of tokens of *fish* will correspond to at least one structure produced by the rules of English grammar. The answer turns out to be yes. To see why, consider the main clause verb for the 6-*fish* example. It is intransitive just like *flee* in (29), hence lacking an overt object. But because the verb *fish* can be used transitively as well, thereby taking an object, the 6-*fish* example can be transformed into a sentence containing seven *fish* simply by adding a noun object *fish* to the main clause predicate phrase. As this procedure can be applied to any sentence with an even number (n) of *fish*, there will be a corresponding sentence with an odd number (n+1) of *fish* (see for example the 7-*fish* construction (22)). Hence any number of *fish* will correspond to a sentence of English.

These *fish* examples illustrate how human language allows us to construct and process some rather complex structures using just one noun and one verb. We've added some drama by choosing a noun and verb that have the same spelling and pronunciation, which creates an opportunity to confuse the two. However, every English speaker can understand naturally the possible interpretations for one, two, three, four, five, or seven *fish*. Moreover, this understanding requires some nontrivial mental computation to assign an interpretation (via a structural description) to a given string of words. This computation involves both overt elements, the words of the sentence that we see or hear, and covert elements that are required for the specification of the meaning, but are not physically present. The precise computations involved and the representations they create will be discussed in detail as we proceed in building a theory of syntactic analysis. All of the examples discussed above demonstrate the computational nature of human language and illustrate the complexity of the computations.

Summary

A linguistic expression consists of a word or string of words in a language that has a pronunciation (PF) and an interpretation (LF) that is related to its syntactic structure. When more than one syntactic structure can be assigned to a single pronunciation of a linguistic expression, the expression is structurally ambiguous. When one of the words in a single syntactic structure can be interpreted in more than one way (e.g. the noun *fish* as singular or plural), the expression involves a lexical ambiguity. In general, ambiguity results when a single PF can be mapped onto more than one LF.

PF is essentially overt, consisting of phonetic features (sounds) that are perceived by ear (or eye in the case of writing or sign). Minus phonetic features, LF consists entirely of covert elements including syntactic labels (e.g. N and V), groupings of words (e.g. as subject and predicate), and meaning, none of which are perceived directly by ear or eye. Imperative sentences, which contain an understood second person subject, provide one instance of a covert element in LF that has no counterpart in PF. The empty position in a relative clause which is linked to the noun it modifies constitutes another. Thus language involves both overt and covert elements.

A simple sentence constitutes a clause structure consisting roughly of a subject and a predicate. Clause structures may be complex, containing another clause structure inside. For example, the noun in a subject may be modified by a clause (a relative clause). A complex sentence constitutes a recursive structure. Grammatically there is no limit to the number of times a clause may be embedded inside another clause structure (e.g. right branching relative clauses (see (28))), but when relative clauses are multiply center embedded the result is unacceptable, presumably because these structures cannot be processed. This suggests that there are parts of human language that are simply not usable. It also suggests that there is a distinction to be made between linguistic expressions that are grammatical (possible given the grammar of a language) and those that are acceptable to speakers, which involves in addition the issue of processability. Most mutilply center embedded constructions are unprocessable and therefore will be unacceptable to speakers.

The mapping between PF and LF usually involves a complex computation that functions primarily in terms of covert elements.

Bibliographical note

See Chomsky 1965, chapter 1 for discussion of the grammatical vs. acceptable distinction and multiple center embedding.

Appendix : Multiple embedding of relative clauses

Notice that (27) involves repeated relative clause formation inside the subject of the sentence. The same difficulty in processing occurs when the subject construction in (27) is placed in the predicate, as in (i).

(i)   John saw the boy the girl the dog bit cursed.

In (i), however, the relative clause *the girl the dog bit cursed* is not strictly speaking center-embedded inside the nominal expression (*the boy*) or the main clause itself (*John saw the boy*). In neither case is there phonetic material to the right that would make the relative clause center embedded in the way it is in (27). (i) shows that we need to formulate a somewhat different characterization of unacceptable examples of multiple embedding. It will not suffice to refer to clause boundaries because this won't distinguish between (27) and (28).

EXERCISE 1.12

Another problem for an analysis of center-embedding concerns the fact that not all multiply center-embedded constructions are unusable. Consider the following example from a novel by Andrew Vachss (for which I am indebted to Jason Merchant).

(i) And the only thing the doctors they had in *there* ever treated was stab wounds. (*Two Trains Running*, p. 250)

a. How is (i) an example of multiple center-embedding?
b. In what ways does it differ from the completely unacceptable (29)?

Consider another example of apparently nondeviant multiple center embedding from Anthony Burgess's *Enderby Outside* on page 224 of the Penguin edition of the Enderby trilogy (for which I am indebted to Pierre Frath).

"Then Shem Macnamara had been very poor, only too ready for a free meal and a quiet sneer at the success of a fellow poet. Then, instead of expensive mouthwash, he had breathed on Hogg-Enderby, bafflingly (for no banquet would serve, because of the known redolence of onions, onions) onions.

'Onions,' said Hogg. He was frowned on in puzzlement. 'Cocktail onions,' he offered. Well just imagine. Shem Macnamara deepened his frown. Something in that voice saying 'Onions?' He did not take any onions."

2   Knowledge of language as an object of inquiry

As the English examples that were partially analyzed in the previous chapter have shown, language has a complex computational structure that involves a mapping between the PF representation of a linguistic expression (its sound/ pronunciation) and its LF representation, which determines its unique interpretation (roughly its meaning). In some cases there appears to be a one-to-one correspondence of elements in PF and LF – for example, the sentence *Fish fish fish*. In others, LF will contain covert elements necessary for interpretation, which do not occur in PF. The command *Fish fish!*, which involves an understood subject "you" at LF, is one such example. The 4-*fish* example is another.

EXERCISE 2.1

On one interpretation of *Fish fish fish fish* the LF representation contains two covert elements, whereas the LF representation of the other interpretation contains only one. Discuss.

In addition, the way in which overt and covert elements are grouped together into syntactic units is also covert information that plays a crucial role in determining the nature of LF representation and thus, by extension, the mapping between PF and LF.

Although linguistic expressions are informally referred to as sentences (e.g. *The pianist arrived late*) and their constituent parts (e.g. the nominal phrase *the pianist* or the single noun *pianist*), it is rather the paired PF and LF representations that fully identify each expression. Their orthographic representation as a linear sequence of written characters, which is a conventional way to represent linguistic expressions, adds no new information and sometimes lacks crucial structural information that distinguishes between distinct PF and/or LF representations (e.g. the 1-*fish* and 5-*fish* examples in the previous chapter, which are structurally ambiguous).

In these particular cases, the structural ambiguity is just an artifact of orthographic representation – i.e. the writing system, which is primarily a product of culture, not biology. Whether this generalizes to other instances of structural ambiguity in English, or more broadly for all human languages, is worth considering. For example, compare the 5-*fish* example with *flying planes can be dangerous*, the example discussed in note 2 of the first chapter, where the ambiguity resides in the interpretation of the phrase *flying planes*. Unlike the 5-*fish* example, where the two LF representations have different PF representations – specifically different intonation contours –, the *flying planes* example seems to have the same PF representation for both LF representations. This issue can be addressed more directly in terms of some basic tools of syntactic analysis that are developed in the next chapters.

From the perspective that is developed in this chapter, the study of language fundamentally concerns the paired PF and LF representations, how they are constructed and how each pair is connected. These representations are assumed to exist in the mind of a speaker, hence they are mental representations that occur in the neural circuitry of the human brain. They constitute a major part of a speaker's knowledge of his or her language and are thereby central to human cognition involving language.

LF and PF representations are constructed out of basic units called **lexical items**. The full set of lexical items in a language constitutes the **lexicon** of the language. The lexicon contains the atomic elements out of which linguistic expressions are constructed. As a preliminary hypothesis, assume that each word that is represented orthographically as a distinct element (i.e. separated from other words by a space at each end) is a separate lexical item (but see also the comments at the beginning of section 1 below).[1] Of course, lexical items so defined can often be broken down into more elementary grammatical parts called **morphemes** – e.g. the verb *walked* can be divided into a stem (or root) *walk-* and a past tense affix *-ed*, where the meaning of the root can be distinguished from the meaning of its tense affix. Whether some or all such morphemes should be treated as distinct lexical items remains to be determined. This issue will arise in subsequent chapters.

Lexical items usually have a sound and a meaning.[2] The sound of a lexical item, its PF representation, is given primarily in terms of phonetic features that identify each sound segment of the item (e.g. the three segments of *fish* or the seven segments of *pianist*). In some cases, this alone is insufficient to distinguish between lexical items. Take for example the verb *permit* compared to the noun *permit*. Although they contain the same consonants and vowels in the same linear order, with the verb the primary stress occurs on the second syllable, but it occurs on the first syllable for the noun.[3] This demonstrates how formal syntactic features are relevant to processes that determine PF (e.g. the assignment of stress).

In addition to syntactic category features that correspond to the traditional notion of word class, lexical items also contain formal features that subclassify items contained in a single word class. For example the noun *pianist* is a concrete noun, one that designates a physical object, as opposed to an abstract noun (e.g. *freedom*), which does not. It is also a count noun, one that can designate a group of countable individuals (e.g. two or three pianists), as opposed to a mass noun, which cannot (e.g. *one sincerity, *two sincerities*). Count nouns can be either singular or plural, as opposed to mass nouns. Note that although *sincerity* and *freedom* are both abstract nouns, the latter is a count noun – e.g. *our* *freedoms under the Constitution*, unlike the former. This shows how the lexicon is organized in terms of cross-classification of features. Count nouns can be either concrete or abstract; abstract nouns can be either countable or not.

These inherent features of nouns lie at the syntax/semantics interface, as do contextual features that identify specific subcategories of lexical items within a single word class. For example, certain verbs must occur with a direct object (e.g. *mention*, where *John mentioned* is a deviant sentence) in contrast to others like *sleep*, which cannot take a direct object (**The mother slept the baby*). Such features are relevant both for interpretation and syntactic distribution.

The semantic features of lexical items are less easily specified and more complicated. The meaning of lexical items, for example a noun like *pianist* or *tiger*, inevitably intersects with a speaker's knowledge of and beliefs about the external world, which are not strictly linguistic in nature. The problem has to do with making a cut between what might reasonably be considered purely linguistic knowledge and the contribution to the meaning of the lexical item that is not purely linguistic. Is the lexical representation of the noun *tiger* in the mind of a speaker who has had personal experience with tigers different from the representation in the mind of a speaker who has not? Is the lexical representation of the noun *gravity* in the mind of a physicist like Stephen Hawking who has written a book on gravitation different from that of a non-physicist who uses the word but lacks the technical scientific understanding? The answer is not known. Although personal experience will certainly contribute a great deal to our understanding and interpretation of various nouns, both concrete and abstract, it's not obvious that the same holds true for most common verbs. It seems probable that every English speaker's understanding of the verb *persuade* is virtually the same. Moreover it seems unlikely that anyone's interpretation of that verb could be dependent on experience in such a way that two speakers would have demonstrably different interpretations based on their different experience with the world. Nonetheless, how to represent the meaning of verbs formally remains a difficult problem. This issue will come up again in Section 2.2 on language acquisition.

In addition to a lexicon, a speaker's knowledge of his or her language must include some mechanism or mechanisms for constructing sentences (linguistic expressions generally) out of lexical items. Such mechanisms form the **computational system of human language** (C_{HL}). The lexicon plus the computational procedures that construct PF and LF representations out of lexical elements constitute a **grammar** of the language. A grammar provides a formal (i.e. explicit) characterization of an individual's knowledge of the language he or she speaks – what is called in linguistics a **generative grammar**. Thus a generative grammar is a formal computational device of a certain sort that maps the lexicon of a language onto paired PF/LF representations that constitute linguistic expressions. In this way, a generative grammar models a speaker's knowledge of his or her language.

From this perspective, a language as defined by a generative grammar is considered to be a system of knowledge in the mind/brain of a speaker. The linguist Noam Chomsky characterizes this view as **internalist**, in contrast to the **externalist** view of language as a phenomenon that can be studied without reference to the mind/brain of individual speakers. Chomsky distinguishes these perspectives using two technical terms. A human language from the internalist perspective is an **I-language**, where "I" indicates internal and individual. I-languages exist in the physical world as structures in the mind/brain of individual speakers – specifically, as a lexicon and a computational system. A generative grammar constitutes a theory of an I-language. From the internalist perspective the notion of grammar is primary and the notion of language as a set of paired PF/LF representations is derivative and hence secondary. This will become clearer in what follows.

In contrast, from the externalist perspective, a human language is an **E-language**, whose definition makes no reference to the mind/brain of any speaker – hence "E" for external to speakers. In practice, E-languages have been characterized in terms of a corpus of utterances, given as a partial list of sentences that is taken to be representative of some portion of the language. The E-language under investigation is taken to be an idealization based on a notion of a homogeneous speech community, which abstracts away from individual differences among speakers in actual speech communities. Given a lexicon and the grammatical mechanisms that account for the structure of sentences in the language, an infinite corpus of syntactic forms can be synthesized to which a sound and a meaning are assigned on the basis of content and form. From this perspective, the primary focus of inquiry is the corpus that is claimed to characterize the language, the grammar being the means by which the infinite corpus that constitutes the E-language is projected.

Unlike the concrete notion of I-language, the notion of E-language involves a very high degree of abstraction. This kind of abstraction is inherent in the way people usually talk about languages. Consider for example the term *English*, where the majority of the inhabitants of the United States and those of Great Britain are all said to speak English – i.e. the same language. Nonetheless, the pronunciation of "English" is different on each side of the Atlantic. Furthermore, pronunciation differs within the two countries, depending on geographical location (north/south; east/west). Moreover, these differences can occur within different parts of the same city (e.g. New York or London). Pronunciation aside, the vocabulary used in Britain is not identical to that used in the United States. For example, the British use the word *serviette* (from French) for what Americans call a "napkin." Notice that these differences concern the phonetic labels of lexical items, which for the most part are arbitrary, primarily accidents of history.

In addition, there are also syntactic differences between what might be called varieties of English. The phrase *give him it* is acceptable in England, whereas it is generally not in the United States (where *give it to him* is the only acceptable version). Another British/American difference concerns the use of the verb *do*. Consider answers to the question: *did George go to the concert?* In the United States one could respond *he might have gone* or *he might have*, but never *he might have done*. The latter is perfectly acceptable in Britain. This is illustrated in the following sentences from the novels of John le Carré.

(a)   And he did these things partly because he always did them and needed
       the steadying familiarity of his own routines, but partly also because he
       was proud of having thrown caution to the winds for once and not found
       twenty-five sound reasons for doing nothing, which these days he might
       have done.
       The Russia House, 1989, *chapter 1.*

(b)   Neither did I ask him which of my languages he considered funny, although
       I might have done if I hadn't been on such a cloud, because sometimes my
       respect for people flies out of the window of its own accord.
       The Mission Song, 2006, p. 38.

Note that in (a) *done* stands for "found twenty-five sound reasons for doing nothing." In (b) *done* stands for "asked him which of my languages he considered
funny."

   Even among speakers of English in the same country (or city) there are differences in syntax. Consider the problem that the following examples, both
reported speech in novels, pose for giving a precise definition of "the English
language."

(1)   a. This ain't no more bad than a night with a girlfriend like to bite.
           (Walter Mosley, *Fearless Jones*, Little, Brown & Co., New York, 2001,
           p. 112)
       b. Dat's right, goes Hardjit, – we b four a us brederens here. An out a
           us four brederens, none a us got a mum an dad wat actually come
           from Pakistan, innit. So don't u b tellin any a us Pakis dat we be Pakis
           like our Paki brederen from Pakistan, u get me. (Gautam Malkani,
           Londonstani, The Penguin Press, New York, 2006, p. 6)

Both examples depart from the properties of what might be called "standard
English."

EXERCISE 2.2

a. Identify three ways in which (1a) differs syntactically from what you consider to
   be standard English.
b. How does the use of the verbal system as illustrated in (1b) differ from standard
   English?

From the perspective of linguistics, they are simply examples from different
varieties (idiolects) of what is called English. However, a definition that must
abstract away from such syntactic differences among speakers is going to be very
abstract indeed. At this point the attempt to characterize "the English language"
begins to lose its coherence along with the notion E-language on which it relies.
From the internalist perspective however, such high-level abstractions are not the
object of inquiry for linguistics.

Notice that the differences under consideration involve varieties of English spoken currently in the early twenty-first century. This involves the **synchronic** description of language – i.e. at a specific point in time. The description of English becomes even more complicated when we consider **diachronic** descriptions, which cover the history of the language. At one point in the history of English, one said *went he to the market?* and not *did he go to the market?* Now, the former is impossible and the latter, which didn't exist in those earlier times, is the only way to ask the question.

The distinction between the I-language and E-language perspectives is crucial for understanding any discussion of language and languages. The two perspectives entail fundamentally different and moreover incompatible assumptions – assumptions which are usually not spelled out. Therefore the first step towards understanding such discussions should be to determine which perspective is being assumed.

The internalist perspective, taking a language to be an I-language, which constitutes a system of knowledge, raises four fundamental questions:

(2)   a.   What is the system of knowledge?
             b.   How does it arise in the individual?
             c.   How is it put to use?
             d.   What is its physical basis?

These questions apply to the specific I-language of each speaker (or I-languages in the case of multilingual speakers). Moreover, it is generally assumed that there is a single answer to each question (2b–d) that holds generally for all I-languages. If this assumption is correct, then the differences between I-languages (especially those that appear on the surface to be very different (e.g. English vs. Japanese vs. Warlpiri)) can have no appreciable effect on how I-language is acquired (2b) or used (2c), or how it is organized in the neural substrate of the brain (2d). Whether the assumption is correct is an empirical question that remains to be answered.[4]

This assumption more or less follows if the answer to question (2a) has significant generality across a wide range of I-languages. Given that the lexicon is demonstrably a source of linguistic variation across I-languages, certainly with respect to the phonetic labels of lexical items but also concerning differences in permissible syntactic constructions in which parallel lexical items can occur,[5] the source of generality, if it exists, must reside in the computational system. In effect, there should be a single uniform computational system underlying all I-languages. At this level, the answer to question (2a) addresses the theory of human language – what is called **Universal Grammar** (henceforth UG), as will be discussed in the following section and developed in detail in the rest of this book.

The existence of UG as well as its form and content are also empirical not theoretical issues, to be addressed by detailed investigations of a wide variety of I-languages. If the properties (especially covert properties) of a substantial range of I-languages can be shown to follow from specific general principles – presumably principles of UG – then the answer to question (2a) will constitute a theory of human language.

2.1   The system of knowledge

From linguistics, the answer to question (2a) above is straightforward. The system of knowledge for each I-language consists of a lexicon and a computational system. The lexicon specifies the lexical items of the language, be they single words or also fixed phrases like idioms (e.g. *kicked the bucket* for "died" – see Jackendoff 2010 for discussion), or their constituent parts (morphological roots and affixes). A lexical item specifies minimally a pronunciation and/or an interpretation. The computational system (C_{HL}) accounts for the pairing of sound (PF) and meaning (LF) for each linguistic expression in the language – specifically those aspects of meaning that are determined by the inherent meanings of lexical items in conjunction with the structural properties of expressions. Note that this abstracts away from whatever contribution to meaning is provided by knowledge of the external world and beliefs – including the real-world context of the utterance, which surely contributes to the overall meaning of a linguistic expression when it is used (the subject matter of the subfield of semantics called **pragmatics**).

Under this view, C_{HL} provides the mechanism that operates on the lexicon to construct PF and LF representations, the pairing of which defines a linguistic expression. The HL subscript designates "human language" on the assumption that significant parts of the computational system, if not all of it, are shared by all human languages. This is of course an empirical assumption. Whether the parts of C_{HL} are unique to human language or shared with other human cognitive faculties (e.g. vision or reasoning) remains a controversial issue. Whether parts of this system exist in non-humans has also been a subject of some controversy. However, there is a biological fact that in the end must be accounted for: humans acquire I-languages and non-humans do not. The postulation of a genetically endowed language faculty that is unique to humans gives one plausible account for this biolinguistic fact.

Consider again, for example, the first example: *Fish*! from Chapter 1. It is multiply ambiguous, where each of the possible LF representations (details aside) is assigned to the same PF representation (assuming that PF contains only phonetic information, but recall the discussion of the verb *permit* vs. the noun *permit* above).

(3)   a. [$_{Noun}$ [$_{-plural}$] Fish]
       b. [$_{Noun}$ [$_{+plural}$] Fish]
       c. [$_{Clause}$ *you*[$_{-plural}$] [$_{Verb}$ Fish]]
       d. [$_{Clause}$ *you*[$_{+plural}$] [$_{Verb}$ Fish]]

Thus *Fish*! orthographically represents four distinct LF/PF pairings, hence four distinct linguistic expressions.

While PF contains primarily overt elements, those that can be perceived with ears and eyes, LF, in contrast, contains covert elements (i.e. invisible to our physical senses) that are crucial for mental computation. The understood subject *you* of imperative sentences is one such element. The categorial designations "noun" and "verb" are likewise covert elements. And moving beyond expressions containing two lexical items, the way in which lexical items combine to form subgroupings within the whole expression also constitutes important information for interpretation not always present in the physical manifestation of the expression. Thus knowledge of the language invariably involves covert as well as overt information.

The extent of a speaker's knowledge of the language(s) he or she speaks is demonstrably unbounded, covering what is essentially an infinite set of linguistic expressions. This can be demonstrated by trying to imagine the longest declarative sentence in English – call it $S_{longest}$. It is trivial to show that our candidate cannot actually be the longest sentence because any sentence of English can be lengthened by embedding it the context (4):

(4)   I know ___.

And of course this sentence could itself be embedded in the context (5):

(5)   He doesn't believe that ___.

The longer sentence that results could again be embedded in the context (4) and that result embedded again in the context (5), giving an even longer sentence. This process could in principle be repeated indefinitely. Given the limitations on human memory and attention, excessively long sentences created in this fashion would soon become difficult to process normally as is done with garden variety linguistic expressions found in speech and writing. Nonetheless, the structure of such sentences will conform to the properties of English syntax even if their extreme length renders them unprocessable by English speakers.

The unbounded nature of human languages entails that a speaker's knowledge of his or her language covers an infinite domain and in this regard can be said to be infinite. Thus a speaker of English has knowledge that allows her to use (i.e. produce or recognize) any one of an infinite number of English sentences (linguistic expressions). In contrast, a speaker's linguistic experience with his or her native language up to the point at which it can be said he or she speaks that language is obviously finite. Therefore infinite linguistic knowledge is in part grounded in finite linguistic experience. Sentences that speakers recognize or produce that go beyond their limited finite linguistic experience constitute **novel utterances** – i.e. utterances new to their linguistic experience. The problem for any account of linguistic knowledge is to account for how a human being, a finite biological entity, can on the basis of finite experience come to have infinite knowledge.

With generative grammar, the solution to the puzzle is simple and straightforward. Let's assume that there are a finite number of atomic units in the mental lexicon. Although the number of sentences of a language is infinite, the number of words in that language is essentially finite. The computational system however involves **recursion**, where a certain syntactic structure α contains another instance of α as a subpart. Thus there must be a computational procedure that allows this. The fact that this procedure is recursive (i.e. can be applied to its own output any number of times) allows for arbitrarily long constructions. This single, hence finite, recursive procedure is capable of yielding an infinite output – for example, the process by which a clause can be embedded inside a predicate phrase as an argument of the verb, as in (4) and (5). Thus the computational system of human language accounts for the mapping of a finite lexicon onto an infinite set of linguistic expressions via a finite number of procedures that can be applied any number of times. In this way, a generative grammar captures Wilhelm von Humbolt's important insight into the nature of language, formulated in 1836 about a century before the requisite technical devices had been developed in mathematics – namely that language "makes infinite use of finite means."[6]

The system of knowledge for a language not only encompasses an unbounded number of linguistic expressions, but also distinguishes between objects constructed from the lexicon of the language that are part of the language and those that are not – typically linguistic expressions that are judged by speakers as not belonging to their language. Consider for example the following pair (from Roberts 1997, as well as those in (9–11) below).

(6)   a.   In the future, everyone will be famous for 15 minutes.
          b.   *Minutes 15 for famous be will everyone future the in.

Reversing the order of the words in the perfectly ordinary sentence (6a), yielding (6b), results in gibberish. It cannot be processed as a normal English sentence; native English speakers cannot assign this string of English words a viable LF or PF (i.e. with normal sentence intonation). If we can demonstrate that (6b) violates some grammatical property or properties, then this constitutes an instance of grammatical deviance.

A comparison of the syntactic analyses of the well formed (6a) with the deviant (6b) provides some insight into why (6b) is grammatically deviant. (6a) contains two prepositional phrases (labeled PP), each consisting of a preposition followed by an object nominal phrase (labeled NP), as indicated in (7).

(7)   a.   [$_{PP}$ in [$_{NP}$ the future]]
          b.   [$_{PP}$ for [$_{NP}$ 15 minutes]]

The sentence also contains a subject *everyone* followed by a predicate consisting of an auxiliary verb *will*, which is in turn followed by the verb *be*, an adjective *famous* and the prepositional phrase (7b). Thus the clause (6a) has a structure along the lines of (8), details aside.

(8)   [$_{Clause}$ [$_{PP}$ in [$_{NP}$ the future]] [$_{Subject}$ everyone] [$_{Predicate}$ will be famous [$_{PP}$ for [$_{NP}$ 15 minutes]]]]

The deviant (6b) actually preserves the grouping properties of (6a). Thus, for example, elements of the prepositional phrase at the end of (6a) show up together at the beginning of (6b) but in reverse order (i.e. with the preposition following its object and inside the prepositional object phrase the number following the noun rather than preceding it).

EXERCISE 2.3

a. Identify the other phrases in (6b) where the grouping properties of (6a) are preserved.
b. Construct another ordering of these words where none of the grouping properties given in (8) are preserved.
c. To what extent, if any, do you find this new construction more deviant than (6b)?

If the grouping properties of (6a) are preserved in (6b), then plausibly the source of the deviance of (6b) is solely its linear ordering properties, i.e. word order.

As a model of knowledge of an I-language, a generative grammar must provide a means for distinguishing (6b) as deviant. One way would be to constrain the mechanisms for creating sentence structure in such a way that examples like (6b) would never be generated. This is the **derivational approach** to identifying grammatical deviance – more precisely, the inability to derive a particular string of lexical items or a structural representation for such strings. Alternatively the mechanisms of sentence construction will generate such examples, but these will be marked deviant because they violate structural constraints that are stated independently of the sentence building machinery – for example, a constraint on prepositional phrases requiring that the preposition precedes its object, where English is one such language governed by this constraint. This constitutes a **representational approach** to characterizing grammatical deviance, where conditions on what constitutes a legitimate syntactic representation exclude certain linguistic structures that result from the otherwise free application of grammatical mechanisms. Notice that either way the grammar, which in the second case includes this constraint, excludes the deviant example and thereby makes the correct distinction between (6a) and (6b).

A generative grammar will also have to distinguish (6a) from the following deviant examples.

(9) a. *In the future will everyone for 15 minutes famous be.
      b. *In the future will be everyone famous for 15 minutes.

(9a–b), in contrast to (6b), contain prepositional phrases that observe the ordering constraint for English. Even though these examples are comprehensible (i.e. not gibberish), they are nonetheless deviant,[7] though apparently less deviant than (6b). If part of knowledge of a language includes being able to distinguish between degrees of deviance, then the first alternative for handling deviance discussed in the preceding paragraph will not suffice because it makes no distinctions among deviant constructions.

Now consider one further deviant example.

(10)   *Future, everyone 15 minutes for famous be will.

(10) like (6b) contains a prepositional phrase that violates English word order among other problems. Like (6b), (10) appears to be gibberish in contrast to (9a–b). However, there is an important distinction to be made between (6b) and (10) as well as the examples in (9). Whereas the linear ordering given in (6b) apparently does not exist in any known language, the orderings given in (9a–b) and (10) do actually obtain in other languages. Thus the ordering in (9a) is exactly the ordering that occurs in German (cf. (11a)). (9b) gives the linear order of the corresponding sentence in Welsh (11b), and (10), the linear order of the corresponding sentence in Japanese (11c).

(11)   a. In der Zukunft wird jeder für 15 Minuten berühmt sein.
            in the future will everyone for 15 minutes famous be
        b. Yn y dyfodol, bydd pawb yn enwog am 15 munud.
            in the future will-be everyone in famous for 15 minutes
        c. Shorai-wa, daremo-ga 15 hun kan yumei-ni naru desho.
            future-TOP everyone-NOM 15 minutes during famous-DAT will-be
            maybe

In Japanese the particle -*wa* indicates a topic (TOP), the particles -*ga* and -*ni* are taken to be overt case markings for nominative (NOM) and dative (DAT) case respectively. These examples show that the computational system for human language must be general enough to account for a certain amount of crosslinguistic variation in word order.

Furthermore, the word order that occurs in English also occurs in other languages, as illustrated in (12).

(12)   a. Dans l'avenir, tout un chacun sera célèbre pendant 15 minutes.
            in the future everyone will-be famous during 15 minutes
        b. V buduscem kazdyj iz nas budet izvestnym na 15 minut.
            in future each of us will-be famous for 15 minutes
        c. Jianglai, mei-ge ren dou hui chuming shiwu fen-zhong.
            In-the-future, every-CL person all will become-famous 15 minutes

(12a) gives the corresponding French version of (6a); (12b), the Russian; and (12c), the Chinese. Thus the word order in English is not in fact peculiar to English, but is rather one of the limited range of possibilities that are available generally for human languages, what are called **parameters** (see Baker 2001 for an extended discussion). As discussed in the following chapters, the specification of linear order can be handled by more general mechanisms than language-specific statements.

Let's turn to another phenomenon that provides further insight into how a generative grammar must account for the distinction between deviant and nondeviant utterances. Consider the pair of sentences in (13).

(13)   a.   John read a novel during spring break.
           b.   Which novel did John read during spring break?

In the statement (13a) the NP *a novel* is construed as the object of the verb *read*. In the question (13b), the interrogative phrase *which novel* is also construed as the object of the verb *read* even though it occurs in PF in clause-initial position. A simple way to account for this construal is to have the interrogative phrase start out in object position of the verb and then be displaced (moved) to the clause-initial position. The LF representation of (13b) will reflect the starting position of the interrogative phrase. In effect, the interrogative phrase is pronounced in one syntactic position, but interpreted in another. This defines the **displacement property** of human languages, another property that is unique to human language – in contrast to artificially constructed systems like computer programming languages or systems of logical notation (see also footnote 3).

A simple computational account would involve a mechanism that moves an interrogative phrase to clause-initial position. Such a mechanism will cover all such interrogatives in English as well as other languages in which interrogative phrases occur clause-initially (see Chapter 8). However, the simple mechanism by itself will generate deviant constructions. Consider (14) where the object phrase is a conjunction of two NPs.

(14)   John read a novel and a play during spring break.

Suppose *which novel* is substituted for *a novel*. A question (15a) formed from this by positioning the interrogative phrase *which novel* at the front of the clause will be deviant.

(15)   a.   *Which novel did John read and a play during spring break?
           b.   *Which novel did John read a play and during spring break?

The pair (15a–b) demonstrates that the order of the two conjuncts does not affect the deviance of the resulting expression.

Rather than complicate the formulation of the displacement rule (i.e. move an interrogative phrase to clause-initial position), a separate constraint that prohibits the displacement of a single conjunct from a coordinate structure, what Ross 1967 and 1984 designates as the **Coordinate Structure Constraint** (henceforth CSC), can be formulated as follows.

(16)   *Coordinate Structure Constraint* (CSC): an interrogative phrase cannot be extracted by itself out of a coordinate structure in which it functions as a conjunct.

While the CSC prohibits (15), it allows (17).

(17)   Which novel and which play did John read during spring break?

In (17) the whole coordinate structure is displaced, not just a single conjunct. Furthermore, the CSC also blocks the extraction of one of the conjuncts by itself when both are interrogative phrases as in (17).

(18)   a.   *Which play did John read which novel and during spring break?
         b.   *Which novel did John read and which play during spring break?

In this way the CSC coupled with the displacement mechanism for interrogative phrases distinguishes deviant constructions like (15) and (18) from nondeviant constructions like (17).

The formulation of the CSC in (16) is however insufficiently general. Consider the following examples containing coordinate structures.

(19)   a.   John has read a novel and written a play during the summer.
         b.   *Which novel has John read and written a play during the summer?
         c.   *Which novel has John written a play and read during the summer?

Under the interpretation of (19a) where the PP *during the summer* modifies both verbs, the two conjuncts in (19a) are *read a novel* and *written a play*. Since the interrogative phrase *which novel* in (19b–c) is not itself a conjunct, but rather is contained in a conjunct, the CSC as formulated in (16) will not exclude these deviant examples. Rather, a more general formulation of the CSC is required, along the lines of (20).

(20)   *Coordinate Structure Constraint* (revised): an interrogative phrase cannot be extracted by itself out of a coordinate structure in which it functions as a subpart.

This formulation now covers both cases where the interrogative phrase is either a conjunct itself or a part of a conjunct.

Displacement in English is not limited to just interrogative phrases. As illustrated in (21b), it also occurs with non-interrogative NPs.

(21)   a.   It seems that Jill's best student adores Mahler.
         b.   Jill's best student seems to adore Mahler.

In both (21a and b) *Jill's best student* is construed as the subject of the verb *adore*. In (21a) *Jill's best student* occupies the syntactic position in which that NP gets its interpretation, whereas in (21b) it occurs in the subject position of the main clause. The proper construal of (21b) can be expressed in an LF representation where the NP *Jill's best student* occurs in the subject position of the embedded clause while in the PF representation of (21b) this NP occurs in the subject of the main clause. (See Chapter 6 for a detailed analysis of these constructions.)

This species of displacement also obeys the CSC, as illustrated in the paradigm (22), where the bracketed coordinate structure *Jill's best student and Jack's professor* is construed as the subject of the embedded clause in each case.

(22)   a.   It seems that [Jill's best student and Jack's professor] adore Mahler.
         b.   [Jill's best student and Jack's professor] seem to adore Mahler.
         c.   *Jill's best student seems and Jack's professor to adore Mahler.
         d.   *Jack's professor seems Jill's best student and to adore Mahler.

(22a) corresponds to (21a), where the phrase construed as the subject of the embedded clause occurs in the subject position of that clause. Assuming that the coordinate structure in (22b) starts out in the subject position of the embedded clause, (22b) demonstrates that the entire coordinate structure can be displaced from the embedded clause subject position to the subject position of the main clause. (22c–d) show that, in contrast, a subpart of a coordinate structure cannot by itself be displaced.

This evidence establishes that the CSC is not limited to the movement of interrogative phrases in English. One might reasonably assume that the CSC applies generally to all displacement in English.

EXERCISE 2.4

How would the CSC (20) have to be reformulated to account for (22c–d)?

The question that arises immediately is whether the CSC applies to other languages. If it does, then this constitutes some prima facie evidence that this constraint is not specific to English and therefore should be considered a part of UG.

EXERCISE 2.5

Identify another language that involves the displacement of interrogative phrases to form questions and determine whether the CSC applies in that language.

There is actually a stronger argument for considering the CSC as part of UG apart from its applicability to other languages, which is discussed in the next section.

The picture that emerges at this point is that knowledge of a language consists of a lexicon and a computational system, where the computational mechanisms for constructing the linguistic expressions of the language are formulated in a general fashion and their output is constrained either by general conditions on the output of the mechanisms (in the case of word order) or by general constraints on their application (in the case of displacement). These general conditions distinguish between deviant and nondeviant linguistic expressions of a language. They are relevant to the second question of how such systems of knowledge arise in the individual.

2.2 Language acquisition

How the system of knowledge that constitutes an I-language arises in the mind of an individual constitutes the issue of first language acquisition. This question of how a child acquires a first I-language can be interpreted in two distinct but related ways. One focuses on the actual process of language acquisition – what happens in a child's mind between having no I-language and having one, assuming that there are identifiable stages. The other addresses the cognitive resources that make it possible for a child to acquire a first language. The second is more basic in that the question "how is it possible?" can be answered without addressing the actual process a child goes through; whereas specifying the actual process presupposes an understanding of the cognitive resources involved. The following discussion focuses on the issue of cognitive resources.

Schematically, the acquisition process can be characterized as a shift from one mental state to another. Thus the mind of a child with no I-language starts in an initial state ($S_{initial}$) that is innate, part of the genetic endowment of humans. That there is an initial state is a fact, not a hypothesis. The mind of every human begins in an initial state with respect to language. The empirical question is: what is the nature (i.e. content and structure) of this initial state? The null hypothesis is that the initial state is identical for all humans (absent some serious pathology). On exposure to language data over a relatively short period of time, the initial state becomes a steady state (S_{steady}), an I-language consisting of a lexicon and a requisite computational system. From this perspective language acquisition can be characterized as (23).

(23) $S_{initial}$ + Experience $\rightarrow$ S_{steady}

The major part of a child's linguistic experience will be the language data the child is exposed to prior to acquiring an I-language – what is called **primary language data** (PLD).

If Experience in (23) is essentially limited to PLD[8] and furthermore S_{steady} designates an I-language, then whatever properties of the I-language acquired there are (i.e. as expressed in the generative grammar of that language) that cannot be derived directly from the PLD must then come from $S_{initial}$. Those properties will be properties of the grammar that by definition are innate (i.e. genetically determined and therefore universal across the species). Thus (23) can be reformulated more specifically as (24), where UG designates Universal Grammar, the innate part of the computational system for human language.

(24)   UG + PLD $\rightarrow$ I-language

Given (24), the answer to question (2b) (i.e., how does a first I-language arise in the mind of an individual?) requires an explanation of how it is possible for a child to convert PLD into an I-language, i.e. a computational system plus a lexicon (in other words, a generative grammar). With PLD as input and an I-language as output, the process of language acquisition involves a mapping from a finite corpus of utterances to an unbounded language – what is called the **projection problem** for language acquisition.

Obviously, PLD, the arbitrary corpus of utterances a child hears, by itself cannot yield an I-language. The PLD is physically a corpus of sound waves, which are continuous rather than discrete. To go from a continuous sound wave to a structured linguistic expression with its discrete parts requires some rather intricate cognitive machinery that belongs to the initial state (by hypothesis, UG). Suppose UG is a function that maps sound waves onto PF/LF pairs, schematized in (25), a process that might be called **The First Miracle of Language Acquisition**.

(25) $UG(\{sw_1, \ldots, sw_n\}) \Longrightarrow \{(PF_1, LF_1), \ldots, (PF_n, LF_n)\}$

With a simple example like the word *tops*, its PF representation specifies four discrete sound segments (phones) of the pattern CVCC (where C = consonant and V = vowel), forming a single syllable. Morphologically the example involves two morphemes, a stem *top* and the plural affix *–s*. How a child extracts this discrete PF representation from the sound wave of *tops* is not obvious.

With the LF representation of *tops* the problem is just as daunting. Although the child's environment will provide crucial clues – e.g. phonetic labels attached to physical objects, nonetheless all the problems of definition still apply. These problems are compounded when we turn to abstract nouns and other parts of speech (e.g. verbs, adjectives, and prepositions). How a child extracts an LF representation from a sound wave is, if anything, a deeper mystery. Nonetheless, a child converts PLD into PF/LF pairs that interact with UG to yield an I-language.

If whatever allows a child to analyze the utterances in the PLD as paired PF and LF representations does not come from the child's experience, then it must come from the child's biology and therefore is innate. Furthermore, this innate component, which is called UG on the grounds that it centrally involves grammatical structure, must provide the requisite mechanisms for constructing the computational system of the I-language acquired. This task is daunting enough just considering any single I-language, but it is actually even more challenging because the initial state must account for the fact that any child can acquire a grammar for any human language that the child is exposed to. The degree of the challenge depends on whether the computational system and lexicon of each language can differ significantly from those of other languages. If all languages share a core computational system and a core lexicon, and are therefore more like variations on a theme rather than fundamentally different systems, then the problem of language acquisition becomes more tractable. This will include that part of the computational system that accounts for deviance (e.g. the Coordinate Structure Constraint) – including degrees of deviance,[9] about which PLD provides virtually no information.

The PLD provides overt and hence direct evidence for the pronunciation of linguistic expressions, including the phonetic label associated with each lexical item. Thus PLD plays a major role in determining which lexicon a child will acquire. A child that is exposed to English data will acquire a lexicon for English, whereas if that same child were raised in Japan, she would presumably acquire a lexicon of Japanese. PLD also contains direct evidence for the linear order of lexical items in linguistic expressions (see Chapter 4), so it will also determine important properties of the syntax that is acquired. However the PLD does not provide direct evidence for covert properties of linguistic expressions, including formal syntactic labels of elements and the grouping properties for strings of lexical items. Thus the covert properties of linguistic expressions must be provided by the initial state, UG, and therefore must be part of an innate cognitive faculty of humans. If UG applies specifically to language, then it is part of a unique

language faculty that is distinct from other cognitive faculties of humans (e.g. reasoning, vision, and audition – apart from their interaction with language).[10]

The covert properties of linguistic expressions provide one example of the impoverished nature of the PLD as a source of information for language acquisition. Another is that PLD is obviously finite whereas the I-language acquired is demonstrably infinite, unbounded in scope and therefore involving novel utterances belonging to the language that are new to the experience of the speaker and possibly to the history of the language itself (cf. E-language). Furthermore, the PLD is not ideal – i.e., it often contains grammatical errors, including sentences that are not completed or sentences that are started one way and finished in another where the two parts do not cohere grammatically. In addition, PLD generally contains no information about deviance (or degrees of deviance), what is referred to as "negative evidence" – e.g. statements that some utterance a child produces (or hears) is deviant. Even if children were told "you can't say it that way" or "say it this way," how would they know whether the problem is grammatical let alone exactly what the grammatical problem with their utterance is? The PLD cannot account for either novel utterances or deviant utterances; and of equal importance, it cannot account for a speaker's ability to distinguish between the two.

The impoverished nature of the linguistic experience of a child acquiring a first I-language is referred to as **poverty of the stimulus**. The phenomenon of poverty of the stimulus creates a problem for any account of the acquisition of knowledge. Chomsky calls this Plato's Problem, in recognition that the Greek philosopher Plato was the first person to discuss it in his writings and try to propose a solution (see Plato's *Meno*). Plato's Problem for linguistics concerns the grammatical knowledge an individual comes to have that cannot be accounted for on the basis of experience alone. The grammatical knowledge a person acquires comes either from their (linguistic) environment or from their biology – i.e. from nurture or from nature. If some aspects of that knowledge cannot be accounted for on the basis of experience, then it follows that these aspects must exist in the individual prior to any experience. In other words they must be innate. The solution to Plato's Problem in linguistics is to posit innate linguistic structure in the mind/brain of the speaker and to assume that this structure is utilized in the acquisition of an I-language, as well as becoming a part of it.

Innateness must therefore be a fact because there is no other plausible way to go directly from a collection of sound waves, the overt part of PLD, to a computational system and a lexicon (especially the covert properties of lexical items). Any viable account of knowledge of language must postulate some innate structure for the human mind that accounts for how an I-language is acquired on the basis of severely impoverished data. Furthermore, any account of human language acquisition must account for the biolinguistic fact that only humans acquire an I-language and therefore there must be something unique about human biology that accounts for this – which again points to innateness. (For further discussion of language acquisition see Yang 2002 and 2006.)

2.3   Language use

The third question (2c) arising from the internalist perspective concerns the use of language, in particular how the system of knowledge that constitutes a language is utilized in linguistic behavior. Language use involves two apparently different processes: production and perception.

Language production starts with what might be called thoughts, which are converted into linguistic expressions – i.e. an LF representation that is paired with a PF representation, presumably mediated by the computational system that links LF representations with their corresponding PF representations (and conversely). Thus language production can be characterized as a mapping of thought to LF and then LF to PF, and finally from PF to speech (including sign) or writing, as indicated in (26).

(26)   thought $\Longrightarrow$ LF $\Longrightarrow$ PF $\Longrightarrow$ speech/writing

Thus LF representations connect directly with the conceptual-intentional systems of human cognition and PF representations connect directly with the perceptual-articulatory systems (i.e. the sensory-motor systems of the brain). These two levels of linguistic representation therefore constitute **interface levels**.

Linguistic production involves the **creative aspect of language use**,[11] which involves the following properties of normal language use: (1) it is innovative in the sense that speakers are constantly producing and interpreting sentences that are new to their experience (**novel utterances**), (2) it is unbounded in the sense that there is no discernible limit to the number of sentences a speaker can produce, (3) it is "free from the control of detectable stimuli, either external or internal," and (4) it is coherent and hence appropriate to the situation. As Chomsky notes, this latter property is difficult to characterize precisely (and may be beyond our intellectual grasp). However, "we can distinguish normal use of language from the ravings of a maniac or the output of a computer with a random element" (Chomsky 2006, p. 11).

Notice that the creative aspect of language use connects with the poverty of the stimulus in a fundamental way. Consider the deviant examples in (15) again. The fact that such sentences have not been heard before does not entail that they are not part of the language. It could have been that the examples in (15) are novel utterances that speakers of English have not yet encountered. The fact that speakers of a language can distinguish between novel utterances and deviant utterances, which share the property "never heard before," demonstrates that the environment is too impoverished to account for our detailed linguistic knowledge.

There is a great deal that remains unknown concerning the interface between language and other cognitive systems. In particular the LF/thought interface remains essentially a mystery. While there are formal and hence explicit theories about LF representations, there are no formal theories (or even formal definitions) of thought. Thought appears to be a rich cognitive stew involving what is known, what is believed, how a speaker thinks/reasons, and other less well defined factors. How this is translated into linguistic expressions is simply unknown. However, it seems clear that any given LF representation presents a kind of bare meaning, in contrast to the richness of the thought it is intended to express, and only reacquires the richness it loses in translation when it is taken into the mind of another speaker, where the interface cognitive systems reinvest it with the same kind of richness – though not necessarily the identical richness.

Language perception proceeds in the reverse direction, as indicated in (27).

(27)   speech/writing $\Longrightarrow$ PF $\Longrightarrow$ LF $\Longrightarrow$ thought

Perception, unlike production, involves the analysis of a linear signal into a hierarchically structured object. On the face of it, it seems that this process, called **parsing**, is very different from the process of production. Moreover, while it is clear that there must be some strong relation between the parser and the computational system that provides a model for knowledge of an I-language, it is not obvious exactly how this works.

2.4   The physical basis for language

It is fair to say that even less is known about the structure and function of language in terms of the neural anatomy and physiology of the brain than is known about language use in general. Given the model of knowledge of a language as a computational system with a lexicon, there are no definitive answers to some of the simplest questions: how are lexical items represented in neural structures? and where precisely are they located in the brain? When we turn to the neural counterpart to the computational system for human language, we encounter the more difficult problem of bridging the apparent disconnect between knowledge and behavior. The computational system does not model our linguistic behavior, but rather what we know about linguistic structure – presumably the paired mental representations of sound and meaning (more accurately PF and LF pairs), which are assumed to enter into language use. But even limiting the query to the paired PF/LF representations nothing concrete is known about how these representations are instantiated in the neural substrate of the brain or where they occur.

The question of how language is represented in the brain concerns a largely future neuroscience that is barely on the horizon. It is a relatively new question in the study of language and its answer surely depends on the answers to the first three questions in (2) above. Chomsky suggests that linguistics and cognitive science more generally may provide crucial concepts for the neuroscience of language in much the same way that nineteenth-century chemistry provided the concepts that made it possible to unify chemistry and physics in the 20th century (see Chomsky 2000b, especially chapter 5, for discussion).

One final caveat is worth bearing in mind: although the object of inquiry in linguistics (from the perspective being investigated here) is the computational system and lexicon that constitutes knowledge of language, there is no direct way to discover exactly what computations are performed when language is used or what representations are produced. In particular, what is occurring in the mind of the speaker is not directly accessible either through introspection (via meditation, psychoanalysis, or hypnosis) or through neuro-imaging via FMRI or PET scan. In short, there are no experiments that can be performed on living human brains that will even distantly approach the rich information that has been gained via linguistic analysis. If, as suggested above, the study of linguistic knowledge and the study of language use intersect at the paired PF/LF representations of linguistic expressions, then for the present the most productive way to study these representations is in terms of the grammatical models proposed in linguistics.

2.5   Summary

From the internalist perspective, a language is a form of knowledge in the mind of the speaker consisting of a lexicon and a computational system (C_{HL}) that maps the lexicon onto linguistic expressions, each with a distinct PF and LF. This lexicon and computational system constitute a grammar or I-language ("I" for "internal" and "individual").

Given the variety of idiolects that exist at the current time (synchronically) or that have existed over time (diachronically), any attempt to define a language coherently without direct reference to the mind of the speaker (i.e. as an E-language ("E" for "external") – for example as a set of sentences) is a hopeless task.

The internalist perspective raises four questions for the study of language:

1. What is the system of knowledge in the mind of the speaker that constitutes a language?
2. How does this system arise in the mind of the speaker?
3. How is this system put to use in the production and perception of speech?
4. What is the biological (neural) basis of this system?

The answers to questions 2–4 will be based on an answer to the first question, which involves specifying what is in the lexicon and what is in the computational system.

Given that there is in principle no longest sentence in a language, C_{HL} must contain a mechanism for creating recursive structures, yielding potentially unbounded output and therefore novel utterances. C_{HL} also must distinguish between linguistic expressions that are part of a language and those that are not (deviant utterances). These latter are those that cannot be produced by the mechanisms of C_{HL} or those that are prohibited because they violate general constraints on the operation or output of those mechanisms (for example, the CSC that applies to displacement phenomena). Variation across languages is accounted for via parameters (e.g. involving word order), also a part of C_{HL}. Thus in addition to mechanisms that map the lexicon onto linguistic expressions, C_{HL} contains both principles and parameters.

Question 2 is all about first language acquisition, which can be characterized as a process by which experience in the form of primary language data (PLD) interacts with an innate initial state of the language faculty in the mind of the speaker to produce a steady state, an I-language. In actuality, this results from the mapping of PLD, consisting of continuous sound waves, onto the discrete paired representations of PF and LF – what can be characterized as the first miracle of language acquisition. The steady state involves substantially more information than PLD provides, a situation referred to as the poverty of the stimulus. The explanation for how language acquisition is possible given poverty of the stimulus relies on the postulation of an innate language faculty with specific mechanisms and principles governing their operation and output.

Question 3 concerns the use of language. In one direction this involves language production, which goes from thought to speech/writing. Thought interfaces with LF; speech and writing with PF. A central problem of language production concerns the creative aspect of language use, which encompasses four properties: language is unbounded, innovative, stimulus-free, and coherent and appropriate. The first two can be explained in terms of the recursive property of the grammatical mechanism. The third concerns free-will, a larger philosophical problem. The fourth remains as much a mystery today as it was when Descartes wrote about it over three centuries ago. Language processing proceeds in the other direction, from speech and writing to thought. Given that there is no formal theory of thought (and may never be), language use remains pretty much an unsolved problem.

About the neural basis of C_{HL} and the lexicon that is addressed in the fourth question, almost nothing is known. Whether a future neuroscience of language can answer any of the basic questions (e.g. where is C_{HL} located?) remains to be determined.

Bibliographical notes

For discussion of the internalist perspective, see Chomsky 2000b. The initial discussion of I-language and E-language occurs in Chomsky 1986. The four questions are discussed in Chomsky 1986 and 1988. For discussion of the creative aspect of language use, see in addition Chomsky 2006 and 2009. See Ross 1984 for more about the CSC. On parameters, see Baker 2001. For more about language acquisition and its relation to C_{HL}, see Yang 2002 and 2006. See Marantz, Miyashita, and O'Neil (2000) and Poeppel and Hickok (2004) for some work on the neural basis of language. For discussion of the problems facing this area of research see Poeppel and Embick (2005) and Boeckx (2010).

3   Categories and constituents

3.1   Syntactic knowledge

Returning now to knowledge of syntax, let us review some points our *fish* examples illustrate.

First, what is known about a sentence crucially concerns the syntactic function of each word in it. Consider (1):

(1)   Fish fish

(1) has several possible interpretations, depending on what syntactic category is assigned to each word. In this example the same phonetic form [f ɪ ʃ] can represent a noun or a verb.[1] If *Fish* in (1) is interpreted as a noun, then *fish* can be interpreted as a verb and the entire construction will be interpreted as a declarative sentence containing an intransitive verb (i.e. lacking an object). If however, *Fish* in (1) is interpreted as a verb, then *fish* can be interpreted as a noun and the entire construction will be interpreted as an imperative sentence, a command, with a covert second person subject (i.e. one that has an LF representation, but no PF representation).

Second, what is known about a sentence crucially concerns the way in which words join together to form syntactic units. Thus (2) has two possible sentential interpretations depending on how the five words join together as units.

(2)   Fish fish fish fish fish

On one interpretation, the fourth word is the verb of the main clause (as opposed to the embedded relative clause), as given in (3).

(3)   [$_{CL}$ [$_{SU}$ Fish [$_{CL}$ fish fish]] fish fish]

Therefore, the fifth word is the object of the verb and the first three words as a unit constitute the subject (SU) of the main clause. Notice that the main clause and the relative clause have the same syntactic label (CL) because in terms of syntactic structure they are the same. On the other interpretation, the second word is the verb of the main clause, as in (4).

(4)   [$_{CL}$ [$_{SU}$ Fish] fish [$_{OB}$ fish [$_{CL}$ fish fish]]]

Therefore, the last three words as a unit constitute the object of the verb (OB) and only the first word is the subject.

The words of a sentence and the syntactic units formed from them are **constituents** of the sentence. Words are **lexical** constituents; the syntactic units created by grouping together two or more words are **phrasal** constituents (or **phrases**). This creates a **hierarchical structure** on top of the linear order of the lexical items in a sentence. This hierarchical structure plus the linear order of elements in phrases constitute the phrase structure of a sentence. The syntax of a language is determined largely by its phrase structure (i.e. its constituent structure).

There are two basic ways to think about the constituent structure of sentences: **top-down** and **bottom-up**.

Top-down analysis starts with the sentence, dividing it into its main subparts (e.g. subject and predicate) and then dividing those subparts into their major subparts and so on until the individual lexical items (roughly "words") of the sentence are reached. Consider the top-down analysis of the simple sentence (5).

(5)   Teachers praise students

(5) consists of two main parts: a subject, the noun *teachers* and a predicate, the phrase *praise students*. Because the predicate contains more than one word, it can be further analyzed as a verb *praise* followed by an object, the noun *students*. The syntactic category of each lexical constituent (the word class to which the lexical item belongs – in more traditional terminology) constitutes the **label** of the lexical item. This phrase structure analysis of the sentence can be represented as a labeled bracket representation (6a) or equivalently as a tree structure (6b) where the syntactic categories of the three words have been made explicit.

(6)   a.   [$_{CL}$ [$_{SU}$ Teachers] [$_{Pred}$ praise [$_{OB}$ students]]]

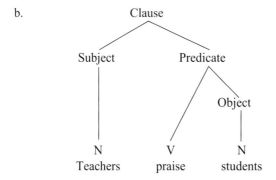

A tree structure consists of a set of elements (in (6b) words identified by their syntactic category) joined together by **branches** (the lines of the tree diagram). When two branches meet they form a **node** that bears a label (e.g. Predicate). The node at which all the branches of the tree meet is called the **root** of the tree. The words at the bottom of the tree are called **terminal** elements. In (6b) the nodes Clause and Predicate involve **binary** branching; the nodes Subject and Object involve **unary** branching. Both the labeled bracket representation in (6a) and the tree representation in (6b) encode the information that the verb and its object N are constituents of the Predicate phrase, and that Subject and Predicate are constituents of the phrase labeled Clause. In this way, a phrase structure tree represents the **hierarchical** constituent structure of a linguistic expression. It also represents the left to right **linear** order of the words and phrases in a sentence. (For example, the N *teachers* precedes the predicate phrase and the lexical items contained in it.) Just as there is only one relation, **precedence**, that holds between elements in the linear structure of a sentence, there is only one relation between elements in the hierarchical structure: **dominance**. For example, in (6b) Predicate dominates the lexical items *praise* and *students* and the phrasal category Object. Furthermore, Predicate **immediately dominates** *praise* and Object, but not *students*. Two constituents that are immediately dominated by the same category are **sisters**. Top-down analysis starts at the root and proceeds down the tree structure to the terminal elements.

Note that under phrase structure analysis the string of words *teachers praise* is not a constituent. Furthermore, neither can the two nouns *teachers* + *students* form an independent phrase. Only continuous linear strings of elements can form constituents. Therefore constituents cannot be discontinuous, where one part of a constituent is separated from another by some element or elements that are not also part of the constituent.

The subject-predicate analysis of clauses, which goes back at least as far as Aristotle, has a certain intuitive naturalness – especially considering the alternative, which would group the subject and verb as a phrase, leaving the object as an independent syntactic element. However, for nominal phrases like (7), it is not immediately obvious how they should be analyzed.

(7)   an insightful analysis

(7) contains three lexical items, an article *an* (labeled Det for **determiner** (the standard categorial designation for what are known in traditional grammar as "articles")), an adjective *insightful* (labeled A), and a noun *analysis* (labeled N as usual) in that linear order. There are three logical possibilities for assigning a phrase structure to the lexical string (7). These are represented in (8) using '+' to indicate a grouping of elements and square brackets to indicate which elements form constituents.

(8)   a.   [an + insightful + analysis]
           b.   [an + [insightful + analysis]]
           c.   [[an + insightful] + analysis]

In (8a) each word constitutes an equal part of the whole phrase. In this case a tree diagram representation would involve a single node with three branches connecting to the three lexical elements, an instance of **ternary** branching. This phrase would have what is called a **flat structure**, where each lexical constituent of a phrase is a sister of every other lexical constituent of the phrase. (8b) contains a constituent *insightful analysis*, whereas in (8c) the determiner and the adjective form a constituent *an insightful*.

EXERCISE 3.1

Consider the phrase in (i).

(i)   an insightful analysis of syntactic structure

a.   Estimate the number of different unlabeled phrase structure trees that could be constructed from this string of lexical items.

b.   Taking *of syntactic structure* to be a PP with the structure (ii),

(ii)   [of [syntactic structure]]

construct as many different unlabeled phrase structure trees for the analysis of (i) as you can discover.

The assignment of labels to the terminal elements is determined by the syntactic category of each lexical item as it exists in the lexicon. In practice, the label of a phrasal constituent under a top-down analysis can be assigned on the basis of function (e.g. Subject or Predicate), structure (e.g. Clause, because it contains a Subject and a Predicate as immediate constituents), or in terms of the most important lexical constituent it contains. For example, labeling (7) as a noun phrase (NP) indicates that the noun constituent in it is the most important element. This is evident given that the determiner and the adjective are optional elements, thus one can talk of *an analysis*, *insightful analyses*, or just *analyses* (without either a determiner or an adjective). Such assignments are relatively straightforward. With the two binary branching analyses in (8b and c) however, there is a question about how the intermediate constituents should be labeled. This issue will be resolved in the discussion of bottom-up phrase structure analysis that follows.

Presumably only one of these analyses is correct. If more than one were possible, then that phrase could be expected to have more than one interpretation, as with cases of pure structural ambiguity like *a review of a book by three professors*. In the next chapter a theory of syntactic structure is developed from which it follows that there is only one syntactic representation for (7).

In contrast to top-down analysis, bottom-up analysis begins with individual lexical items (e.g. words), forming constituents by **concatenating** (joining together) either (a) pairs of lexical items, or (b) pairs consisting of a lexical item and a group of lexical items that have already been concatenated to form a syntactic constituent, or (c) pairs of syntactic units so formed (e.g. [subject + predicate] in (6) above). As an illustration, consider a bottom-up analysis of (9) as given in (10).

(9)   A picture of Mary is hanging in the office.

(10)   a.   the + office => [the office]
           b.   in + [the office] => [in [the office]]
           c.   hanging + [in [the office]] => [hanging [in [the office]]]
           d.   is + [hanging [in [the office]]] => [is [hanging [in [the office]]]]
           e.   of + Mary => [of Mary]
           f.   picture + [of Mary] => [picture [of Mary]]

g.   a + [picture [of Mary]] => [a [picture [of Mary]]]
h.   [a [picture [of Mary]]] + [is [hanging [in [the office]]]]] => (i)
i.   [[a [picture [of Mary]]] [is [hanging [in [the office]]]]]]

The syntactic structure derived from (10) contains only binary branching, but that is because only two syntactic objects (lexical items or the phrases formed from them) are concatenated at each step. The following discussion is based on the working hypothesis that constituent structure is basically binary in nature. Whether it involves more (e.g. ternary with three branches from a single node) is an empirical question for which a positive answer requires either strong empirical evidence or strong theoretical considerations. See Section 3.3 and Section 4.3 for a possible exception to binary branching involving coordinate structures.

The groupings of lexical items into constituents can also be analyzed on the basis of type, in terms of a syntactic label. In general, a label of a phrasal constituent is determined by the syntactic category of one of the lexical constituents it contains. In (10a), for example, the two constituents of the phrase *the office* bear the labels Det and N. Traditionally, such phrases have been analyzed as noun phrases, in which case the syntactic object constructed from the concatenation of these two lexical elements bears the category label N. In effect the lexical constituent N **projects** its label onto the phrasal constituent formed by concatenating the noun with a determiner. The lexical constituent that projects its label in this way is designated as the **head** of the phrasal constituent formed. With the phrase *the office*, the noun *office* functions as the head of that phrase. The phrase itself is an N phrase or more commonly NP. When a preposition P is concatenated with a NP, as in (10b), the result is a prepositional phrase (PP); hence the phrase bears the categorial label P of its head, the preposition *in*. When a verb (e.g. *hanging*) is concatenated with a PP, the result is a verb phrase (VP) that bears the categorial label V.

EXERCISE 3.2

The analysis of the sentence in (9) given in (10) yields an unlabeled phrase structure tree.

a. Give the tree.
b. Assign labels to the nodes of the tree in terms of the heads of the phrases constructed. What issues arise?

Given the bottom-up analysis, the functional labels Subject, Object, and Predicate as illustrated in (6) are not viable. That is because such labels are not determined by or related to the intrinsic syntactic properties of their lexical constituents. This is obvious in the case of Subject and Object where the noun phrases they label are often interchangeable (e.g. *students praise teachers*). However, in the case of the label Predicate, a verb is almost always the head so the categorial label V (or VP for verb phrase) is sufficient to identify the phrase as a predicate and necessary because verbs need to be distinguished from the other lexical classes (e.g. N, P, and A). The hierarchical structure of a phrase structure tree with only labels derived from lexical items can then be used to identify the grammatical functions of the constituents without recourse to functional labels of any sort. Thus the subject of a clause is the NP that is immediately dominated by Clause; the predicate of a clause is the VP immediately dominated by Clause; and the object of the verb is the NP immediately dominated by VP. This illustrates how functional designations can be identified solely on the basis of configurational relations in purely categorial representations (see Chomsky 1965 for discussion).

This analysis of labels now raises a question about the label *Clause*, because it is not related to the label of either of its immediate constituents. This issue is resolved in Chapter 5, where the phrase structure analysis of clauses is developed.

Consider (7) again within a bottom-up analysis. (7) consists of a determiner *an* followed by an adjective *insightful* followed by a noun *analysis*, as given in (11).

(11)   Det   A   N
            an   insightful analysis

It is important to notice that the lexical item in each case is an instantiation of its syntactic category, not a constituent of that category. This distinction is signified by using lines only to indicate the constituent structure relation of dominance. When *insightful* and *analysis* are concatenated the question that arises is: what is the label of the newly constructed syntactic unit? Assuming the simplest answer: that it is the syntactic category of one of the two constituents concatenated, then the label of *insightful analysis* must be either A or N. In this case, the adjective modifies the noun and hence is functionally/semantically subordinate to the noun in this construction. Moreover, when the adjective is eliminated a viable phrase (*an analysis*) remains, but not the other way round (hence *an insightful*). Therefore the noun provides the categorial label of the phrase – it is a noun phrase (NP).

The same kind of analysis can be given for the concatenation of the determiner *an* with the phrase *insightful analysis*. The label of the phrase (7) could be either Det or N. Traditionally, N has been taken to be the label of phrases like (7) on the grounds that the determiner acts as a modifier of the noun. For example, as with other modifiers (e.g. adjectives) it seems to be optional given that NPs can apparently occur without a determiner as in *insightful analyses*.

Bottom-up analysis involves a principle of labeling such that the label of each phrasal constituent is determined by the label of one of the lexical items it contains. In effect, one of the lexical items in each phrase will **project** its label to be the label of the phrase. The lexical element that projects its label constitutes the **head** of the phrase; the phrase itself is a **phrasal projection** of that head. The highest phrasal projection of a head is the **maximal phrasal projection** of

that head. A constituent whose label is determined by a lexical head is called
endocentric. Chapter 5 extends this analysis to clausal constructions, which
prior to the mid 1980s were considered to be **exocentric** (i.e. without an identifiable head).

EXERCISE 3.3

Construct a complete analysis of (7).

a. Add labels to the three trees you constructed for (8).
b. How precisely does our theory choose (8c) over (8a) and (8b)?
c. What effect does our theory have on the analysis of (i) from Exercise 3.1?

3.2   Constituents and displacement

Recall that, in contrast to artificial formal "languages" that have been
constructed for various technical purposes (e.g. logic or computer programming),
natural human languages contain syntactic constructions in which a constituent
pronounced in one position in a sentence (at PF) is actually interpreted as if it
occupied a different position (at LF), the **displacement property**. Consider the
construction in which an object NP in a simple declarative sentence like (12a) is
pronounced at the beginning of the sentence, as in (12b).

(12)   a.   I did not assign the book about syntactic analysis by Joenz for this
                course.
           b.   The book about syntactic analysis by Joenz, I did not assign for this
                course.

In (12b) the NP *that book about syntactic analysis by Joenz* is interpreted as
the topic of the sentence as well as the object of *assign*. Thus (12b) is a **topicalization** construction. This displacement of the NP *that book about syntactic
analysis by Joenz* in (12b) can be viewed as the result of a process of syntactic
movement of the displaced constituent from its grammatical function position
(e.g. object of a verb), where it receives its interpretation, to another position in
a sentence where it is pronounced. (See Chapters 6–8 for detailed discussion of
displacement in syntax.)

In simple cases like (12b), the displaced element is a phrase – namely, a NP.
This NP consists of a head noun *book*, a determiner *the*, and two prepositional
phrases (PP) *about syntactic analysis* and *by Joenz*, each containing a preposition
and a noun object. The specific constituent structure for the whole NP of course
depends on how these elements are constructed with each other. Keeping to the
working hypothesis of binary branching, (13) gives one analysis for the syntactic
object in (12a).

(13)   [$_{NP}$ the [$_N$ [$_N$ book [$_{PP}$ about [$_{NP}$ syntactic analysis]]]][$_{PP}$ by Joenz]]]

EXERCISE 3.4

a. Give (13) as a tree diagram.
b. State the steps by which it is constructed (e.g., step 1: concatenate *syntactic* and *analysis* to form NP).

Given this structural analysis, the strings of lexical items listed in (14) form phrasal constituents as well as the string *that book about syntactic analysis by Joenz*.

(14)   a.   syntactic analysis   =NP
                     b.   about syntactic analysis   =PP
                     c.   by Joenz   =PP
                     d.   book about syntactic analysis   =N
                     e.   book about syntactic analysis by Joenz   =N

This means that the following substrings of lexical items, among others, do not constitute constituents.

(15)   a.   the book
                     b.   the book about
                     c.   the book about syntactic analysis
                     d.   the book about syntactic analysis by
                     e.   book about
                     f.   book about syntactic analysis by

Whether (13) is the correct phrase structure for the NP under discussion and moreover the only correct structure will be addressed in the following chapter.

EXERCISE 3.5

a. Give two additional substrings that are not constituents.
b. Explain why they are not constituents given the analysis of the string in (13).

The analysis can be used to test the hypothesis that non-constituents (i.e. strings of lexical items that do not form a single constituent) are not subject to displacement. If the hypothesis is correct, then the displacement of a non-constituent should produce a deviant construction, as it does – illustrated in part with the examples in (16) as compared with (12b). The underlined blank space indicates the position from which the italicized string of lexical items has been displaced.

(16)   a.   *The book*, I did not assign _____ about syntactic analysis by Joenz for this course.
                     b.   *The book about*, I did not assign _____ syntactic analysis by Joenz for this course

This analysis assumes that the string of lexical items that has been displaced to the front of the clause in a topic position has been extracted out of a NP constituent of the form (13) that occurs as the object of the verb *assign*. (16a) shows the displacement of non-constituent (15a), and (16b) involves the non-constituent (15b).

The constraint on displacement formulated above is, however, not strong enough to rule out other cases that do not occur. For example, although the string in (14d), *book about syntactic analysis by Joenz*, constitutes a single constituent, it alone cannot be displaced in a passive construction corresponding to (12b) (cf. (12a)).

(17)   *Book about syntactic analysis by Joenz*, I did not assign the _____ for this course.

As (17) illustrates, when the NP object of the verb *assign* is displaced in the derivation of the topicalized construction, the determiner *the* cannot be stranded. In effect, displacement applies to the maximal projection of the head of the phrase, in this case *book*, not any non-maximal projection of the head. This also covers the impossibility of moving just (14c) in the derivation of a passive construction, because (14c) is also an intermediate constituent of the NP (13).

Although maximal phrasal projections are candidates for displacement, not all maximal phrasal projections can be displaced. Only the entire NP object of the verb *assign* can be legitimately topicalized. Thus compare (12b) to the deviant examples (18a–b).

(18)   a.   *Syntactic analysis*, I did not assign the book about _____ by Joenz for this course.
            b.   *About syntactic analysis*, I did not assign the book _____ by Joenz for this course by me.

In (18a) the NP *syntactic analysis*, consisting of the adjective *syntactic* and the noun *analysis*, which is the object of the preposition *about*, has been displaced; while in (18b) it is the PP *about syntactic analysis* which has been topicalized. Neither result is legitimate, so therefore while the constraint on the application of displacement to maximal phrasal projections is necessary, by itself it is not sufficient to separate all the illegitimate from the legitimate cases.

The analysis above establishes three important points about how displacement can be used as a diagnostic for constituent structure. First, a non-constituent is not subject to displacement; therefore a legitimate instance of displacement serves as a diagnostic for identifying strings of lexical items that form constituents. Second, a constituent that is not the maximal phrasal projection of its head is not subject to displacement; therefore displacement serves as a diagnostic for a string of lexical items that constitutes a maximal phrasal projection. And third, not every maximal phrasal projection is subject to displacement however; thus there are other constraints on displacement beyond the requirement that the displaced syntactic material form a constituent that is a maximal phrasal projection.

Topicalization can also affect PP as well as NP. Consider (19).

(19)   a.   John ran *out the door*.
            b.   *Out the door*, John ran.

Given that (19b) is a possible variant of (19a) where the lexical string *out the door* has been displaced to the front of the sentence before the syntactic subject, by hypothesis this string must be a constituent and also a maximal phrasal projection. Taking *out* to be a preposition, the displaced phrase is analyzed as a PP. The PP *out the door* in both (19a) and (19b) is interpreted as a locative phrase specifying where John ran. This locative phrase in (19b) has been topicalized – i.e. promoted to the prominent initial position of the sentence; thus (19b) is also a topicalization construction.

The topicalization of PP can also be used to test constituency. Compare (19) to (20).

(20)   a.   John threw *out the door*.
            b.   *Out the door*, John threw.

Both (19a) and (20a) contain what appears to be an identical string *out the door*. However, (20b) shows that this string in (20a) cannot be topicalized and therefore one explanation for the deviance of (20b) is that the string *P-Det-NP* does not form a single constituent. In contrast, the same string in (19a) must be a single constituent because it can be topicalized.

It is worth noting that (21), in contrast to the deviant (20b), is also a possible topicalization construction.

(21)   *The door*, John threw out _____.

The deviance of (20b) in conjunction with the nondeviance of (21) suggests that the string *threw out* must form some kind of constituent because *out* must be concatenated with the verb *threw* independently of and prior to the incorporation of the NP *the door* into the syntactic structure. The analysis of *throw out* is investigated in the next section.

Cleft constructions also manifest displacement. Two examples are given in (25), where the italics mark the focus position and the underline marks the position in which the element in focus position is interpreted.

(22)   a.   It was *the thief* that [the police arrested _____].
            b.   It would have been *to Mary* that [Bill gave the book _____].

These constructions have the schematic structure (23).

(23)   *it* BE XP *that* Clause

In clefts, *it* is pleonastic and hence non-referential. BE stands for some form of the copula *be* with or without auxiliary verbs (e.g. *was* or *would have been*), and XP marks the phrase that constitutes the focus of the sentence, the element that receives emphatic stress. The syntactic analysis of *that* and Clause is given in Chapter 5.

The constituent Clause, marked with brackets in (22), is designated as "open" because it contains an empty (i.e. phonetically null) position that is linked to the constituent in the focus position. Thus (22a) *the thief* is interpreted as the object of *arrested* even though it does not appear in that position at PF (as in *the police arrested the thief*). (22b) demonstrates that the focus position can take PP as well as NP (unlike the subject position of a passive construction, as illustrated in the paradigm in (24)).

(24)　　　a.　John gave Mary a book.
　　　　　b.　John gave a book to Mary.
　　　　　c.　*A book* was given _____ to Mary by John.
　　　　　d.　*Mary* was given _____ a book by John
　　　　　e.　**To Mary* was given a book _____ by John.
　　　　　f.　**Mary* was given a book to _____ by John.
　　　　　g.　**Mary* was given a book by John to _____.

In (24a) *Mary* occurs as a NP object of *gave*, while in (24b) the same N with the same semantic relation to the verb occurs as the NP object of the P *to*. As the contrast between (24d) and (24e) shows, *Mary* can be displaced to the subject position in a passive construction when the NP occurs as an object of V, but not as the object of P where the entire PP is displaced. (24f–g) show that when *Mary* functions as the object of the preposition *to*, the NP cannot be displaced to the syntactic subject position either.

Notice that although the prescriptive prohibition against ending a sentence with a preposition could apply to (24g), it does not cover (24f). Moreover, presumably the problem concerns the extraction of the NP from the PP, so whatever rules out (24f) will inevitably generalize to (24g). See Section 6.3 for a single general principle that rules out (24e–g).

Given the previous discussion, displacement comes in at least two varieties, one that affects only NPs (e.g. movement to the syntactic subject position in passive constructions) and another that can affect either NPs or PPs (e.g. topicalization and cleft constructions). As (25) illustrates, only NP and PP can occur in the focus position of a cleft construction.

(25)　　　a.　*It was *very happy about his new book* that [John was _____].
　　　　　b.　*It is *going to the party* that [John is _____].
　　　　　c.　*It was *go to the party* that [John did _____].
　　　　　d.　*It was *that the proof was flawed* that [the mathematician
　　　　　　　thought _____].

(25a) demonstrates that an AP cannot occur in the focus position of a cleft. (25b–c) and (25d) demonstrate the same point about VP and clause respectively. Topicalization however allows for a broader class of displacements. (26) illustrates that it is possible to topicalize an AP, and (27) shows that a VP can be topicalized as well.

(26)　　　*Very happy about his new book*, John isn't _____.

(27)　　　*Go to the museum*, John did/would/can _____.

However, interestingly, cleft sentences do not seem to be able to undergo topicalization.

(28)   *_This book_, it would have been _to Mary_ that [Bill gave _____ _____].

Why this is so is raised again in Chapter 8 (see exercise 8.27), which develops an analysis of interrogative constructions and their kin.

3.3   Constituents and coordination

In addition to displacement constructions, **coordinate** constructions, in which two lexical items or groups of lexical items are joined together by a conjunction (e.g. _and_), also provide a reliable test for whether or not a given string of words forms a constituent. A coordinate construction contains the form (29) as a subpart of a clause, including when X and Y constitute coordinated main clauses.

(29)   X and Y

We call X and Y **conjuncts** of the coordination. The coordinating conjunction _and_ simply joins the conjuncts together, but does not indicate any more specific relationship between them.

A sentence consisting of a coordination of two or more independent clauses is called a **compound sentence**. This is a special case. There are also coordinate constructions that are not compound sentences – that is, when X and Y are either single lexical items or non-clausal phrases. The examples in (30) provide three distinct cases.

(30)   a.   syntax and semantics
              b.   the syntax of case in Finnish and the semantics of quantifiers in
                   English
              c.   syntax and the semantics of quantifiers in English

(30a) involves the coordination of two lexical items, the nouns _syntax_ and _semantics_. (30b) consists of a coordination of two NPs, _the syntax of case in Finnish_ and _the semantics of quantifiers in English_. (30c) contains the coordination of a single noun _syntax_ with a NP _the semantics of quantifiers in English_. In all three cases, N is the head of each conjunct.

There are parallel constructions involving conjuncts headed by adjectives and also verbs. The examples in (31) constitute APs, the italicized phrases in (32) are VPs.

(31)   a.   surprised and happy
              b.   surprised about the result of the experiment and happy for the members
                   of the lab
              c.   surprised and very happy for the members of the lab

(32)   a.   John _writes and edits_.
              b.   John _writes plays and edits novels_.
              c.   John _edits novels and writes_.

In (31–32), the a-examples involve a coordination of single lexical items, the respective heads of each conjunct; the b-examples coordinate two phrasal conjuncts; the c-examples contain coordinations of a single lexical item with a phrasal constituent. This set of examples demonstrates that conjuncts in a coordinate construction form constituents. If this must be the case, then there must be a general constraint on conjuncts that requires them to be constituents, call this the **Constituency Constraint on Conjuncts**.

The possibility of coordinating lexical heads as well as phrases can lead to ambiguity. (33) has two different interpretations.

(33)   John edits and writes novels.

On one interpretation (33) is synonymous with (34).

(34)   John edits novels and writes novels.

Under this interpretation (33) is analyzed syntactically as (35), where the NP *novels* is the object of the conjoined verb *edits and writes*.

(35)   John [$_{VP}$ [$_V$ edits and writes] novels]

Alternatively, (33) can be interpreted as synonymous with (36) where the first conjunct is unambiguously a VP (*writes novels*).

(36)   John writes novels and edits.

On this interpretation, (33) is analyzed as a coordination of a V and a VP, as given in (37).

(37)   John [$_{VP}$ edits and [$_{VP}$ writes novels]].

Under the first interpretation, John edits novels as well as writes them; under the second, what sort of work John edits is unspecified.

Notice that (33) can be punctuated in a way that disambiguates the two readings.

(38)   John edits, and writes novels.

The comma indicates a pause, hence the PF of (38) will be distinct from the PF of (33) under the interpretation that John both edits novels and writes them where there is no pause between *edits* and *and*. In the case of (33) then, it appears that the ambiguity results from the orthographic representation of the sentence – that is, without the comma, both readings are possible. Whether the two interpretations have distinct PF representations is not obvious. However, as such standard cases of ambiguity as *flying planes can be dangerous* show this is not always the case (see also the following examples).

EXERCISE 3.6

Discuss the ambiguity involved in each of the following examples.

   (i)   Students and professors from Los Angeles are welcome to attend.
   (ii) We were surprised and happy about the results of the experiment.

  a. Provide two different syntactic analyses of the coordinate constructions in
     each example and identify which syntactic structure corresponds to which
     interpretation.
  b. Consider whether the PFs of the two interpretations of (i) and (ii) are distinct,
     and whether punctuation can be utilized to create unambiguous versions of these
     sentences.

Ambiguity can also arise with a modifier to the left of a pair of coordinated
Ns, as (39) illustrates.

(39)   Brilliant students and professors are welcome to attend.

The adjective *brilliant* can be interpreted as modifying either just the noun
students or the coordination *students and professors*. The difference in interpretation involves the **scope** of the modifier – whether it modifies only one noun or
both. The scope of the adjective when it modifies both nouns is wider than when
it modifies only one of them. The two readings are distinguished as wide-scope
vs. narrow-scope. Moreover the two interpretations of the ambiguous subject in
(39) can be represented with distinct syntactic structures, as given in (40). (Note
that these syntactic structures for coordination involve ternary rather than binary
branching (see Section 3 of Chapter 4 for arguments against using binary branching for coordinate constructions).)

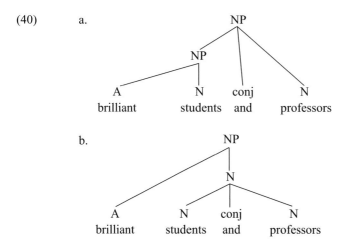

(40)   a.

(40)   b.

This ambiguity is purely structural, so scope can be defined in structural terms.
In the narrow-scope reading represented in (40a), the A *brilliant* is in a sister
relation with the N *students*, but not with the N *professors*. In the wide-scope
reading represented in (40b), the A *brilliant* is a sister of the constituent that
contains both nouns.
    Using the sister relation, scope can be defined syntactically in terms of phrase
structure relations. These relations involve hierarchical structure and are characterized using the notion of **constituent-command** (henceforth **c-command**).

(41)   **c-command:** A constituent α *c-commands* a constituent β if and only if β is either a sister of α or contained in (dominated by) a sister of α.

Thus when *brilliant* c-commands *professors* (as in (40b)), then that noun is in the scope of the adjective, and when the adjective does not c-command the noun (as in (40a)), the noun is not in the scope of the adjective.[2]

EXERCISE 3.7

Now consider what happens when the two ambiguous NPs *students and professors from Los Angeles* and *brilliant students and professors* are combined into a single NP:

(i) brilliant students and professors from Los Angeles

This should lead to a four-way ambiguity as represented in the following table.

INTERPRETATION	*brilliant*	*brilliant*	*from Los Angeles*	*from Los Angeles*
	students	professors	students	professors
1	yes	no	no	yes
2	yes	yes	yes	yes
3	yes	yes	no	yes
4	yes	no	yes	yes

Each one of these interpretations can be matched to a specific phrase structure representation (tree diagram).

a. Provide a phrase structure representation for each interpretation.
b. For the second interpretation, the phrase structure representation you gave is not the only one possible. What is the other?
c. There are other assignments of yes/no in an extension of this table that do not yield possible interpretations: no – yes – yes – yes, for example. Why is this interpretation impossible? How many other impossible patterns can you identify? Why are these also excluded?
d. And last but certainly not least, which of the four possible interpretations do you actually get/recognize? Are they all equally accessible or are some easier to access than others?

EXERCISE 3.8

The same kind of multiple ambiguity occurs with a coordination of adjectives. The AP italicized in (i) is ambiguous.

(i) We were *surprised and happy about the results of the experiment.*

a. Give an unambiguous paraphrase of the AP for each interpretation.

b.   Demonstrate how the ambiguity of the AP is purely structural by providing two
     distinct phrase structure trees for this italicized string. (Assume the coordination
     to be ternary branching.)
c.   How is c-command involved in the disambiguation/interpretation of (i)?

Now consider a more complicated example: the result (ii) from adding a single word
to (i).

   (ii) We were *very surprised and happy about the results of the experiment.*

d.   Given that lexical items and the phrases constructed from them are grouped in
     a binary fashion (i.e. only two at each step) to build phrase structure, how many
     distinct structures can be assigned to the underlined AP?
e.   Give each structure and match it to a distinct interpretation which you give as an
     unambiguous paraphrase of the AP.
f.   Identify how c-command is involved in each interpretation.

Given the examples above, coordinate constructions may contain a
coordination of single lexical items or phrases or the combination of a single
lexical item and a phrase. They conform to a general constraint on coordinate
constructions: each conjunct must be a single constituent. There are others, as
will be discussed below, using data from the paradigm for double object verbs
in English.

(42) provides a paradigm for double object verbs like *write* which can take both a
direct object (*a letter*) and an indirect object (*Mary*) – see (42a) and (24a) above.

(42)   a.   John wrote Mary a letter.
          b.   John wrote a letter to Mary.
          c.   John wrote Mary.
          d.   John wrote to Mary.
          e.   John wrote a letter.
          f.   John wrote.

Such verbs also have a corresponding construction in which the NP that can
show up as the indirect object (between the V and the direct object) can also
occur as the object of a prepositional phrase following the direct object (see
(42b)). Furthermore, neither the direct object nor the indirect object (either as a
NP object of the verb or the NP object of a preposition) is obligatory, as illustrated
in (42c–f). As expected, the direct object and the indirect object may involve a
coordinate structure as illustrated in (43).

(43)   a.   John wrote a letter and a postcard.
          b.   John wrote Mary and Fred.
          c.   John wrote to Mary and to Fred.

However, as (44) shows, a coordination of a NP and a PP is prohibited.

(44)   a.   *John wrote to Mary and a letter.
          b.   *John wrote a letter and to Mary.

The deviance of (44) could motivate a constraint on the coordinate construction where the conjuncts must bear the same syntactic label, a **Syntactic Symmetry Constraint** on coordinate constructions.

Consider however an alternative hypothesis about these deviant coordinate constructions in (44). Suppose instead that the coordination is ruled out on the semantic grounds that the two NPs in the two conjuncts (*Mary* and *a letter* in (42)) serve different semantic functions since Mary is the intended recipient of the letter being written. While this is certainly a plausible alternative hypothesis, the syntactic constraint is still necessary. The semantic hypothesis would allow a coordination of a NP and a PP if they shared the same semantic function. However when two different constituents with the same semantic function are coordinated, a deviant construction results, as in (45).

(45)   *John wrote Mary and to Bill.

The semantic hypothesis does not exclude (45), whereas the syntactic constraint, which generalizes across (44) and (45), does.

EXERCISE 3.9

Now consider the following example.

   (i) John wrote to Mary and her best friend.

a.   One syntactic analysis that could be assigned to this example would violate the Syntactic Symmetry Constraint. Give the analysis and explain how it violates the constraint.
b.   However there is an alternative analysis that satisfies the constraint. Give that analysis and explain how it conforms to the constraint.

With coordination in double object constructions there is one other case to consider.

(46)   *John wrote Mary and a letter.

In (46) an indirect object *Mary* is coordinated with a direct object *a letter*. Since both are NPs, the coordinate construction satisfies the Syntactic Symmetry Constraint. The deviance of (46) must then arise from some other factor. One possible source might be the lack of semantic parallelism of the two conjuncts. If this is the relevant factor, then (46) provides empirical evidence for a **Semantic Parallelism Constraint** on coordinate constructions and thus it appears that both the syntactic and the semantic constraint are necessary.

There are however other examples that call into question whether a Semantic Parallelism Constraint on coordinate structures is the right approach to the deviance of (46). Consider the passive constructions in (47).

(47)   a.   ?The letter was written to Mary and by John.
            b.   ?The letter was written by John and to Mary.

Although these coordinate structures are somewhat odd because there are more standard variants (cf. (48)), they are not as strongly deviant as (46).

(48)   a.   The letter was written to Mary by John.
         b.   The letter was written by John to Mary.

(46) provides solid motivation for a Semantic Parallelism Constraint unless there is a viable alternative account. (47) suggests that it might be necessary to find one.

So far, it has been assumed that conjuncts must be constituents – i.e. either a single lexical item or a single phrase, but never a string of words that does not form a single phrase. This can be illustrated using the pair of sentences (19a) and (20a), repeated here as (49).

(49)   a.   John ran out the door.
         b.   John threw out the door.

As demonstrated above with displacement phenomena, the string *out the door* constitutes a single constituent, a PP, in (49a), but not in (49b). Thus it is possible for this string to occur as a conjunct in a coordinate construction, whereas it is impossible for the same string to function as a conjunct in a coordinate structure following the verb *threw*.

(50)   a.   John ran out the door and down the street.
         b.   *John threw out the door and away the window.

(50a) can be analyzed as a coordination of PPs, whereas (50b) cannot – which raises the question of the analysis of (50b).

The deviance of (50b) could be analyzed as a violation of the Constituency Constraint on Conjuncts. Thus the conjunct *away the window*, for example, cannot be analyzed as a single constituent. However, as discussed below, there is nonetheless a way to analyze the conjuncts in (50b) as single constituents; therefore an explanation for the deviance of (50b) must be found elsewhere.

The analysis of (50b) must be related to the analysis of the nondeviant examples in (51).

(51)   a.   John threw out the door.
         b.   Mary threw away the window.

The previous section raised the possibility that the string *threw out* formed a constituent. Furthermore, the NP *the door* functions straightforwardly as a direct object of the verb. Thus it can occur as the syntactic subject in the passive counterpart to the active (51a), where it is nonetheless interpreted as the object of the verb.

(52)   The door was thrown out by John.

If object NPs are interpreted in a configuration where the object is concatenated with a V as in (53), then *threw out* would be properly analyzed as a complex verb, a verb-particle construction – i.e. a single lexical constituent.

(53)   [$_{VP}$ V NP]

The syntactic label of the particle remains to be determined. It is not obvious that the particle is a species of preposition, say an intransitive P. Interpretatively it specifies a direction or location, functionally a locative of some sort. If this analysis is correct, then the orthographic convention of spelling this construct as two separate words simply masks the syntactic reality that the verb-particle construction constitutes a single lexical item.

Further evidence that supports the single lexical item analysis of the verb-particle construct comes from another major phenomenon that affects syntactic analysis, **deletion**. Consider the following pair of sentences.

(54)   a.   Bernie bought a new car and Adam bought a used bike.
        b.   Bernie bought a new car and Adam, a used bike.

Both examples are compound sentences. The first contains two finite clauses each of which could stand on its own as a sentence. Furthermore, the order of the two conjuncts could be reversed and the result would still be a viable sentence. In the second example, however, only the first conjunct can occur on its own as a sentence. The second conjunct *Adam, a used bike* does not constitute a viable sentence. Furthermore, if the order of the two conjuncts is reversed, the result is deviant.

(55)   *Adam, a used bike and Bernie bought a new car.

While the PF representations of (54a) and (54b) are different, their interpretation is the same; therefore they have the same LF representation. This follows if both have the same syntactic representation along the lines of (54a), but that in PF, the second instance of the verb *bought* is silenced (i.e. not pronounced). Thus the PF representation of (54b) would be (56), where the element with the strikethrough represents the silenced verb.

(56)   Bernie bought a new car and Adam ~~bought~~ a used bike.

This constitutes the essence of deletion phenomena in syntax, where an element that has a (non-null) PF representation in the lexicon is interpreted at LF even though it is not pronounced at PF.

The deletion of the verb in the second clausal conjunct of (54b) is called **gapping**, where the deletion of the finite verb creates a gap in the PF of the sentence. This kind of deletion can also occur with compound sentences that contain verb-particle constructs.

(57)   a.   Bernie threw out his old clothes and Adam threw out his old computer equipment.
        b.   Bernie threw out his old clothes and Adam ~~threw out~~ his old computer equipment.

This follows if *threw out* is a single lexical V. If however *threw* inside the lexical V *threw out* can be deleted independently as a V, then the analysis of gapping must be complicated to handle the deletion of the particle in (57b). Furthermore, an explanation would be needed for why the verbal part of these constructions (e.g. *threw*) cannot delete under gapping, as illustrated by the deviance of (58).

(58)   *Bernie threw out his old clothes and Adam ~~threw~~ away his old computer equipment.

The simpler analysis thus provides evidence for treating the verb-particle construct as a single lexical item. Furthermore the deviance of (58) provides empirical evidence for a constraint that prohibits deletion from applying to phonetic material that does not constitute at least a lexical constituent.

This analysis also suggests a way of analyzing the deviance of (50b). Instead of treating the two conjuncts of the coordinate structure in (50b) as non-constituents, hence in violation of the Constituency Constraint on Conjuncts, (50b) can be analyzed as a coordination of VPs as in (59), where the head of VP is the verb+particle construction *threw away*.

(59)   John [$_{VP}$ threw out the door] and [$_{VP}$ ~~threw~~ away the window]

Under this analysis, (50b) only violates the constraint on deletion that prohibits the deletion of subparts of lexical items.

EXERCISE 3.10

The following material may seem simple on the surface, but it gets complicated when trying to spell out all the analytical assumptions.

The verb-particle construction has an alternant realization in which the particle is separated from its verb by showing up in PF to the right of the direct object NP.

(i)   a.   He let in the cat.
     b.   He let the cat in.

Just as with the examples above, the particle plus the direct object cannot be coordinated, as in (ii).

(ii)   *He let in the cat and out the dog.

However the NP plus the particle can be coordinated when the particle occurs to the right of the NP, as in (iii).

(iii) He let the cat in and the dog out.

a.   Given this analysis of examples like (ii), how might that analysis be extended to (iii) in a way that allows (iii)?

3.4   Summary

The phrase structure of sentences involves how lexical constituents (words) are grouped together and labeled as constituent phrasal parts of the whole and how they are ordered linearly within phrasal constituents. This creates a hierarchical structure for sentences in addition to the linear order of the words they contain. This structure can be constructed either top-down (from sentence to words) or bottom-up (from words to sentence). Top-down analysis has historically involved some category labels of constituents that have no relation to the lexical constituents they contain (e.g. sentence, subject, predicate). In contrast, bottom-up analysis involves the labeling of phrases on the basis of the labels of the lexical constituents they contain. The label of the lexical constituent that labels a phrasal constituent identifies the head of the constituent. From the bottom-up perspective, a head projects its label.

The displacement property of language, in which a constituent is interpreted in a syntactic position (in LF) that is not the position in which it is pronounced (in PF), involves single constituents and not strings of words that do not form a single constituent. Therefore, displacement can be used as a diagnostic for constituents. For example, displacement in topicalized constructions can be utilized to test the constituent structure of complex NPs. Coordination provides another diagnostic given that conjuncts in a coordinate construction must be single constituents.

Syntactic ambiguity in coordinate constructions involves the scope of modifiers (wide, if they modify both conjuncts and narrow, if they only modify the adjacent conjunct). Scope can be captured in terms of c-command, a relation based on hierarchical structure between two elements in a precedence relation. The conjuncts in a coordinate construction must meet two general constraints, one syntactic and the other semantic. The former is a symmetry constraint that requires both conjuncts to be constituents of the same type (i.e. with the same syntactic label). The latter is a semantic parallelism constraint whereby the two conjuncts are interpreted as filling the same semantic function.

Verb-particle constructions provide an apparent counter-example to the constituent constraint on conjuncts. However, such constructions appear to involve deletion (gapping) so that their derivation actually conforms to this constraint.

Bibliographical notes

Most of the topics discussed in this chapter are covered more extensively in the next. See the bibliographical notes in the following chapter for details.

See Chomsky 1965 for a discussion of how relational notions like "subject," "object," and "predicate" can be interpreted from hierarchical syntactic structures, where for example a subject is a NP that is an immediate constituent of S (for sentence) and an object is a NP that is an immediate constituent of VP and a sister to V.

The relation c-command is first proposed and developed for a theory of anaphoric relations in Reinhart 1976. It is essentially the same as the relation "in construction with" in Klima 1964 (see Culicover 1976 for discussion).

4   Phrase structure theory

4.1   The fundamentals

From the bottom-up perspective discussed in the previous chapter, the creation of phrase structure representations consists of two procedures, **grouping** and **labeling**:

(i)   concatenate two (or possibly more) syntactic elements into a single syntactic object, a phrase;

(ii)   label the phrase created, using the category label of one of the syntactic elements in the phrase constructed by (i).

(i) and (ii) together constitute a single syntactic operation called **Merge**. The steps by which the phrase structure of a linguistic expression is constructed is called its **derivation**. Each derivation will therefore involve several successive applications of Merge to the lexical items contained in the expression and to the syntactic objects constructed by the previous applications of Merge. In this way, Merge re-applies to its own output and is therefore a **recursive procedure**, thereby providing the grammatical mechanism by which the computational system of human language (C_{HL}) can produce arbitrarily long sentences. That is, in principle there is no limit to the number of times Merge can apply in the derivation of a sentence, thereby yielding infinite use of finite means: the single recursive procedure Merge applied to the finite lexicon.

Consider, as an example, the derivation of the NP in (1) via Merge.

(1)   a brilliant student of linguistics from Princeton

The order in which the seven lexical items in (1) are merged is constrained in part by the **linear order** of the string. A pair of lexical items that are merged will create a syntactic object in which the two are adjacent and one precedes the other in Phonetic Form (PF). By hypothesis Merge is a binary operation, thus restricted to merging just two syntactic objects at each step. This pair of lexical items will remain adjacent (and sisters) throughout the derivation. Thus Merge cannot apply for example to *a* and *student* in (1) because they are not adjacent in the expression under analysis.

EXERCISE 4.1

Given no further constraints on linguistic structure, there are several different ways to merge the seven lexical items in (1), only some of which will yield a viable syntactic structure. One such derivation involves merging lexical elements pairwise starting from the left. Thus the first step would merge the determiner *a* with the adjective *brilliant*. The label of the syntactic object created could be either Det or A. Since this is not a viable syntactic structure in the first place, it really does not matter which label is choosen. (This, of course, means that for the wrong derivations, the categorial labeling of the illegitimate syntactic structures generated could be more than one way, thereby greatly increasing the number of illegitimate syntactic representations derivable from a completely unconstrained procedure.)

a. Construct an unlabeled tree structure that results from merging the lexical items in (1) from left to right.
b. Discuss how the labeling procedure could yield more than four different syntactic representations.
c. Construct the unlabeled tree structure that results from merging the lexical items in (1) from right to left.
d. In contrast to the previous procedure, this one yields a viable structure in the first step, a PP. What about the second, third, fourth, and fifth steps?

To fully understand the nature of the computational procedures proposed here, it is useful to see how they can misfire when unconstrained.

A viable derivation of the syntactic structure of (1) will contain two PPs *of linguistics* and *from Princeton*. Therefore, at some point in the derivation these distinct phrasal constituents will be constructed from their lexical elements via Merge before they are merged with other constituents of the NP. Given that neither PP is a constituent of the other, the order in which they are constructed makes no difference.

EXERCISE 4.2

In contrast, consider the NP (i).

(i) a photo of Charles with his dog

a. Given that the PP *with his dog* modifies *Charles* and not *photo*, what must the constituent structure of this NP be?
b. Given this structure, what must be the order of Merge with respect to the two PPs?

As a first step, the merger of the P *from* and the N *Princeton* yield a PP *from Princeton*, as represented in (2).

(2)

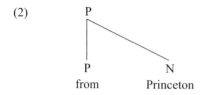

(2) shows that the merger of the P and the N results in a phrase labeled P.
Thus the preposition *from* **projects** its categorial label onto the syntactic object
created by the merger. This label marks the phrase created as a **phrasal projection** of the preposition, hence a prepositional phrase. The lexical element that
projects its label constitutes the **head** of the phrase. One of the most fundamental relations in phrase structure representations concerns a head and its (phrasal)
projections.

Not only does Merge create syntactic structure, but it also performs **lexical
insertion** as the operation that introduces lexical items into a syntactic derivation. Thus Merge links the computational system with the lexicon.

The next step in the derivation will not involve the PP just constructed for
two reasons. First, there are no further elements to add to the internal structure
of the PP. It is just a preposition *from* followed by its object, a single noun
Princeton. Second, it does not form a constituent with the adjacent noun *linguistics* to its left because it does not modify that noun in any way (cf. *student
of the linguistics of the Prague School*, where the PP *of the Prague School* does
modify what sort of linguistics referred to and therefore would be merged with
the N *linguistics*). Instead, the P *of* and the N *linguistics* will merge to form a
new PP. Then this PP will merge with the N *student* to form a phrase *student
of linguistics*. Given that *student* is the head of this phrase, the phrase will be
labeled N, thus a noun phrase. At this point the PP *from Princeton* that was
first constructed can be merged with this NP to construct a larger NP *student
of linguistics from Princeton*, where that PP now modifies the head of the NP,
student.

At this point, and only at this point, the adjective (A) *brilliant* merges
with the NP to create an even larger NP *brilliant student of linguistics from
Princeton*. And finally, the indefinite determiner *a* merges with that NP to create a still larger NP, the phrase in (1). The derivation yields the representation
in (3). Purely for clarity, all the phrasal projections from a head are represented
by vertical lines. The diagonal lines represent other syntactic relationships that
will be explicated shortly.

In (3) (see next page) the **maximal phrasal projection** of *student* (i.e. the
highest), given as NP for notational convenience, has several levels of phrasal
projection, in contrast to the PPs headed by *of* and *from*, which each have only
one, identical to the maximal projection.

(3)

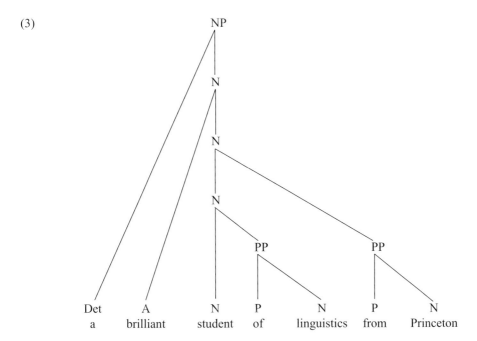

The phrases labeled N between the maximal projection and the head are **intermediate** phrasal projections. Thus (3) contains three constituents that constitute noun phrases (given in (4)) in addition to (1), which is the maximal phrase.

(4)   a. student of linguistics
        b. student of linguistics from Princeton
        c. brilliant student of linguistics from Princeton

The prepositional phrases in (1) contain only one level of phrasal projection, so that is the maximal projection, hence labeled PP (again for notational convenience).

Notice that a maximal phrasal projection can be easily identified configurationally as the highest projection of the category label of its head, including both the NP and the PP in (3). If labels of syntactic representations can be limited to just the category labels of the lexical items that constitute the heads of constituents, then syntactic representations might meet a **Condition of Inclusiveness**, where any structure formed by the computational system is limited to elements that already exist in lexical items. This prohibits the use of labels to categorially distinguish a head from any level of its phrasal projection, including the maximal level. The Inclusiveness Condition also affects the analysis of displacement, see Section 6.1 for details. However, for purely pedagogical purposes the maximal phrasal projection of a category X will be designated as XP.

Merge does not allow unary branching in principle. There is no way to construct a phrasal projection without concatenating at least two syntactic objects. If so, then what is the status of a bare head, which involves no levels of phrasal projection, as is the case for the adjective *brilliant* and the nouns *linguistics* and *Princeton* in (3)? These elements are indeed constituents of the larger NP. In terms of labeling there is no principled distinction between a lexical constituent and a phrase (whether it be an intermediate or maximal projection). Therefore the label of a bare head, by definition, marks the maximal phrasal projection even though the head does not project its label to another level of phrasal projection.

The order of steps in a derivation is not necessarily fixed uniquely. In the derivation of (1) *of* could have merged with *linguistics* and the resulting PP with *students* before merging *from* with *Princeton*. However, it is assumed that the hierarchical order in a tree representation determines the linear order of the elements in PF to a significant extent. Two elements that are merged together (hence sisters) must be adjacent in linear order and remain so unless one is moved to another part of the structure or deleted. In other words, there can be no crossing branches in tree structures. If this were possible then hierarchical structure would place virtually no constraints on the linear order of elements in the representations constructed.

A further constraint specifies that merger takes place only at the root. In other words, Merge cannot embed a syntactic element within a syntactic object – i.e. a phrase that has already been constructed. In effect, Merge can only extend a syntactic object by adjoining material to its right or left edge – that is, merging at the root. This constraint follows from the natural requirement for efficient computation that the merger of two syntactic objects leaves the two objects unchanged, what is called the **No Tampering Condition** (henceforth NTC, see Chomsky 2007, 2008). Once a sister relation between two syntactic elements is established in a derivation it cannot be modified either by adding additional sister constituents or by eliminating an existing sister relation.

Phrase structure is constrained by the following conditions:

(5)   i.   Each phrase has a unique head (i.e., it has a head and only one).
          ii. Each constituent has a unique parent (i.e. one category that
               immediately dominates it).[1]

Given (5.i), each constituent in a phrase structure representation is **endocentric** (i.e. it has an identifiable head), and therefore no syntactic constituent is **exocentric** (i.e. without a head). As will be discussed in the next chapter, this holds for clause structures as well as NPs and PPs. It follows from the formulation of Merge, specifically the projection function. Given (5.ii), each constituent will be immediately dominated by one and only one syntactic category in phrase structure representation. There is only one exception to this: the root, which is not a constituent of any other category in syntactic representation and therefore has no parent.

EXERCISE 4.3

Using Merge, give a derivation for the NP (i).

> (i) an exceedingly distinguished professor of mathematics from Harvard with a
> gray beard

a. Discuss how the resulting phrase structure (tree) conforms to the constraints
    in (5).
b. Identify at least two additional derivations of this phrase structure (i.e. where
    the order of merger of elements is different from the one you gave). It is not
    necessary to give full derivations, just enough to indicate how they differ.

4.2 Syntactic evidence for binary Merge in NPs

The binary branching structure for (1) given in (3) conforms to our
working hypothesis that Merge is a binary operation. As a consequence, NPs
with two or more constituents in addition to the head will have intermediate
levels of phrasal projection. Some evidence that supports the postulation of such
intermediate projections and hence the kind of binary constituent structure this
involves will be discussed below.

This syntactic evidence involves the phenomenon of **anaphora**, where a single
lexical item can stand in for another lexical item or a larger constituent – i.e. its
antecedent. Personal pronouns are one example. In (6), for example, the pronoun
he can stand in for the NP *a student who is majoring in linguistics at Princeton*
under the interpretation of (6) as a sentence about a single person.[2]

(6)   A student who is majoring in linguistics at Princeton thinks that he would
        like to pursue a graduate degree in the field.

While most pronominal forms can only stand in for maximal projections, there is
one instance in English where a pronoun can stand in for intermediate levels of
projection. Thus compare the following examples.

(7)   a. I met an old friend of John's and Mary met a new one.
        b. *I met an old friend of John's and Mary met a new him.
        c. I met an old friend of John's and Mary met him too.
        d. I met an old friend of John's and Mary met one too.

(7a) demonstrates that the pronoun *one*, in contrast to the personal pronoun *him*
in (7b), can stand in for a constituent that is smaller than the maximal projection – in this case, the constituent *friend of John's*. (7b) shows that a personal
pronoun cannot do this. (7c–d) demonstrate that *one* like a personal pronoun (e.g.
the third person singular *him*) can also take a maximal NP as an antecedent.

Given that *one*, like other pronouns, only substitutes for a single constituent,
constructions with *one* can be used to dissect the internal structure of NPs. To see
how this works, consider the paradigm in (8).

(8)   Mary met an eccentric professor from Princeton with a gray beard and
           Bill met
      a.   a conventional one.
      b.   a conventional one with a black beard.
      c.   a conventional one from Harvard with a black beard.

In (8a) *one* stands in for a subpart of the full NP object of *met, professor from Princeton with a gray beard*, itself labeled N. In (8b) *one* stands in for the N constituent *professor from Princeton*, and in (8c) *one* stands in for the N constituent *professor*, the head of the entire NP. Thus the pronoun *one* can stand in for a variety of phrasal projections of N, including the head. (8b–c) demonstrate the functionality of our analysis, which predicts the existence of these sub-constituents within the whole NP.

EXERCISE 4.4

a. Give the phrase structure representation as tree structure for the object of *met* in the second conjunct in (8a–c).
b. How do these analyses provide evidence for the analysis of the object of *met* in the first conjunct?

Furthermore, these constructions provide crucial evidence on how the derivation under Merge must proceed. Thus in order to derive (8a), the two PPs *from Princeton* and *with a gray beard* must merge with the head N *professor* and its phrasal projection before the A *eccentric* is merged. Recall that this requirement is based on the assumption that the pronoun *one* can only take a single constituent as an antecedent.

   The pronoun *one* can apparently also substitute for the entire NP as well, as illustrated in (9).

(9)   Mary met an eccentric student from Princeton with purple hair and Bill also
           met one.

In (9) the antecedent of the pronoun *one* is the entire NP object of the first conjunct, *an eccentric student from Princeton with purple hair*. Interestingly, (9) actually has two distinct readings. In addition to the reading of *one* as a pronoun, hence N, *one* can also be interpreted as a number. The two readings have different PF representations. On the pronominal reading, the verb *met* is more strongly stressed than *one*. On the numeral reading, the verb *met* and the numeral *one* receive equal stress or alternatively the numeral has greater stress than the verb. On the numeral reading *one* can be replaced with any numeral, as in (10).

(10)   Mary met two eccentric students from Princeton with purple hair and Bill
           met three.

(10) is synonymous with (11), which spells out the full NP object of the second conjunct.

(11)   Mary met two eccentric students from Princeton with purple hair and Bill
              met three eccentric students from Princeton with purple hair.

Taking (11) as a closer approximation to the LF representation of (10) as well as
(11), the PF of (10) would result from deletion as indicated in (12).

(12)   Mary met two eccentric students from Princeton with purple hair and Bill
              met three ~~eccentric students from Princeton with purple hair~~.

The deleted string constitutes a single constituent in the whole NP, a sister of the
numeral, and furthermore this deleted constituent is identical in structure and
lexical content to an identical constituent in the first conjunct. This constitutes
another example of deletion under identity (cf. the discussion of coordinate constructions in the previous chapter).

   Before continuing with this analysis, there are two important points to note
about the deletion operation. First, it appears to be optional. If it doesn't apply,
a legitimate sentence is still derived. Second, the fact that the PF representation
of a sentence can diverge significantly from its LF representation entails that
at some point in a derivation the path to PF diverges from the path to LF. See
Chapter 6 for further discussion.

EXERCISE 4.5

Notice that deletion can also affect a set of subparts of the deleted phrase in (10).
a.   Construct the phrase structure for (i).

     (i) three eccentric students from Princeton with purple hair

b.   Now demonstrate that there are two other structurally distinct cases where
     deletion can affect smaller phrases in this structure – i.e. construct the relevant
     examples and discuss how their analysis shows this.

EXERCISE 4.6

Given the analysis above, there could be a similar ambiguity regarding the pronoun/
numeral distinction in phrases like *one from Harvard* as in (i).

     (i) Mary met an eccentric student with purple hair from Princeton and Bill met
          one from Harvard.

a.   What are the two possible syntactic analyses for the phrase *one from Harvard*?
b.   How do these relate to the syntactic analysis of the phrase in the first conjunct *an
     eccentric student with purple hair from Princeton*?

   One way to disambiguate between the pronominal *one* and the numeral *one*,
which have the same PF (they are homophones) but are syntactically distinct
(one is a N and the other a numeral that can modify a noun), is to use the plural
counterpart of the pronoun, *ones*. This plural pronoun behaves in exactly the
same way as its singular counterpart, as demonstrated in (10).

(13)   Mary assisted the eccentric professors from Princeton with gray beards and
          Bill assisted
          a. the conventional ones.
          b. the conventional ones with black beards.
          c. the conventional ones from Harvard with black beards.

The antecedent of *ones* is *professors from Princeton with gray beards* in (10a),
professors from Princeton in (10b), and *professors* in (10c). However, *ones* cannot stand in for an entire NP like its singular counterpart (cf. (9)), as illustrated
by the deviance of (14) in contrast to the acceptability of (15).

(14)   *Mary met many eccentric professors from Princeton and Bill also met
          ones.
(15)   Mary met many eccentric professors from Princeton and Bill also met some.

(15) would be derived via deletion, as illustrated in (16).

(16)   Mary met many eccentric professors from Princeton and Bill also met some
          ~~eccentric professors from Princeton~~.

Furthermore, *ones* cannot be interpreted as a numeral in these constructions; thus
an expression like *the ones from Yale* in (17) cannot have a deletion analysis as in
(18), but instead must have the pronominal analysis in (19).

(17)   Marjorie invited the professors from Princeton and Bill invited the ones
          from Yale.
(18)   Marjorie invited the professors from Princeton and Bill invited [$_{NP}$ the ones
          ~~professors~~ from Yale].
(19)   Marjorie invited the professors from Princeton and Bill invited [$_{NP}$ the [$_{N}$
          ones [$_{PP}$ from Yale]]].

EXERCISE 4.7

This contrasts with the deletion analysis required for (i), which is synonymous
with (ii), where the head N of the direct object in the second conjunct has not been
deleted.

   (i) Marjorie invited the professors from Princeton and Bill invited the two from
        Yale.
   (ii) Marjorie invited the professors from Princeton and Bill invited the two
        professors from Yale.

Now consider the following more complicated examples.

   (iii) Marjorie invited the professors with gray beards from Princeton and Bill
        invited the two from Yale.
   (iv) Marjorie invited the professors with gray beards from Princeton and Bill
        invited the two professors with gray beards from Yale.

a. What is the syntactic analysis of the direct object NP in the second conjunct of
    (iii)?

b.   What is the syntactic analysis of the direct object NPs in both conjuncts of the following example (v)?

   (v) Marjorie invited the two professors with gray beards from Princeton and Bill invited the ones from Yale.

c.   Why can't the pronoun *ones* take as its antecedent the constituent beginning with *two*?

If the deletion in (18) is reversed, the result (20) is deviant.

(20)   *Marjorie invited the professors from Princeton and Bill invited [$_{NP}$ the ones professors from Yale].

This is because *ones* can only be interpreted as a pronoun that cannot modify the head of the NP, *professors*. Assuming that (20) approximates the LF representation that corresponds to the PF representations of (18) as well as (20), the analysis in (18) can be ruled out. Thus (19) is the only viable analysis of (17).

   (13) shows how the pronoun *ones* can take as an antecedent just a head N or a phrase consisting of the head N plus various modifiers to its right. (21) demonstrates that *ones* can also stand in for the head N plus a modifier to its left as an antecedent. The phrase structures of the object NPs in both conjuncts is given in (21b-c).

(21)   a.   Mary assisted the eccentric professors from Princeton and Bill assisted the ones from Yale.

b.

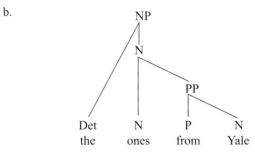

c.

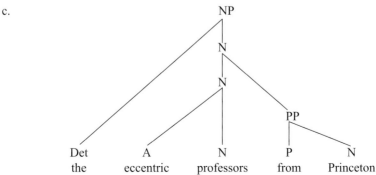

In (21a) the antecedent of *ones* is interpreted as *eccentric professors* – i.e. A + N. Given our assumption that the antecedent of a pronoun must be a single constituent, this requires that the A *eccentric* must merge with the N *professors* before the PP *from Princeton* as in (21c). In contrast, the reverse order of merger must occur in the derivation of (22), where the antecedent of *ones* is the single phrase *professors from Princeton*.

(22)   Mary assisted the eccentric professors from Princeton and Bill assisted the conventional ones.

(21) in conjunction with (22) demonstrate that the order of merger must be variable in some cases.

Both the prenominal adjectives (e.g. in (21–22)) and the postnominal PP like *from Princeton* and *with a gray beard* are modifiers of the head N. Such modifiers are called **adjuncts**. Thus (21) in conjunction with (22) constitutes empirical evidence that adjuncts can be merged in any order. In the case of the AP and PP, this only affects the hierarchical structure; the linear order of elements will be AP – N – PP in either case. With modifiers on the same side of the head, the variable order of merger will also affect the linear order of these modifiers, as illustrated in (23).

(23)   a.   professors from Princeton with gray beards
            b.   professors with gray beards from Princeton

Both examples in (23) are equally acceptable, so both derivations must be legitimate. (23) demonstrates again that the order of merger for adjuncts is variable.

EXERCISE 4.8

Given that the order of merger for adjuncts is unconstrained, the NP in (i) is susceptible to more than one analysis of its hierarchical structure.

(i) the mildly eccentric professors from Yale with black beards

a.   Identify the adjuncts in (i).
b.   Give these analyses in terms of phrase structure trees.
c.   Use the *ones*-constructions to validate your analyses.

Although the freedom with which Merge applies to adjuncts is functional and therefore necessary, unconstrained Merge will in other circumstances yield deviant constructions. Consider, for example, the deviance of the expressions in (24).

(24)   a.   *these eccentric professor from Yale
            b.   *this eccentric professors from Yale

The problem with these examples is pretty obviously a mismatch between the number features of the demonstrative determiner and the head of the NP that it marks. The determiner *these* is inherently plural in number (hence [+plural]) whereas the N *professor* is in the singular (hence [-plural]). Designating the determiner as a **specifier** (following standard terminology), the deviance of (24a) can be characterized as a failure of **Specifier-Head Agreement**. Changing the Determiner to the singular form *this* or alternatively changing the head to the plural form *professors* eliminates the deviance of the construction.[3]

We take Specifier-Head Agreement to be a condition on representations, rather than a constraint of derivations under Merge. Thus Merge will produce constructions like (24), but their syntactic representations will be marked as deviant because they violate the Specifier-Head Agreement condition.

The specifier is a special type of modifier because it enters into an agreement relation with the head of the smallest maximal projection in which it is a constituent. Given that it is the leftmost modifier and furthermore appears to take scope over the rest of the NP, it is plausible that it is merged last in the derivation of the NP and therefore would c-command the rest of the NP (see Section 3.3).

The previous discussion establishes a specific order for Merge in the derivation of NP. First, adjuncts are merged with the head or a syntactic object consisting of a head and one or more of its adjuncts. Next, the specifier is merged last. From this last property it will follow that the specifier of a head will always c-command the adjuncts of that head and therefore take scope over them. How this ordering for the merger of constituents generalizes to other maximal phrasal projections will be discussed in the next chapter.

So far the word "modifier" has been used to describe both adjectival and prepositional phrase constituents of NPs. As demonstrated above there is empirical evidence demonstrating that the order of merger of these constituents within the NP is variable. This raises a question whether all PP constituents within a NP are adjuncts. If so, then PPs should be susceptible to free linear ordering within the NP. This turns out to be false. Consider the following examples.

(25)   a.   brilliant students of mathematics at Princeton
         b.   *brilliant students at Princeton of mathematics

Granting that the phrase *of mathematics* is in fact a PP, it cannot be merged after the adjunct PP *at Princeton*, and therefore does not share this defining property of adjuncts.

EXERCISE 4.9

The PP *at Princeton* is essentially the same as the PP *from Princeton*. Nonetheless, it is always good to be able to provide empirical evidence for claims of this kind. Using the examples discussed previously, construct an empirical argument for this claim.

Even so, *of mathematics* seems to perform a modifying function in that it picks out a subset of students in much the same way that the PP *at Princeton* picks out a subset of students. This illustrates the necessity for exercising care in using terminology. The two PPs may be modifiers in function, but the empirical evidence shows that they have a different status in terms of phrase structure.

This evidence suggests that there must be a class of constituents that must be merged before adjuncts. Such constituents are designated as the **complements** of the head. In VP and PP the identification of complements is much more straightforward. The grammatical objects of V and P are considered to be complements. In the following PPs and VPs the grammatical objects (and hence complements) of V or P are given in boldface.

(26)   a.   of **mathematics**
         b.   from **South America**
         c.   write **a book**
         d.   construct **a proof**
         e.   give **Eloise presents**

The verb *give* takes a double object, an indirect object *Eloise* and a direct object *presents*. Both are complements of the verb. Furthermore, the indirect object can also show up in a PP.

(27)   give presents **to Eloise**

In this case the PP is then a complement of the verb. In general, complements of a verb involve NPs and PPs that occur as constituents of VP and answer the questions *who?* and *what?* (see the examples in Exercise 4.11).

Given that grammatical object NPs are always complements, the PP *of mathematics* can be identified as a complement of the N *students* on the basis of the parallelism between the N *students* and the V *studies*. This is illustrated in (28), a tautology but a well-formed sentence nonetheless.

(28)   Students of mathematics study mathematics.

Taking *students* to be a nominalization of the verb *study*, then semantically *mathematics* bears pretty much the same relation to the N as to the V. If it is a complement NP to the V, then the PP containing it would be a complement to the N.

This argument may not apply in every case where the PP headed by *of* is a complement to a noun. Thus for *professors of mathematics* it is stretching a point to argue that the noun is a nominalization of the verb *profess* since the sentence *professors of mathematics profess mathematics* sounds a lot less natural than (28). Nonetheless, there is sufficient evidence that such PPs share a marked parallelism with direct objects of verbs (e.g. *destruction of the city, rejection of the plan, rebuttal of the argument*). Furthermore, the N *professors* cannot merge with a locative PP (e.g. *from Princeton*) before merging with the *of*-phrase. Thus *professors from Princeton of mathematics* is deviant, presumably because its derivation merges an adjunct before a complement.

Another piece of evidence showing that the phrase *of mathematics* behaves differently from standard adjuncts concerns the distribution of the pronouns *one/ones* in NP. When the head of phrase is adjacent to a following PP adjunct, the head alone can be replaced by the pronoun, as in (29).

(29)   Mary met all of the students in my class and Bill met all of the ones in Professor Katz's class.

However, when the head is followed by a PP complement, it alone cannot be replaced by the pronoun.

(30)   a.   *Mary met all the students of mathematics in my class and Bill met all the ones of physics in Professor Katz's class.
          b.   *Mary met a student of linguistics and Bill met one of physics.

An explanation for this behavior remains to be determined, but the phenomenon is useful in distinguishing between complements and adjuncts.

Given that the merger of multiple adjuncts in NP can occur in any order, consider whether this also applies to complements. As evidence for the affirmative, consider the following examples.

(31)   a.   Mary's gift of a book to Bill
          b.   Mary's gift to Bill of a book

The NPs in (31) to be nominalized correspond to the sentence (32a), which is a variant of the double object construction in (32b).

(32)   a.   Mary gave a book to Bill.
          b.   Mary gave Bill a book.

In (31), the PP *of a book* corresponds to the direct object complement in (32) and the PP *to Bill* corresponds to the indirect object complement in (32b). Thus (31) shows that the order of merger for complements in NPs is variable.

EXERCISE 4.10

a. Discuss what the following examples demonstrate regarding the order of merger in NP.

  (i)   a.   the gift of a book for services rendered
         b.   *the gift for services rendered of a book

b. Add the PP that corresponds to the indirect object and construct the full paradigm of examples for this nominal (i.e. *gift*).
c. Discuss how this paradigm either conforms or fails to conform to the analysis under consideration.

So far binary Merge always involves a head or a phrase that bears the label of the head of the constituent under construction. The other element that is merged has one of three distinct relations with respect to that head: either as a complement, an adjunct, or a specifier. The order of merger of these elements is given in (33).

(33)   Order of merger: complements > adjuncts > specifier

Complements are always merged first, adjuncts are merged after complements, and the specifier is merged last. This constitutes a working hypothesis and first approximation.

EXERCISE 4.11

The actual facts of English syntax may not be so well behaved and therefore might require modification and sharpening of our analyses. Along these lines, consider the following examples.

(i)   a.   Susie talked to Charles about Eddie.
      b.   Susie talked about Eddie to Charles.
(ii) a.   Susie talked to Charles about Eddie for an hour.
      b.   Susie talked about Eddie to Charles for an hour.

The PP *for an hour* modifies the verb *talked* by specifying a duration for the action. The other two PPs do not modify the verb. Instead they specify two of the participants in the action designated by the verb, the subject being the other participant. Being internal to the VP, these two PPs might reasonably be analyzed as complements.
   Now consider the following paradigm:

(iii) a.   Susie talked for an hour to Charles about Eddie.
      b.   Susie talked to Charles for an hour about Eddie.
      c.   Susie talked for an hour about Eddie to Charles.
      d.   Susie talked about Eddie for an hour to Charles.

a. Compared to the examples in (ii), what is the acceptability of each example in (iii)?
b. Do your judgments support or contradict the hypothesis for the order of merger under discussion? If the latter, is there some way to adjust our proposal to accommodate the counterexamples or to explain how these examples are only apparent counterexamples (e.g. they have special intonation)?

The phrase structure of example (1) in this chapter has a fairly rich functional structure as annotated in (34).

(34)

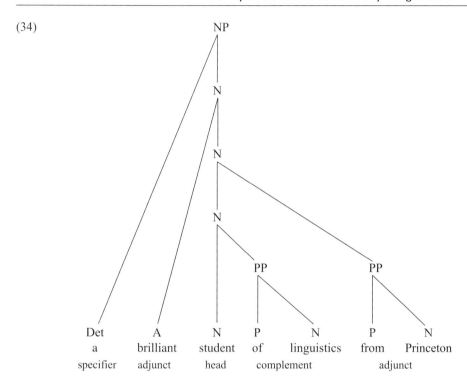

This functional structure in NP appears to be only partially manifested in projections of other lexical categories like P, A, and V (italicized in (35)).

(35)   a. The paper airplane sailed *right out the window*.
         b. Jill was *very proud of her new apartment*.
         c. Harry *quietly left the room in a big hurry*.

The PP in (35a) contains a modifier *right* and a complement *the window*. The lexical item *right* is designated as a specifier rather than an adjunct because even though it does not enter into an agreement relation with the prepositional head of the phrase, it narrowly modifies just the head. The AP in (35b) contains a complement *of her new apartment* and what is taken to be an adverbial degree modifier *very*. Whether *very* is analyzed as a specifier or an adjunct, it is still going to be merged after the complement of the adjective. Given that it does not enter into an agreement relation with the head it modifies – i.e. the adjective *proud*, the choice between designating *very* a specifier as opposed to an adjunct may be more arbitrary than one would like. The VP in (35c) contains a complement, the object *the room*, and a PP adjunct *in a big hurry*. The adverb *quietly* is also most likely an adjunct rather than a specifier. Notice that it can occur to the right of the verb, as in (36), which is something that specifiers cannot do.

(36)   Harry left the room quietly.

At this point, nothing important hangs on the assignment of functional designations for these examples.

As demonstrated in the next chapter, the functional structure that occurs in
NPs also applies straightforwardly to clauses. This suggests that the constituent
structure of all phrases in a linguistic expression conforms to the basic pattern
outlined in (37), where "hp" designates a phrasal projection of a head, whatever
its categorial designation (i.e. h).

(37)

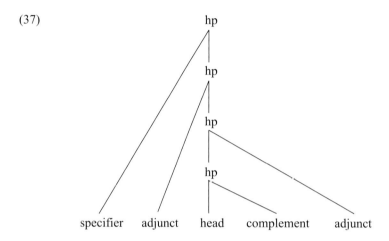

Although there is empirical evidence to support the binary nature of Merge when
h is N, whether there is also strong empirical evidence with respect to other categories remains to be determined.

4.3   A coda on coordinate constructions

Applying binary Merge to the analysis of coordinate constructions
runs into several potentially serious problems. They indicate that perhaps merger
in the derivation of coordinate constructions involves more than just two syntactic objects at each step, as assumed for non-coordinate constructions.

As a point of departure, consider the phrase structure analysis of the simplest
case of coordination: the coordination of two nouns.

(38)   syntax and semantics

The binary branching hypothesis would impose one of the following analyses
on (38).

(39)   a.   [syntax [and semantics]]
            b.   [[syntax and] semantics]

It would entail that either *and semantics* (as in (39a)) or *syntax and* (as in (39b))
is a constituent. The next question concerns the labels of these groupings. If the

conjunction *and* bears a category label of Conj, then under the Inclusiveness Condition (see footnote 1) the label of *and semantics* in (39a) must be either N or Conj. Whichever label projects will be the designated head of the construction. If *and* is analyzed as the head of the phrase, then the phrase is labeled Conj. Presumably this would extend to the whole coordinate construction when the first conjunct *syntax* is merged with the ConjP *and semantics*. One problem with this analysis concerns the functional roles of the two conjuncts with respect to the conjunction. The relations complement, adjunct, and specifier do not apply. Furthermore, the two coordinated nouns should bear the same relation to the conjunction. But syntactically the first c-commands the second. Unfortunately, the same problem occurs when one of the noun conjuncts is analyzed as the head of the coordinate structure. Thus suppose that the N *semantics* is the head that projects its label. Then structurally the conjunction *and* would be either a complement or an adjunct; but again neither relation fits.[4]

EXERCISE 4.12

The problem of identifying the structural relations between the parts of a coordinate construction becomes even more difficult with more complicated cases – e.g. the coordination of two larger NPs in (i).

(i) the syntax of Russian case and the semantics of English quantifiers

Taking the N *semantics* to be the head of the entire construction, what problems arise in designating the structural relations of the conjunction *and* and the first conjunct *the syntax of Russian case*?

One approach to identifying the head of a coordinate construction is through an analysis of phenomena that bear on identification of head. One such phenomenon is subject/verb agreement in English (and many other languages). In English, a finite verbal element agrees in number and person features with its subject. This shows up most strikingly with personal pronoun subjects.

(40)   a. I am studying Scarlatti.
        b. He is studying Scarlatti.
        c. We are studying Scarlatti.
        d. They are studying Scarlatti.

The progressive auxiliary verb *be* shows up in three distinct suppletive morphological forms, depending on the features of the subject. In both (40a–b) the subject is singular but differs in person features, first person for (40a) and third person for (40b). There is no first vs. third person feature distinction for the plural form – both occur as *are*. Nonetheless, there is a morphological distinction between singular and plural in the first person, and also singular and plural in the third person. Agreement between the subject and the finite verbal element specifically involves the head of the subject NP.

(41)   a.   The author of those quirky papers on the Barnhouse effect is/*are
                    going to speak at our conference.
              b.   The authors of that quirky paper on the Barnhouse effect are/*is going
                    to speak at our conference.

Both subjects in (41a–b) contain a singular N and a plural N, but clearly verbal
agreement is determined by the number feature of the N that is the head of the
subject NP.

(42) gives the agreement paradigm for subjects containing coordinated N
heads.

(42)   a.   The professor and his student are/*is joining us for dinner.
              b.   The professor and his students are/*is joining us for dinner.
              c.   The professors and their student are/*is joining us for dinner.
              d.   The professors and their students are/*is joining us for dinner.

In every case, agreement involves a plural subject, but only the subjects in
(42b–d) contain plural nouns. However if the plural N is designated as the head
of the coordinate subject construction, the problems noted previously arise.
Furthermore, there is the question of which plural N would be the head in (42d).
With (42a) neither N is plural, so designating either head would give the wrong
result for agreement. Alternatively, the conjunction *and* could be designated as
the head of this phrase on the grounds that it is inherently plural – which would
solve the agreement issue for this paradigm.

Unfortunately this solution does not generalize to other conjunctions – in particular, *or*. Consider just the two examples from the paradigm for *or* that correspond to (42a) and (42d).

(43)   a.   The professor or his student is/*are joining us for dinner.
              b.   The professors or their students are/*is joining us for dinner.

In (43a) the subject contains a disjunction of singular Ns and the finite verbal
form occurs in the singular. However it does not follow from this that *or* is inherently singular because in (43b), where the two Ns are plural, the verb must show
plural agreement; so if the conjunction *or* is the head of the subject phrase then
it must have the feature [+plural]. Therefore *or* cannot be inherently singular or
plural. What appears to be determining the number agreement morphology on
the finite verb is the number features of the two conjuncts (or disjuncts) together.
If this holds for the conjunction *or*, then it generalizes to the conjunction *and* –
even if there is only one possible result with *and*. The problem encountered when
or conjoins two NPs whose heads do not match in number also indicates that the
determination of agreement depends on both Ns.

EXERCISE 4.13

Now consider the two cases in the paradigm for *or* where the two Ns do not match in
number. The Ø indicates that these examples are not marked for acceptability.

(i)   a.   ØThe professor or his students is joining us for dinner.
      b.   ØThe professor or his students are joining us for dinner.
(ii) a.   ØThe students or their professor is joining us for dinner.
      b.   ØThe students or their professor are joining us for dinner.

a. Were you ever taught a rule to cover these cases? If yes, what is the rule?
b. Consulting your own grammatical intuitions (and disregarding the rule if possible), do you find either example in (i) acceptable? or distinctly preferable to the other? What are the details?
c. Perform the same experiment with (ii).
d. Pose this problem to three other people and collect the data.
e. What would you conclude on the basis of this (obviously limited) sample?

One possible solution to these problems is to treat both heads of the coordinated NPs as heads of the coordinate construction. This violates the constraint that every phrase has a unique head; but as demonstrated above, trying to satisfy this constraint in the analysis of coordinate constructions leads to seemingly intractable problems. Coordinate constructions may simply be fundamentally different from non-coordinate constructions.

Pursuing this second option, it appears that if in the coordination of two nouns (e.g the object of the verb in (44)) both Ns are heads, then they would presumably be merged at the same step in the derivation.

(44)   They are eating bread and cheese.

Therefore Merge must apply to three lexical items at once, yielding a structure (45).

(45)

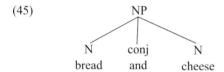

Merge can also apply to two larger phrases and a conjunction, as (46).

(46)   They are eating the bread from New York and the cheese from Paris.

The resulting structure would presumably be something like (47).

(47)   [$_{NP}$ [$_{NP}$ the bread from New York] and [$_{NP}$ the cheese from Paris]]

The phrases *the bread from New York* and *the cheese from Paris* are in some sense maximal phrasal projections of their respective heads. At the same time they combine with a conjunction to create a larger species of NP.

This is in fact the only kind of analysis for coordinate structures that is compatible with the Syntactic Symmetry Constraint discussed in the previous chapter. The empirical evidence for this concerns the phenomenon of layered conjunctions. Consider the sentence (48), which is ambiguous.

(48)   They will invite David and Charles or Susie to the party.

The coordinate object *David and Charles or Susie* has two distinct interpretations, either as (49a) or (49b).

(49)   a.   either David and Charles or Susie
         b.   David and either Charles or Susie

In (49a) the conjunction of David and Charles functions as a constituent of the disjunction, whereas in (49b) the disjunction of Charles or Susie functions as a constituent of the conjunction. Under interpretation (49a) it is possible that only one of the three people named will be invited to the party. Under the interpretation (49b), this is not possible; two of the three will be invited to the party in either case. In terms of phrase structure analysis the interpretation in (49b) would correspond to the structure (50).

(50)   [David and [Charles or Susie]]

Adding labels, yields (51).

(51)   [$_{NP}$ David and [$_{NP}$ Charles or Susie]]

The disjunction of *Charles* and *Susie* coordinates the two Ns, as a NP. And the conjunction of this NP with the N *David* is also a coordination of NPs, hence a NP. This conforms to the Syntactic Symmetry Constraint for coordinate structures because the category designations of the phrases coordinated at each level are identical. Now consider the structure (52) that would result if the conjunction were taken to be the syntactic head of the coordinate structure.

(52)   [$_{ConjP}$ David and [$_{ConjP}$ Charles or Susie]]

In the embedded coordinate structure of (52), the disjunction *Charles or Susie*, the two coordinated parts are structurally identical – both Ns. However in the larger phrase, a noun is being coordinated with a ConjP, in violation of the symmetry constraint. In this way, the Syntactic Symmetry Constraint serves as the basis for an argument against the binary branching hypothesis as applied to coordinate constructions.

4.4   Summary

Merge is the single recursive operation in C$_{HL}$ that creates phrase structure. It has two basic functions: grouping and labeling.

Grouping is essentially binary with the possible exception of coordinate constructions. Another constraint on grouping concerns the functional relations between a head and the constituents contained in its maximal phrasal projection. There is a basic order to merger where a head must combine with its complement(s) before any adjunct, and a specifier must be merged last as the immediate constituent of the maximal phrasal projection. A third constraint involves the No Tampering Condition, which prohibits Merge from changing the hierarchical structure of a syntactic object that has been constructed in the derivation.

Labeling is constrained by the Inclusiveness Condition, an effect of which is to prohibit any label that is not derived from a label that already exists as part of a lexical entry in the lexicon.

Empirical evidence for binary Merge is provided by complex NPs that contain pronominal *one* and *ones*, which can be anaphoric on subparts of other complex NPs. These constructions demonstrate that in the case of adjuncts which occur on either side of a head N, the order of Merge can vary, producing two viable and necessary distinct syntactic structures, but with no apparent difference in interpretation.

Applying binary Merge to coordinate constructions creates problems for labeling, and in layered coordinate constructions violates the Syntactic Symmetry Constraint on conjuncts.

Bibliographical notes

The bottom-up analysis of phrase structure was originally designated X-bar theory because of the way the notation was handled. In the original theory (Chomsky (1970)) a head X (or X^0, so-called X-zero) was thought to project a category X (or X'-bar – i.e. a category label X with a single bar on top). The next higher projection would have two bars (or two primes) and so on to the highest (hence maximal) phrasal projection of the category. At another stage of the theory, the complicated number of bar levels were reduced to three: the head (X), all intermediate projections (X'), and the maximal projection (XP). Given the Inclusiveness Condition (Chomsky 1995b, 2000b, 2001) all bar-level distinctions are illegitimate in phrase structure representations.

For discussion in favor of the generalized binary nature of Merge, see Kayne 1984, 1994 and Chomsky 1995a. The operation Merge is first proposed in Chomsky 1995a. The No Tampering Condition is first proposed in Chomsky 2005, see Chomsky 2007, 2008 for discussion, but the discussion of tampering goes back to Chomsky 2000a, where a similar constraint is proposed but not labeled as such.

For discussion about whether labels are predictable and therefore can be eliminated from syntactic representations, see Chomsky 2000b and Collins 2002.

5   The structure of clauses

In the previous chapter the discussion of phrase structure focused primarily on the structure of NPs, with some discussion of PP and AP. This chapter turns to the phrase structure of clauses, in which VPs constitute a significant part.

5.1   The phrase structure of VP

The internal structure of the maximal phrasal projection of V (i.e. VP) is essentially identical to that of the other maximal phrasal projections that have been analyzed in the previous chapters. Thus a V merges first with its complement(s), then with its adjuncts, and finally with its specifier.[1] To see how this works in detail, an investigation of the distinction between complements and adjuncts in VP is required.

In the previous chapter it was simply stipulated that any NP that occurs as an object of a head (e.g. V or P) is a complement. This is axiomatic. In PP the number of complements is limited to just one because P can take only one NP object, whereas a VP may contain up to two because of double object verbs (e.g. *give* and *write* as mentioned in Chapter 3, Examples (24a) and (42a)), which can occur with both an indirect object and a direct object.

(1)   a.   Len gave Kathleen a painting.
        b.   Susan wrote John a letter.

Given binary Merge, the structure of the VPs in (1) would be (2).

(2) $[_{VP} [_V$ V NP $]$ NP $]$

The NP adjacent to V in these constructions is always interpreted as the indirect object and the following NP as the direct object. Both objects specify participants involved in the action or event designated by V. In this way they are distinct from adjuncts, which generally modify the V by adding additional information about how, where, when, and why. As noted in the previous chapter, complements provide information about who and what.

The notion of participant involved in the action or event designated by the V also extends to the subject NP of a clause. Take a simple case like (3).

(3)   John hit the ball.

John and *the ball* are participants in the action of hitting. On the model of predicate logic, they are designated as **arguments** of the **predicate** *hit*. As a constituent dominated by VP *the ball* is internal to VP in contrast to the subject *John* which is presumably outside the VP. Thus the direct object *the ball* is an **internal** argument of V, while the subject *John* is an **external** argument. In the case of double object constructions (e.g. (1)), there are two internal arguments, hence two complements of V.

As noted previously, the double object construction has a variant in which the indirect object occurs as the NP object of a P following the direct object of V. (4) thus corresponds to (1b).

(4)   Susan wrote a letter to John.

John is still an internal argument of *wrote*, but in this construction the PP containing *John* is the complement of V. The class of double object verbs provides two patterns for verbal complements, [___ NP NP] and [___ NP PP].

The material inside the square brackets indicates the contexts in which double object verbs can occur. The underline indicates the position of the V, hence [V NP NP]. Given that PP can be a complement of V, there are also verbs that can take two PP complements, as in (5).

(5)   The committee talked to the applicant about her resumé.

Both *the applicant* and *her resumé* are internal arguments and therefore the two PPs in which they occur are complements of the verb *talked*.

The different strings of possible complement patterns identify the different contexts in which various verbs can occur. These contexts constitute properties that distinguish various subclasses of verbs. They subcategorize the class of verbs into their various subclasses and thus provide **subcategorization features** that form part of the lexical entries for verbs.

Such features can be utilized either as restrictions on the application of Merge or as constraints on its output – in other words, as constraints on derivations or conditions on representations. For example, the verb *mention* can occur with two internal arguments – one of them an object NP, as illustrated in (6).

(6)   Bill mentioned the problem to us.

Thus the subcategorization feature for *mention* will be [___ NP PP]. However, unlike double object verbs (e.g (1)), *mention* cannot also occur in the context [___ NP NP].

(7)   *Bill mentioned us the problem.

Subcategorization features can account for the deviance of (7) in terms of the mismatch between the subcategorization feature of the verb and the actual context in which it occurs. Alternatively, Merge could be prohibited from applying to the second NP object *the problem* because this would create a context that does not match the subcategorization feature of the verb.

The subcategorization contexts in which various verbs can occur allow for some variation. In particular, it is possible for some of the verbs mentioned above to occur without one or both of their internal arguments.

(8)   a.   Susan wrote a letter.
          b.   Susan wrote John.
          c.   Susan wrote to John.
          d.   Susan wrote yesterday.
          c.   The committee talked about the applicant's resumé.
          f.   The committee talked to the applicant.
          g.   The committee talked yesterday.

In (8a) the indirect object argument (either as NP or PP) is missing, while in (8b–c) the direct object argument is. In (8d) both internal arguments are absent. The same applies to (8g). Of the two internal arguments of *talk*, one is missing in (8e) and the other in (8f). A complement that can be left out is **optional**.[2] When it must occur, it is **obligatory**, as illustrated in the paradigm for *recommend* in (9).

(9)   a.   John recommended that book to me at the party.
          b.   John recommended that book at the party.
          c.   *John recommended to me at the party.
          d.   *John recommended at the party.

(9) shows that the verb *recommend*, which in (9a) takes two internal arguments *that book* and *me*, has one obligatory complement (the NP object) and one optional complement (the PP *to me*). This can be represented in a subcategorization feature by using parentheses to indicate optionality. Thus the subcategorization feature for *recommend* will be [___ NP (PP)].

EXERCISE 5.1

These facts can be stipulated in terms of binary contextual features. For example, the fact that the verb *recommend* requires a NP complement can be stated in terms of a positive contextual feature: [+___ NP]. The same context can be used to account for the fact that some other verbs (e.g. *sleep*) cannot occur with a NP complement by changing the plus sign for a minus sign, hence [–___ NP].

a. Formulate the full set of contextual features that will account for the examples in (1–9).
b. Adding the verbs *buy* and *sell* to this group, construct the full paradigms and discuss how well they fit the patterns of the other verbs.

With the verbs examined so far, it appears that PP complements are generally optional. This is not always the case, as the paradigm for *put* shows.

(10)   a.   Susan put the letter in the mailbox.
          b.   *Susan put the letter.
          c.   *Susan put in the mailbox
          d.   *Susan put.

This paradigm demonstrates that both the NP and PP complements are obligatory. What does seem to be true, however, is that when a verb takes an obligatory PP complement as well as a NP complement, the NP complement will be obligatory too.

EXERCISE 5.2

Returning to the issue of the order of merger between complements and adjuncts, consider the following paradigm.

(i) a.   Eloise carefully put the book on the shelf.
  b.   Eloise put the book on the shelf carefully.
  c.   *Eloise put carefully the book on the shelf.
  d.   Eloise put the book carefully on the shelf.
  e.   *Eloise put on the shelf the book.

Given our hypothesis about the order of Merge, the apparent acceptability of (i.d) is a problem.

a. State what the problem is.
b. What other examples in this paradigm are not covered by the hypothesized order of merger?
c. If this hypothesis is abandoned, what examples are no longer accounted for?

In addition to NP and PP complements, there are also clausal complements (underlined in (11)).

(11)   a.   They think *that John is brilliant.*
        b.   They persuaded Mary *that John is brilliant.*

Thus *think* takes a single clause as a complement, whereas *persuade* takes both an object NP and a clause. Again the subcategorization features [+__ Clause] for *think* and [+__ NP Clause] for *persuade* are needed to account for the deviant examples in (12), where the two verbs occur in the wrong contexts.

(12)   a.   *They persuaded that John is brilliant.
        b.   *They think Mary that John is brilliant.

The examples in (12) violate the subcategorization features of their main clause verbs because the context specified by the feature does not match the actual context of the verb. Clausal complements are considered in the next section, which develops the phrase structure analysis of clauses.

The head-complement relation also involves linear order. Consider the following pairs of expressions, where one is obviously English and the other is not even though it contains the same English words.

(13)   a.   i.   John goes to school.
              ii.   *John school to goes.
        b.   i.   study of mathematics
              ii.   *mathematics of study

The structural analysis of the VPs in (13a) and the NPs in (13b) are given in (14a) and (14b) respectively.

(14)   a. i. [$_{VP}$ goes [$_{PP}$ to school]]
            ii. [$_{VP}$ [$_{PP}$ school to] goes]
        b. i. [$_{NP}$ study [$_{PP}$ of mathematics]]
            ii. [$_{NP}$ [$_{PP}$ mathematics of] study]

The legitimate English sentence (13a.i) has the analysis (14a.i) where the VP contains a PP complement. In both the VP and the PP, the head precedes its complement. This is called **head-initial** order. (13a.ii) also contains a VP with a PP complement, given our analysis in (14a.ii). The order of elements in this VP is the mirror-image of that in (13a.i). In terms of head-complement order, the heads in the VP of (14a.ii) follow their complements, thus are **head-final**. English is obviously head-initial and therefore the head-final order of constituents in (13a.ii) sounds like gibberish. However, the head-complement order in (13a.ii) is exactly what occurs when (13a.i) is translated into Japanese, the corresponding sentence given in (15).

(15)   John-ga gakkou ni ikuwasa.
        John school to goes

(The particle *ga* marks the subject in Japanese.)

EXERCISE 5.3

In Japanese (13b.ii) translates as (i).

(i) suugaku   no benkyou
    mathematics of study

a. Give the phrase structure analyses for the Japanese examples in (15) and (i).
b. What do these examples tell us about head-complement order in Japanese?

This difference in head-complement order is called a **parameter**, in this case the **Head Parameter**. It is generally assumed that the Head Parameter is set for a particular value for all the head-complement relations in a given language. Of course, if the Head Parameter is set differently for different heads, this information will be readily available from the primary language data a child encounters while acquiring the grammar of the language. Nonetheless, there appear to be only two settings for the Head Parameter with respect to the languages of the world. That is, there seems to be no evidence that a head can occur between two complements when it occurs with more than one.

The Head Parameter accounts for correlations between types of constructions among the world's languages. These correlations are identified in the study of language typology, which attempts to characterize the languages of the world into distinct types based on the kinds of constructions each contains. The syntactic branch of this study was pioneered by the late Joseph Greenberg, a linguist at

Stanford University, who extensively studied the syntactic patterns of numerous languages in a search for generalizations across languages. These statements, which bear his name, are called **Greenberg universals**.

To see how the Head Parameter accounts for some of the Greenberg universals, let's begin with the fourth.

(16)   Universal 4: With overwhelmingly greater than chance frequency, languages with normal SOV order are postpositional. (Greenberg 1966, p. 79)

SOV order refers to the linear order of the subject (S), the object (O), and the verb (V). The term "postpositional" refers to a prepositional phrase in which the P follows its NP complement. In traditional grammar the P would be called a postposition rather than a preposition. Modern generative grammar makes no such distinction; P is a preposition whether it occurs before its object or after it.

Setting aside the qualification in the initial prepositional phrase of (16), Greenberg's fourth universal can be reformulated as an implicational statement (17), where $\Rightarrow$ indicates an implication.

(17)   SOV $\Rightarrow$ [$_{PP}$ NP P]

Given the phrase structure analysis developed above, it should be immediately clear that the PP is head-final, so all that is left to do is figure out how SOV constructions are also head-final. But that is also obvious. The V must merge first with its complement O, forming a VP (18) that is also head-final.

(18)   [$_{VP}$ NP V]

Thus (16) reduces to the fact that a language with head-final VP will have head-final PP, which is precisely what the Head Parameter predicts. Note further that Japanese is such a language, as the examples in (15) and (i) in the last exercise show.

Greenberg's second universal is similarly easy to reduce to the Head Parameter.

(19)   Universal 2: In languages with prepositions, the genitive almost always follows the governing noun, while in languages with postpositions it almost always precedes. (Greenberg 1966, p. 78)

Genitive refers to a case distinction that is manifested in the morphology of nouns, adjectives, and determiners of languages where case is realized overtly in morphology. Old English, like other Germanic languages, manifested a rich morphological case system; in contrast, modern English manifests no case distinctions with the marked exception of the personal pronouns (e.g. *he* (nominative) vs. *him* (objective) vs. *his* (genitive)). In contrast to English, German provides clear examples of the genitive constructions that (19) refers to.

(20)   a.   die   Studie   der   Mathematik
              the-NOM study-NOM the-GEN mathematics-GEN
              "the study of mathematics"
         b.   die   Studie   des   Romans
              the-NOM study-NOM the-GEN novel-GEN
              "the study of the novel"

c. die   Student   der   Medizin
the-NOM student-NOM the-GEN medicine-GEN
"the student of medicine"

Unlike English, German has just a NP following the head noun instead of a PP. In
(20) the NPs following the head N are all complements and they all occur in the
genitive case. The difference between (20b) and the other two examples is that
Roman is a masculine noun, whereas *Mathematik* and *Medizin* are both feminine.
Thus *der* is the genitive form of the feminine article, while *des* is the genitive
form of the masculine article.

Given this analysis, the second Greenberg universal can be reformulated as the
pair of implications in (21).

(21)   a. $[_{PP} \text{ P NP}] \Rightarrow [_{NP} \text{ N NP}_{GEN}]$
          b. $[_{PP} \text{ NP P}] \Rightarrow [_{NP} \text{ NP}_{GEN} \text{ N}]$

But in terms of head-complement order, (21a) just says that head-initial order in
PP implies head-initial order in NP, which again is exactly what is expected given
the Head Parameter. And (21b) says exactly the same thing with respect to head-
final order. Once again, the Greenberg universal reduces to the Head Parameter
under the appropriate syntactic analysis.

EXERCISE 5.4

Consider Greenberg's thirteenth universal in (i).

   (i) Universal 13: If the nominal object always precedes the verb, then verb
        forms subordinate to the main verb always precede it. (Greenberg 1966,
        p. 84)

a. The first part of the universal clearly implicates the Head Parameter. Explain.
b. Consider (ii).

    (ii) They know he made a mistake.

    Given that the underlined string of lexical items form a subordinate clause, how can
    the second part of (i) be interpreted so that it also implicates the Head Parameter?
c. The formulation of this universal is less general than it needs to be. Reformulate
    the universal so that it is as general as possible.

If the linear order of heads and their complements is determined by the setting of
a parameter, then this order need not be stipulated in subcategorization features.
Thus the feature [+___ NP] in the lexical entry of a verb simply indicates that the
verb occurs with a NP complement either to its left or its right, depending on the
setting of the head parameter. Thus the phrasal categories mentioned in a subcategorization feature merely indicate the context with respect to complements in
which the verb may occur.

Although subcategorization features provide a basis for constraining the effects of free Merge by prohibiting such deviant examples as (22), they cannot account for other effects as illustrated in (23).

(22)   a. *John talked Mary about Bill.
           b. *Mary recommended us the movie.
           c. *They gave of books to Mary.

(23)   a. *They put the books to the closet.
           b. *John recommended the movie at us.
           c. *Mary sold a book into Bill.

EXERCISE 5.5

Using (22–23),

a. discuss in detail how subcategorization features account for the deviance of the examples in (22);

b. discuss how the deviant examples in (23) satisfy the subcategorization feature of their respective verbs.

The deviance of (23a) rather obviously concerns the choice of the lexical preposition. Substituting *in*, *into*, *inside*, or *outside* for *to* results in a grammatical sentence, whereas changing *to* to *for*, *from*, or *at* doesn't change the deviant status of the resulting sentence. Merge by itself cannot prohibit such deviant examples and the addition of subcategorization features does not affect this result. However it is clear that the V determines the choice of the lexical head of its PP complement. In this way V **selects** P. This selection must also be specified as a property of the lexical head – i.e. as a **selectional feature**, which is another type of contextual feature associated with heads. Whereas the subcategorization feature characterizes the relation between a head and its complement, the selectional relation is a **head-to-head** relation between a head and the head of its complement (for each complement if there are more than one).

Selectional restrictions also apply between verbs and their NP objects, as illustrated in (24) compared to (25).

(24)   a.   The student frightened the professor.
           b. *The student frightened the textbook.
           c. *The student frightened justice.

(25)   *The student frightened.

(25) shows that the verb *frighten* requires an object NP, hence has a subcategorization feature [+___ NP]. The deviant examples in (24b–c) satisfy this feature but are nonetheless deviant. This is accounted for by postulating a selectional feature for *frighten* which requires that the head of its NP complement meet certain conditions. These conditions involve distinguishing the noun *professor* from

the nouns *textbook* and *justice* in terms of their inherent features. For example, *professor* designates an animate entity as opposed to *textbook* and *justice,* which are not. Taking the noun *professor* to be inherently animate, its lexical entry will contain the feature [+animate], in contrast to *textbook* and *justice* which will be marked [–animate]. The verb *frighten* will then have the selectional feature [+___ [+animate]], which is violated in (24b–c).

Another area of syntax involving selection concerns the verbal system, which consists of a main verb and its verbal auxiliaries. Consider the following paradigm.

(26)   a.   Mary could have been writing her thesis.
          b.   Mary could have written her thesis.
          c.   Mary could be writing her thesis.
          d.   Mary could write her thesis.
          e.   Mary had been writing her thesis.
          f.   Mary had written her thesis.
          g.   Mary was writing her thesis.
          h.   Mary wrote her thesis.

While (26h) contains but a single main verb inflected in the past tense, (26a) contains three additional verbal auxiliaries: a modal *could,* the perfective auxiliary *have,* and one form of the progressive auxiliary *be* (cf. (26c) and (26g)). Modal verbs in English form a special class that are neither aspectual like perfective *have* and progressive *be* nor are they main verbs that can stand on their own in a sentence. In English the modal verbs are: *will, would, shall, should, can, could, may, might,* and *must.* The modal *will* is used in English to express future tense, unlike Romance languages – i.e. Latin and its descendents, where the future tense occurs as a special conjugation of the main verb. With the modal and the two aspectual auxiliaries there are six combinations in which the main verb and the three verbal auxiliaries may occur in addition to the one that contains only the finite main verb.

The paradigm (26) illustrates several descriptive generalizations about the syntax of the verbal system.

(27)   a.   The first (leftmost) verbal element is marked for tense.[3]
          b.   If the verbal string contains a modal, the verbal form that follows occurs in its uninflected form (i.e. identical to its infinitival form).
          c.   If the verbal string contains the perfective auxiliary *have,* then the verbal form that follows is inflected as the past participle.
          d.   If the verbal string contains the progressive auxiliary, the verbal form that follows is inflected as the present participle.

Putting aside (27a) for a moment, the remaining three (27b–d) can be reduced to a more general statement (28).

(28)   The morphological form of a verbal element will be determined by the verbal element that precedes it if there is one.

The dependencies are as follows:

(29)   a.   modal: V + Ø
            b.   *have*: V + -*en*
            c.   *be*: V + -*ing*

Ø indicates a phonetically null affix. A verbal element with a Ø affix shows up at
PF in its **bare** form, the "uninflected" form of the infinitive (e.g. *be* in *to be*). The
morphological forms of the past participle involve some variation, for example:
had walked consisting of the uninflected verbal stem *walk*– plus the affix – *ed*;
had fallen consisting of the uninflected verbal stem *fall*– plus the affix –*en*; *had
sung* consisting of a phonological variant of the verbal stem *sing*–; and *had stolen*
consisting of a phonological variant of the verbal stem *steal*– plus the affix –*en*.
The corresponding morphological forms of present participle are invariant: the
verbal stem plus the affix –*ing*. The dependencies listed in (29) are prima facie
relationships between two lexical items. In the case of the main verb, which is
the head of a VP, this is therefore a dependency between a lexical item and the
head of a phrase.

If the verbal auxiliary is analyzed as the head of a phrasal projection, then
these dependencies become head-to-head relations, namely selection. It follows
that the VP projected by the main verb is a complement of the verbal auxiliary to
its left. Thus (26c) would involve roughly the following partial phrase structure.

(30)

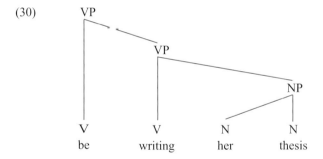

Analyzing nonfinite forms of auxiliaries as V is standard, motivated in part by
a desire to avoid proliferating syntactic categories unnecessarily. The analysis of
the finite form of the verbal auxiliary (and also the main verb) will be discussed
later because it is more complicated.

The analysis of the verbal system depends to a large extent on the form of verbal elements when they enter a derivation. Like other lexical items, verbal elements enter a derivation via Merge. The question that remains is what form they
take in the lexicon. For example, does the lexical entry for the verb *walk* contain
the form *walking* and *walked* (as a past participle)? If so, then these forms can
be merged directly into a derivation. If not, then there are at least two distinct
alternatives: (1) a morphological process of inflectional affixation applies to the
uninflected form in the lexical entry, producing the inflected form which is then
inserted in a derivation via Merge, and (2) the verbal element is merged as an
abstract form which then undergoes inflectional affixation at some later point

in the derivation as a morphosyntactic operation. In effect the first alternative is identical to having inflected forms in lexical entries. In what follows it will be assumed that all verbal elements enter a derivation fully inflected. (But see Chapter 7 for a modification of this approach.)

In the paradigm for the verbal system in English there is only one correct linear order of elements, namely (31).

(31)   modal > perfective > progressive > main verb[4]

Unconstrained, Merge will construct strings of verbal elements in this order, but it can also produce combinations of verbal elements that are deviant. Thus in addition to (26a), Merge could also produce the deviant examples in (32).

(32)   a.   *Mary could has been writing her thesis.
        b.   *Mary could have be writing her thesis.

Given Merge, the verbal strings in (32) would have the same syntactic analysis as (30). (33) gives a more complete (though schematic) analysis including the modal auxiliary.

(33)   [$_{XP}$ could [$_{VP}$ HAVE [$_{VP}$ BE [$_{VP}$ WRITE her thesis]]]]

HAVE represents all forms of the perfective auxiliary, BE the forms of the progressive auxiliary, and WRITE the forms of the main verb *write*. The syntactic category of the modal auxiliary is left open, but will be discussed below.

Given that each VP is a complement of the lexical auxiliary it merges with, there is a selectional relation between each auxiliary and the head of its VP complement where the auxiliary selects the head of its VP complement. With this much analysis in place the deviance of examples like (32) which preserve the correct linear order of verbal elements can now be explained. The selectional relation between *been* and *writing* is satisfied because the progressive auxiliary *been* selects a verb in the present participle form – in this case *writing*. Similarly the selectional relation between the perfective auxiliary *has* and the progressive auxiliary *been* is satisfied because the former selects the past participle form of the latter. However, the selectional relation between the modal *could* and the perfective auxiliary is violated in (32a). The modal auxiliary selects the bare form of the head of its complement, but in (32a) the head of its complement, the perfective auxiliary, is inflected for tense.

EXERCISE 5.6

a. Construct two additional examples of deviant verbal strings that nonetheless preserve the correct linear order.
b. Discuss in detail how selectional constraints account for the deviance of (32b) and the two additional examples you have constructed.

Unconstrained Merge can also generate illegitimate orderings of these verbal elements – any one of the twenty-three possible. Therefore these deviant orderings must also be prohibited by some grammatical mechanism. For example, consider the illegitimate order (34a) of which (34b) constitutes a specific instance.

(34) a. perfective > modal > progressive > main verb
      b. *Mary has will been sailing for three hours.

The verbal string in (32b) would have a structure (35) along the lines of the analysis of the examples in (32) as given in (33).

(35)   [$_{VP}$ has [$_{XP}$ will [$_{VP}$ been [$_{VP}$ sailing for three hours]]]]

The complement of the progressive auxiliary *been* is the VP *sailing for three hours*, thus *been* selects the progressive participle *sailing*. This satisfies the selectional feature of the progressive auxiliary. In this structure, the modal *will* selects the progressive auxiliary *been*, which violates the selectional feature of the modal because the modal always selects the bare form of the head of its complement. The auxiliary *been* is inflected as the past participle. Thus (34b) is prohibited because it violates a selectional feature of one of its verbal elements. Substituting *be* for *been* eliminates this problem, but the result (36) remains deviant.

(36) a. *Mary has will be sailing for three hours.
      b.   [$_{VP}$ has [$_{XP}$ will [$_{VP}$ be [$_{VP}$ sailing for three hours]]]]

In (36) the selectional features of the modal *will* and the progressive auxiliary *be* are both satisfied. The deviance of the example is now restricted to the selectional relation between *has* and *will*. The perfective auxiliary *have* selects a past participle form. Modals have no such form. This ordering of verbal elements is therefore prohibited by the selectional features of the verbal elements.

EXERCISE 5.7

a. Select another deviant order of verbal elements and construct an example; then give its phrase structure analysis.
b. Now explain how this order is prohibited by the necessary selectional features on the verbal elements.

This analysis of the verbal system depends in part on the inventory of legitimate verbal forms in the lexicon. For example, modals do not have past or present participle forms and therefore cannot head the complement of the perfective or progressive auxiliary. Similarly, to account for the deviance of (37), there should be no present participle form for the perfective auxiliary *have*.[5]

(37)   *Mary will be having sailed for three hours.

Otherwise, (37) satisfies all the selectional features of its verbal elements.

EXERCISE 5.8

Discuss how the sectional restrictions on the verbal elements in (37) are all satisfied.

This approach to the illegitimate ordering of verbal elements generalizes to the other deviant orders. Therefore given three necessary selectional features (on modals and the perfective and progressive auxiliaries), we can account for not only the illegitimate insertion of the wrong form of the four verbal elements (including the main verb) but also for merging them in an illegitimate order.

EXERCISE 5.9

There is one further problem with free Merge that remains to be solved: the merger of multiple instances of the same verbal element (e.g. two modals or two perfective auxiliaries).

a. Construct two examples using different verbal elements.
b. Give a detailed structural analysis of these examples and discuss whether they can be prohibited on the basis of selectional features.
c. Discuss whether it makes any difference whether the multiple instances are adjacent or separated by at least one other verbal element.

5.2   The phrase structure of clauses beyond VP

The selectional analysis of the verbal system leads directly to the phrase structure analysis of clauses. A modal auxiliary selects the bare form of the verbal head of its complement and the infinitival marker *to* does too. Compare the pairs of examples in (38) and (39).

(38)   a.   Mary should be studying for the exam.
        b.   I expect Mary to be studying for the exam.
(39)   a.   Mary should study for the exam.
        b.   I expect Mary to study for the exam.

Given this selectional analysis, the VPs *be studying for the exam* and *study for the exam* must be complements of infinitival *to*, which is therefore the head of the phrases *to be studying for the exam* and *to study for the exam*. The infinitival *to* is a realization of the category T (for tense), where T involves the feature [±finite]. The infinitival marker *to* is designated as [−finite]. The feature [+finite] involves another feature [±past], where [+past] marks the past tense and [−past] marks the present tense. Thus the infinitival phrase (38b) would have the syntactic analysis given in (40).

(40)   [$_{TP}$ to [$_{VP}$ be [$_{VP}$ studying for the exam]]]

The infinitival verbal construction is thus a TP. This analysis generalizes to the corresponding finite verbal construction headed by the modal *should* in (38a), as in (41).

(41)   [$_{TP}$ should [$_{VP}$ be [$_{VP}$ studying for the exam]]]

Given (41), the category XP in (33) and (35) is therefore TP.

Under the traditional analysis of a clause discussed in the first chapters, the finite TP in (41) corresponds to the designation "predicate." In (38a) that leaves the subject *Mary*, so merging *Mary* with the TP (41) yields the full clause. Given the constraints on Merge, the syntactic label of the clause must be either T or N. If N were the designated head of the clause construction, then the TP (41) would be either a complement or an adjunct of N. Neither analysis has anything to recommend it. Alternatively, T is the head and the clause itself is a TP. If the subject NP is analyzed as a specifier, then subject/verb agreement in finite clauses becomes a species of specifier-head agreement. Thus finite and infinitival clauses have the same phrase structure (42).

(42)

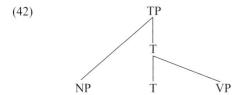

Given (42), T is the head of a clause, VP is the complement of T, and the subject NP constitutes the specifier of TP (henceforth Spec-TP).

The analysis being developed is based on an assumption that infinitival *to*, which is clearly a grammatical formative that represents [−tense], and the English modal auxiliaries are members of the same syntactic category. There are two pieces of evidence for this assumption. First, the two cannot co-occur in the same verbal string and therefore are in complementary distribution, as (43) demonstrates.

(43)   a.   We expect John to study for the exam.
           b.   We expect John will study for the exam.
           c.   *We expect John to will study for the exam.
           d.   *We expect John will to study for the exam.

(43a–b) show that either *to* or *will* can show up in the same context, while (43c–d) show that both cannot occur together. In contrast, both the perfective and progressive auxiliaries can co-occur with either.

(44)   a.   We expect John to be studying for the exam.
           b.   We expect John will be studying for the exam.
           c.   We expect John to have studied for the exam.
           d.   We expect John will have studied for the exam.

Next, both infinitival *to* and modal auxiliaries impose the same selectional restriction – that is, both require that the head of their complement be the bare form.

EXERCISE 5.10

Discuss how selection might be used to account for both of the deviant examples in (43).

In addition to these shared properties, it is plausible that both are marked T in the lexicon because when they occur in indicative (as opposed to interrogative) clauses, they always occur in the T position adjacent to the subject of the clause.

The next question for this analysis concerns clauses in which some other auxiliary (i.e. the perfective or progressive) is inflected for tense. In this regard, consider the following pair of sentences.

(45)   a.   Mary should have studied for the exam.
         b.   Mary has studied for the exam.

In (45a) the perfective auxiliary occurs as the head of the complement of the modal *should* and shows up in its bare form, thus not inflected for tense. The modal is in the T position, the perfective auxiliary is clearly in some other position. Given it is a species of verb, hence V, in this position it functions syntactically as a V and thus heads a VP. In (45b) however the perfective auxiliary is inflected for tense and occurs in the T position. This is necessary in order to account for specifier-head agreement. Further evidence for this analysis concerns negative and interrogative constructions, discussed in Chapter 7. The perfective *has* is the form for third person singular, as opposed to present tense *have*, which covers first and second person singular and plural as well as third person plural. Thus (46) violates specifier-head agreement.

(46)   a.   *Mary have studied for the exam.
         b.   *I/we/you/they has studied for the exam.

Assuming that *has* in the lexicon is marked as V, how does it become T?

The simplest answer is that *has* merges directly as T, projecting its syntactic label. This would require that in the lexicon the auxiliary verb *has* is also marked as T, whereas the uninflected forms of the perfective auxiliary are only marked as V. V constitutes a **lexical** category label, whereas T is a **functional** category. Lexical categories designate homogeneous sets of lexical items (e.g. verbs vs. nouns vs. adjectives). Functional categories (e.g. T) are heterogeneous, given that T covers verbal auxiliaries as well as infinitival *to*, which is not similarly verb-like.

EXERCISE 5.11

Construct a pair of examples for the progressive auxiliary similar to (45) and discuss the analysis of the finite form of this auxiliary.

The final case to consider involves finite clauses without verbal auxiliaries.

(47)   a.   Mary writes novels as a hobby.
         b.   Mary laughed.

The phrase *writes novels as a hobby* is a VP, with the V *writes* as its head. The N *novels* constitutes the direct object complement of the verb. To generate this structure, *writes* must be merged as a V that projects its lexical category label.

Nonetheless, we still want to analyze the sentence as a TP with *Mary* as the specifier and the VP as a complement of the head of TP. Since there is no overt element T distinct from the verb itself (i.e. one that is pronounced/has a PF realization), it is assumed that T in this construction is covert.

This raises two further questions: (1) where does this covert T come from? and (2) what does it contain? Being covert it has no phonetic features, but this does not preclude that it has other grammatical features. Minimally it has the features that constitute the functional category T. Furthermore, it must at some point contain the relevant agreement features of person and number (henceforth "phi-features" which will be designated with the Greek letter ϕ as is standard in the literature) to account for the agreement between the subject and the finite verb, spec-head agreement in our analysis. That is, the agreement features of person and number must be present in T to verify subject-verb agreement, for example in the paradigm (48).

(48) a.   Mary laughs.
      b.   I/we/you/they laugh.
      c.   *Mary laugh.
      d.   *I/we/you/they laughs.

So the answer to the second question is straightforward: T must contain the features that designate T plus the relevant ϕ-features.

Since these features already exist in the finite main verb itself, the minimal answer to the first question about the source of T would be finite V in the lexicon. Given this analysis, the derivation of TP for (47a) would proceed as follows, starting with the VP (49).

(49)   [$_{VP}$ writes novels for a hobby]

The next step involves the placement of the tense and agreement features that constitute T at the left edge of VP, forming a new syntactic object labeled T. This operation involves merging the tense and agreement features in finite V with VP to create the structure (50).

(50)

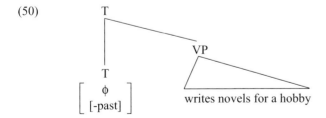

Exactly how (50) is derived is discussed in Chapter 7.

The analysis of clause structure developed above is anchored on the main verb and based on selectional phenomena. The cases under consideration have all concerned constructions in which the main verb is the head of the complement of some other element in the verbal system (including T). Extending this analysis of clause structure to the clausal complements of main verbs leads to a more highly articulated analysis of clause structure.

The verbs *think* and *believe* both take finite clause complements, but as illustrated in (51) these complements come in two distinct variants.

(51)   a. i.   We think John will arrive on time.
            ii. We think that John will arrive on time.
        b. i.   We believe John will arrive on time.
            ii. We believe that John will arrive on time.

All the examples in (51) contain a finite subordinate clause *John will arrive on time* – a TP. The second examples in (51a) and (51b) contain an additional lexical item *that*, not to be confused with the demonstrative determiner *that* (e.g. *that book*) or demonstrative pronoun (e.g. *that is annoying*). This element *that,* which introduces a finite TP that functions as a clausal complement, is called a **complementizer**, having a syntactic category label C; in effect it introduces a clause that functions as a complement. The i-examples in (51) show that an overt finite clause complementizer is optional.

The complementizer *that* also shows up in relative clauses (e.g. (52a)) and cleft constructions (e.g. (52b)).

(52)   a.   a topic that Mary can investigate
        b.   It was to Mary that John gave the book.

In these constructions, the finite clause that *that* introduces is not the complement of any head. However, like clausal complements, such constructions are subordinate clauses. So *that* functions as a subordinating particle. From here on, the term "complementizer" will be used to designate these subordinating particles, whether or not clauses that follow are actual complements of some head.

Subordinate clauses can also be infinitival – i.e. headed by T *to*. Alongside the finite clause complement of *expect* in (53a) there is a corresponding infinitival complement (53b).

(53)   a.   We expect (that) Mary will be successful.
        b.   We expect Mary to be successful.

Thus the complement *Mary to be successful* is analyzed as a TP with the same structure as the corresponding finite subordinate clause in (53a). The presence of the complementizer *that* in (53a) is optional, as indicated by the parentheses. In some idiolects of English the infinitival complement can also occur with a complementizer *for*.

(54)   a.   We expect for Mary to be successful.
        b.   We want for Mary to be successful.

This complementizer is obligatory when the matrix verb is separated from its clausal complement by an adverb phrase.

(55)   a.   We want very much for Mary to be successful.
        b.   *We want very much Mary to be successful.

It appears that even speakers who find examples like (54) marginal or worse recognize that (55b) is strongly deviant while in contrast, (55a) is not.

The complementizer *for* also shows up in infinitival relative clauses, where it is obligatory when the subject of the relative clause is overt.

(56)   a.   a topic for us to investigate
        b.   *a topic us to investigate

(See Section 6.3 for an explanation of the deviance of (56b).) The infinitival relative clause in (56a) is roughly synonymous with the finite relative clause in (57).

(57)   a topic that we should investigate

This synonymy follows if the pronouns *us* and *we* have the same syntactic function – i.e. Spec-TP of a clause whose main verb is *investigate*, and thus the same semantic function and of course a parallel LF representation.[6]

The two complementizers *that* and *for* merge with TP to form subordinate clauses of various types. When C merges with TP, either C or T must be the head that projects its label on the resulting syntactic object. Which is the head depends on the relation between C and TP, and more particularly between C and T. Just as there are two instances of C, there are also two instances of T, finite and infinitival. As the following paradigm for relative clauses demonstrates, not all combinations are possible.

(58)   a.   a topic that Mary should investigate
        b.   a topic for Mary to investigate
        c.   *a topic that Mary to investigate
        d.   *a topic for Mary should investigate

(58) shows that there are co-occurrence restrictions on which C can occur with which T. C *for* pairs with T *to* and C *that* pairs with finite T. If C is the head of the phrase C+TP, these restrictions can be analyzed as another instance of selection. Thus TP is the complement of C and therefore C-to-T is a selectional head-to-head relation.

EXERCISE 5.12

In syntactic analysis to more fully understand the strengths and weaknesses of a given analysis, it is useful to consider the alternatives. In this case, that would involve taking T as the head of the phrase C+TP.

a. Can selection still be used to account for the co-occurrence restrictions? If not, why not?
b. Could the Spec-head agreement relation possibly be used to explain these co-occurrence restrictions?
c. What potential problems does this alternative analysis involve?
d. And how does it compare to the analysis in which C is the head of C+TP?

Taking clausal complements to be CPs, then the main verb selects C. This gives us a set of selectional relations in clause structure that can iterate indefinitely.

(59)   V > C > T > V ...

There is however the question of whether V always selects C or only when C has phonetic content and is therefore overt. That is, when the lexical complementizer is optional and does not occur in the PF representation, is the clausal complement of V a CP or a TP? Given the already ample evidence for covert grammatical structure in syntax, postulating a covert C is not problematic. There are several ways to account for the covert analysis. One possibility would be to posit a phonetically null counterpart for each lexical (i.e. phonetically realized) C. Alternatively, the absence of lexical C could be handled by a deletion operation. Thus at LF there would be no difference between the two examples in (60).

(60)   a.   Mary thinks that Bill may be right.
          b.   Mary thinks Bill may be right.

At LF, (60b) will have the same representation as (60a) – i.e. with the lexical complementizer represented. Whereas at PF, the complementizer would be deleted as in (61).

(61)   Mary thinks [$_{CP}$ ~~that~~ [$_{TP}$ Bill may be right]].

For now, assume the deletion analysis to account for the optionality of lexical complementizers. From this it follows that all clausal complements and subordinate clauses more generally are CPs. If this is correct, the structural analysis for all embedded clauses will be uniform. (See Chapters 6 and 8 for further discussion of covert C in the analysis of clauses.)

The alternation in (60) follows because the deletion of C *that* is optional, as are the other cases of deletion previously discussed. However, there are constructions in which the deletion of *that* is not permissible. In this regard, consider the following paradigm.

(62)   a.   It is unlikely that John will arrive on time.
          b.   It is unlikely John will arrive on time.
          c.   That John will arrive on time is unlikely.
          d.   *John will arrive on time is unlikely.

The finite clause CP is a complement of the predicate adjective *unlikely*, where the C *that* may optionally delete as in (62b). When the subordinate clause occurs at the beginning of a sentence, the subordinating complementizer cannot be deleted.

An optional deletion analysis works less well for the complementizer *for*. As noted above for (54), infinitival clause complements with a *for* complementizer are not generally acceptable in the same way that finite clause complements headed by a *that* complementizer are. Furthermore, some verbs that take an infinitival clause complement can never take an infinitival clause headed by *for* even marginally.

(63)   a.   We believe George to be lying.
          b.   *We believe for George to be lying.

An optional deletion analysis predicts that (63b) ought to be possible for some native speakers of English at least marginally. The fact that this is not the case suggests that there may be two distinct infinitival complementizers, *for* and a null phonetic element designated as ø. Thus *believe* selects ø not *for*. This analysis generalizes to other infinitival constructions where *for* never occurs. Consider for example the case of *persuade*.

(64)   She persuaded the committee to interview Herman.

In (64) *the committee* has a dual semantic interpretation as both the object of *persuade* and the subject of *interview*. The NP *the committee* must be merged with the verb in the canonical object position in order to be interpreted as the object of *persuade*. This leaves the subject position of the infinitival clause empty (without phonetic material and hence covert), in contrast to the near paraphrase of (64) in (65) using a finite clause complement.

(65)   She persuaded the committee that they should interview Herman.

The dual interpretation for *the committee* arises from taking this NP as the antecedent of the pronoun *they* in subject position of the finite clause. Given this interpretation, the matrix VP in (64) should have the analysis in (66).

(66)   a.   [$_{VP}$ [$_V$ persuaded [$_{NP}$ the committee]] [$_{CP}$ C [$_{TP}$ PRO to interview
                Herman]]]

          b.

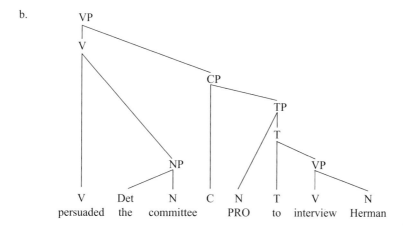

PRO here designates the null subject of the infinitival clause, another covert syntactic element, following standard practice. If C in (66) is *for*, then deletion would have to be obligatory. However, *persuade* never occurs with a *for* C. Therefore it is plausible that *persuade* does not select *for* but rather the null phonetic alternate ø.

EXERCISE 5.13

Consider the following paradigm, including (64–65).

    (i)   She persuaded the committee that Fred should interview Herman.
    (ii) *She persuaded the committee for Fred to interview Herman.
    (iii) *She persuaded the committee for them to interview Herman.

a. What are the facts concerning the anaphoric relationship between the object of *persuade* and the subject of its clausal complement?
b. What does this paradigm show regarding the two clausal complementizers?
c. How can selection be used to rule out (ii-iii)?

EXERCISE 5.14

Another argument can be made that the analysis of *persuade* involves a covert infinitival subject PRO as in (66), based on the fact that active/passive construction pairs generally have the same interpretation with respect to truth conditions. Thus consider (i).

    (i)   a. The committee interviewed Herman.
          b. Herman was interviewed by the committee.

If (i.a) is true, then (i.b) must also be true – and conversely. This finite clause pair has an infinitival counterpart, as illustrated in (ii).

    (ii) a. She expected the committee to interview Herman.
          b. She expected Herman to be interviewed by the committee.

a. What are the truth condition relations between (ii.a) and (ii.b)?
b. How does this relate to the pair in (i)?

Now consider the pair in (iii) where the verb *persuaded* has been substituted for *expected*.

    (iii) a. She persuaded the committee to interview Herman.
          b. She persuaded Herman to be interviewed by the committee.

c. If (iii.a) is true, is (iii.b) necessarily also true?
d. How does the analysis in (66) conform to these facts about the semantics of (iii)?

The inventory of complementizers now includes finite *that* and two infinitivals, the overt *for* and the covert ø. To these the question particles *whether* and *if* which occur in indirect yes/no question complements can be added.

(67)   a. Mary wonders whether John will arrive on time.
          b. Mary wonders if John will arrive on time.
          c. (see next opage)

(68)   a. It is unclear whether John will arrive on time.
          b. It is unclear if John will arrive on time.

c.

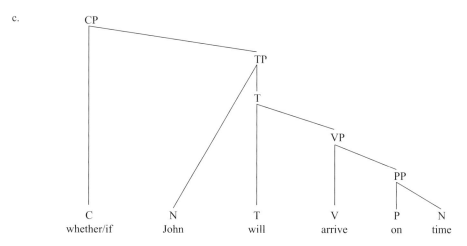

The clausal complements of the verb *wonder* in (67a–b) and of the predicate adjective *unclear* in (68) consist of the lexical items *whether* or *if* followed by a finite TP *John will arrive on time*, as represented in (67c). Taking them to be complementizers, *whether* and *if* impose a question interpretation on the TP that follows. Thus this TP is understood as a yes/no question (69).

(69)   Will John arrive on time?

(69) is a direct question, in contrast to the clausal complements under analysis, which are indirect questions. The clausal complements of *wonder* and *unclear* have the familiar analysis of C+TP, a CP as in other cases. Given that C selects T, both *if* and *whether* select finite T as (67–68) illustrate. However they are syntactically distinct (as opposed to merely phonetically distinct) in that *whether* but not *if* can occur with an infinitival TP.

(70)   a.   Mary wonders whether to rebuild after the floods.
              b.   It is unclear whether to rebuild after the floods.
(71)   a.   *Mary wonders if to rebuild after the floods.
              b.   *It is unclear if to rebuild after the floods.

(67a), (68a), and (70) demonstrate that *whether* selects both finite and infinitival T, whereas (67b), (68b), and (71) show that *if* selects only finite T.

    While the verb *wonder* takes indirect question clausal complements, CPs headed by *whether* or *if*, it cannot occur with other (non-interrogative) clausal complements.

(72)   a.   *Mary wonders that John has arrived on time.
              b.   *Mary wonders to arrive on time.
              c.   *Mary wonders for Bill to arrive on time.

The interrogative complementizers *whether* and *if* can be distinguished from their non-interrogative counterparts (*that, for*, and ø) in terms of a binary feature [±Q], where [+Q] designates the interrogative members. The verb *wonder* therefore selects a [+Q] C.

EXERCISE 5.15

Consider the variety of verbs taking clausal complements that have been discussed above.

a. List these verbs and state their selectional features.
b. Identify additional verbs that have the same selectional features. Be sure to provide the appropriate paradigms that establish this.
c. Can you identify any other verbs that take clausal complements but require different selectional features from the ones discussed so far?
d. Consider clausal complementation in some other language. What similarities and/or differences occur for the verbs corresponding to your list for (a) above?

EXERCISE 5.16

Consider clausal complements of predicate adjectives – i.e. adjectives that can occur in the context: NP BE Adj CP.

a. Give the paradigms for the adjectives *unclear*, *possible*, and *happy*.
b. State their selectional features and discuss how these account for the paradigms you have given.
c. Answer (a) and (b) for some other language and then discuss how this language is similar to or different from English.

There is another variant of indirect question which does not have an overt complementizer. Examples are given in (73), where (73a) contains a finite indirect question and (73b) contains an infinitival version.

(73)   a.   John has wondered which novel by Updike he should read next.
        b.   John has wondered which novel by Updike to read next.

In (73a) the complement of *wonder* is interpreted along the lines of the direct question in (74).

(74)   Which novel by Updike should he read?

The infinitival indirect question in (73b) is interpreted similarly. Both involve an interrogative wh-phrase (in this case *which novel by Updike*, but alternatively *what* or *who*). The interpretation of these questions are distinct from the yes/no question interpretation (cf. (69)) that holds when there is an overt complementizer. The interrogative wh-phrase and the overt yes/no question complementizer cannot occur in the same clause.

The analysis of this second kind of indirect question is somewhat more complicated than that of the first. The first (e.g. (67a)) contains straightforwardly a C plus a TP. The second (e.g. (73a)) contains an interrogative NP (e.g. *which novel by Updike*) followed by a TP *he should read next*. This NP is interpreted as the object of the verb *read* in TP. Therefore, the fact that this NP is pronounced at the beginning of the indirect question complement construction indicates that displacement is involved. Given that *wonder* requires an indirect question complement, which in the case of an indirect yes/no question involves an overt complementizer, it is natural to extend this analysis for wh-questions as in (73) by postulating a covert question complementizer [+Q] that is also selected by the verb. The derivation of the indirect question complement as a CP starts with the construction of the interrogative NP *which novel by Updike* via Merge. This NP is then merged with the V *read* to form a VP, and so on until the subject *he* is merged as Spec-TP. At this point in the derivation the TP constructed is merged with a covert C [+Q], creating a CP, as shown in (75).

(75)   [$_{CP}$ [+Q] [$_{TP}$ he should [$_{VP}$ read [$_{NP}$ which novel by Updike]]]]

In the next step in the derivation the NP that was merged as object of *read* is merged with (75) to create (76). (A more precise account of how this operation applies is given in Section 6.1.)

(76)   a.   [$_{CP}$ [$_{NP}$ which novel by Updike] [$_C$ [+Q] [$_{TP}$ he should [$_{VP}$ read [$_{NP}$ which novel by Updike]]]]]

          b.

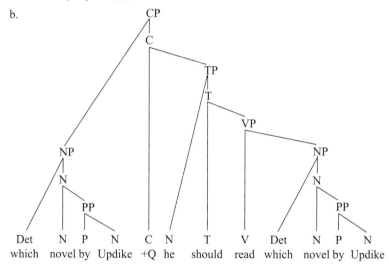

The pair of identical NPs that occur in (76a–b) are treated as *copies* of a single NP that was constructed once by Merge.

   The resulting CP now has another phrasal position in addition to its head C and its complement (TP) to the right. Furthermore, there is evidence suggesting that the NP merged with CP occupies a specifier position. Compare (73a) with the deviant (77).

(77)   *John has wondered the novel by Updike he should read next.

Given that the covert C in (77) is [+Q], thereby satisfying the selectional requirement of *wonder*, how then could (76) be prohibited? The two NPs differ in that *which novel by Updike* is interrogative, hence [+Q], whereas *the novel by Updike* is not and therefore [−Q]. If the displaced NP is in the specifier position of CP, then the interrogative NP matches the [+Q] feature of C whereas the non-interrogative NP does not. (77) therefore violates spec-head agreement.

The analysis of clause structure developed above involves two distinct heads T and C. Both T and C take a phrasal complement and a phrasal specifier.

(78)   a. $[_{TP}$ NP $[_T$ TVP$]]$
        b. $[_{CP}$ XP $[_C$ C TP $]$ $]$

The specifier for TP is usually a NP (but not always, as will be discussed in the next chapter), whereas the interrogative phrase in CP could also be a PP (e.g. *to which student*) or an AP (e.g. *how angry*). The phrase structure of clauses is thus (79).

(79)

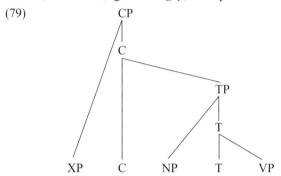

This structure holds for the full set of clausal complements. The question that arises is whether it also holds for non-complement subordinate clauses (e.g. relative clauses) and extends to main clauses. This question is investigated in Chapters 7 and 8. (In case you have any doubts the answer is yes.)

The phrase structure analysis of the clause developed in this chapter is empirically motivated by the set of co-occurrence restrictions that hold for English and other languages. These restrictions come in two varieties both of which involve the head of a phrase: selection, which also involves the head of its complement, and spec-head agreement, which also involves the specifier phrase. This analysis is theoretically grounded in the concept of phrasal projection and the special relations between a head and the constituents it merges with.

The structure (79) contains two specifier positions, one for CP and another for TP. Both are involved in displacement phenomena. A large part of the syntax of infinitival constructions concerns the distribution of overt vs. covert elements in Spec-TP. This topic is investigated in detail in the next chapter, along with other issues concerning the distribution of NPs in syntax more generally.

5.3   Summary

The architecture of the system of grammar presented in this chapter is as follows:

a.   Mechanisms of the computational system:
            Merge
            Contextual features:

    i. subcategorization
   ii. selection

Parameters:
   The Head Parameter

In terms of head-complement relations, the VP are more complicated than NP, PP, or AP. Verbs take a variety of complement constructions. Verbs can be sub-categorized on the basis of what complements they can occur with. These contexts can be formulated as contextual features, subcategorization features, that restrict the occurrence of specific verbs to specific contexts. Furthermore, there is a linear relation between a head and its complements that in most languages holds across categories. Thus if a VP is head-initial, with the V preceding its complement(s), then the same relation will hold in NP, PP, and AP. Thus there appears to be a Head Parameter that holds in languages where there are two settings, head-initial and head-final. Many of the Greenberg Universals, which identify correspondences between constructions across languages, can be reduced to the Head Parameter.

Another head-complement relation involves selection where a head will deter-mine the properties of the head of its complement. The selectional constraints on verbal elements in the verbal system of English predicts not only the proper form of verbal elements (auxiliaries and main verb) but also their linear order. Selection also establishes that modal auxiliaries and infinitival *to* share the same selectional property as well as being in complementary distribution. Given that infinitival *to* is an instance of a functional category T, in which case infinitival clauses are instances of TP, modals can also be analyzed as instances of T. Thus finite clauses as well as infinitival clauses will be TPs. In finite clauses, if the sub-ject NP is a specifier of TP, then "subject-verb agreement" follows as an instance of Spec-head agreement. When a finite clause contains only a finite main V, there must be a covert T head of TP. Subordinate finite clauses can occur with an overt complementizer C. That C cannot occur with an infinitival T, which again can be handled via selection (C selects T, and therefore TP is a complement of C). Finite and infinitival CPs also occur in NP as relative clauses. Subordinate CP in VPs function as complements of V. V will also select specific C elements, therefore V selects C. Thus selection of V to C to T to V constitutes the structural spine of clauses. The optionality of overt C can be accounted for by positing a phonetically null (hence covert) lexical C. In the case of indirect questions (e.g. the clausal complement of *wonder*), either the C is overt (e.g. *whether*) or it is covert ([+Q]) and then requires the displacement of a wh-phrase in TP to a Spec-CP position.

Bibliographical notes

The original discussion of the contextual features involved in subcategorization and selection occurs in Chomsky 1965. The analysis of the English verbal mor-phology system has a long and intricate history. See Chomsky 1957 for the origi-nal proposal; Lasnik 2000 and Freidin 2004 for critical discussion.

6   The syntax of Spec-TP

Having established the fundamentals of clause structure in the previous chapter, we turn now to the syntactic analysis of the elements in clauses that are involved in displacement phenomena. This chapter investigates displacement of non-interrogative NPs and also CPs; Chapter 7, of verbs and auxiliaries; and Chapter 8, of interrogative phrases (including NPs) and related elements. The first section of this chapter examines the mechanisms of the computational system that produced displacement constructions. As discussed in Chapter 2, displacement involves a mismatch between PF and LF representations: a phrase that is pronounced in one position in a sentence is interpreted as if it occupies another. Thus displacement is centrally concerned with issues of semantic interpretation. The second section of this chapter deals with constraints on argument structure that place restrictions on possible displacement constructions. The third section of this chapter explores the notion of syntactic Case and how it can be utilized for the formulation of additional constraints on displacement constructions. Given our analysis of infinitival complements in the previous chapter, this question generalizes to covert NPs not involved in displacement – namely PRO (see (66) in Chapter 5). The final section of this chapter takes up the issue of the limitations on the syntactic distance between an overt NP and the corresponding covert position in which it is interpreted.

6.1   Displacement and the computational system

Inter-clausal NP displacement provides a paradigm case with which to begin an investigation of the syntactic and semantic properties of displacement, starting with a comparison of the two sentences in (1).

(1)   a.   It seems that the students are enjoying their new laptops.
            b.   The students seem to be enjoying their new laptops.

In both examples the NP *the students* is interpreted as the subject of the verb *enjoying*, but only in (1a) does this NP occupy the subject position for that verb, Spec-TP of the clausal complement of *seem*. In (1b) *the students* occurs in Spec-TP of the matrix clause, the subject position for the main clause verb *seem*. An account of the interpretation of *the students* in (1b) as the subject of the verb *enjoying* requires that at some point in the derivation of (1b) *the students* actually occurs in the Spec-TP of the infinitival complement clause and then apparently "moves" from there to the Spec-TP position of the matrix (root) clause. Thus at one stage in the derivation of (1b) the following structure occurs.

(2)   [$_{TP}$ [$_{NP}$ the students] [$_{T}$ to [$_{VP}$ be [$_{VP}$ enjoying [$_{NP}$ their new laptops]]]]]

To derive (2), the NP *the students* is first merged with the TP *to be enjoying their new laptops* via Merge.

At this point the syntactic derivation of (1b) raises a nontrivial issue. The clausal complement of *seem* in (1a) is clearly a CP with an overt head, the C *that*, whereas the infinitival clause complement of *seem* in (1b) has no overt C and as (3) shows, could not.

(3)   *It seems for the students to be enjoying their new laptops.

Therefore the infinitival complement of *seem* could at most have a covert C ø, as discussed in the previous chapter. But obviously whether it does must be motivated on the basis of something other than PF, where it doesn't exist. As a working hypothesis, assume from now on that all clauses are CPs, infinitival as well as finite, regardless of the presence of an overt head. (Note that this applies as well to the variant of (1a) that lacks the overt complementizer.) Motivation for this hypothesis is discussed later in this chapter and also in Chapter 8.

Given that infinitival clauses are CPs and therefore would contain a covert C if no overt C occurs, the next step in the derivation of (1b) after (2) is (4) where the covert infinitival C ø is merged with (2).

(4)   [$_{CP}$ ø [$_{TP}$ [$_{NP}$ the students] [$_{T}$ to [$_{VP}$ be [$_{VP}$ enjoying [$_{NP}$ their new laptops]]]]]]

The derivation continues with the merger of this CP (4) with the matrix verb *seem* to form VP. The step after this involves the construction of TP by merging the T-features of *seem*, tense and agreement (number and person) with the VP, to create the T position as discussed in the previous chapter. This yields a TP with the internal structure (5) (see the following page). Merging the NP *the students* in the Spec position of the matrix TP yields a displacement construction.

(5)

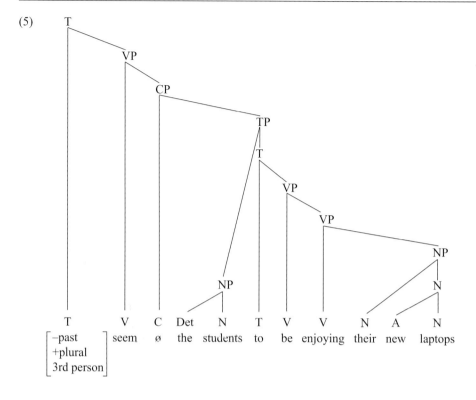

T
[−past
  +plural
  3rd person]
seem   ø   the   students   to   be   enjoying   their   new   laptops

Consider the technical process that accounts for displacement. It involves merging the NP *the students* as the Spec-TP of the infinitival complement of *seem*
in (5), and then merging that same NP as the Spec-TP of the root clause in (6),
where φ stands for the agreement features [+plural] and [3rd person].

(6)   [$_{TP}$ [$_{NP}$ the students] [$_{T}$ [−past, φ] [$_{VP}$ seem [$_{CP}$ ø [$_{TP}$ [$_{NP}$ the students] [$_{T}$ to [$_{VP}$
           be [$_{VP}$ enjoying [$_{NP}$ their new laptops]]]]]]]]]]

One useful way to think about displacement phenomena is that a single syntactic object occurs in multiple syntactic contexts. In (6) the NP *the students* occurs
in the context of both the TP *to be enjoying their new laptops* and the TP [−past,
φ] *seem the students to be enjoying their new laptops*. When this NP, which is
constructed by Merge independently of its two contexts in (6), is merged with
a context, either the NP is not part of the context (**external Merge**) or it is
part of the context (**internal Merge**). Internal Merge creates multiple **copies** of
the constituent that is merged (e.g. *the students* in (6)), one inside the context
and the other outside. Both options for Merge are available without stipulation;
in fact it would require an additional prohibitive stipulation to exclude either
option. Given Merge, the phenomenon of displacement follows.

The two copies of the NP *the students* in (6) form a nontrivial **chain**, which
can be represented either as a set of copies (7a) or alternatively as a set of contexts in which the copies occur – i.e. their sister constituents as in (7b).

(7)   a.   {[$_{NP}$ the students], [$_{NP}$ the students]}

        b.   {[$_T$ [−past, ϕ] seem to be enjoying their new laptops], [$_T$ to be enjoying
             their new laptops]}

Under the working hypothesis that Merge is binary for everything except coordinate structures, a copy can be uniquely identified by its context. For ease of explication, the copy that is overt in PF can be distinguished from the other copies that are not by designating the latter as **traces**. (7) is an example of a two-member chain. Given the representation of chains in terms of contexts, it follows that every constituent in a phrase structure representation is associated with at least a one-member chain, what is called a **trivial chain**. The largest context identifies the **head of the chain**, thus the first member in both (7a) and (7b). A nontrivial chain contains one or more links. A chain **link** consists of a pair of adjacent copies in the chain. Thus a three member chain will contain two links; a four member chain, three links; and so on.

   The phenomenon of displacement is often described in terms of the notion "movement." Given the analysis in the preceding paragraph, this description is purely metaphorical. Nothing actually moves in a derivation. However, the metaphor is pervasive in the syntax literature and therefore it is useful to know how it applies to examples like (6). Under the movement analysis the NP *the students* is said to move from a complement Spec-TP position, where it is first merged, to a matrix Spec-TP position. This is considered to be inter-clausal movement, referred to as **raising**.

   The derivation of (6) involves another grammatical operation that deletes one of the copies of the NP *the students* to yield the proper PF, as illustrated in (8), where the strikethrough indicates the deletion.

(8)   [$_{TP}$ [$_{NP}$ the students] [$_T$ [−past, ϕ] [$_{VP}$ seem [$_{CP}$ Ø [$_{TP}$ [$_{NP}$ ~~the students~~]
        [$_T$ to [$_{VP}$ be [$_{VP}$ enjoying [$_{NP}$ their new laptops]]]]]]]]]

Given this analysis, our theory of the computational system for human language C$_{HL}$ contains two **elementary operations**, listed in (9).

(9)   a.   Merge
        b.   Delete

Merge is structure-building and Delete appears to be structure-destroying. The application of Delete in (8) reduces a nontrivial chain to a trivial chain, what can be called **chain reduction**. This results in a unique linear order for the syntactic objects in a construction, a basic requirement for a well-formed PF representation. Thus chain reduction results in the **linearization** of the phonetic elements in a syntactic object. Delete also accounts for ellipsis phenomena, as illustrated in (10b).

(10)   a.   John bought a bicycle and Mary bought a computer.
        b.   John bought a bicycle and Mary ~~bought~~ a computer.

These two mechanisms account for possibly all of syntax.

In terms of how these elementary operations actually apply in a derivation, both Merge and Delete appear to operate independently. This suggests a general constraint on the formulation of grammars – that grammatical operations, which create steps in a derivation, cannot compound elementary operations.

This constraint against compounding elementary operations is the strongest type of condition that can be imposed on a theory of grammar because it restricts the class of possible grammars by restricting the class of possible grammatical operations.

Merge can be further constrained by a No Tampering Condition (see Chapter 4) that prohibits Merge from altering the internal structure of any syntactic object it applies to. That is, Merge cannot change any sister relations that have been established by prior applications of Merge. This forces Merge to apply to the roots of the two syntactic objects involved. In effect, Merge always extends the syntactic objects to which it applies by adding material at their edges.

The fact that the infinitival subject is absent in PF but presumably must exist in LF for semantic interpretation tells us a derivation must at some point split into two parts, one that leads to PF and the other that leads to LF, creating a three-part derivation as illustrated in (11).

(11)

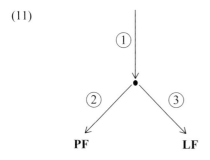

Part 1 mainly involves the insertion of lexical items via Merge (including displacement) that affects both PF and LF. Part 2 concerns syntactic operations that affect only pronunciation (PF representation) – in particular, deletion (see Chapter 9 for detailed discussion). Note also that part 2 cannot involve the introduction of any element with semantic content because such an element would not reach LF for interpretation. Likewise, part 3 cannot involve the merger of any element with phonetic content because such an element would never be pronounced. This suggests that the point at which the derivation splits into two independent tracks, one to PF and the other to LF, involves the separation of phonetic and semantic features.

The existence of this point, called **Spell-Out**, can be motivated by more general considerations. Recall that PF and LF interface with different cognitive components of the brain: PF with the sensory/motor systems and LF with conceptual/intentional systems. They are therefore interface representations that connect the language faculty with the rest of cognition. Suppose that interface representations need to be "pure" in the sense that they contain no superfluous elements. An element is superfluous at an interface if it does not contribute information that the interface cognitive systems are concerned with. For example, to the cognitive systems that process linguistic meaning the phonetic features of lexical items are superfluous. Likewise, the semantic features of lexical items are superfluous for the cognitive systems that process linguistic sound. This suggests a general constraint on representations that prohibits superfluous elements, what is called **Full Interpretation**.

(12)   Full Interpretation: there can be no superfluous symbols in representations.
           (Chomsky and Lasnik 1993, p. 514)

(12) operates as a condition on the two interface representations PF and LF. From (12) Spell-Out follows as a consequence.

While Spell-Out imposes a separation of phonetic from semantic features, whether syntactic features are also affected is not clear. Obviously syntactic structure significantly determines interpretation at LF. Whether it is also present in PF representations is less obvious. Evidence that it might be comes from ambiguous examples like (13).

(13)   Mary has plans to leave.

(13) can be interpreted in two distinct ways, each of which corresponds to a different syntactic analysis. The NP *plans to leave* can be analyzed along the lines of (14).

(14)   Mary plans to leave.

Under this interpretation the verb *leave* in (13) is intransitive (like the same verb in (14)). In contrast, the verb *leave* in (13) can be interpreted as being transitive, with a covert object linked to the N *plans*. On this latter interpretation the infinitival *to leave* constitutes a relative clause modifying the N *plans*, whereas on the former interpretation the same infinitival indicates what the plans are. (See Chapter 8 for further analysis of relative clauses.)

EXERCISE 6.1

a. Give the full syntactic analysis of the NP *plans to leave* assuming that the complement of *plans* is a CP.
b. Discuss how the following example has the same dual analysis.

(i)   Mary has plans for John to leave.

The two readings of (13) are thus disambiguated via syntactic structure at LF, one contains a covert object of *leave* while the other doesn't, and they are also disambiguated at PF. Under the complement interpretation of *to leave*, *leave* receives heavier phonological stress than *plans*, but under the relative clause interpretation *plans* receives the heavier stress. As this example shows, intonational patterns based on the assignment of phonological stress depends on syntactic structure. If this assignment occurs after Spell-Out, then PF must contain syntactic features. See Chapter 9 for further discussion.

While part 2 of a derivation as schematized in (11) concerns the overt elements in a linguistic expression as manifested in PF, part 3 is exclusively concerned with semantic interpretation based on the semantic features of lexical items within the expression and their syntactic organization. Given Spell-Out, which removes all phonetic features from this part of the derivation, what is processed between Spell-Out and LF is entirely covert.

Part 3 of a derivation concerns the construction of a LF representation that determines the semantic interpretation of the linguistic expression under analysis. In the LF for (1a), where *seems* functions as a one-place predicate that takes a single argument, the CP *that the students are enjoying their new laptops* constitutes the clausal complement of *seems*. The other syntactic object in the sentence is the lexical item *it*. Although this *it* is orthographically (and phonetically) identical to the third person singular neuter pronoun *it*, this word does not function as a pronoun (i.e. standing in for some antecedent referential expression), rather it is non-referential. This element, also referred to as **expletive** *it* to distinguish it from the pronoun *it*, has no inherent semantic features. Expletive *it* is thus a pleonastic element, essentially a placeholder occupying the subject position (Spec-TP) of the clause. Although *it* is the syntactic subject of the verb *seems*, this expletive bears no semantic function because the verb *seem* only assigns one argument in (1a) – i.e. to its complement.

6.2   Displacement and interpretation

Consider the interpretations of the two examples in (1). Because (1a) contains an expletive that contributes no information to semantic interpretation, the expletive element at LF will be virtually invisible. After Spell-Out expletive *it* has only syntactic features, a category feature N and the agreement features [-plural] and [3rd person] which are notated as **N** in (15).

(15)   [$_{TP}$ **N** [$_T$ [−past, ϕ] [$_{VP}$ 'seems' [$_{CP}$ 'that' [$_{TP}$ [$_{NP}$ 'the students'] [$_T$ 'are' [$_{VP}$ 'enjoying' [$_{NP}$ 'their new laptops']]]]]]]]]

The single quotes around lexical items/strings are to indicate that they are without phonetic features. If **N** violates Full Interpretation at the LF interface, it would have to be removed from the representation after Spell-Out on the LF-side of the derivation via an LF-deletion operation.

The LF representation of (1b) is more complicated. The first thing to note is that in terms of truth conditions, (1b) and (1a) are equivalent: (1a) is true if and only if (1b) is true. Thus the truth values of (1a) and (1b) always match. Given this it might be expected that (1a) and (1b) have the same LF representation.

This is going to be true at least in part because in both examples the matrix verb *seem* takes a single clausal argument. This follows given our derivation of (1b) where the infinitival clause (4) is the complement of *seem*. (4) is taken as roughly equivalent semantically to the corresponding finite clause (16).

(16)   [$_{CP}$ that [$_{TP}$ [$_{NP}$ the students] [$_T$ are [$_{VP}$ enjoying [$_{NP}$ their new laptops]]]]]

EXERCISE 6.2

a. What are the (obvious) differences between (4) and (16)?
b. Discuss whether they constitute significant differences in meaning.

If the assignment of semantic functions to arguments by predicates is all that is relevant to determining the LF representations of (1a) and (1b), then the LF of (1b) should be virtually identical to (15) – e.g. (17).

(17)   [$_{TP}$ N [$_T$ [–past, φ] [$_{VP}$ 'seems' [$_{CP}$ ø [$_{TP}$ [$_{NP}$ 'the students'] [$_T$ 'to' [$_{VP}$ 'be' [$_{VP}$ 'enjoying' [$_{NP}$ 'their new laptops']]]]]]]]]

If so, then the displaced infinitival subject *the students* in the matrix Spec-TP must be deleted from the LF representation and therefore Delete, now applied to semantic features, must apply in part 3 of a derivation.

However, there is a difference in interpretation between (1a) and (1b) that goes beyond truth conditions. (1b) is a statement about *the students* in a way that (1a) is not. That is, under the interpretation of (1b) in terms of topic vs. comment, *the students* as subject of the main clause is the topic of the sentence, while the VP *seems to be enjoying their new laptops* functions as a comment. In (1a) *seems that the students are enjoying their new laptops* is not interpreted as comment about anything. The syntactic subject of the main clause, being a semantically empty expletive, cannot be interpreted as a topic. If this is correct, then the LF of (1b) must represent this in some way – most naturally by showing a copy of *the students* in main clause subject position at LF, as in (18).

(18)   [$_{TP}$ [$_{NP}$ 'the students'] [$_T$ [–past, φ] [$_{VP}$ 'seems' [$_{CP}$ ø [$_{TP}$ [$_{NP}$ 'the students'] [$_T$ 'to' [$_{VP}$ 'be' [$_{VP}$ 'enjoying' [$_{NP}$ 'their new laptops']]]]]]]]]

Thus the LF representations of (1a) and (1b) are different.

The number of active English verbs that pattern like *seem* is very small, limited to *seem*, *appear*, and *happen* – possibly also *begin* as in *the cider began to ferment*. However, the syntactic properties of *seem* also extend to a subset of passive verbs (*reported*, *believed*, *expected*, *suspected*, *acknowledged*), as illustrated in (19).

(19)   a.   It was reported that the students are enjoying their new laptops.
        b.   The students were reported to be enjoying their new laptops.

Expletive *it* occurs in the matrix subject position of (19a) as indicated by the agreement morphology of the finite passive auxiliary that heads the main clause

TP (*was*, but **were*). Therefore the Spec-TP position in this construction is one that is not assigned an argument function by the verb in the root clause, *reported*. In (19b) the NP *the students* is interpreted as the subject of *enjoying* in the complement clause and therefore assigned an argument function by the predicate of that clause. The complement clause itself is assigned an argument function by *reported*.

This property of passive predicates that they do not assign an argument function to Spec-TP generalizes to single clause constructions.

(20)   a.   The company has reported huge profits.
         b.   Huge profits have been reported by the company.
         c.   Huge profits have been reported.

In (20a) the NP *huge profits* is assigned the argument function associated with the verbal object position. In (20b–c) this NP occurs in Spec-TP as indicated by the difference in agreement with the finite auxiliary, but it is still interpreted as the object of *reported*. In this way a single clause with a passive predicate also involves displacement – in this case between the complement of V and Spec-TP.

In passive constructions the assignment of the argument function associated with the Spec-TP position in active sentences is assigned to the object of passive preposition *by*, when it occurs. Truncated passive constructions like (20c) demonstrate that this PP argument is optional in much the same way that other PP complements can be optional (cf. *talk about NP to NP* where either PP can be left out).

EXERCISE: 6.3

Given this displacement analysis of single clause passive constructions,

a. provide the syntactic analysis of (20b) by listing the steps in the derivation of (20b) needed to generate the PF and LF representations for this example.
b. Discuss how the derivation of (20a) differs from that of (20b).
c. State the derivation for (20c). How does it relate to that of (20a)?

Displacement also occurs inside of certain NPs. Just as the active sentence in (21a) has a corresponding nominalization (21b), its passive counterpart (22a) also has a corresponding nominalization (22b).

(21)   a.   The invaders destroyed the city.
         b.   the invaders' destruction of the city
(22)   a.   The city was destroyed by the invaders.
         b.   the city's destruction by the invaders

In both examples in (21) the NP *the invaders* is assigned the same argument function by the predicates *destroy/destruction*. The same holds for the NP *the city*. In (22a) *the city* has been displaced from verbal object position where it is assigned its argument function to a Spec-TP position to which no argument function is assigned. An account of the interpretation of *the city* in (22b) requires a similar displacement operation from the object position of the nominalized *destruction*. Thus the LF representation of (22b) would be (23).

(23) $[_{NP} [_{NP}$ 'the city'$]$ $[_N [_N$ 'destruction' $[_{NP}$ 'the city'$]]$ $[_{PP}$ 'by' $[_{NP}$
          'the invaders'$]]]]]$

In (23) there are three NP positions but only two argument functions assigned, agent (i.e. in this case, destroyer) and target (also called "patient"). The NP *the city* that is merged with the nominal *destruction* is structurally a complement and as such is assigned the complement function of target. The NP *the invaders* occurs as the object of the passive preposition *by* and as in clausal passives is assigned the subject function of the predicate (i.e. the nominalization *destruction*), hence agent.[1]

The other copy of *the city* that occurs in the Spec-NP position is not assigned either argument function. That of course fits the interpretation of (21b), but the question is why is this the only interpretation? For example, since a copy of *the city* occurs in Spec-NP position and that position can be assigned the agent function as in (21b), why couldn't (22b) have an interpretation roughly equivalent to (24), where *the city* is assigned both the agent and target argument functions?

(24)   the city's destruction of itself

As this interpretation of (22b) is impossible, the computational system must prohibit this assignment of argument functions. Notice that under this impossible interpretation, the chain (25) would be assigned two argument functions.

(25) $\{[_{NP}$ the city$], [_{NP}$ the city$]\}$[2]

The head of the chain would be assigned the agentive function and the other member would be assigned the target function. Such chains can be ruled out by a general principle of grammar that prohibits multiple assignments of argument functions.

(26)   **Argument Uniqueness:**
          No chain can bear multiple argument functions.

Note that the formulation of (26) does not distinguish types of argument functions from tokens of the same function; thus if a chain is assigned the same argument function twice, the resulting chain still constitutes a violation of Argument Uniqueness.

As formulated in (26), the principle of Argument Uniqueness functions as a condition on representations, a filter on the output of derivations. Given that there are only two levels of linguistic representation – PF and LF –, and further that chains, being superfluous objects at the PF interface, are not present in PF representations under Full Interpretation, it follows that Argument Uniqueness applies solely to LF representations. Depending on how and when in a derivation argument functions are assigned to arguments, this may be the only possibility (as will be discussed below).

EXERCISE 6.4

Argument Uniqueness generalizes to other impossible cases of displacement. For example, consider the deviant sentence (i).

> (i)   *Mary mentioned.

Given displacement there are actually two different syntactic representations that can be assigned to (i). In one, (i) violates the subcategorization property of the verb *mention*; in the other, this property is satisfied, but Argument Uniqueness is violated.

a.   Give the two syntactic representations
b.   What would the interpretation of (i) have to be under the second analysis?

Now consider (ii).

> (ii)   John shaved this morning.

Notice that (ii) is synonymous with (iii).

> (iii)   John shaved himself this morning.

c.   Under what analysis is (ii) a counterexample to Argument Uniqueness? Be sure to spell out what assumptions you are making.
d.   Is the analysis necessarily correct, and if so then how is the deviance of (i) under the displacement analysis accounted for?

EXERCISE 6.5

Argument Uniqueness will also rule out raising between two positions that are assigned independent argument functions.

a. Construct an example (deviant of course) involving raising between two Spec-TP positions that demonstrates this.
b. Show how this extends to raising to Spec-TP from any other position in a complement clause.

The fact that the Spec-NP position can be assigned an argument function directly by a nominalized predicate creates another issue in the analysis of these NP constructions. Consider first that when there is only one argument in Spec-NP of a nominalization construction, the example is ambiguous because there are two possible interpretations.

(27)   the invaders' destruction

The sole NP argument of *destruction* can be interpreted as either agent or target.

EXERCISE: 6.6

The two interpretations correlate with two distinct LF representations.

a. Construct these representations.
b. Discuss how each corresponds to a unique interpretation.

Now consider the possible analyses of (28), which is merely (27) with an added passive *by*-phrase.

(28)   the invaders' destruction by the army

Under the normal interpretation, *the invaders* is assigned the target argument function and *the army* is assigned the agent function. This requires that the NP *the invaders* originates as the complement of *destruction* and then undergoes displacement. Furthermore, it is not directly assigned any argument function in Spec-NP. This derivation produces a representation that contains a nontrivial chain. However, suppose that *the invaders* is merged directly as Spec-NP and furthermore is assigned the agent argument function. The passive preposition *by* also signals that its object is interpreted as the agent. This would yield a LF representation (29) that contains only trivial chains.

(29) $[_{NP}$ the invaders' $[_N$ destruction $[_{PP}$ by $[_{NP}$ the army$]]]]$

That such interpretations are generally impossible means that the representation (29) must be deviant and suggests that there is another general principle of grammar that accounts for this. This principle can be formulated as follows.

(30)   **Unique Assignment of Argument Functions:**
             Each argument function of a predicate can only be assigned once.

So (30) will prohibit (29) when both NPs are assigned the same argument function. But what if only one NP is assigned an argument function? On this analysis the LF representation (29) would not violate Unique Assignment. Nonetheless, this LF representation cannot serve as a viable analysis for (28). The representation can be prohibited by another plausible general principle (31).

(31)   **Argument Relatedness:**
             Each argument must be assigned an argument function by a predicate.

Thus (29) must violate either Unique Assignment or Argument Relatedness, depending on how argument functions have been assigned.

EXERCISE 6.7

Nominalization constructions also allow a form that has no clausal counterpart.

(i) a.   the destruction of the city by the invaders
    b.   *was destroyed the city by the invaders

Nor is there a sentential passive counterpart to (i.a) with an expletive subject.

(ii) *It was destroyed the city by the invaders.

(i.a) shows that the passive *by*-phrase must undergo Merge just like other constituents. If so, then Merge could (erroneously) introduce a passive *by*-phrase in an active sentence.

(iii) *The police arrested the kidnapper by the FBI.

Since passive *by*-phrases can never occur in active sentences, (iii) requires an explanation. The analysis just outlined for nominalizations involving principles governing the assignment of argument functions generalizes to sentential constructions.

a. Show how it applies to (iii).

EXERCISE 6.8

The analysis developed for nominalization constructions also generalizes to double object constructions in the following way. As already noted, the indirect object of a double object verb may also show up as the object of a prepositional complement, as in the pair (i).

(i) a. Fred gave Sheila a book.
     b. Fred gave a book to Sheila.

However, what cannot occur is a double object verb that has both an indirect object and the corresponding PP complement. Hence (ii) is deviant.

(ii) *Fred gave Sheila a book to Mary.

a. Discuss how the two principles in (30) and (31) account for the deviance of (ii).

Combining the principles of Argument Uniqueness and Argument Relatedness yields a general requirement that any constituent with semantic content occurring in an "argument position" must be assigned one and only one argument function of a predicate. In general, argument position can be characterized in terms of grammatical functions – in particular, subject, object, indirect object, object of a preposition where the PP is a complement, and clausal complement. But the notion of grammatical function position is of limited use in identifying arguments of a predicate because the same argument can occur in a variety of grammatical function positions. Consider the examples in (32).

(32)   a. Rosie gave a book to Herman.
        b. Rosie gave Herman a book.
        c. Herman was given a book by Rosie.

Although *Herman* has the same argument function in all three examples, this NP occupies a different grammatical function position in each. Given that the three sentences are roughly synonymous, a somewhat different vocabulary is needed to account for this.

This vocabulary concerns the **argument structure** of the three sentences in (32), which is identical because the predicate involved in each is the verb *give*, a verb denoting motion. With respect to the concept of motion, each argument fills a specific role. *The book* is the object that moves between Rosie and Herman. Call this role the **theme**. The theme moves from a **source**, the position the theme starts from, to a **goal**, the position to which the theme is moved. In each example in (32), *a book* is the theme, *Rosie* is the source, and *Herman* is the goal. The same argument structure analysis holds for (33), where *a book* occurs in the syntactic subject position.

(33)   A book was given to Herman by Rosie.

(32) and (33) illustrate how arguments may have a variety of grammatical relations to their predicate, while their **thematic relations** (also called θ-**roles**) remain the same.

This kind of argument structure analysis allows us to account for the near synonymy of sentences that have different verbs. Consider the pair of sentences in (34).

(34)   a.   Rosie sent a book to Herman.
            b.   Herman received a book from Rosie.

Both *send* and *receive* are verbs of motion, thus their argument structure involves the θ-roles theme, source, and goal. The three arguments *Rosie*, *Herman*, and *a book* are assigned the same θ-roles as they are in (32–33).

Note that (34b) entails (34a), but not conversely. Rosie could have sent Herman a book but he didn't receive it because it was lost in the mail or stolen, etc. There is also a difference in the interpretation of *Rosie* in the two sentences. In (34a) Rosie is the instigator of the action, hence an agent as well as the source, so the θ-role assigned to *Rosie* is actually agentive source, a single θ-role because it is the argument function that *send* assigns its subject. In (34b) Rosie is not the instigator of the action designated by the verb *receive* (and neither is Herman), so *Rosie* has no agentive interpretation.

EXERCISE 6.9

Consider the following paradigm for the verb *sell*.

    (i) a.   Rosie sold a rare book to Herman.
        b.   Rosie sold Herman a rare book.
        c.   Herman was sold a rare book by Rosie.
        d.   A rare book was sold to Herman by Rosie.

a. Taking *sell* to belong to the class of motion verbs, what is the argument structure analysis of these examples in terms of θ-roles?

b. Construct the corresponding paradigm for the verb *buy*.
c. Now discuss the relations between the two paradigms in terms of

    i.   argument structure (i.e. θ-roles)
    ii. truth conditions
    iii. topic/comment relations

Given this new vocabulary, we can now distinguish between argument positions to which θ-roles are assigned as **θ-positions**, as opposed to argument positions to which no θ-role is assigned, **nonθ-positions**. All complements of predicates (e.g. verbs and predicate adjectives) constitute θ-positions and only specifier positions (i.e. in TP and NP) can be nonθ-positions. NPs with semantic content (as opposed to expletives, which have none) always merge first to a θ-position. Displacement always involves a nonθ-position. Furthermore, the principles governing argument structure can now be recast in terms of θ-roles.

(35)   a.   Argument Uniqueness: no argument chain can bear multiple θ-roles.
            b.   Unique Assignment: each θ-role can be assigned only once.
            c.   Argument Relatedness: each argument chain must bear a θ-role.

If all complements (internal arguments) are θ-positions and first Merge always involves a θ-position, it would follow from Argument Uniqueness that there is no movement to complement positions.

The theory of derivations concerning θ-role assignment can be simplified if the lexical entry of each predicate contains a finite set of θ-roles that can be assigned to arguments. There is no reason to assume that this set involves multiple copies of any θ-role, therefore it would make no sense to assume that any θ-role could be assigned more than once. If so, then every potential violation of Unique Assignment (35b) must in fact be construed as a violation of Argument Relatedness (35c). Given two distinct arguments that could both be assigned the same θ-role (e.g. the indirect object and object of the preposition *to* with the verb *give*), only one argument will actually be assigned that θ-role and the other will have none. In this way the empirical effects of a Unique Assignment principle are derived from Argument Relatedness. Argument Relatedness is, like Argument Uniqueness, a condition on representations, presumably applying at LF.

Argument Uniqueness and Argument Relatedness can be unified in terms of θ-roles as a single condition on chains.

(36)   Each argument chain must bear one and only one θ-role.

(36) constitutes a simplified version of the **θ-Criterion** which also requires that each θ-role be assigned to one and only one argument (see Chomsky 1981b).

There is one further class of raising constructions involving predicate adjectives rather than verbs, for which a θ-theoretic analysis of argument structure as expressed in (36) has interesting consequences. The adjective *likely* shares the syntactic properties of the *seem*-class of verbs.

(37)   a.   It is likely that Fred will succeed
            b.   Fred is likely to succeed.

The presence of expletive *it* in the matrix Spec-TP of (37a) shows that *likely* does not assign a θ-role to its syntactic subject. Thus in (37b) the only θ-role assigned to *Fred* is the one assigned by *succeed* to its subject in the local Spec-TP. This of course requires that the NP *Fred* be merged as Spec-TP of the infinitival complement clause first and then merged to create the matrix Spec-TP position. The derivation of (37b) yields (38).

(38)   [$_{TP}$ Fred [$_T$ is [$_{AP}$ likely [$_{CP}$ ø [$_{TP}$ Fred [$_T$ to succeed]]]]]]

In (38), {*Fred, Fred*} forms a nontrivial chain that bears a single θ-role, where the θ-role of the subject of *succeed* is assigned to the second member of the chain. The first member of the chain is assigned no θ-role. Since (38) is not deviant, it presumably does not violate the θ-Criterion (36), specifically Argument Relatedness. Thus the θ-Criterion functions as a condition on chains (including of course trivial chains).

   This simplified θ-Criterion (36) accounts for the paradigm for raising adjectives given in (37), to which we add an additional example (39c).

(39)   a.   It is likely that Fred will succeed.
            b.   Fred is likely to succeed.
            c.   *Mary is likely that Fred will succeed.

While (39a–b) conform to the two θ-theoretic principles combined in (36), (39c) violates the Argument Relatedness part of the θ-Criterion.

EXERCISE 6.10

The paradigm in (39) extends to the two other cases of raising constructions involving active and passive verbs (e.g. *seem* and *reported* respectively).

a. Construct the corresponding paradigms for these two other cases.
b. Discuss how the a–b examples conform to our θ-theoretic principles and how the c-examples constitute a violation.

EXERCISE 6.11

Compare (39) to the following paradigm:

(i) a.   It is certain that Fred will succeed.
    b.   Fred is certain to succeed.
    c.   Mary is certain that Fred will succeed.

a. How is this paradigm different from (39)?
b. How is it the same?
c. Suppose that (i) conforms to our θ-theoretic principles. What problems arise if it is assumed that there is a single lexical adjective *certain*?

d. Suppose that there are two distinct lexical adjectives *certain₁* vs. *certain₂*. What would be the differences between these two lexical items in terms of argument structure and complement structure?

e. How would the analysis you provided in (d) account for (i)?

Under our analysis of the argument structure for a single argument predicate adjective like *likely*, its sole θ-role is assigned to a clausal complement and the subject position is a nonθ-position. (39a–b) show that this position can contain either a semantically null expletive *it* or an argument that has been displaced from a θ-position elsewhere in the sentence. This extends to constructions in which the entire complement occurs in Spec-TP of the minimal clause containing the adjective. (40) provides another part of the paradigm for these predicate adjectives.

(40)   a.   That Fred will succeed is likely.
         b.   *That Fred will succeed it is likely.
         c.   *is likely that Fred will succeed.

Given that the θ-role of the clausal argument of *likely* is assigned to the complement position (cf. (39a–b)), the θ-role of the clausal argument in (40a) should be assigned to the same syntactic position. Therefore, (40a) must constitute a displacement construction, where the finite clausal argument is first merged as the complement of *likely* and then merged as the Spec-TP of the matrix clause. The LF representation of (40a), given in (41a–b), thus contains a nontrivial chain (41c).

(41)   a.   [TP [CP that Fred will succeed] [T is [AP likely [CP that Fred will succeed]]]]

         b.

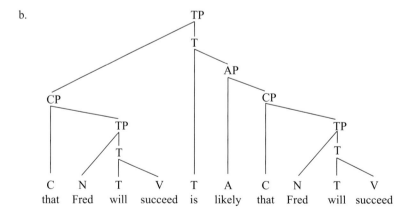

         c.   {[CP that Fred will succeed], [CP that Fred will succeed]}

This explains why expletive *it* cannot co-occur with the clausal argument in clause initial position: they both occupy the same syntactic position and therefore only one syntactic object can occur in that position.

EXERCISE 6.12

The displacement analysis of (40a), while plausible, depends crucially on our underlying assumptions about syntactic analysis. Consider two alternative derivations for (40a), given as (I) and (II).

I.   the subordinate CP is merged directly as Spec-TP of the root clause.
II. the subordinate CP merges with expletive *it* and the NP that is created then merges as Spec-TP of the root clause. (Cf. Rosenbaum (1967).)

a. How would our analytic assumptions have to be revised if (I) were the correct derivation?
b. Given (II), what further operations would be needed to derive both (37a) and (40a)?
c. Under (II), what would the PF and LF representations of (37a) and (40a) be?

EXERCISE 6.13

Analyzing clause initial subordinate CP as occurring in Spec-TP raises some issues for Spec-head agreement. Consider the following paradigm.

(i) a.   That Mary will succeed is likely.
    b.   *That Mary will succeed are likely.
    c.   That Mary will succeed and that Fred will fail is likely.
    d.   That Mary will succeed and that Fred will fail are (equally) likely.
    e.   That Mary will succeed or that Fred will fail is likely.
    f.   *That Mary will succeed or that Fred will fail are likely.

a. What might be the explanation for the very clear difference between (i.a) and (i.b)?
b. Do you find a difference in acceptability between (i.c) and (i.d)? If so, what is it? If not, is there a difference in meaning between the two examples. (If you modify *likely* with *equally* in (i.c), does the acceptability (or meaning) change?)
c. These examples seem to show that a default agreement analysis in which a finite verb always occurs in third person singular when it occurs with a clausal Spec-TP cannot be maintained. Discuss.

(40c) in conjunction with (40a–b) demonstrates that either the semantically null expletive or the displaced complement clause must occur in Spec-TP of the minimal clause containing the predicate adjective. In effect, a clause must have some element that occupies the subject position – i.e. Spec-TP. To account for the deviance of (40c), the following has been proposed as a general principle of grammar.

(42)   **Extended Projection Principle (EPP)**: every clause (finite or infinitival) must have a subject (i.e. Spec-TP) in its syntactic representation.[3]

(40c) violates the EPP under the assumption that its syntactic representation does not contain a covert Spec-TP in the matrix clause.

EXERCISE 6.14

As formulated the EPP constitutes a condition on representations. Covert elements like silent copies must satisfy the EPP, otherwise the complement clause in (1b) which contains a covert Spec-TP would violate the principle. Still there is the question of which level or levels must satisfy the EPP: LF or PF, or both.

a. Identify what evidence, empirical or theoretical (i.e. given the theory so far constructed and the assumptions on which it is based) if any, might bear on the choice between the three alternatives.

EXERCISE 6.15

There are three additional syntactic representations that could be assigned to (40c).

(i) a. $[_{TP}$ PRO $[_{T}$ is $[_{AP}$ likely $[_{CP}$ that Fred will succeed]]]]

b. $[_{TP}$ it $[_{T}$ is $[_{AP}$ likely $[_{CP}$ that Fred will succeed]]]]

c. $[_{TP}$ $[_{CP}$ ~~that Fred will succeed~~] $[_{T}$ is $[_{AP}$ likely $[_{CP}$ that Fred will succeed]]]]

a. None of these violates the EPP. Explain.
b. (i.a) is prohibited by one of our θ-theoretic principles. Explain.
c. The problems with (i.b) and (i.c) do not concern LF representations. Explain.
d. Somehow the deletions indicated by the strikethroughs in (i.b–c) must be prohibited. Discuss what is involved and try to speculate about how this might be achieved.
e. How does your analysis of the three representations in (i) affect your answer to the previous exercise?

The displacement of finite clausal complements of predicate adjectives involving Spec-TP is common to virtually all predicate adjectives that take finite clause complements. Consider in addition the adjectives *probable* and *possible*, both of which allow the displacement of a finite complement clause, as illustrated in (43) and (44).

(43)   a.   It is probable that Fred will succeed.
         b.   That Fred will succeed is probable.
(44)   a.   It is possible that Fred will succeed.
         b.   That Fred will succeed is possible.

The a-examples correspond to (37a) and the b-examples, to (40a). Note further that in terms of meaning there is a set of one-way entailments between the three adjectives. The adjective *probable* entails the interpretation *possible*, but not conversely. If an event is probable then it must be possible, but a possible event may not be probable. Moreover, an event that is likely must also be probable, but a probable event, while certainly possible, is not necessarily likely.[4]

Although the syntactic properties of these adjectives, which are close in meaning, are virtually identical with respect to finite CP arguments, there is considerable variation with infinitival arguments. With respect to the overt infinitival complementizer *for*, only *possible* takes an infinitival complement that has it.

(45)   a.   *It is likely for John to arrive on time.
       b.   *It is probable for John to arrive on time.
       c.   It is possible for John to arrive on time.

As expected, only *possible* allows the infinitival argument to also occur in the Spec-TP of the minimal clause that contains the predicate adjective.

(46)   a.   *For John to arrive on time is likely.
       b.   *For John to arrive on time is probable.
       c.   For John to arrive on time is possible.

Furthermore, *possible* can occur with a bare infinitival clause (i.e. lacking both an overt C and an overt subject) complement, whereas *likely* and *probable* cannot. In (47a) the subject of the root clause must be construed as an expletive, and presumably that same construal holds for the deviant examples in (47b–c).

(47)   a.   It is possible to arrive on time.
       b.   *It is likely to arrive on time.
       c.   *It is probable to arrive on time.

Again as expected, the bare infinitival complement of the adjective may occur in the Spec-TP of the minimal clause containing the adjective, as illustrated in (48).

(48)   a.   To arrive on time is possible.
       b.   *To arrive on time is likely.
       c.   *To arrive on time is probable.

Given the pair (45c) and (46c) as well as the pair (47a) and (48a), displacement of the infinitival complement in Spec-TP appears to be optional for adjectives like *possible*.

EXERCISE 6.16

Note that the apparent optionality for the displacement of the finite clausal complement of the predicate adjectives *possible* and *probable* to the Spec-TP position of the main clause (e.g. (43b) and (44b)) is in fact illusory. Consider the derivation of the following constructions.

   i. a.   *Is probable that Fred will succeed.
      b.   *Is possible that Fred will succeed.

a. Explain how the derivations of (i.a–b) satisfy the θ-Criterion (35).
b. What principle of grammar do these two deviant constructions violate?

c. Explain how the analysis in (b) extends to the following two deviant constructions.

   ii. a.   *Is possible for John to arrive on time.
       b.   *Is possible to arrive on time.

d. Would this principle still apply if the derivations of (i-ii) involved a displacement from Spec-TP position to a clause final position?
e. Would the derivations in (d) pose a problem for the θ-Criterion?

In contrast, displacement of the subject of the infinitival complement of *likely* is obligatory.

(49)   a.   Mary is likely to arrive on time.
         b.   *It is likely Mary to arrive on time.

And moreover, even though the subject position with *possible* is a nonθ-position, as illustrated by both interpretation (i.e. an expletive subject) and the possible displacement of both forms of clausal complement (cf. (44b), (46c), and (48a)), it does not allow subject displacement as in (50a) and (51a).

(50)   a.   *Mary is possible for to arrive on time.
         b.   [$_{TP}$ Mary [$_T$ is [$_{AP}$ possible [$_{CP}$ for [$_{TP}$ (Mary) to arrive on time]]]]]

(51)   a.   *Mary is possible to arrive on time.
         b.   [$_{TP}$ Mary [$_T$ is [$_{AP}$ possible [$_{CP}$ ø [$_{TP}$ (Mary) to arrive on time]]]]]

These are the bare facts concerning the syntactic properties of these adjectives.

    We are concerned with two separate but related questions: (1) what is the syntactic analysis of this data? and (2) how much of this analysis follows from general principles of grammar vs. how much must be stipulated as properties that are idiosyncratic to specific lexical items? Note the assumption that the locus of idiosyncratic properties is the lexicon.

    (45c) shows that *possible* can take an infinitival complement with a *for* complementizer. Hence the analysis of (45c) is (52).

(52)   [$_{TP}$ it [$_T$ is [$_{AP}$ possible [$_{CP}$ for [$_{TP}$ John [$_T$ to [$_{VP}$ arrive on time]]]]]]]

The adjective *possible* selects a *for* complementizer, whereas *probable* and *likely* do not; therefore (45a–b) constitute selectional violations. This analysis generalizes to (46) since displacement of the clausal complement does not affect the selectional relations between these predicate adjectives and the heads of their CP complements (in this case the C *for*).

    To account for the paradigm in (47), start with the derivation of the one legitimate sentence (47a). Given the EPP, Spec-TP of the infinitival complement of *possible* must contain a covert element, presumably PRO, a phonetically null N that bears the subject θ-role of *arrive*. As noted previously, the absence of an overt infinitival C (i.e. *for*) in the complement clause can be analyzed in two ways. Either the C *for* is deleted at PF as in (53a), or (47a) involves the phonetically null C ø as in (53b).

(53)   a.   [$_{TP}$ it [$_T$ is [$_{AP}$ possible [$_{CP}$ ~~for~~ [$_{TP}$ PRO [$_T$ to [$_{VP}$ arrive on time]]]]]]]
          b.   [$_{TP}$ it [$_T$ is [$_{AP}$ possible [$_{CP}$ ø [$_{TP}$ PRO [$_T$ to [$_{VP}$ arrive on time]]]]]]]

Given Spell-Out the two alternatives will be identical at LF, unless the semantics of *for* and *ø* differ – which seems doubtful. The derivation with (53a) involves one more step than the derivation of (53b) – namely, the deletion of *for*. Therefore (53b) might be preferable on considerations of derivational economy – i.e. preferring derivations with fewest steps.

Regarding the deviant examples in (47), (47c) might constitute a violation of selection. The adjective *probable* can never occur with an infinitival complement in any form. This explanation applies to (48c) as well. However selection does not account for (47b) because, as already noted, *likely* does take an infinitival complement, as in (49a). In fact, if *it* in (47b) is construed as the third person neuter singular pronoun instead of the semantically null expletive, then (47b) is a legitimate sentence with a representation (54) – e.g., something we might say about a package we are expecting to be delivered to us.

(54)   [$_{TP}$ it [$_T$ is [$_{AP}$ likely [$_{CP}$ ø [$_{TP}$ (it) [$_T$ to [$_{VP}$ arrive on time]]]]]]]

Both (49a) and (54) involve displacement. (47b) is nonetheless deviant if *it* is construed an expletive and the complement subject is construed as PRO, as in (55).

(55)   *[$_{TP}$ it [$_T$ is [$_{AP}$ likely [$_{CP}$ ø [$_{TP}$ PRO [$_T$ to [$_{VP}$ arrive on time]]]]]]]

EXERCISE: 6.17

There are two other possible analyses of (47b) to consider, both yielding deviant constructions.

(i)   a.   [$_{TP}$ it [$_T$ is [$_{AP}$ likely [$_{CP}$ ø [$_{TP}$ PRO [$_T$ to [$_{VP}$ arrive on time]]]]]]]
      b.   [$_{TP}$ it [$_T$ is [$_{AP}$ likely [$_{CP}$ ø [$_{TP}$ (it) [$_T$ to [$_{VP}$ arrive on time]]]]]]]

(i.a) is similar to (55) except that *it* is construed as the referential pronoun, not the expletive. (i.b) is similar to (55) except that *it* is construed as the expletive.

a. For each of the three analyses (47a) and (i.a–b), discuss whether it would be prohibited by the theory of grammar developed so far. If so, how? If not, why not and how might our theory be elaborated to exclude these cases?

(55) and (54) together demonstrate that displacement involving the subject of the infinitival complement and the main clause Spec-TP position is obligatory, in contrast to the optional displacement involving the CP complements (finite or infinitival) of *possible* and the main clause Spec-TP position.

The principles of grammar presented thus far do not account for the deviance of (55). (54) and (55) together show that the two covert NP types trace and PRO are in complementary distribution. This generalizes to the analysis of *possible* where the reverse situation holds: PRO yields a legitimate sentence while trace does not. ((56b/c) are identical to (53b).)

(56)   a.   *[$_{TP}$ it [$_T$ is [$_{AP}$ possible [$_{CP}$ ø [$_{TP}$ (it) [$_T$ to [$_{VP}$ arrive on time]]]]]]]

     b.   [$_{TP}$ it [$_T$ is [$_{AP}$ possible [$_{CP}$ ø [$_{TP}$ PRO [$_T$ to [$_{VP}$ arrive on time]]]]]]]

     c.

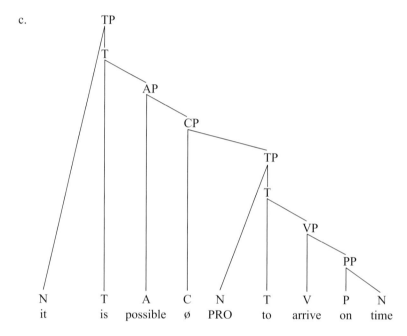

This complementarity between PRO and trace is so far just a descriptive statement. If this follows from general principles of grammar, then there is an explanation at the level of theory. If not, then the complementarity will be idiosyncratic, holding for some languages but not others – in which case we are stuck with a description of phenomena. There is also the related issue of whether this complementarity is based on structural or lexical properties – or possibly some combination of the two.

6.3   Displacement and Case

Consider another apparent complementarity with the Spec-TP position of an infinitival complement involving phonetically null NP vs. NP with phonetic content. There is an infinitival construction where NP in Spec-TP can have phonetic content – i.e., where C is *for*. In all other infinitival constructions discussed so far (e.g. (47a), (48a), and (49a), but see below for another class of exceptions) Spec-TP must be phonetically null at PF, either PRO or a trace (i.e. an unpronounced copy). Moreover, when infinitival CP is headed by C *for*, NP in Spec-TP cannot be phonetically null; thus neither a trace (as in (50b) and (56a)) nor a PRO (as in (57b) – at least in what is considered standard English) can occur in Spec-TP in this configuration.

(57) a. *It is possible for to arrive on time.
      b. *[_TP it [_T is [_AP possible [_CP for [_TP PRO [_T to [_VP arrive on time]]]]]]]

This complementarity between phonetically null and phonetically realized NP in the Spec-TP of infinitival clauses extends to raising constructions, whose matrix predicates (V (e.g. *seem*) or A (e.g. *likely*)) typically do not select C *for*. In these constructions the infinitival complement subject with phonetic content must have a copy that is pronounced in some other position at PF. Thus the obligatory nature of displacement in raising constructions is linked to whatever accounts for this complementarity.

The two positions in which the subject argument of an infinitival clause complement can occur at PF are both Spec-TP positions; they have distinct properties. This can be seen by using personal pronouns as subjects, as illustrated in (58).

(58) a. It is possible for him to arrive on time.
      b. He is likely to arrive on time.

Both *he* and *him* are third person masculine singular pronouns, therefore they share the same syntactic/semantic features but differ in their PF representations. The difference is linked to the different syntactic contexts in which they occur. The pronoun *he* can only occur in Spec-TP of a finite clause (e.g. (58b)), in contrast to *him*, which occurs as the object of a verb (e.g. (59a)) or a preposition (e.g. (59b)) – or in Spec-TP of an infinitival complement of C *for* (e.g. (58a)).

(59) a. The committee recommended him for our short list.
      b. Mary threw the ball to him.

Thus the morphological shape of the word designating the third person masculine singular pronoun is determined by the syntactic context in which it occurs. These morphological differences are called **Case** distinctions. The form *he* is the **nominative** form of this pronoun, while *him* is the **objective** form.

If the pronouns in (58) are switched, the result is deviant.

(60) a. *It is possible for he to arrive on time.
      b. *Him is likely to arrive on time.

If *he* and *him* exist in the lexicon as distinct forms, then they are inherently Case-marked and Merge could produce the deviant constructions in (60). The contrast between (58) and (60) shows that the distribution of Case forms is determined by syntactic context. The nominative form occurs only in the Spec position of a TP headed by finite T. As illustrated in (58) and (59), the objective form occurs as a complement of V or P, but also in Spec-TP of an infinitival CP headed by C *for*. This latter context is a special situation to which we will return. The mismatches in (60) between the inherent morphological Case of the pronouns and their syntactic contexts produces the deviance in these examples. The context licenses a particular kind of morphological Case.

Furthermore, there are constructions in which a personal pronoun cannot occur.

(61)   *It is likely her/she to arrive on time.

The context in which the pronoun occurs in this construction, Spec-TP of an infinitival clause that is a complement of a predicate adjective, does not license any Case at all. The deviance of (61) can be explained in terms of Case by imposing the following general constraint.

(62)   **Case Filter**: *NP, where a NP containing phonetic features is not licensed for Case.

Even though the pronoun in (61) is morphologically marked for Case, it nonetheless violates the Case Filter. The Case Filter analysis generalizes to NPs whose head is not a personal pronoun and therefore not morphologically marked for Case. The deviant example that results from changing the pronoun in (61) to a nonpronominal N (a name, as in (63)) also violates the Case Filter.

(63)   a. *It is likely Elizabeth to arrive on time.

Unlike (61), there is no issue of morphological Case for (63). Instead, the issue for this construction concerns the syntactic context that licenses the occurrence of Case, what can be thought of as **abstract Case**.

Given Spell-Out, phonetic features will not occur in LF and therefore the Case Filter as formulated in (62) would have to apply to PF representations. The filter applies straightforwardly to NPs that constitute trivial chains. This extends to legitimate constructions in English involving NP displacement, given that such nontrivial chains will be reduced to trivial chains via Delete, which will eliminate the phonetic features of covert copies in the chain.

EXERCISE 6.18

To see how this works, consider the derivation of the following examples.

(i)   a.   It seems to us that Mary is having a problem with Bill.
      b.   Mary seems to us to be having a problem with Bill.

(ii) *It seems to us Mary to be having a problem with Bill.

a.   Discuss how the Case Filter analysis applies to the derivation of the non-deviant constructions in (i).
b.   Discuss how the Case Filter accounts for the deviance of the construction in (ii).

The Case Filter (62) also prohibits infinitival complement constructions where the complement clause subject must be PRO (as in (64a) with the analysis (56b)), but is instead a phonetically realized NP (as in (64b) with the analysis (64c)).

(64)   a.   It is possible to arrive on time.
          b.   *It is possible Sam to arrive on time.
          c.   [$_{TP}$ it [$_T$ is [$_{AP}$ possible [$_{CP}$ ø [$_{TP}$ Sam [$_T$ to [$_{VP}$ arrive on time]]]]]]]

The context of the N *Sam* does not license any Case and therefore (64b) violates the Case Filter. In this way the filter contributes to an account of the complementarity of phonetically null PRO and NP with phonetic features.

One half of the Case Filter account involves syntactic contexts where a Case feature cannot be licensed. The other half concerns the specification of the contexts in which Case features are licensed. We turn now to an analysis of the syntactic contexts in which the three distinct morphological Cases of English ([NOM], [OBJ], and [GENITIVE] (henceforth [GEN])) are licensed.

In English, [NOM] is licensed on a NP that occurs as the Spec-TP of a finite T. If T is infinitival *to*, [NOM] will not be licensed and cannot be checked in that configuration. Thus [NOM] is licensed by the specific features of a syntactic head, in this case T. However, finite T also contains agreement features (ϕ-features). Because both tense and ϕ features occur together in English finite T, it could be that one or the other (or even the combination of both) that licenses [NOM].

Data from English will not decide the issue for [NOM], but data from other languages can. Portuguese, for example, has two distinct infinitival clause constructions, one in which the infinitival verb form is uninflected for agreement (as in all other Romance languages) and another, unique to Portuguese, in which the infinitival form of the verb is inflected for agreement just like finite verbal forms. The paradigm for these constructions is revealing. (Portuguese data are from Quicoli 1996.)

(65)   a.   É necessario nós terminarmos a tarefa.
              is necessary we-NOM to-finish.1st.PL the-task
              "it is necessary for us to finish the task"
          b.   *É necessario nós terminar a tarefa.
          c.   É necessario terminar a tarefa.
              "it is necessary to finish the task"

The inflected infinitive verb *terminarmos* in (65a) (i.e. *terminar + mos*) occurs with an overt nominative subject *nós*, while the corresponding uninflected verb *terminar* in (65b) cannot. (65b) violates the Case Filter, whereas (65c) where the infinitival subject is phonetically null PRO does not. Thus in Portuguese it is the presence of ϕ-features rather than tense that licenses the occurrence of [NOM]. This paradigm also demonstrates the complementarity between phonetically null NP and NP with phonetic features under investigation.

Another piece of evidence that ties [NOM] to the ϕ-features of T comes from Russian. In a regular active sentence the NP in Spec-TP position is inflected for [NOM] Case; the verb is inflected with ϕ-features that agree with those of the NP in Spec-TP; and the direct object of the verb is inflected for accusative Case (ACC), as illustrated in (66).

(66)   Pulja ranila inostranca.
         Bullet-NOM.FEM.SG wounded-FEM.SG foreigner-ACC
         "A bullet wounded a foreigner."

In the passive counterpart to (66) the Russian lexical item for "foreigner" shows up in Spec-TP in the nominative, and the finite passive auxiliary agrees with the φ-features of this nominative, as demonstrated in (67).

(67)   Inostranec byl ranen pulej.
         Foreigner-NOM.MASC.SG was-MASC.SG wounded-MASC.SG bullet-INST.FEM.SG
         "A foreigner was wounded by a bullet".

There is another possibility in which the lexical item for "foreigner" shows up in Spec-TP inflected as ACC, as illustrated in (68).

(68)   Inostranca ranilo pulej.
         Foreigner-ACC.MASC.SG wounded[−AGR] bullet-INST.FEM.SG
         "A foreigner was wounded by a bullet".

The lack of φ-features on the verb that agree with those on the N *inostranca* in Spec-TP allows this noun to occur in the accusative. If *inostranca* in (68) is changed to the nominative form *inostranec*, the result is deviant.

(69)   *Inostranec ranilo pulej.
         Foreigner-NOM.MASC.SG wounded[−AGR] bullet-INST.FEM.SG
         "A foreigner was wounded by a bullet".

In this way, the paradigm (66)–(69) shows how [NOM] is dependent on φ-features of T as opposed to the context of Spec-TP for a finite TP.[5]

    (68) creates a potentially serious problem for the formulation of the Case Filter in (62). Given that [ACC] is licensed in a complement position in VP, the NP chain created in (68) has the opposite properties of all the other NP chains considered so far. In this chain, the silent copy is in a position that is licensed for Case and the pronounced copy is not. Therefore (68) incorrectly violates the Case Filter as formulated in (62).

    One solution to the problem is to reformulate the Case Filter as a well formed-ness condition on NP chains, as in (70).

(70)   **(revised) Case Filter:**

         *NP chain, where it contains phonetic features and no member is licensed for Case.

(70) applies to both trivial and nontrivial chains. Given Spell-Out, it cannot apply at LF because there are no phonetic features at that level of representation. If Full Interpretation rules out nontrivial chains at PF, then (70) cannot apply at PF either. One alternative is to apply the Case Filter at Spell-Out, where non-trivial NP chains and the phonetic features of copies that become silent at PF still exist.

    The **genitive** form of the third person masculine singular pronoun *his* occurs as a constituent of a NP where it is distinct from the head of that NP.

(71)   his book

Like other third person pronouns, *his* can stand in for a nonpronominal N as in
(72a) or a NP as in (72b).

(72)   a.   Albert's book
           b.   her professor's book

If (71) is interpreted as equivalent to (72b), then *his* is anaphoric on the NP
her professor. The genitive pronoun cannot occur with a determiner, as illustrated in (73).

(73)   a.   *the his book
           b.   *his the book
           c.   *the her professor's book
           d.   *her professor's the book

This complementarity of a determiner and a genitive pronoun in English suggests
that the pronoun may function syntactically as a specifier of NP.

    If the genitive NP functions as a specifier, then it enters into a Spec-head rela-
tion with the head N. This corresponds to the Spec-head relation involved in the
licensing of the [NOM] Case feature via the ϕ-features of T, though there is no
overt agreement between a head N and its genitive specifier. This contrasts with
the apparent head-complement relation involved with [OBJ] as discussed below.
However, [GEN] differs from the other two Case features in English. In (72) the
non-pronominal nouns *Albert* and *professor* are inflected with the affix *'s*. As the
deviance of (74) shows, this is obligatory.

(74)   a.   *Albert book
           b.   *her professor book

The *'s* affix appears to be an overt realization of [GEN]. One piece of evidence
comes from the fact that a genitive personal pronoun, which carries the [GEN] feature inherently, cannot also be inflected with this affix; thus the deviance of (75).

(75)   *his's book

But unlike the Case features of the personal pronouns, the genitive affix is actually attached to the phrasal NP, not its head. English orthography is misleading
here, as can be seen from a consideration of more complicated NPs.

(76)   a.   the king of England's hat
           b.   a student who is diligent's reward
           c.   a friend of his's publishing company

Assuming that genitive Case in these constructions indicates a relation of
"possession," we do not, for example, interpret the hat in (76a) as belonging
to England, but rather to the king, the head of the NP *the king of England*.
Therefore the syntactic analysis of (76a) would be (77).

(77)   [NP [NP the [N king [PP of England]]]'s hat]

EXERCISE 6.19

a. How does this analysis apply to (76b and c)?
b. Why doesn't (76c) contradict what has been said about (75)?

This genitive affix functions as an inflection of the NP it attaches to, rather than as sister to a projection of N (which would have to be an immediate constituent of the maximal projection of N).

EXERCISE 6.20

Like the third person masculine singular pronoun, the first person singular pronoun also has a nominative, objective, and genitive form – i.e. *I*, *me*, and *my*, respectively. However it also has a fourth form *mine* as in (i).

(i)   a friend of mine

(i) is essentially equivalent to (ii).

(ii)   my friend

Obviously *mine* constitutes a fourth morphological Case form (which might be called "the second genitive" to distinguish it from the prenominal genitive forms like *my* etc.).

a. What are the forms of the second genitive for the other English personal pronouns?
b. How is the third person masculine singular pronoun different from the other forms? And what issue does this raise for the analysis of these forms?
c. Note that this second genitive form must always occur with the P *of*.

(iii)   *a friend mine

What issue(s) does this form raise for our analysis of Case?
d. What is the analysis of (iv) and does this example raise any problems for our analysis of Case?

(iv)   a friend of mine's production company

The Case [OBJ] is licensed when the N that contains it is the head of a complement of V (as in (59a)) or P (as in (59b)). However, when we turn to the infinitival C *for*, which also licenses [OBJ] on the NP specifier of its TP complement, the head-complement relation no longer applies. In this construction OBJ is licensed across a TP clause boundary, as illustrated in (78).

(78)   a.   It is possible for him to arrive on time.
            b.   [$_{TP}$ it [$_T$ is [$_{AP}$ possible [$_{CP}$ for [$_{TP}$ him [$_T$ to [$_{VP}$ arrive on time]]]]]]]

In this way, the licensing of the [OBJ] is exceptional, often referred to as **exceptional Case marking** (henceforth **ECM**, terminology derived from earlier analyses involving specific morphosyntactic rules assigned a specific Case to a NP based on its syntactic context). This is one of two configurations in which ECM occurs. The second involves a matrix V that licenses [OBJ] on the NP specifier of a TP in its clausal complement, as in (79).

(79)   a.   Mary reported him to have arrived on time.
        b.   [$_{TP}$ Mary [$_T$ [+past, ɸ] [$_{VP}$ reported [$_{CP}$ ø [$_{TP}$ him [$_T$ to [$_{VP}$ have [$_{VP}$ arrived on time]]]]]]]]]

The analysis of this configuration of ECM given in (79b) shows that the licensing of [OBJ] appears to cross both a TP and a CP boundary, in contrast with the configuration in (78b), where assignment only crosses a TP boundary.

The class of ECM verbs includes (in addition to *report*) *believe, expect, want, suspect*, and *acknowledge*. Their ECM property appears to be a lexical property. It does not hold for all English verbs and moreover it is extremely rare for corresponding verbs in other languages, including those most closely related to English (i.e. German and French). Furthermore, this property does not function in the passive forms of these verbs, as illustrated in (80).

(80)   a.   The press reported her to be lying.
        b.   She was reported to be lying.
        c.   *It was reported her to be lying.

(80a) is a viable ECM configuration, but (80c) is not. The difference is that *reported* in the former is an active form of the verb, while in the latter it is a passive past participle. When an infinitival clause with an overt NP subject is the complement of a passive verb, displacement of the NP to a Case position, as in (80b), is obligatory. In this way passive verb form is functionally equivalent to a predicate adjective (e.g. *likely*), which also cannot license [OBJ].

The Case Filter motivates NP displacement in several constructions. Consider for example (80a–c). Their PF representations would be (81a–c) respectively.

(81)   a.   [$_{TP}$ the press [$_T$ T [$_{VP}$ reported [$_{CP}$ ø [$_{TP}$ Jane [$_T$ to [$_{VP}$ be lying]]]]]]]]
        b.   [$_{TP}$ Jane [$_T$ was [$_{VP}$ reported [$_{CP}$ ø [$_{TP}$ ~~Jane~~ [$_T$ to [$_{VP}$ be lying]]]]]]]]
        c.   *[$_{TP}$ it [$_T$ was [$_{VP}$ reported [$_{CP}$ ø [$_{TP}$ Jane [$_T$ to [$_{VP}$ be lying]]]]]]]]

The active form of *report* has an ECM property that allows the verb to license [OBJ] Case across a TP clause boundary. Thus both trivial NP chains in (81a), {*the press*} and {*Jane*}, satisfy the Case Filter (70). Given that the passive predicate *reported* does not have or cannot utilize this ECM property that holds for its active counterpart, the *Jane* in the infinitival Spec-TP position in (81b) is not licensed for Case, and therefore must occur in another context that licenses Case, forming a nontrivial chain. Otherwise, this copy would violate the Case Filter (70) as *Jane* does in (81c). Therefore the Case Filter motivates the displacement of the NP in infinitival Spec-TP to a Spec-TP context that is licensed for Case – in this case Spec-TP of a finite clause, but a Spec-TP in an ECM context is another possibility. The analysis generalizes automatically and without modification to single clause passive constructions.

EXERCISE 6.21

Consider the following paradigm.

(i) a.   The committee praised him.
     b.   He was praised by the committee.
     c.   *It was praised him by the committee.
     d.   *It was praised he by the committee.

a. Discuss the Case analysis for each example.
b. How is the Case Filter satisfied for (i.a–b) but violated for (i.c–d)?

NP displacement in English occurs between a Caseless position and one that is licensed for Case. The obligatory character of NP displacement follows from the Case Filter. This contrasts with the optional character of the CP displacement phenomena discussed previously, i.e. as in (82b) (as compared with (82a)).

(82)   a.   It is likely that John will arrive on time.
          b.   That John will arrive on time is likely.

In the case of (82b), recall that CP displacement is motivated by the EPP.

EXERCISE 6.22

Consider the Russian paradigm given in (66–69).

a. Given the theory and analysis developed so far, how does the assignment of θ-roles work for these examples?
b. What motivates the displacement of the ACC argument in (68)?
c. How does this compare to the motivation for displacement in raising constructions (e.g. (49)?

In contrast, NP displacement involving two Case positions is generally prohibited. Thus a raising construction cannot involve two Spec-TP positions where each TP is finite.

(83)   a.   *John is likely that will travel by train.
          b.   *John is likely will travel by train.

Taking *that* in (83a) as a complementizer, the examples in (83) would have the following syntactic analyses.

(84)   a.   *[TP John [T is [AP likely [CP that [TP ~~John~~ [T will [VP travel by train]]]]]]]
          b.   *[TP John [T is [AP likely [CP ç [TP ~~John~~ [T will [VP travel by train]]]]]]]

The derivations of (83a–b) and the representations (84a–b) do not violate any principle of grammar presented so far. In particular, because the displacement of *John* in these examples involves one θ-position and one nonθ-position, the nontrivial chains in the LF representations of (83a–b), which would be similar to (84a–b), do not violate the Argument Uniqueness constraint of the θ-Criterion.

Furthermore these chains satisfy the Case Filter (70). So what accounts for the deviance of (83) requires a solution.

Given the analysis of displacement, the nontrivial chains in (84) contain two members, each of which is licensed independently for ([NOM]) Case. The difference between a legitimate raising construction (e.g. (82a)) and the deviant raising constructions in (83) is that only in the latter does the NP chain involve multiple contexts that license Case. Thus the deviance of the constructions in (83) can be ruled out by a constraint on NP chains involving multiple instances of Case licensing. This would constitute a **Case Uniqueness Constraint** on chains, formulated as (85).

(85)   **Case Uniqueness:** *NP chain, where it contains multiple members that are licensed for Case.

Like the Case Filter as formulated in (70), the Case Uniqueness condition applies to NP chains at Spell-Out.

EXERCISE 6.23

Case Uniqueness applies to other configurations involving displacement from non-Spec-TP positions. Consider the following deviant examples.

(i) a.   *He is likely that Mary will meet.
   b.   *He is likely that Mary will give a book to.

a. Discuss the derivation of (i.a) with specific attention to what happens regarding Case. How is (i.b) different; how is it the same?

The conditions on argument structure and Case proposed above place strong constraints on the properties of NP displacement structures. However, there remains one case of prohibited interclausal NP displacement that is apparently not covered. Consider (86a) where *John* has been displaced from Spec-TP of a finite clause to an unlicensed Spec-TP position of an infinitival complement.

(86)   a.   *It seems John to be likely will travel by train.
         b.   *It seems [TP John [T to [VP be [AP likely [CP ç [TP John [T will [VP travel by train]]]]]]]]]

(86b) violates neither the Case Filter (70) nor Case Uniqueness (85). Furthermore, (86a) appears to share the same properties as the nondeviant Russian construction in (68), which involves NP displacement from a Case licensed position to a Caseless position. Moreover, the displacement in Russian is to a Spec-TP whose T lacks agreement which is similar to (86a) given that infinitival *to* also lacks agreement. However there are several dissimilarities between the two constructions. For one, the displacement in Russian is obligatory (see Lavine & Freidin 2002 for details), whereas there is an alternative derivation in English that yields a legitimate outcome, namely (87).

(87)   a. It seems to be likely John will travel by train.
        b. It seems [$_{TP}$ it [$_T$ to [$_{VP}$ be [$_{AP}$ likely [$_{CP}$ ç [$_{TP}$ John [$_T$ will [$_{VP}$ travel by train]]]]]]]]

For another, the displacement in Russian is local, within the same clause, whereas the English example involves interclausal displacement. Thus in the Russian, T and V are connected via selection if nothing else. But in the English construction, there is no connection between the two Ts of the two clauses. Therefore, what prohibits the English construction in (86) may be a locality constraint governing NP displacement from a Case licensed position to a Caseless one.

6.4   Locality

With the exception of (86–87), we have been examining constructions with only one level of clausal embedding. In more complex constructions, containing more than one level of embedded clauses, the same principles involving Argument Uniqueness and Case Uniqueness still apply. Consider the contrast between (88a) and (88b) as one illustration.

(88)   a. It was reported that Mary had said John would mention her.
        b. *John was reported that Mary had said would mention her.

(88a) contains two verbs that take clausal complements, *reported* and *said*. The verb *said* is the main verb of the clausal complement of the verb *reported*, thus (88a) has the syntactic structure (89).

(89)   [$_{TP}$ It [$_T$ was [$_{VP}$ reported [$_{CP}$ that [$_{TP}$ Mary [$_T$ had [$_{VP}$ said [$_{CP}$ that [$_{TP}$ John [$_T$ would [$_{VP}$ mention her]]]]]]]]]]]

If, instead of merging the expletive *it* as the final step in the derivation of (88a), Merge had applied to *John*, the result would be (88b) with the syntactic structure (90).

(90)   *[$_{TP}$ John [$_T$ was [$_{VP}$ reported [$_{CP}$ that [$_{TP}$ Mary [$_T$ had [$_{VP}$ said [$_{CP}$ ç [$_{TP}$ John [$_T$ would [$_{VP}$ mention her]]]]]]]]]]]]

The chain {*John, John*} bears only one θ-role, so it satisfies Argument Uniqueness. However, the chain contains two instances of a checked Case feature, in violation of the Case Uniqueness Principle.

EXERCISE 6.24

Construct examples involving multiple embedded clauses that violate Argument Uniqueness:

a. one that violates only Argument Uniqueness and
b. another that violates Case Uniqueness as well.
c. Discuss the syntactic analyses of these examples, showing exactly how they violate the relevant principles.

The derivation and syntactic representation of sentences with multiple embedded clauses can create further problems that cannot be solved by either Argument Uniqueness or Case Uniqueness. Consider first the following legitimate constructions.

(91)   a. It was reported that it is likely that Charles will help us.
        b. It was reported that Charles is likely to help us.

(91a) contains two expletive non-referential pronouns *it*, which occupy two nonθ-positions. As they are overt at PF, each occupies a Case position. In (91b) *Charles*, the subject of *help*, has been displaced to a Case position – the Spec-TP of the higher clause. Now suppose that instead of merging *Charles* as specifier of T *is*, the expletive *it* is merged instead and then *Charles* is merged at the root as specifier of T *was*, yielding (92a) with the syntactic analysis (92b).

(92)   a. *Charles was reported that it is likely to help us.
        b. *[$_{TP}$ Charles [$_T$ was [$_{VP}$ reported [$_{CP}$ that [$_{TP}$ it [$_T$ is [$_{AP}$ likely [$_{CP}$ ∅ [$_{TP}$ (Charles) [$_T$ to [$_{VP}$ help us]]]]]]]]]]]]

This deviant example violates neither Argument Uniqueness nor Case Uniqueness.

EXERCISE 6.25

Nor does (92a) violate the Case Filter or the EPP.

a. Discuss how this example satisfies these four constraints.

Therefore another way is needed to prohibit such derivations and/or the syntactic representations they create.

Both (91b) and (92a) involve a single instance of NP displacement, thus the syntactic analysis of both will have a nontrivial chain with two members, {*Charles*, *Charles*}, forming a single link. The two members of each chain can be distinguished if they are identified by their syntactic context, which can be done in terms of the constituent that merges with each copy of *Charles*. Thus the chain for (91b) will be (93a) while the chain for (92a) will be (93b).

(93)   a. {[$_T$ is likely …], [$_T$ to help us]}
        b. {[$_T$ was reported …], [$_T$ to help us]}

These two chains differ with regard to the syntactic distance between their two members. Measuring syntactic distance in terms of clause boundaries crossed – e.g. TPs, note that the link in (93a) crosses only one TP whereas the link in (93b) crosses two. A link in a chain **crosses** a TP only if one member of the link is a constituent of that TP and the other is not. In this way, clause boundaries can be used to distinguish legitimate from illegitimate instances of displacement.

The deviance of (92a) can be accounted for by postulating a general constraint that prohibits the creation of chain links that cross more than one clause boundary. These clause boundaries are designated as **bounding categories** (or nodes).

Two syntactic objects that are separated by no more than one clause boundary are **subjacent**. Thus two syntactic objects that are separated by no clause boundaries are subjacent, as are two syntactic objects that are separated by only one such boundary, as in (91b). Given this definition a general condition on the application of (internal) Merge can be formulated that prohibits displacement to non-subjacent positions.

(94)   **Subjacency Condition:** Merge cannot displace a constituent to a non-subjacent position.

Alternatively, the Subjacency Condition can be reformulated as a well-formedness constraint on chains.

(95)   **Subjacency Condition:** the pair of members in each link of a nontrivial chain must be subjacent.

(94) and (95) are equivalent, hence indistinguishable in terms of empirical coverage. As formulated in (94), Subjacency is a condition on derivations; whereas as formulated in (95) it is a condition on representations. Either way, it imposes a locality constraint on movement by limiting the syntactic domain in which single movements can occur. (See Chapters 7 and 8 for further applications of this condition, and Chapter 9 for further discussion of how it should be implemented in the computational system.)

EXERCISE 6.26

The following example involves two chains, each with two members.

(i)   It seems to have been reported that Charles is likely to help us.

a.   Give the syntactic analysis of (i), showing all copies.
b.   Identify the two nontrivial chains.
c.   Show how each satisfies the Subjacency Condition.

Now consider the deviant example (ii).

(ii)   *Charles seems to have been reported that it is likely to help us.

d.   Give the syntactic analysis of (ii), assuming that *Charles* is the subject of *help*.
e.   Identify the nontrivial chain for this analysis.
f.   Assume instead that *it* is a referential pronoun rather than an expletive and further is the subject of *help*. Under this analysis, what principle or principles of grammar does this construction violate?

EXERCISE 6.27

Multiple embedded clause constructions raise further interesting issues. Consider first the property of raising constructions where a finite clause complement can be raised to matrix Spec-TP.

(i)   a.   It is unlikely that John will arrive on time.
    b.   That John will arrive on time is unlikely.

Suppose the examples in (i) are embedded as the complements of an ECM verb.

(ii)   a.   They reported that it is unlikely that John will arrive on time.
    b.   ?They reported that that John will arrive on time is unlikely.

(ii.b) is somewhat degraded compared to (ii.a). Recall that the C *that* is optional, so that (iii) is a viable alternative to (i.a).

(iii)   It is unlikely John will arrive on time.

However, when the clause is preposed to Spec-TP as in (i.b), the C *that* is obligatory (i.e. the null finite C ç is not a viable alternative), as (iv) illustrates.

(iv)   *John will arrive on time is unlikely.

Now consider (v), which is close to but less degraded than (ii.b).

(v)   They reported that John will arrive on time is unlikely.

a. Given our analysis of clauses, there are two possible structural analyses for the C *that*. What are they? Are both equally viable or is only one possible? If the latter, which one?

Now consider what happens when *is unlikely* is changed to the infinitival *to be unlikely*.

(vi)   a.   They reported it to be unlikely that John would arrive on time.
    b.   ?They reported that John would arrive on time to be unlikely.
    c.   *They reported John to arrive on time to be unlikely.
    d.   They reported for John to arrive on time to be unlikely.

b. What is the syntactic analysis of (vi.b), especially the position of the C *that*?
c. Give the syntactic analysis of (vi.c). Are the verb *reported* and the noun *John* subjacent?
d. Discuss whether (vi.c) violates the Case Filter.

Now compare the following three examples in (vii).

(vii)   a.   It was reported to be unlikely that John would arrive on time.
    b.   *It was reported that John would arrive on time to be unlikely.
    c.   That John would arrive on time was reported to be unlikely.

e. Give the syntactic analyses for the three examples in (vii).
f. How would our analysis of Case have to be revised to account for the deviance of (vii.b)?
g. How might such an analysis be used to also account for (iv) and (vi.c)?

Consider now a somewhat more complicated case of NP displacement.

(96)   Charles was reported to be likely to help us.

Charles is interpreted as the subject of *help*, hence as Spec-TP of the most deeply embedded clause. And *Charles* is pronounced as the Spec-TP of the main clause. The distance between these two positions crosses more than one TP boundary, as you can easily verify. Yet this example is not deviant and therefore cannot have violated Subjacency. The solution to this apparent problem is to analyze this example as involving not a two member chain, which would inevitably violate Subjacency, but rather a three member chain. In other words, (96) involves two instances of NP displacement – in which case (96) would have the analysis (97a–b).

(97)   a.   [$_{TP}$ Charles [$_T$ was [$_{VP}$ reported [$_{CP}$ ø [$_{TP}$ (Charles) [$_T$ to [$_{VP}$ be [$_{AP}$ likely
            [$_{CP}$ ø [$_{TP}$ (Charles) [$_T$ to [$_{VP}$ help us]]]]]]]]]]]]

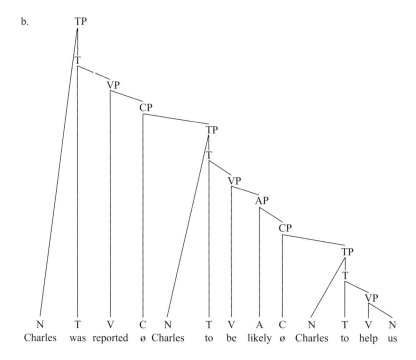

(97a–b) contains a three member chain (98) with two links (99a) and (99b).

(98)   {[$_T$ was reported ...], [$_T$ to be likely ...], [$_T$ to help us]}
(99)   a.   ([$_T$ was reported ...], [$_T$ to be likely ...]),
          b.   ([$_T$ to be likely ...], [$_T$ to help us])

Both links satisfy Subjacency; therefore (96) does not violate the condition.

EXERCISE 6.28

Suppose that (96) were instead derived via a single instance of displacement and thus has the representation given in (i).

(i) [$_{TP}$ Charles [$_T$ was [$_{VP}$ reported [$_{CP}$ ∅ [$_{TP}$ to [$_{VP}$ be [$_{AP}$ likely [$_{CP}$ ∅ [$_{TP}$ (Charles) [$_T$ to [$_{VP}$ help us]]]]]]]]]]]

This representation would violate two principles of grammar.

a. What are they?
b. How exactly are they violated by (i)?

Note that the analysis of (96) in (97) involves an occurrence of *Charles* that appears to be neither pronounced nor interpreted and therefore is not directly involved in what has been characterized as displacement. That is, the step in the derivation of (97) involving the two covert occurrences of *Charles* cannot be called displacement. For lack of a better term, let us refer to the connection between these two positions as an instance of "movement," noting again the metaphorical nature of the term. Thus the relation of any two members of a chain that form a link can be called movement. And based on this, the derivation of a chain link can be described as involving a "movement operation," in reality Merge.

In the legitimate derivation of (96) given in (97), NP movement first applies to the smallest TP domain in which it can apply. Then it applies to the next larger TP domain – i.e. the smallest TP in which the first TP domain is embedded. The next larger TP domain is the root TP domain. Each TP domain in which NP displacement occurs constitutes a cyclic domain (or **cycle**) in the derivation. Thus NP movement via Merge applies cyclically, starting with the smallest TP domain and proceeding successively through the next minimal TP domain that contains the first, and so on until all TP domains have been considered. NP movement is therefore **successive cyclic**. In the derivation of (89) NP movement does not occur in the smallest cyclic (i.e. TP) domain, in contrast to a monoclausal passive construction where it does. Subjacency imposes successive cyclic derivations on all nondeviant constructions involving **long-distance** displacement – i.e., where the position in which a constituent is pronounced at PF is separated by multiple clause boundaries from the position in which the constituent is interpreted (i.e. assigned an argument function (θ-role)). In this way, Subjacency constitutes part of the definition of the syntactic cycle, which like Merge in general processes syntactic structure bottom-up.

The No Tampering Condition also enforces strictly bottom-up construction of syntactic structure. Given the NTC Merge can only affect the roots of the two syntactic objects it applies to. Thus a derivation will not only involve only successive cyclic operations but furthermore these operations will be **strictly cyclic** in the sense that they cannot affect subdomains of the current cycle.

EXERCISE 6.29

The following example involves a four member chain.

(i) Charles was reported to be likely to be awarded a prize.

a.   Give the syntactic analysis for this example.
b.   Identify the nontrivial chain and each of its three links.
c.   Show how each link satisfies Subjacency.

EXERCISE 6.30

Consider the following as an extension of Exercise 6.26.

a. What is the syntactic analysis of (viii)?

(viii) That John will arrive on time seems to have been reported to be unlikely.

b. How does this analysis satisfy the Subjacency Condition?

The investigation of NP movement phenomena in this chapter has demonstrated that some instances of long-distance displacement yield grammatical constructions whereas others result in deviance. The deviant cases demonstrate that NP movement is syntactically bounded, while the legitimate cases suggest the opposite. This paradox is resolved by postulating a principle that imposes boundedness on Merge (hence the operation is indeed bounded and there is no actual long-distance "movement") and at the same time allowing for covert instances of movement to occur in a derivation. Legitimate long-distance displacement thus arises from a series of covert local operations (henceforth referred to as "movement") each satisfying the Subjacency Condition. In this way, NP displacement phenomena provide another case for the conclusion that syntax is not WYSIWYG.

6.5   Summary

The architecture of the system of grammar presented in this chapter is as follows:

a.   Mechanisms of the computational system:
   i.   Merge
   ii. Delete
b.   Constraints on derivations and representations:
   i.   No compounding of elementary operations
   ii.   No Tampering Condition
   iii. Full Interpretation
   iv.   Argument Uniqueness (θ-Uniqueness)
   v.   Argument Relatedness (θ-Relatedness)
   vi.   EPP (Extended Projection Principle)

This chapter has been concerned with the analysis of displacement, starting with interclausal displacement from the Spec-TP of an infinitival clausal complement to the matrix Spec-TP position. There are two elementary grammatical operations involved in this phenomenon: Merge and Delete. Merge constructs the displaced constituent in two distinct syntactic contexts, one of which is interpreted but not pronounced and the other of which is pronounced, hence overt at PF. Like other applications of Merge, this one is also constrained by a No Tampering Condition that prevents Merge from altering the internal phrase structure of any syntactic object that has been constructed in a prior part of the derivation. The two copies of the displaced constituent that result from Merge form a chain, where adjacent pairs of members form a link. The copy that is pronounced at PF, hence overt, is designated the head of the chain. The other copies are covert because they are erased by Delete at PF, which reduces a nontrivial chain (i.e. with multiple members) to a trivial chain, thus linearizing the constituents in the PF representation. Merge and Delete cannot be compounded to form a single grammatical operation – i.e. where the two operations apply simultaneously. This follows if in the organization of derivations, the two elementary operations are segregated in distinct parts. Delete affects PF, but not LF. Therefore there must be a point (or points) in a syntactic derivation where the derivation of PF separates from the derivation of LF. This is called Spell-Out. Delete applies to the derivation of PF after Spell-Out, given that what is deleted at PF must still be interpreted at LF. Spell-Out is further motivated by Full Interpretation, a constraint on interface representations such that they must contain no superfluous elements, which would be illegible to the cognitive components that interface with PF and LF. From this it follows that Spell-Out separates phonetic features and semantic features, sending the former to PF and the latter to LF.

In the case of a nontrivial NP chain, which results from displacement, the most deeply embedded covert copy occupies a syntactic position to which an argument function of a predicate (a θ-role) is assigned. All subsequent contexts in which a copy of the constituent is merged constitute non-argument positions (i.e. positions to which a θ-role is not assigned). This results from Argument Uniqueness, a general constraint on argument structure that prohibits chains with multiple θ-roles. This constraint on argument structure is supplemented by Argument Relatedness, which prohibits Merge from creating trivial chains in positions that are not assigned a θ-role. These principles generalize to other constructions involving NP displacement, including single clauses (passives) and NPs involving a nominalized N that corresponds to a V.

Some non-argument positions contain an overt expletive element (in English, non-referential *it*). This position can be utilized for NP displacement out of infinitival complement clauses under certain conditions. It can also be used for displacement of finite and infinitival clausal complements (i.e. CP). However, this non-argument Spec-TP position cannot be covert at PF. Thus a further constraint that requires every clause to have a Spec-TP (the EPP) appears to be necessary.

Another property of NP displacement concerns a notion of Case. The context in which a displaced NP is pronounced turns out to be the context in which a particular Case is licensed (e.g. nominative in the Spec-TP of a finite T). In contrast, the silent copies of a constituent occupy contexts that do not license any Case. Thus displacement connects a Caseless position to a Case position. So in addition to argument structure principles that govern the properties of displacement, there are also Case principles that further constrain these properties.

Given that all Ns enter a derivation with an abstract Case feature, only those that occur in the appropriate context for Case at PF (i.e. an N that is pronounced) will have their Case feature checked (i.e. licensed and then eliminated). Those Ns with phonetic content at PF whose Case feature remains unchecked will violate the Case Filter. Thus displacement cannot be to a Caseless position. Furthermore, displacement cannot create chains containing a Case feature that has been checked more than once (Case Uniqueness).

While these principles of argument structure and Case place severe restrictions on the properties of displacement, there remain possibilities that nonetheless need to be prohibited. These involve long-distance displacement across multiple clause boundaries. They are ruled out by the Subjacency Condition. Given this condition, long-distance displacement must be the result of multiple intermediate "movements" where each link in a NP-chain satisfies Subjacency. In this way, legitimate long-distance displacement must be derived via a series of successive cyclic local movements. Furthermore, given the No Tampering Condition, all operations of syntactic Merge will be strictly cyclic, hence not affecting subdomains of a syntactic object that has already been constructing.

Bibliographical notes

The constraint against compounding elementary operations was originally proposed in Chomsky 1980, though for a different theory of elementary operations and in a different framework. For the No Tampering Condition see the bibliographical notes in Chapter 4. Full Interpretation is proposed in Chomsky 1986 and elaborated in Chomsky 1991; see also Chomsky 1995b. Argument Uniqueness and Relatedness are first formulated in Freidin 1978. The prohibition against multiple assignments of a single θ-role for a predicate is first formulated in Freidin 1975: footnote 20. For the θ-Criterion, see Chomsky 1981b. See Gruber 1965 and Jackendoff 1969, 1972 for the original discussions of thematic relations. The EPP (by that name) is first proposed in Chomsky 1982; see Lasnik 2001 for background and commentary. The Case Filter is first proposed in Chomsky 1980, based on ideas of Jean-Roger Vergnaud in a letter (now published as Vergnaud 2008) to Chomsky and Lasnik about their manuscript for "Filters and Control" (1977); see Lasnik 2008 for background and commentary. The formulation of the Case Filter in terms of chains occurs in Chomsky 1981b, p. 334. For a recent discussion of morphological vs. abstract Case, see Legate 2007. The Subjacency Condition is first proposed in Chomsky 1973 and modified in Chomsky 1977 and 1981a. For interpreting Subjacency as a condition on representations, see Freidin 1978. For the initial discussion of strictly cyclic derivations, see Chomsky 1973, which proposes a Strict Cycle Condition and Freidin 1978, which attempts to derive the empirical effects of this condition from other independently motivated principles of grammar (including conditions on argument structure). See also Chomsky 1993 for a reformulation of strict cyclicity as an Extension Condition, which enforced merger at the root (see also the No Tampering Condition, which has roughly the same effect). For discussion and commentary on the concept of cyclic derivation, including its history, see Freidin 1999 and Lasnik 2004.

7 Head movement and the structure of root clauses

Chapter 5 established that embedded (hence subordinate) clauses are CP structures. This chapter will show how this analysis generalizes to root clauses.

Although it is obvious that a clausal complement with an overt C cannot occur as a root clause (e.g. as in (1) below), and also that indicative root clauses are conspicuously missing an overt element that might be designated as occupying a C position, the analysis of interrogative constructions provides clear evidence that this species of clause must be more than a simple TP.

(1)   a. *That the student has been helpful to them.
           b. *For the student to be helpful to them.

Thus consider the syntactic structure of a direct yes/no question (2a) as compared to the corresponding indicative (2b).

(2)   a. Has he been helpful?
           b. He has been helpful.

In the interrogative the finite auxiliary *has* occurs to the left of the subject *he*, in contrast to its position following the subject in the indicative. Given that (2b) is a TP with a syntactic structure (3), the Spec-head agreement relation will account for the deviance of (4a).

(3) $[_{TP}$ he $[_T$ has $[_{VP}$ been helpful$]]]$
(4)   a. *He have been helpful.
           b. *Have he been helpful.

Presumably the source of deviance in (4b) is essentially the same as that of (4a). If so, then the derivation of (4b) must at some point involve a TP structure like (3), where the finite verbal element occurs as a head T. Given this analysis, two separate but related questions arise:

(5)   a. What syntactic position does the finite auxiliary verb occupy in (4b)?
           b. How does it get from T to that position?

The answers to these questions apply as well to the analysis of the legitimate yes/no interrogative (2a).

7.1   The analysis of yes/no questions

One way to approach these questions is to consider not just the PF representations of yes/no interrogative questions but also their LF representations. In particular, we want to compare the LF representation of a direct yes/no question, for example (2a), with that of its indirect counterpart, the complement CP as in (6).

(6)   They wonder whether he has been helpful.

Taking the complementizer *whether*, the head of that CP, to be the question operator, which will be represented as a question mark, the LF of the complement clause in (6) will be a structure (7).

(7)   a.   [$_{CP}$? [$_{TP}$ he [$_T$ has [$_{VP}$ been helpful]]]]

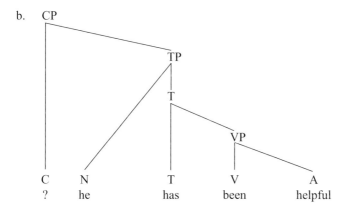

(7) is also the simplest representation that could be posited for the LF representation of the direct yes/no interrogative (2a). Thus at LF the representations of a direct yes/no question and its indirect counterpart are identical. This suggests that if two linguistic expressions have essentially the same interpretation, they will have the same LF representation in spite of differences between their PF representations. Let us call this the **LF representation criterion** (see Section 6.2 for further discussion).

   Under this analysis, the derivation of a direct yes/no question must inevitably involve the merger of a covert element ?, which in indirect yes/no questions is a lexical element C with phonetic features (i.e. *whether*). Given that non-interrogative C in clausal complements has two covert variants, ø for infinitival clauses and ç for finite clauses, it is not surprising that interrogative C would also have a covert variant. Obviously ? is not a "complementizer" in the sense that it marks its clausal complement TP as a complement of some external head. Rather it is an operator that takes scope over the clause that functions as its complement. This suggests that what we have been calling complementizers (e.g. *that* and *for*) are also clausal operators. Following standard practice, these operators will continue to be designated as C.[1]

Turning now to the derivation of (2a), given that (7) is the target representation at LF, the simplest derivation of LF would involve (7) and nothing more. If so, then whatever is involved in deriving a PF representation of (2a) would occur in the part of the derivation after Spell-Out, part 2 of the schema for derivations given in (8) (= (11) in Chapter 6).

(8)

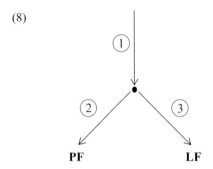

Recall that Spell-Out is the point in a derivation where the syntactic representation bifurcates into one that carries the phonetic features but not semantic features and another that carries the semantic features but no phonetic features. Under this analysis, the finite verbal auxiliary is interpreted as T, but pronounced in sentence-initial position – another instance of displacement. The answer to (5b) therefore would appear to involve the application of Merge to the finite auxiliary verb.

How Merge functions in this part of the derivation depends on what the PF representation of (2a) is taken to be. The standard assumption is that the fronted finite verbal auxiliary occupies the C position and that displacement involves two head positions T and C – what is referred to as **head movement** because it involves displacement between two head positions, in contrast with **phrasal movement** where displacement involves two phrasal positions (usually complement and specifier). If this is correct, then the finite auxiliary – in this case *has* – is merged as T and then it is adjoined to the C ?. This second operation cannot be merger at the root as in displacement involving phrases. Instead, the finite verbal auxiliary must combine with ?. Presumably the resulting element is still a head not a phrase – in other words, not a phrase (9a), where the label of ? (i.e. C) projects, but rather (9b) where + is a morpheme boundary within a lexical head labeled C.

(9)   a.   [c has C]
       b.   has + ?

Under this analysis, head movement affects linear order and morphological structure, but not the composition of phrases and therefore does not violate the No Tampering Condition.

One way to instantiate this analysis is to consider ? to be a morphological affix of some kind that adjoins to the finite verbal auxiliary to form a single lexical unit with the syntactic feature C. In effect, ? functions like a derivational affix that determines the label of the lexical item formed by adjoining it to a root (e.g the nominalizing affix *–ity* in *electricity* that turns an adjectival stem *electric* into a N). From this perspective, what is called head movement appears to involve some sort of morphological operation – which would be appropriate for the derivation of PF representations.

Some empirical evidence in support of this proposal comes from an analysis of yes/no questions in Russian. As illustrated in (10), the indirect yes/no question (italicized in (10a)) has the same syntactic structure as its direct question counterpart in (10b).

(10)   a.   Ja ne znagu *budet li on čitat' knigu.*
                I not know will ? he be-reading book
                "I don't know whether he will be reading the book"
          b.   Budet li on čitat' knigu?
                will ? he be-reading book
                "Will he be reading the book?"

In (10) *li* functions as a question operator (like the C *whether* in English) where the following clause is interpreted as a yes/no question. Moreover, the auxiliary *budet*, which carries the tense of the clause occurs to the left of the question particle *li*. Taking *li* to be an affix labeled C, it must be adjoined to some stem to form a legitimate morphological construction – under the assumption that there can be no free affixes in PF (henceforth the **No Free Affix Condition** (NFAC)). Thus in (10), *li* functions as a suffix on *budet*. Thus *budet-li* has the same structure as the preposed finite verbal auxiliary in English (cf. (9b)), as indicated in (11) where *budet* replaces *has* and *li* replaces the covert ?.

(11)   [$_C$ budet + li]

This analysis provides an explanation for the deviance of the examples in (12), which differ from those in (10) only in that the finite verbal element has not been preposed to the left of *li*.

(12)   a.   *Ja ne znagu li on budet čitat' knigu.
          b.   *Li on budet čitat' knigu?

In contrast, the LF representations of both the direct and the indirect yes/no questions in (10) will be (13), where PF *li* represents as the semantic operator ?.

(13)   [$_{CP}$? [$_{TP}$ on [$_T$ budet [$_{VP}$ čitat' knigu]]]]

The LF representations of these yes/no questions will be essentially identical to the deviant CPs in (12). Thus the source for the deviance of the examples in (12) involves PF rather than LF. Moreover given that the phonetic features of the words in the sentence do not exist at LF, the LF representation (13) is essentially equivalent to the LF representation of the corresponding direct and indirect yes/no questions in English.

The prohibition against free affixes in PF representations, formulated in the NFAC, provides an explanation for the obligatory nature of head movement in Russian yes/

no questions. Thus the obligatory application of head movement in this case follows from a general principle of grammar and therefore need not be stipulated as part of the rule. This account generalizes to English direct yes/no questions.

Both English and Russian involve a process of head movement in the derivation of direct yes/no questions, specifically displacement between T and C. It has been suggested that this operation occurs after Spell-Out on the grounds that it affects solely PF representations. If head movement applies prior to Spell-Out, then the derivation of the LF representations postulated would require the deletion of the preposed finite verbal auxiliary in T. This deletion is not required if head movement occurs after Spell-Out. Therefore on economy grounds – specifically the **economy of derivations**, which prefers derivations with the fewest steps, the post Spell-Out analysis of head movement is preferable.

In Russian a finite main verb may also be preposed to clause-initial position in both direct and indirect yes/no questions, as illustrated in (14).

(14)   a.   On postroil dom.
              he built house
              "he built a house"
        b.   Postroil-li on dom?
              built-? he house
              "did he finish building a house"
        c.   Ja ne znagu postroil-li on dom
              I not know built-? he house
              "I don't know whether he built a house"

Thus any finite verbal element, including a main verb, may be displaced to clause-initial position. This stands in marked contrast with English, where a finite main verb is prohibited from occurring in clause-initial position in direct yes/no questions.

(15)   *Built he the house?

Thus it appears that Russian allows both V-to-C and T-to-C movement whereas English only allows the latter.[2]

At this point two questions arise. First, what is the actual derivation of V-to-C movement in Russian? Second, what prohibits the corresponding derivation in English?

Given the existence of T-to-C movement in Russian, there are two logically possible derivational paths for the V-to-C displacement found in yes/no questions (14b–c). Either displacement could occur directly between V and C, or it could occur indirectly with an intermediate movement from V-to-T and a final movement from T-to-C. The indirect movement derivation faces two substantial problems. First, the movement from V-to-T would have no effect at PF. In essence, there seems to be no PF reason for having such a movement, in contrast to the movement to C, which is motivated by the NFAC. Moreover, in terms of derivational economy, the extra derivational step makes such derivations less preferable than the direct V-to-C movement.

If however there were some general grammatical constraint against one-step V-to-C movement, then that would motivate the two step derivation in spite of its apparent problems with economy considerations. To this end, let's consider the impossibility of V-to-C movement in English, as (15) illustrates. With (15) there are also two possible derivations, one that involves displacement directly from V-to-C in one step and another that involves two movements – one from V-to-T and another from T-to-C. In the literature of generative grammar, one-step movement from V-to-C is prohibited generally by the **Head Movement Constraint** (HMC).

(16)   **Head Movement Constraint:**
           A head can only move to the closest c-commanding head position.

With the HMC, V could only reach the C position if it is moved first to the T position. Both C and T c-command V, but T is the closer (hence closest) c-commanding head. In the case of C, T, and V, our analysis of clause structure postulates that T selects V and also that C selects T. So it appears that a head can only move to the position of the head that selects it. In this way the HMC functions as a locality condition on head movement in much the same way that the Subjacency Condition (see (94–95) in Chapter 6) constrains the locality of movement to Spec-TP.

However, for English, the two-step derivation of head movement involving a main V must also be prohibited. Therefore the fact that in English a main verb is inert needs to be accounted for; it cannot move even to the closest c-commanding head position – i.e. T. But given the inertness of main V in English, there is no need to rely on the HMC to rule out (15). And if the HMC isn't required for English, then there may be no point for positing it for Russian, where V-to-C movement occurs. (See below for further discussion.)

It is worth noting that the prohibition against V-to-C movement in English also extends to auxiliary verbs that do not bear tense. Thus the only viable yes/no question corresponding to (17a) is (17b), (17c–e) being deviant.

(17)   a.   Howard could have been writing for five hours.
           b.   Could Howard have been writing for five hours?
           c.   *Have Howard could been writing for five hours?
           d.   *Been Howard could have writing for five hours?
           e.   *Writing Howard could have been for five hours?

Assuming that (17c–e) are derived via head movement, where the moved auxiliaries are first merged in their overt positions in (17a), then each movement is an instance of V-to-C. In contrast, (17b) is an instance of T-to-C movement. Thus (17c–e) would be prohibited by the HMC and therefore might be taken as independent evidence for the constraint.

Alternatively, the impossibility of displacing nonfinite verbal forms (including the main verb) could be accounted for in another way. Suppose that the interrogative C **attracts** only a finite verbal element. Under this conceptualization, displacement/movement involves an attracting element (a **probe**) that targets a specific kind of syntactic object (a **goal**), a copy of which is attached near the probe. In this case, the probe C ? attracts a syntactic object bearing finite tense. Under this analysis, the deviance of (17c–e) would follow from the inability of ? to attract a nonfinite form. Note that a separate explanation for impossibility of displacing a finite main verb to C via T still has to be provided.

Another consideration that might bear on a two-step derivation of V-to-C movement concerns whether there is any evidence for overt V-to-T movement. The placement of French adverbs provides an important case. Consider the following paradigm comparing English constructions to their French counterparts.

(18)   a.   John often kisses Mary.
         b.   *Jean souvent embrasse Marie.
(19)   a.   *John kisses often Mary.
         b.   Jean embrasse souvent Marie.

Given that the adverb *often* is a VP adjunct because it modifies the verb *kisses*, that Adv is merged at the left edge of VP and after V merges with its complement, the object *Mary*. Assuming that the constraints on merger are the same across languages, the VP in French should have the same internal structure as English even though the PF of the French counterpart to the English example involves a different word order. If the LF representations of (18a) and (19b) are identical, then the difference in word order will be a PF effect.

Under this analysis, both the English and the French examples have the structure (20) at Spell-Out.

(20) $[_{TP}$ NP $[_T$ T $[_{VP}$ Adv $[_V$ V NP]]]]

The following examples establish that an adverb in French can occur at the left edge of a VP.

(21)   a.   Jean a souvent embrassé Marie.
              Jean has often kissed Marie
         b.   Souvent paraître triste pendant son voyage de noce, c'est rare.
              often to-appear sad during one's honeymoon, it is rare
              "to often appear sad during one's honeymoon is rare"

In (21a) the adverb appears between T and V. Given that VP is the complement of T because of the selectional relation between the perfective auxiliary and the past participle form of the main verb, the adverb is naturally analyzed as a constituent of the VP. In (21b) the adverb occurs before the infinitival form of the verb, which it modifies. Again the simplest analysis is to take the adverb to be an adjunct within the infinitival VP.

Given (20) as the underlying (i.e. before Spell-Out) representation for the VPs in both (18a) and (19b), English and French VPs will have the same LF representation in spite of the difference in their PF representations. However, where English retains the same word order at PF, French shows that the V must show up to the left of Adv. This order can be created by a PF operation that adjoins V-to-T as in (22).

(22) $[_{TP}$ NP $[_T$ V+T $[_{VP}$ Adv $[_V$ ~~V~~ NP]]]]

One way to instantiate this analysis is to relocate a copy of V at the T locus. The copy of V to the right of Adv would then undergo deletion as part of chain reduction at PF. As a purely PF operation, this movement may also be morphologically motivated. That is, just as movement to C in yes/no questions is driven by the morphological properties of C, the movement of V-to-T might also be driven by the morphological properties of T. The difference between French and English in these constructions would then rest on the difference between the morphological properties of T. Presumably the tense feature of T would be identical for English and French, in which case the difference between the two languages must involve the agreement features. Under this morphological analysis, the displacement of V-to-T would not constitute a violation of the NTC (see note 5).

EXERCISE 7.1

V-to-T movement in French can also be motivated by considering the syntactic analysis of the following English/French paradigms.

(i)   a.   *John likes not Mary.
      b.   Jean (n') aime pas Marie.
      c.   John does not like Mary.
      d.   *Jean ne pas aime Marie.
(ii) a.   My friends all love Mary.
      b.   *Mes amis tous aiment Marie.
      c.   *My friends love all Mary.
      d.   Mes amis aiment tous Marie.

a. Taking *pas* in (i) to be the French counterpart to the negative *not* and assuming that *not* is a VP adjunct modifying the verb, how can the analysis of this paradigm be assimilated to the analysis of (18–19) given above?
b. How does the paradigm in (ii) relate to this analysis? Consider the possibility that the English sentences might involve the underlying order *all my friends* and correspondingly *tous mes amis* in French.

  Head movement is also involved in the formation of direct yes/no questions in French, as illustrated with the interrogative counterparts for the indicative root clauses in (23–24).[3]

(23)   a.   Il a souvent embrassé Marie.
                 he has often kissed Mary
            b.   A-t-il souvent embrassé Marie?
                 has he often kissed Mary

(24)   a.   Il embrasse souvent Marie.
              he kisses often Mary
              "he often kisses Mary"
         b.   Embrasse-t-il souvent Marie?
              kisses he often Mary
              "does he often kiss Mary?"

In (23a) the finite perfective auxiliary constitutes the head of the clause as T. In its yes/no question counterpart (23b), the auxiliary occurs as the C head of CP. Thus the derivation of (23b) involves displacement between T and C, while the main verb *embrassé* remains in VP as a sister to its object complement and to the right of the adverb *souvent*, which is a VP adjunct. Given that the main verb is merged first with its complement NP as the head of VP, the displacement that occurs in a direct yes/no question with no verbal auxiliary (e.g. (24b)) involves at a minimum the V and C positions.

The question that arises is whether the V-to-C displacement in French constructions like (24b) involves one-step movement from V directly to C, or movement in two steps, from V-to-T and then from T-to-C. The answer depends in part on whether the morphological property of T that forces overt V-to-T movement in an indicative clause without auxiliaries (e.g. (19b)) is also present in an interrogative clause like (24b), which also lacks any auxiliary verb. However the answer to this follow-up question is not obvious given that this V-to-T movement at PF has no overt effect. Furthermore, since the overt V does not remain in T but moves on to C, the V that would be satisfying the morphological requirement of T would be a silent copy. Also from the perspective of economy of derivations, the two-step derivation would be the less preferable.

Another factor to consider in answering the question about how many steps are involved in V-to-C displacement is whether languages that manifest such displacement manifest V-to-T displacement as well. Russian is a case in point. It shows V-to-C displacement in both direct and indirect yes/no questions, as illustrated above in (14b–c) respectively. However, as the paradigms given in (25–26) demonstrate, V-to-T displacement is not allowed in indicative clauses – either in root or subordinate clauses.

(25)   a.   Ivan často celuet Masha.
              Ivan often kisses Masha
         b.   *Ivan celuet často Masha.
              Ivan kisses often Masha

(26)   a.   Boris skazal, čto Ivan často celuet Masha.
              Boris said that Ivan often kisses Masha
         b.   *Boris skazal, čto Ivan celuet často Masha.
              Boris said that Ivan kisses often Masha

Thus, finite T in Russian lacks the property that in French requires the displacement of V-to-T. So it appears that the after Spell-Out movement of V-to-C in Russian would not involve an intermediate movement of V-to-T, which further undermines the motivation for the HMC.

EXERCISE 7.2

The HMC can also be used to account for another locality restriction on head movement, namely that there appears to be no interclausal head displacement. Consider the following examples.

(i) a. The child who is crying is unhappy.
   b. Is the child who is crying unhappy.
   c. *Is the child who crying is unhappy.

a. Give the phrase structure analysis of (i.a).
b. Give the phrase structure analysis of (i.b)
c. Explain how the HMC blocks the derivation of (i.c).
d. Discuss whether the Subjacency Condition might also block (i.c) and how this affects the motivation for the HMC.

7.2   The auxiliary *do*

Because English lacks V-to-C displacement in any form, the yes/no question corresponding to (27a) cannot be (27b) [= (15)], but is instead (27c).

(27)   a.   He wrote a book.
           b.   *Wrote he a book?
           c.   Did he write a book?

The element *did* in (27c) functions like an auxiliary verb to the extent that it carries tense and agreement features rather than the main verb.

EXERCISE 7.3

Consider the following paradigm:

(i) a.   Does he write books?
     b.   *Do he write books?
(ii) a.   Do they write books?
     b.   *Does they write books?

a. Assuming the b-examples are violations of spec-head agreement, discuss the derivations of the examples in (i–ii) and explain how this analysis is captured in these derivations.

Unlike the main verb *do* (illustrated in (28)), auxiliary *do* is otherwise semantically empty.

(28)   a.   They did it again.
           b.   Did they do it again?

As shown in (28b), both auxiliary *do* and main verb *do* can occur in the same clause.

Auxiliary *do* shares two properties with modal auxiliaries and infinitival *to*. First, it can only occur with the bare (overtly uninflected) form of the following verb (cf. the legitimate (27c) in contrast with the deviant examples in (29)).

(29)   a.   *Does he writes a book?
          b.   *Did he writing a book?
          c.   *Did he written a book?

Thus compare (27c) and (29) to the paradigms in (30) for infinitival *to* and (31) for modal auxiliaries.

(30)   a.   They want him to write a book.
          b.   *They want him to writes a book.
          c.   *They want him to writing a book.
          d.   *They want him to written a book.
(31)   a.   He will write a book.
          b.   *He will writes a book.
          c.   *He will writing a book.
          d.   *He will written a book.

The properties of the paradigms (30–31) follow under the analysis that the modal *will* and infinitival *to* select the form of the following verb. In Chapter 5, both were analyzed as instances of T on the grounds that infinitival *to* is clearly an overt tense element. Since modal auxiliaries are in complementary distribution with infinitival *to*, they are also instances of T. This analysis extends automatically to auxiliary *do* because it is also in complementary distribution with infinitival *to* and modal auxiliaries.

   Auxiliary *do* only occurs in finite (i.e. [±past]) forms, hence it has no bare form; so it could not occur with an infinitival *to*, which selects a bare form. Having no bare form is also a property of modal auxiliaries. Therefore a modal auxiliary cannot be selected by auxiliary *do*, nor can it select another auxiliary *do*.

   Although all of the examples of auxiliary *do* examined above occur in C rather than T, the auxiliary *do* can also occur in T, as illustrated in a negative declarative sentence like (32).

(32)   He did not write a book.

Given that the bare form of the main verb *write* in (32) occurs as the head of VP, then the auxiliary *did* must be in T, where T selects V. If so, then *not* must be analyzed as a VP adjunct. (See below for further discussion on the analysis of negative sentences.)

   One way to account for the three-way complementary distribution of modal auxiliaries, infinitival *to*, and auxiliary *do* is to analyze them as three instances of lexical T. If one occurs as the T of a clause, then the other two cannot because a clause can contain only one T, which follows from the fact that T selects V, never another T, and from the nature of Merge in that every phrase has a unique head. Furthermore, a lexical T selects the bare form of the head of its complement, so any construction with successive adjacent lexical Ts would violate selection.

In contrast to modal auxiliaries and infinitival *to*, auxiliary *do* has a more limited distribution. As illustrated in the paradigms (33–35), while the first two can occur with one or both aspectual auxiliaries, auxiliary *do* cannot.

(33)   a.   Bill will be studying for the exam.
       b.   Bill will have studied for the exam.
       c.   Bill will have been studying for the exam.
(34)   a.   Mary expects Bill to be studying for the exam.
       b.   Mary expects Bill to have studied for the exam.
       c.   Mary expects Bill to have been studying for the exam.
(35)   a.   *Bill did not be studying for the exam.
       b.   *Bill did not have studied for the exam.
       c.   *Bill did not have been studying for the exam.

The limited distribution of auxiliary *do* cannot be attributed to selection because in all the examples in (35), the VP complement of T *do* is headed by an auxiliary in the bare form.

An account of the limited distribution of auxiliary *do* depends crucially on how this auxiliary enters a derivation. There are two distinct analytic assumptions to consider.

(36)   a.   Auxiliary *do* exists as an item in the lexicon and therefore is subject to Merge like other auxiliary elements.
       b.   Auxiliary *do* is not an item in the lexicon, hence not inserted via Merge but instead is introduced into a derivation only under the special circumstances in which it is required.

Under (36a), the lexicon contains the finite forms of auxiliary *do* (*does*, *do*, *did*), which, when Merged as T, select the bare form of the head of its complement. The limited distribution of *do* remains to be explained. The syntactic analysis of auxiliary *do* under (36b), in contrast, does not necessarily involve this selectional restriction. Nonetheless, the limited distribution of *do* under (36b) must be handled by the operation that inserts it into the derivation.

The precise formulations for the analyses based on (36a–b) crucially depend on how verbal elements are represented in the lexicon. This goes beyond the question of whether auxiliary *do* is a lexical item that undergoes Merge or not. The question can be divided into two parts, one dealing with auxiliaries (excepting *do*), and the other with main verbs. With modals and aspectual auxiliaries, it is assumed that they are fully inflected in the lexicon. For example, the perfective auxiliary *have* will have its thirteen morphologically distinct forms listed, as given in the representation (37).

(37)

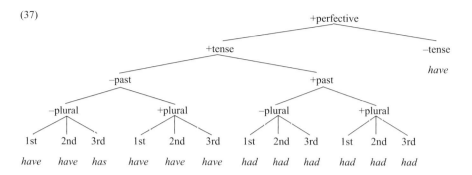

This paradigm involves considerable **syncretism**, where morphologically distinct items share the same PF. The paradigm for progressive *be* would include one additional form for the past participle *been*. With main verbs, the lexicon contains at least the bare form along with the past and present participles. For example, the lexical entry for the verb "build" will contain *build* (the bare form as in *to build*), *built* (the past participle as in *has built*), and *building* (the present participle as in *is building*).

The question that remains is whether the finite forms of "build" (i.e. the six present tense forms and the six past tense forms) are also represented in the lexicon in a form that undergoes Merge like the nonfinite forms. In Chapter 5, where the phrase structure of clauses was first explicated, a fully inflected finite main verb was merged as the head of VP and the TP structure of a clause with such a finite main verb resulted from merging the tense and φ features of V as a T with VP. As will be discussed below, this analysis creates a problem for an account of auxiliary *do*.

Alternatively, the complex of tense and φ features could occur in the lexicon as a separate lexical item, a morphological affix that merges directly as T. Its VP complement would be headed by the bare form of V; presumably this affix selects the bare form of V because under this analysis the lexicon would not contain inflected finite verbs. The feature complex in T would adjoin to V, an operation called **affix-hopping**. Merging a copy of the tense and agreement features of V into the T position is essentially affix-hopping in reverse, call it **affix-raising**.

One way to evaluate the affix-raising versus the affix-hopping analyses is to consider the LF representations of a declarative sentence with a finite main verb and its corresponding yes/no question. To meet the LF Representation Criterion (LFRC), the declarative TP must have the same structure as a complement of C ? in the interrogative.

Consider the pair of examples (38).

(38)   a.   He builds houses.
          b.   Does he build houses?

Under the affix-raising analysis, the LF representation of the declarative (38a) would be (39), where **F** stands for the feature complex [[−past], 3rd person, [−plural]].

(39) $[_{TP}$ (he) $[_T$ **F** $[_{VP}$ (build)+**F** (houses)]]]]

The two copies of **F** form a nontrivial chain, so **F** is only interpreted once. The corresponding LF representation of the interrogative is (40).

(40) $[_{CP}$? $[_{TP}$ 'he' $[_T$ **F** $[_{VP}$ 'build'+**F** 'houses']]]]]

Therefore the affix-raising analysis meets the LFRC.

In contrast, the LF representation of (38a) under the affix-hopping analysis would be (41), the difference being that (41) contains a trivial affix chain whereas (39) does not.

(41) $[_{TP}$ 'he' $[_T$ **F** $[_{VP}$ 'build' 'houses']]]

The LF representation for the corresponding interrogative (38b) under the affix-hopping analysis is (42).

(42) $[_{CP}$? $[_{TP}$ 'he' $[_T$ **F** $[_{VP}$ 'build' 'houses']]]]

Here too the LFRC is satisfied.

Both analyses meet the LFRC under the assumption that auxiliary *do* is not merged as a lexical auxiliary, but rather is added to the derivation after Spell-Out by a separate operation called **do-Support** that applies on the PF side. This operation adjoins an uninflected auxiliary *do* to the feature complex **F**. To derive the actual phonetic form, *do* + **F** would be assigned the appropriate phonetic features – e.g. *does* for *do*+[−past, 3rd person, −plural] and *do* for [−past, 1st person, +plural]. In contrast to Merge and Delete, this operation is language-specific.

Interestingly, the alternative analysis based on (36a), where the actual phonetic forms of *do* are merged directly into the derivation, fails the LFRC. Under this analysis, (38b) will have the LF representation (42) because at LF *does*, which is merged directly as T, would have no phonetic features and therefore would be just **F**. Furthermore this auxiliary *do* selects the bare form of V. In contrast, the corresponding declarative (38a) would have the LF representation (39). As a result, the TPs in the two LF representations would not match.

Under the *do*-Support analysis based on (36b), auxiliary *do* does not directly select the bare form of a main V. It occurs with the bare form of the main verb for different reasons depending on whether main verbs are fully inflected in the lexicon or not. If finite main verbs are fully inflected in the lexicon, then the interrogative (38b) involves (40), and at PF the copy of **F** attached to V is deleted via chain reduction. In this derivation, the main verb is not the bare form, but only comes to resemble it because its tense and agreement features do not contribute to its pronunciation. In contrast, if **F** constitutes a lexical item that is independent from the main verb, then inflected main verbs are not in the lexicon, only their bare forms and participial forms. In this case, **F** selects the bare form of V, the situation in (42). In either case, the LFRC is met.

As in previous chapters, elements that are syntactically present but silent at PF are subject to deletion at PF. One form of deletion involves the elimination of nontrivial chains at PF (**chain reduction**) on the grounds that such objects are uninterpretable at the PF interface (thus superfluous and therefore in violation of Full Interpretation). Assume that this also holds for affix chains. Thus the representation of (38a) after Spell-Out will involve a nontrivial chain {**s**, **s**}, where **s** now stands for the finite inflection of *builds*, including its phonetic features.

(43)   [$_{TP}$ he [$_T$ **s** [$_{VP}$ builds houses]]]

Deletion would apply to the affix in T, yielding (44).

(44)   [$_{TP}$ he [$_T$ **s** [$_{VP}$ builds houses]]]

What happens in the corresponding negative sentence is that the affix on the verb is deleted, as illustrated in (45).

(45)   [$_{TP}$ he [$_T$ **s** [$_{VP}$ not builds houses]]]

At this point, the only inflectional affix **s** in the PF representation is free, and therefore *do*-Support must apply to save the derivation from violating the NFAC. With nontrivial affix chains, affixes adjacent to the verb are deleted if there is another affix that is nonadjacent. However, when both copies are adjacent to the verb (as in (43)), then the free affix in T is deleted. This generalizes to interrogatives (cf. the analysis of (38b)).

EXERCISE 7.4

Consider the analysis of the negative interrogative (i).

(i) Does he not build houses?

a. Identify the nontrivial affix chain in this example.
b. What operations apply in the derivation of (i) and in what order?
c. Show how *do*-Support could apply at two different points in the derivation.
d. Discuss how chain reduction via deletion applies, and in particular whether our discussion above generalizes to this case.

The alternation of *builds*/*build* makes it easy to visualize that a verbal affix with a specific phonetic form is actually moving from one syntactic position to another. However, with other verbs this is not at all apparent. With the past tense of "build" we have *built* vs. *build* and with the past tense of "buy" yields an alternation between *bought* and *buy*, as illustrated in the pair in (46).

(46)   a.   They bought a house.
         b.   Did they buy a house?

For these cases it is not possible to assign a specific PF to the inflectional feature complex of [[+past], ϕ] for verbs like *bought*.

We have been assuming that when a lexical item is inserted into a derivation by Merge, it comes with its full set of semantic, syntactic, and phonetic features.

But examples like (46) raise questions about this assumption. Consider, for example the derivation of the TP (46a). To create the TP, the inflectional features of *bought* are copied and merged with the VP *bought a house*. Because there is no obvious candidate for the PF of this feature complex, it seems likely that this complex has no PF. Whether chain reduction must occur in this case is an open question because without phonetic features the copy is automatically silent. Now consider the derivation of (46b). Up to a point, the derivation is the same as the one for (46a). After Spell-Out, the copy of the feature complex in T adjoins to ? in C. *do*-Support then renders C as *did*, which of course has a distinct PF. But in terms of a PF for the interrogative, this derivation would yield the deviant (47), not (46b).

(47)   *Did they bought a house?

This derivation makes the wrong prediction about the PF of the interrogative counterpart to (46a).

EXERCISE 7.5

One solution to this problem would be to treat all English verbs as if they were regular and thus had inflectional affixes with distinct (if not unique) PFs. Thus *bought* would be inserted as *buy + ed*. After chain reduction, a form that comes out as *buy+ed* would be replaced by its irregular form *bought*.

a. Discuss how this would work for the derivation of the following paradigms.

(i)   a.   He sells houses.
      b.   He does not sell houses.
      c.   Does he sell houses?
(ii) a.   They sold houses.
      b.   They do not sell houses.
      c.   Did they sell houses?

The problem with (47) is that the derivation allows the phonetic form associated with the relevant inflectional feature complex to be manifested twice, where it should only be expressed once. One solution to this problem is to restrict the way in which the inflectional feature complex can be assigned. Given that it is the derivation that determines whether a verb will ultimately express a tense inflection or not, main verbs should not be inflected for tense and agreement in the lexicon (as suggested above). Rather this feature complex constitutes its own lexical entry and is merged as T in a derivation. This proposal goes back to Chomsky's original analysis of the English verbal system in Chomsky 1957.

To see how this works, consider the derivation of a simple declarative sentence like (38a). The derivation of (38a) would require adjoining the tense and agreement feature complex **F** in T to the uninflected main verb *build*, via affix-hopping. The V and its affix are then rendered as the appropriate PF of the inflected form.

If the inflectional feature complex in T is a free affix, then affix-hopping is also motivated by the NFAC.

The derivation of the interrogative (38b) after T-to-C movement yields the structure (48).

(48) $[_{CP}$ [[−past], ϕ]+? $[_{TP}$ he $[_T$ [[−past], ϕ] $[_{VP}$ build houses]]]]

Here again the derivation produces multiple copies of the inflectional feature complex, which was the source of the problem of the deviant (47). Obviously there can only be one inflectional feature complex at PF. With (48) this can be accomplished via chain reduction. How chain reduction must function is determined by the NFAC, which forces the deletion of the feature complex in T. The feature complex in C will then undergo *do*-Support, yielding the desired result (38b).

EXERCISE 7.6

a. What would be the result if the feature complex in C deletes instead of the feature complex in T? Discuss derivational possibilities.

EXERCISE 7.7

a. Give the derivation for (46b).
b. Discuss how the analysis that yields this derivation prohibits the deviant (47).

Under the affix-hopping analysis, the derivation of negative sentences poses a potential problem. This can be illustrated with the following paradigm.

(49)   a.   She did not leave the room.
         b.   *She not left the room.
         c.   She quickly left the room.
         d.   *She did quickly leave the room.[4]

(49a) demonstrates that *do*-Support must apply to the inflectional feature complex in T, while (49b) shows that affix-hopping is inapplicable in such constructions. One might try to account for this difference in terms of adjacency, where the inflectional feature complex in T is adjacent to the main verb in the affirmative counterpart to (49a) (e.g. *She leaves on time*, using present tense to show the affix) in contrast to the negative (49a) where it is not. Under this analysis, (49b) couldn't be derived because the *not* would block affix-hopping. However, affix-hopping applies in the derivation of (49c) where the adverb *quickly* intervenes between T and V. And furthermore, *do*-Support cannot apply in such constructions. Note however, that the adverb *quickly* in (49c) can also occur at the right edge of the VP, as in (50).

(50)   She left the room quickly.

In contrast, *not* cannot similarly occur at the right edge of VP as (51) shows.

(51)   *She left the room not.

One possible explanation for the difference is that (49c) is derived from the structure underlying (50) so that affix-hopping applies prior to the operation that relocates the adverb at the left edge of VP.

EXERCISE 7.8

Another solution that has been proposed involves analyzing *not* as the head of NegP in which VP is a complement of *not*, as opposed to the adverb which is not the head of a phrase in which the VP is a complement. (See Haegeman and Zannutini 1991 for discussion.) Then affix-hopping could be blocked by the HMC. However, this is not viable given the assumption that the bare form of V is selected by T, in which case VP not NegP must be its complement.

a. If NegP were the complement of auxiliary *do*, which of the following examples are problematic?

(i)   a.   *She did not leaving the room.
      b.   *He did not stolen the book.
(ii) a.   She is not leaving the room.
      b.   He has not stolen the book.

EXERCISE 7.9

a. Discuss the syntactic derivations of the following declarative and its corresponding yes/no interrogative using the affix-hopping and *do*-Support analysis.

(i)   a.   John left.
      b.   Did John leave?

b. How can this analysis be extended to account for the following paradigm involving negation?

(ii) a.   John did not leave.
      b.   *John not left.

c. Discuss the derivations of the following. Be explicit about what you assume to be the source of the contraction *didn't*.

(iii) a.   Did John not leave?
      b.   John didn't leave.
      c.   Didn't John leave?

d. How can the deviance of the following examples be accounted for?

(iv) a.   *Did not John leave?
      b.   *Did John n't leave?

Let us turn finally to how an analysis involving *do*-Support accounts for the nonoccurrence of auxiliary *do* with the bare form of the aspectual auxiliaries, as illustrated in (35). Given **F** as a lexical item, there is the possibility that **F** and a bare aspectual auxiliary could be merged. If *do*-Support applies to **F**, then the deviant construction is derived. However, the lexical item **F** constitutes a head T and therefore occurs in a selectional relation with the head of its complement VP. If **F** selects only main verbs and specifically not aspectual auxiliaries, then auxiliary *do* cannot take a complement VP headed by an aspectual auxiliary. It follows from this analysis that the finite forms of the aspectual auxiliaries must be merged fully inflected – hence no affix-hopping of **F** could apply in their derivation. Furthermore, under this analysis there is no motivation for merging a finite aspectual auxiliary as V and then merging a copy as T. Instead, a finite aspectual auxiliary is merged directly as T. Thus there is no way the lexicon and the computational system can produce the co-occurrence of auxiliary *do* and an aspectual auxiliary.

7.3   VSO languages

In the Celtic languages (e.g. Irish, Welsh, and Breton) the word order in simple declarative sentences involves a finite verb preceding both the subject and the object, a word order that is designated as VSO. For example, Welsh contains the following examples (from R. Borsely, M. Tallerman, and D. Willis 2007, p. 33; (59) is courtesy of D. Willis (personal communication)).

(52)   a.   Gwellodd Rhiannon ddraig.
             see-PAST-3s Rhiannon dragon
             "Rhiannon saw the dragon"
        b.   Mae Rhiannon wedi gweld ddraig.
             be-PRES-3s Rhiannon PERF see-INF dragon
             "Rhiannon has seen a dragon"

Given the general syntactic analysis developed in this and the previous chapters, it would appear that these examples involve some form of head movement.

Consider first the analysis of (52a). The main verb is separated from its complement object *ddraig* by the subject *Rhiannon*. Assuming that at some level of analysis the main verb and its object form a VP constituent because Merge applies first to a head and its complements, then (52a) cannot be simply the result of merging the verb once in the derivation – i.e. with its complement NP. Furthermore, (52b) shows clearly that the main verb can take a complement object to its right (i.e. in the phrase *gweld ddraig*), hence VP is head-initial in Welsh. Given that a head merges first with its complement, the derivation of (52a) would have to involve a corresponding VP with the structure (53).

(53)   [VP gwellodd ddraig]

Taking the finite clause (52b) to be structurally a TP (as in other languages), then (53) would be the complement of a T element, as in (54).

(54)   [T T [VP gwellodd ddraig]]

How (54) is mapped onto (52a) now crucially concerns where the subject *Rhiannon* is merged into the derivation. If the subject is merged as Spec-TP, then the main verb must move to some head position outside TP to generate (52a). Alternatively, the subject could be merged inside VP – what is called the **VP-internal subject hypothesis**, yielding the structure (55).

(55)   [$_T$ T [$_{VP}$ Rhiannon [$_V$ gwellodd ddraig]]]

Given (55), (52a) could be derived from a simple V-to-T movement.[5]

   (52b) shows that the VP-internal subject hypothesis is not enough to account for the position of subjects in Welsh. Under this hypothesis, the derivation of (52b) would involve the VP (56) where the subject is adjacent to the main verb, which it isn't in (52b).

(56)   [$_{VP}$ Rhiannon [$_V$ gweld ddraig]]

Rather the subject occurs in PF adjacent to the verbal element that bears the finite tense and agreement features. (52b) contains three verbal elements, *mae*, *wedi*, and *gweld* (the main verb). The perfective auxiliary *wedi* selects the infinitival (bare) form of the main verb. The perfective auxiliary is itself selected by the finite auxiliary *mae*. Thus each verbal element is the head of a phrase and at some level of analysis expresses the appropriate head-complement relations, as in (57) which leaves aside the position of the subject.

(57)   [$_{TP}$ mae [$_{VP}$ wedi [$_{VP}$ gweld ddraig]]]

The agreement features on the verbal element *mae* must match those on the subject, presumably as a form of Spec-head agreement. Under this analysis, the finite verbal element would be merged as T and the subject as its Spec, yielding (58).

(58)   [$_{TP}$ Rhiannon [$_T$ mae [$_{VP}$ wedi [$_{VP}$ gweld ddraig]]]]

Given this, then the derivation of (52b) from (58) would have to involve a movement from T to some head outside of TP.

   If the subject *Rhiannon* in (52) occupies Spec-TP, then the derivation of (52b) could involve a simple T-to-C movement. If this analysis is correct, then the simplest analysis of (52a), which contains only a finite main verb, would be to posit V-to-C movement as in Russian. However this won't suffice because a VSO structure can occur as the complement of an overt C. This is illustrated in (59), where the overt C *y* is possible, but not normally present in spoken Welsh (D. Willis, personal communication).

(59)   Dwi'n meddwl (y) bydd Rhiannon yn gweld draig.
            be.pres.1s PROG think.INF (C) be.FUT.3S Rhiannon PROG see.INF dragon
            "I think (that) Rhiannon will be seeing a dragon"

The clausal complement of C *y* is a VSO construction, where the finite verbal auxiliary *bydd* precedes the subject *Rhiannon*, which is followed by the object *draig*. The matrix clause main verb *meddwl* takes a CP complement, the matrix VP having a structure (60).

(60)   [$_{VP}$ meddwl [$_{CP}$ y [$_\alpha$ bydd [$_{\beta P}$ Rhiannon [$_\beta$ (bydd) [$_{VP}$ yn [$_{VP}$ gweld draig]]]]]]]

(59) demonstrates that the finite V *bydd* occurs in a head position between C and the subject, the head of α in (60). Furthermore, it has presumably been displaced from a head position to the right of the subject, the head of β in (60). The subject *Rhiannon* would be in Spec-βP, and in this position establishes a spec-head agreement relation with the finite V.

This analysis raises the question of the labels of the heads α and β in (60). One solution involves a **split-inflection analysis** where T is split into two functional heads, one solely for tense and the other solely for agreement, the two sets of features that occupy T in our previous analyses of clause structure. Given that spec-head agreement is verified in βP, it is natural to take β as a functional category AGR (for agreement) and α as the category T, now designating tense and not tense plus agreement features. Whether the split inflection analysis is sufficient to account for VSO syntax generally (e.g. in other VSO languages) remains to be determined. And how the split inflection analysis applies to the English verbal system is also a topic for further discussion.

7.4   Summary

The architecture of the system of grammar presented in this chapter is as follows:

a.   Mechanisms of the computational system:
   i.   Head movement
   ii. affix-hopping
   iii. *do*-Support

b.   Constraints on derivations and representations:
   i.   No Free Affix Condition
   ii. Head Movement Constraint

This chapter has been concerned with the analysis of the system of verbal morphology, primarily in English but with some attention to French and Russian, as it involves the derivation of yes/no interrogatives. Applying the LF Representation Criterion to the relation between direct and indirect yes/no questions in English results in an analysis of head movement (T-to-C) after Spell-Out on the PF side. This operation appears to be morphological in character unlike Merge. This analysis is supported by data from Russian. The movement involved is motivated by a No Free Affix Condition, which will be violated unless the movement from T-to-C occurs.

In English, main verbs cannot undergo movement to C. One possible analysis of this fact involves the Head Movement Constraint, which blocks direct movement from T-to-C. This presupposes that movement from V-to-T is also blocked. However, in French, the position of a manner adverb between a verb and its object in PF argues for movement of a main verb from V-to-T so that the order of Merge not be violated. French also allows a main verb to move to C in yes/no questions. However, Russian, which also allows main verb movement to C in yes/no questions, does not have the same distribution of manner adverbs as French and thus no empirical evidence to support movement from V-to-T. This undermines the Head Movement Constraint. The fact that only finite verbal forms move to C in yes/no questions can be accounted for by conceiving movement in terms of attraction where a probe, the interrogative C, attracts a goal, a finite verbal element, which would only occur in T. This further undermines the Head Movement Constraint analysis.

Because main verbs in English are inert with respect to head movement, the affixal analysis of covert yes/no interrogative C requires a special strategy to avoid violating the No Free Affix Condition. This requires that the tense and agreement features on main verbs enter the derivation as a separate element in T. If the derivation does not involve covert interrogative C (in direct yes/no questions), then this feature complex attaches to the main verb (affix-hopping). If the derivation contains a covert interrogative C in the root clause, these features attach to C via T-to-C movement and then this complex must be adjoined to an auxiliary *do* via a language specific rule of *do*-Support to avoid a violation of the No Free Affix Condition.

The third and final section of this chapter extends the analysis of head movement to VSO languages, where a finite main verb can be displaced out of VP to a position to the left of a subject. A preliminary analysis of Welsh suggests that this cannot be completely explained under the VP-internal Subject Hypothesis. The fact that a VSO construction can occur as the complement of an overt C suggests instead that VSO languages might require a split-inflection analysis where T is analyzed as two distinct functional heads, one for tense and the other for agreement.

Bibliographical notes

Head movement, affix-hopping, and *do*-Support have a long and rich history in syntactic theory, starting with Chomsky's *Logical Structure of Linguistic Theory* 1955–56 (published in 1975) but mostly known via Chomsky 1957. For a detailed commentary on the history of this analysis up through the 1990s, see Lasnik 2000, and for some critical discussion and an analysis of the English verbal system that attempts to eliminate the rules of affix-hopping and *do*-Support, see Freidin 2004. For more recent analysis of head movement, see Roberts 2010. The No Free Affix Condition is first proposed in Lasnik 1981. The Head Movement Constraint originates in Travis 1984. The VP-internal subject hypothesis originates from Stowell 1978 and is developed in Manzini 1983 and Fukui

1986 and Speas 1986; see Takano 1995 for discussion of how this hypothesis can be used to account for some anaphor/antecedent relations.

See Pollock 1989 for the original proposal of a split inflection analysis of clauses and Chomsky 1991 for further discussion and modification. For empirical evidence that T takes AgrP as a complement, see Roberts 2000 and Tallerman 2005. See also Koizumi 1995 and 2006, which propose a split VP analysis that eliminates the need for VP-internal subjects.

8   Wh-movement

Chapter 7 used the analysis of yes/no interrogatives to establish that certain root clauses are CP structures. This chapter extends this analysis to another class of interrogative constructions, those involving interrogative pronouns (e.g. *who* and *what*) and related questions words like *where*, *when*, *why*, *how*, and *which*.

8.1   The displacement of wh-phrases

The comparison of declarative sentences and their corresponding yes/no interrogatives leads to the hypothesis that the latter are CP structures where the clause-initial finite verbal element occurs in the C position.

(1)   a.   My student is reading the textbook.
          b.   Is my student reading the textbook?

There is another interrogative construction that corresponds to the declarative (1a). This involves replacing one of the NPs in (1a) with an interrogative pronoun, yielding for example the question (2).

(2)   What is my student reading?

Although the interrogative pronoun *what* is pronounced at the beginning of the clause, it is interpreted as the object of the verb *reading*. Thus (2) involves displacement. Displacement involving interrogative lexical items in this way is generally referred to as **wh-movement**. Clauses like (2) are called **wh-questions**, in contrast to yes/no questions like (1b).

Both (1b) and (2) are direct questions. Like yes/no questions, wh-questions also have an indirect question counterpart where the interrogative clause is embedded as a complement of some lexical head, for example a V as in (3a) or an A as in (3b).

(3)   a.   I wonder what my student is reading.
          b.   It is unclear what my student is reading.

The direct wh-question differs from its indirect counterpart in that the former also involves T-to-C movement whereas the latter does not. It is generally assumed that the T-to-C movement that occurs in direct wh-questions is the same syntactic operation that occurs in direct yes/no questions. If so, then presumably it too occurs after Spell-Out as discussed in Chapter 7.

The derivation of (2) would then start with the merger of the V *reading* and the interrogative pronoun *what* to form a VP. This VP is then merged with the T element *is* forming a T phrase, which is then merged with the subject *my student* (the pronoun and noun having merged independently to form a NP) to form a larger T phrase. This TP would be the complement of a covert [+Q] C. This C phrase would then merge with *what* to produce the root CP, as given in (4).

(4)   [$_{CP}$ what [$_C$ [+Q] [$_{TP}$ [$_{NP}$ my student] [$_T$ is [$_{VP}$ reading what]]]]]

After Spell-Out, (4) maps onto (5), where T *is* combines with [+Q] to form a viable morphological unit (an affix bound to a root) and the two nontrivial chains created are reduced to trivial chains via deletion.

(5)   [$_{CP}$ what [$_C$ is+[+Q] [$_{TP}$ [$_{NP}$ my student] [$_T$ ~~is~~ [$_{VP}$ reading ~~what~~]]]]]

The PF representation of (2) that is given in (5) is relatively straightforward because it is based on the occurrence of overt elements, as is its relation to the PF representation of the corresponding yes/no question (1b).

   The LF representation of (2) is a more complicated issue. As noted above, the interpretation of the interrogative pronoun *what* is linked to the object of the V *reading*. In effect, the θ-role that *reading* assigns to its NP object is linked to *what*. But there must be more to the LF representation of (2) to distinguish it from the interpretation of the yes/no interrogative (1b) because the wh-question is not (also) a yes/no question. The LF representation of (1b) is (6) under the analysis in the previous chapter.

(6)   [$_{CP}$? [$_{TP}$ [$_{NP}$ my student] [$_T$ is [$_{VP}$ reading [$_{NP}$ the textbook]]]]]

The C ? is taken to be a question operator that gives the "yes/no" interpretation. However, given that the LF representation of (2) would involve a structure like (6), but where the interrogative *what* replaces the NP *the textbook* as in (7), the [+Q] in the LF representation of (2) cannot be interpreted as "yes/no."

(7)   [$_{CP}$ [+Q] [$_{TP}$ [$_{NP}$ my student] [$_T$ is [$_{VP}$ reading what]]]]

Moreover, as discussed below, the LF representation of (2) involves more than (7) provides.

   If the displacement of the interrogative pronoun in (2) contributes to the LF representation of the question, then the question operator C is no longer a focal point for the difference in interpretation between yes/no questions and their wh-question counterparts. That is, wh-movement applies before Spell-Out, in contrast to T-to-C movement. Thus the LF representation of (2) would involve (8) rather than (7).

(8)   [$_{CP}$ what [$_C$ [+Q] [$_{TP}$ [$_{NP}$ my student] [$_T$ is [$_{VP}$ reading what]]]]]

[+Q] in (8) represents a question operator, but is not interpreted "yes/no." In what follows, the notation ?? will be used for the wh-question operator to constrast with ?, the yes/no question operator.

The LF representation of the wh-question can be further articulated by spelling out the interpretation of the interrogative pronoun *what*. What this involves can be seen more easily by considering first the more complicated interrogative phrase in (9).

(9)   which book on the course reading list

Replacing *what* in (2) with (9) results in a question (10) which asks about a specific book on the course reading list.

(10)   Which book on the course reading list is my student reading?

(9) can be interpreted as a kind of quantificational expression (11), which binds a variable, so that its interpretation with respect to (10) can be expressed as (12).

(11)   (for which x, x = a book on the course reading list)
(12)   [$_{CP}$ (for which x, x = a book on the course reading list) [$_C$?? [$_{TP}$ [$_{NP}$ my student] [$_T$ is [$_{VP}$ reading x]]]]]

Under this analysis, x in VP is a variable bound by the quantificational expression (11), which occupies the Spec position of the root CP. The quantificational expression limits the domain over which the variable ranges by restricting it to "a book on the course reading list". Given this analysis, wh-questions differ from yes/no questions in that they involve quantifier/variable constructions at LF, whereas yes/no questions do not.

Under this analysis, the interrogative pronoun *what* would be interpreted roughly as a quantificational expression "for which x, x = an inanimate object." The LF representation of (2) would therefore be (13), lexical items in single quotes are used to represent interpretations without phonetic features.

(13)   [$_{CP}$ (for which x, x = an inanimate object) [$_C$?? [$_{TP}$ [$_{NP}$ 'my' 'student'] [$_T$ 'is' [$_{VP}$ 'reading' x]]]]]

The derivation of this LF representation involves two steps: (1) the replacement of the wh-phrase in the VP, the position to which a θ-role is assigned, with a variable, and (2) the replacement of the wh-phrase in Spec-CP with its interpretation as a quantificational expression.

This analysis generalizes to the other wh-questions that can be derived from (1a) by substituting an interrogative pronoun for the subject – in this case, *who* for *my student*, yielding (14).

(14)   Who is reading the textbook?

Interpreting *who* as (15) yields the LF representation (16) for (14).

(15)   (for which x, x = a person/persons)
(16)   [$_{CP}$ (for which x, x = a person/persons) [$_C$?? [$_{TP}$ x [$_T$ 'is' [$_{VP}$ 'reading' [$_{NP}$ 'the' 'textbook']]]]]]

If the LF representation (16) is derived in the same way that (13) is derived, then the syntactic derivation of (14) will also involve wh-movement to Spec-CP before Spell-Out even though this movement doesn't affect the linear order of overt elements and is therefore "string vacuous."

The interrogative pronouns *who* and *what* share an interpretive property that can be designated as a feature [+wh]. This feature determines the interpretation "for which *x*," the restriction on the quantifier follows from the inherent interpretive features of *who* vs. *what* – i.e. roughly person vs. non-person. In the case of the interrogative determiner *which* in (9), the restriction on the variable *x* is provided by the rest of the NP that *which* modifies as the Spec of NP. As Spec-NP, *which* c-commands the rest of the NP and therefore takes scope over this material (see the analysis of scope and c-command in Chapter 3).

As illustrated above, interrogative expressions come in two varieties. One is a bare interrogative pronoun that can occur by itself in clause-initial position (e.g. *who* and *what*); the other is an interrogative determiner that cannot (i.e. *which*, e.g. (10)). The interrogative construction (9) constitutes a NP whose lexical head is *book*. This phrase is standardly referred to as a **wh-phrase**. The interrogative pronouns *who* and *what* are also wh-phrases, albeit wh-phrases consisting of only a lexical head. When wh-movement involves a phrase containing more than the interrogative lexical element, the phenomenon is called **pied-piping** (from Ross 1967, after the famous fairy tale "The Pied Piper of Hamelin"). In (10) the string/phrase *book on the course reading list* is pied-piped along with *which* under wh-movement. See below for further discussion of this and related phenomena.

When a wh-phrase merges with a C-phrase headed by a question operator ?? (vs. the yes/no question operator ?), the operation establishes a syntactic relation with C. This relation has the general character of specifier-head to the extent that the wh-phrase in this CP position can only occur with certain C heads, as noted at the end of Chapter 5. As an illustration, consider the analysis of the following examples.

(17)   a.   Mary wondered whether Bill is hiding something.
        b.   *Mary wondered that Bill is hiding something.
        c.   Mary wondered what Bill is hiding.
(18)   a.   Mary thinks that Bill is hiding something.
        b.   *Mary thinks whether Bill is hiding something.
        c.   *Mary thinks what Bill is hiding.

The analysis developed at the end of Chapter 5 distinguishes the two overt Cs *whether* and *that* in terms of the feature [±Q], where the former is [+Q] and the latter is [−Q]. The verb *wonder* selects a [+Q] C, whereas the verb *think* selects a [−Q] C. The deviance of both (17b) and (18b) results from a selectional violation. In this way the selectional properties of a verb determine whether its clausal complement can be interrogative or declarative. The deviance of (18c), however, is not obviously the result of a selectional violation. If the covert C of the clausal complement is analyzed as [−Q], then this analysis of (18c) satisfies the selectional property of *think*. Under this analysis, (18c) can be analyzed as a spec-head agreement violation because the interrogative *what* is also marked [+Q] and thus conflicts with the [−Q] feature of the covert C. The alternative analysis of (18c), where C is analyzed as [+Q], would not constitute a spec-head agreement violation, but would violate selection. The same analysis holds for the case where the C is overt, as in (19).

(19)   *Mary thinks what that Bill is hiding.

In contrast, (17c) satisfies both the selection requirement of the matrix verb and spec-head agreement between the covert C and its specifier *what*. Under this analysis, wh-movement is, like the phrasal movements discussed in Chapter 6 (i.e. of NP and CP), movement to a Spec-position.

Exercise 8.1

a. Discuss whether the spec-head agreement analysis extends to the following case.

   (i)   *Mary wondered what whether Bill is hiding.

Consider the analysis of (ii).

   (ii) *Mary wondered what if Bill is hiding.

There are actually two distinct analyses that could be assigned to (ii). One is related to the analysis of (iii).

   (iii) What if Bill is hiding?

b. To determine the analysis of *what if*, compare (iii) to the complement CPs in (iv).

   (iv) a.   Mary wondered what Bill is hiding. [=(17c)]
        b.   Mary wondered if Bill is hiding.
        c.   What do the following examples tell us about the analysis of *what if* in (iii)?
   (v)   a.   *It is unclear what if Bill is hiding.
        b.   *Mary wondered what if Bill is lying.

Note that the deviance of (v.b) appears to lessen if the *what-if* clause is separated from *wondered* by a pause. However, a pause before the same clause in (v.a) has no corresponding effect.

Exercise 8.2

a. Discuss how the spec-head agreement analysis generalizes to complement CPs with an overt infinitival C (i.e. *for*).

   Although a verb like *think* cannot occur with an interrogative clausal complement, it is nonetheless possible for an interrogative wh-phrase to be merged as part of the clausal complement of *think*. When this happens, the wh-phrase is normally moved to the Spec-CP of the matrix clause in which the complement clause is embedded. Compare, for example, (20) with the deviant (18c).

(20)   What will Mary think Bill is hiding?

The derivation of (20) involves the merger of the interrogative pronoun *what* with the main verb *hiding* as its complement object. The derivation of (20) involves a syntactic structure (21a) before Spell-Out, and at LF, the representation (21b).

(21)   a.   [$_{CP}$ what [$_C$?? [$_{TP}$ Mary [$_T$ will [$_{VP}$ think [$_{CP}$ [–Q] [$_{TP}$ Bill [$_T$ is
              [$_{VP}$ hiding what]]]]]]]]]

        b.   [$_{CP}$ (for which x, x = a thing) [$_C$?? [$_{TP}$ 'Mary' [$_T$ 'will'
              [$_{VP}$ 'think' [$_{CP}$ [–Q] [$_{TP}$ 'Bill' [$_T$ 'is' [$_{VP}$ 'hiding' x]]]]]]]]]

In this way, selection constrains wh-movement. The [–Q] C in this construction prohibits intra-clausal movement as in the deviant (18c), leaving inter-clausal wh-movement (e.g. (20)) as the only viable possibility.

In contrast, the verb *ask*, which like *wonder* (cf. (17)) takes an indirect question complement, blocks inter-clausal wh-movement and requires intra-clausal wh-movement within its clausal complement. Compare, for example, (22) and (23).

(22)   Bill asked them which books Mary had ordered.

(23)   *Which books did Bill ask them Mary had ordered?

The deviance of (23) appears to be connected to the selectional requirement of *ask*. That requirement is satisfied either by an overt [+Q] C (*if* or *whether*) or an overt wh-phrase in Spec-CP. What is excluded is the case where the C is covert and there is no overt wh-phrase in Spec-CP of the complement clause. Exactly why (23) is prohibited in grammatical terms depends on how the grammar assigns a syntactic representation to (23).

Exercise 8.3

Consider the following paradigm in addition to (22–23):

    (i)   *Bill asked them which books whether Mary had ordered.
    (ii)   *?Which books did Bill ask them whether Mary had ordered?
    (iii) *Which books did Bill ask them that Mary had ordered?

a.   What would be the syntactic representation of (i) at Spell-Out?
b.   What accounts for the deviance of (i)?
c.   What accounts for the deviance of (iii)?
d.   (ii) seems to some speakers to be less deviant than (i) and (iii). Do you agree? What accounts for the relative deviance of (ii)?
e.   Given the analysis developed in (a–d), how might it account for the deviance of (23)?

In addition to predicates that either require or prohibit indirect question complements, there are verbs and predicate adjectives that select either a [+Q] or [–Q] C – *know* and *unclear* for example.

(24)   a.   Bill knows that Mary bought an expensive painting.
          b.   Bills knows whether Mary bought an expensive painting.
          c.   Bill knows what Mary bought.

(25)   a.   It is unclear that George will meet Susan.
          b.   It is unclear whether George will meet Susan.
          c.   It is unclear who George will meet.

In both (24c) and (25c) the wh-phrase is interpreted as the object of the clausal complement main verb (i.e. *bought* and *meet*). Under the analysis of the clausal complement C as [–Q], the wh-phrases must move inter-clausally, yielding (26).

(26) a.   What does Bill know (that) Mary bought?
      b.   Who is it unclear (that) George will meet?

The syntactic analysis of inter-clausal wh-movement is discussed in the next section.

The discussion above illustrates how selectional properties determine the possibilities for wh-movement in languages like English, where a wh-phrase is displaced to the clause-initial position, Spec-CP. There are also languages that have no wh-phrase displacement in wh-questions. Instead, the interrogative wh-phrase is pronounced in the syntactic position in which it is first merged in a derivation. This phenomenon is referred to as **wh-phrase *in situ*** (Latin for "in the original position," literally "in place"). Chinese and Japanese are wh-*in situ* languages.

Like English, Chinese has SVO word order, as illustrated in the simple sentence (27). (The following data is from Huang 1982 and Jim Huang (personal communication)).

(27)   ni xihuan Lisi
          you like Lisi
          "you like Lisi"

Replacing the name *Lisi* with an interrogative pronoun *shei* ("who") yields (28a) but not (28b).

(28) a.   ni xihuan shei
           you like who
           "who do you like?"
      b.   *shei ni xihuan
           who you like

This demonstrates that Chinese does not have wh-phrase displacement in wh-questions.

(28) shows what the PF representation of the Chinese sentence corresponding to the English question "who do you like?" must be. Yet this is only one piece of evidence for determining the syntactic derivation of wh-questions like (28a). Given the three part architecture of derivations in (29), the LF representations of wh-questions also play a role in determining the syntactic derivation for these constructions.

(29)

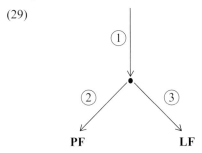

For the LF representation of the Chinese wh-question (28a), the null hypothesis would be that the interpretation of *shei* ("who") in Chinese is identical to the corresponding interrogative pronoun *who* in English; therefore the LF representation of the Chinese interrogative pronoun will also be a quantificational expression that binds a variable. In effect, the LF representations of the Chinese wh-question (28a) and its English counterpart will be identical – i.e. (30), because Full Interpretation guarantees the absence of phonetic features in LF representations.

(30) $[_{CP}$ (for which x, x = a person/persons) $[_C$?? $[_{TP}$ 'you' $[_T$ T $[_{VP}$ 'like' $x]]]]]$

Single quotes in (30) are used to indicate semantic interpretations without phonetic features. In English the LF representation (30) is derived via wh-movement that happens to be overt at PF; therefore it must occur in part 1 of (29). In Chinese (30) also implicates wh-movement, but in this case there is no PF effect and hence wh-movement in Chinese is covert. These are minimal assumptions.

Granting that the derivation of wh-questions in wh-*in situ* languages involves covert wh-movement, there are at least two options for deriving their PF and LF representations. Under one option, the absence of wh-displacement in PF reflects the absence of any wh-movement – overt or covert – in part 1. Under this analysis, the derivation of LF representation (30) for the Chinese example (28a) would require that wh-movement in Chinese occurs only after Spell-Out and only in part 3. In this way, the interpretation of wh-questions in wh-*in situ* languages argues that wh-movement actually applies in these languages, but only covertly in that part of the derivation that does not affect PF, i.e. in part 3.

This option will be problematic for the derivation of indirect wh-questions in wh-*in situ* languages. Such question constructions are embedded structures; thus wh-movement after Spell-Out would violate the No Tampering Condition because it would change the internal syntactic structure of the syntactic element that merges with the wh-phrase. This doesn't happen with wh-movement in the root clause.

The other derivational option for wh-questions in wh-*in situ* languages involves the application of wh-movement in part 1 of the derivation, just as in languages with overt wh-movement (i.e. wh-displacement). Then the derivation of (28a) at Spell-Out would yield (31).

(31) $[_{CP}$ shei $[_C$?? $[_{TP}$ ni $[_T$ T $[_{VP}$ xihuan shei $]]]]]$

In order to derive the appropriate PF for (28a), chain reduction would require the deletion of the interrogative pronoun in Spec-CP, shown in (32).

(32) $[_{CP}$ ~~shei~~ $[_C$?? $[_{TP}$ ni $[_T$ T $[_{VP}$ xihuan shei $]]]]]$

Thus in Chinese, the *in situ* copy is retained in PF representation, whereas in English this copy is eliminated. The difference between wh-displacement and wh-*in situ* is relegated to a difference in PF options – i.e. which elements of a wh-chain are deleted under chain reduction.

This analysis shows how the syntactic derivation of linguistic expressions, part 1 in particular, is determined by both PF and LF requirements – i.e., what is overt and thus perceived directly for PF and equally by what is required for interpretation that goes beyond the physical signal. This analysis of Chinese wh-questions, which is motivated in part by the LF representation criterion discussed in the previous chapter, provides further evidence that syntax is not WYSIWYG.

The interpretation of Chinese interrogative pronouns in complex sentences provides further evidence for a wh-movement analysis of a wh-*in situ* language. Consider the Chinese verb for "remember," which like its English counterpart can take either an indirect wh-question or a finite declarative clause as a complement. In English, the two possibilities have different word orders, as illustrated in (33).

(33)   a.   Bill remembers what Mary bought.
        b.   What does Bill remember that Mary bought.

In both examples, *what* is construed as the object of *bought*. The indirect wh-question complement in (33a) involves intra-clausal wh-movement, in contrast to the inter-clausal wh-movement in (33b), which is a direct wh-question where the clausal complement of the main clause verb *remember* is interpreted as a finite declarative subordinate clause. In Chinese, because there is no overt wh-movement, the counterpart to (33a) would be (34).

(34)   Bill jide Mary mai-le shenme.
        Bill remembers Mary bought what

For the same reason, (34) is also the Chinese counterpart to (33b). Nonetheless, given that (33) has two distinct interpretations, there must be two distinct and unambiguous LF representations that map onto a single PF representation for (34). There are two ways to disambiguate (34). If either the wh-phrase is stressed or the question particle *ne* occurs at the end of the sentence, then the direct question is the only interpretation possible because the question particle cannot occur in a subordinate clause.

The ambiguity of (34) follows automatically under the wh-movement analysis of simple wh-questions proposed above. Under this analysis (34) associates with the two distinct syntactic structures given in (35), where C in (35a) is [-Q].

(35)   a.   [$_{CP}$ shenme [$_C$?? [$_{TP}$ Bill [$_T$ T [$_{VP}$ jide [$_{CP}$ C [$_{TP}$ Mary [$_T$ T [$_{VP}$ mai-le
              shenme]]]]]]]]]]
        b.   [$_{TP}$ Bill [$_T$ T [$_{VP}$ jide [$_{CP}$ shenme [$_C$?? [$_{TP}$ Mary [$_T$ T [$_{VP}$ mai-le
              shenme]]]]]]]]]]

Interpretation of the interrogative pronoun *shenme* "what" in (35) as a quantificational expression, which includes the replacement of the copy in the complement VP with a variable, yields the LF representations (36).

(36)   a.   [$_{CP}$ (for which x, x = a thing) [$_C$?? [$_{TP}$ 'Bill' [$_T$ T
              [$_{VP}$ 'jide' [$_{CP}$ C [$_{TP}$ 'Mary' [$_T$ T [$_{VP}$ 'mai-le' x]]]]]]]]]]]

    b.   [$_{TP}$ 'Bill' [$_T$ T [$_{VP}$ 'jide' [$_{CP}$ (for which x, x = thing)
          [$_C$?? [$_{TP}$ 'Mary' [$_T$ T [$_{VP}$ 'mai-le' x]]]]]]]]

Ignoring the phonetic features of lexical items, which don't exist in LF representations, these LF representations in (36) will also match the corresponding English examples in (33).

Exercise 8.4

Now consider the Chinese counterpart to a verb like *ask*, which in English requires an indirect question complement.

    (i)   Bill wen wo Mary mai-le shenme.
         Bill ask me Mary bought what

(i) has an interpretation (ii.a), but cannot be interpreted as (ii.b), a direct question.

    (ii) a.   "Bill asked me what Mary bought"
        b.   "what did Bill ask me that Mary bought?"

a.   Give the LF representation for (i) under the correct interpretation (ii.a).
b.   What would the LF representation of (i) be under the incorrect interpretation (ii.b)?
c.   Before Spell-Out, how do the syntactic derivations of these two LF representations differ?
d.   How are these two distinct syntactic derivations mapped onto the same PF representation (i.e., what happens to each after Spell-Out)?
e.   What prohibits interpretation (ii.b)?
f.   How does this analysis relate to the corresponding sentences in English?

The Chinese counterpart to the English verb *believe* yields a similar phenomenon. Thus consider (iii).

    (iii) Bill xiangxin Mary mai-le shenme
         Bill believe Mary bought what

In contrast with the Chinese verb *wen* "ask," *xiangxin* "believe" cannot take an interrogative clause complement. Therefore (iii) can only be interpreted as a direct wh-question.

g.   Using (a–f) above as a guide, provide a detailed analysis of (iii).

    The analysis of Chinese wh-questions reveals how there can be significant mismatches between PF and LF representations of sentences. wh in English wh-questions, in contrast (cf. for example (10) and (12)), shows how PF representation can mirror LF representation. Nonetheless, this asymmetry between PF and LF representations is not restricted to wh-*in situ* languages; it occurs in English as well.

    Consider the analysis of a wh-questions containing the genitive form of "who" – i.e. *whose* as in (37).

(37)   Whose proposal will she support?

The syntactic derivation of (37) involves wh-movement: the wh-NP *whose proposal* is first merged as the complement object of *support* and then it is merged as the

Spec-CP of the root clause. The second merger of the wh-NP constitutes an instance of pied-piping. At Spell-Out (37) has the syntactic structure (38a) which is then converted to the PF representation (38b) after Spell-Out via the T-to-C movement of the modal auxiliary *will* and two instances of chain reduction via deletion.

(38)   a. $[_{CP}$ $[_{NP}$ whose proposal] $[_C$?? $[_{TP}$ she $[_T$ will $[_{VP}$ support $[_{NP}$ whose proposal]]]]]]

          b. $[_{CP}$ $[_{NP}$ whose proposal] $[_C$ will + ?? $[_{TP}$ she $[_T$ ~~will~~ $[_{VP}$ support $[_{NP}$ ~~whose proposal~~]]]]]]

The displaced wh-phrase consists of a genitive pronoun *whose*, hence a N syntactically, and a noun *proposal*, which is syntactically the head of the wh-phrase even though it itself is not interrogative. However in terms of interpretation, the genitive form *whose* and its objective Case counterpart *who(m)* are identical; both are interpreted as the quantificational expression (39).

(39)   (for which x, x = a person/persons)

The LF representation of (40a) is (40b).

(40)   a.   Who(m) will she support?

          b. $[_{CP}$ (for which x, x = a person/persons) $[_C$?? $[_{TP}$ 'she' $[_T$ 'will' $[_{VP}$ 'support' x]]]]]

Similarly, the LF representation for (37) is (41).

(41) $[_{CP}$ (for which x, x = a person/persons) $[_C$?? $[_{TP}$ 'she' $[_T$ 'will' $[_{VP}$ 'support' $[_{NP}$ x's 'proposal']]]]]]

Although the N *proposal* is pronounced as part of the wh-phrase in Spec-CP, it is not interpreted as part of the quantificational expression at the LF interface, but rather in its original position as the complement of the V *support*. This phenomenon is often referred to as **reconstruction**.

Exercise 8.5

Although *which* and *whose* both induce pied-piping and thus manifest the same behavior with respect to PF, they appear to have distinct LF properties.

a.   Discuss this using the analyses of (10) and (37).

The same syntactic behavior occurs with the interrogative *how*, as illustrated in the analysis of (42).

(42)   How angry was he?

At Spell-Out (42) has a syntactic structure (43).

(43) $[_{CP}$ $[_{AP}$ how angry] $[_C$?? $[_{TP}$ he $[_T$ was $[_{AP}$ how angry]]]]]

(43) is mapped onto a PF representation (44) in the usual way.

(44) $[_{CP} [_{AP}$ how angry] $[_C$ was + ?? $[_{TP}$ he $[_T$ ~~was~~ $[_{AP}$ ~~how angry~~]]]]]

Like the other interrogative lexical items, *how* is also interpreted as a quantificational expression (45).

(45)   (to what degree *x*)

Thus the LF representation of (42) would be (46).

(46) $[_{CP}$ (to what degree *x*) $[_C$?? $[_{TP}$ he $[_T$ was $[_{AP}$ *x* angry]]]]]

The quantificational expression (45) binds a variable inside the predicate AP.

With a somewhat more complicated predicate AP construction, there is more
than one PF option. Consider the two wh-questions in (47).

(47)   a.   How angry at Mary was he?
        b.   How angry was he at Mary?

Mary is an internal argument of the adjective *angry* and *he* is the external argument. The PP *at Mary*, which contains the internal argument, is the complement
of the adjective *angry*. The interrogative adverb *how* constitutes a modifier of the
adjective, hence an adjunct. The predicate adjective phrase thus has the syntactic
structure (48).

(48) $[_{AP}$ how $[_A$ angry $[_{PP}$ at Mary]]]

The derivation of (47a) is identical to that of (42). In contrast, the derivation of
(47b) is not straightforward. While the LF representations of the two sentences in
(47) would be identical, there are various options for deriving the PF representation of (47b), including what happens derivationally before Spell-Out (part 1 of
the derivational architecture (29)).

The comparison between (47a) and (47b) suggests that the pied-piping of the
PP *at Mary* is in fact optional (in contrast to the obligatory pied-piping that occurs
in (10) and (37)). However, (48) shows that the string *how angry* does not by itself
constitute a phrase and therefore wh-movement cannot operate on just this string.
Wh-movement will therefore create the structures in (49) before Spell-Out. (See
also (49b) on the following page.)

(49)   a. $[_{CP} [_{AP}$ how $[_A$ angry $[_{PP}$ at Mary]]$[_C$?? $[_{TP}$ he $[_T$ was $[_{AP}$ how $[_A$ angry
        $[_{PP}$ at Mary]]]]]]]]

As long as the adjective *angry* must be pied-piped, then given that movement affects
phrases and not strings that do not form a single phrase, the PP complement of A
must also be pied-piped. In effect, pied-piping of the entire wh-AP is obligatory for
the derivation of (47b) in spite of the misleading appearance to the contrary.

Given (49) at Spell-Out, there are at least two options to consider for deriving
the PF representation of (47b). One plausible derivation involves complementary
deletions in each copy of the AP, as shown in (50).

(50) $[_{CP} [_{AP}$ how $[_A$ angry $[_{PP}$ ~~at Mary~~]]$[_C$?? $[_{TP}$ he $[_T$ was $[_{AP}$ ~~how~~ $[_A$ ~~angry~~
        $[_{PP}$ at Mary]]]]]]]]

Both instances of deletion would be deletion under identity. If this analysis is
viable, then deletion (unlike Merge) can apply to strings that do not form single

(49)   b.

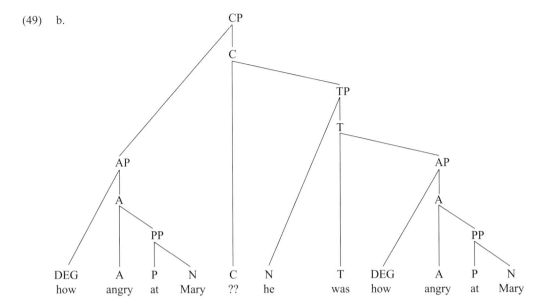

constituents (e.g. *how angry*). Alternatively, the entire AP complement of T could be deleted and then the PP *at Mary* could be "extraposed" – i.e. presumably merged at the end of the clause. Then the remaining PP in Spec-CP would be deleted via chain reduction. This would yield (51).

(51)   [CP [AP how [A angry [PP at Mary]]][C ?? [TP he [T was [AP how [A angry [PP at Mary]]]]] [PP at Mary]

This extraposition derivation involves one of the same deletions that the derivation of (50) uses. However in addition to a second deletion, like (50), (51) also involves an additional movement operation, the merger of the PP at the end of the clause (though how exactly is left open). Thus on simple economy grounds, where the derivation with fewest steps is preferable, (50) provides the more attractive analysis.

Exercise 8.6

Compare the following set of examples.

  (i)   a.   How angry was he at Mary during the meeting?
        b.   *How angry was he during the meeting at Mary?
        c.   He was very angry at Mary during the meeting.
        d.   *He was during the meeting very angry at Mary.

a.   Give a detailed analysis of the PF representation for (i.a) under an analysis along the lines of (50).
b.   What problems arise for an extraposition analysis of (i.a) along the lines of (51)?
c.   How can (i.b–d) be used to argue for the pure deletion analysis of (50) and against the extraposition analysis of (51)?

Exercise 8.7

Consider the following pair of examples.

(i)   a.   Whose photograph that Mary hadn't seen did Bill admire?
      b.   Whose photograph did Bill admire that Mary hadn't seen?

Take the relative clause *that Mary hadn't seen* to be a CP structure.

a.   What is the syntactic representation for these two examples at Spell-Out?
b.   Starting with the answer to (a), give the derivations for the PF representation of each example.
c.   If *which* is substituted for *whose* in (i), what changes in the answers to (a–b)? What remains the same?

(ii) a.   Which photograph that Mary hadn't seen did Bill admire?
      b.   Which photograph did Bill admire that Mary hadn't seen?

Pied-piping constructions occur in indirect as well as direct questions. For example, if the syntactic structures (38a) and (43) are merged as complements of a verb that selects a [+Q] C like *know*, sentences like (52) are derived.

(52)   a.   They don't know whose proposal she will support.
          b.   They don't know how angry he was.

The derivations of these indirect question CP complements in (52) are identical to their direct question counterparts (37) and (42) except for the T-to-C movement that occurs in the latter after Spell-Out. Their LF representations are identical.

The CP *whose proposal she will support*, which is merged as the complement of a verb in (52a), can also be merged as a constituent of a NP.

(53)   They just met [$_{NP}$ the senator [$_{CP}$ whose proposal she will support]]

In (53) the wh-CP contains a relative pronoun *whose* (hence [−Q] in contrast to the [+Q] interrogative pronoun with the same PF in (37)). The relative pronoun takes the N head of the relative clause as its antecedent. The relative pronoun *whose* is thus interpreted as "the senator." The relative clause functions as a modifier of the noun it is interpretively linked to. In terms of its syntactic structure, the relative clause is virtually identical to its indirect wh-question counterpart. Thus the derivation of a relative clause like the derivation of an indirect wh-question involves wh-movement. Designating both interrogative and relative pronouns as [+wh] captures this property. The two types of pronoun diverge in terms of their [±Q] property, which determines how each is interpreted.

The relative pronoun is analyzed along the same lines as an interrogative pronoun, as a kind of logical operator that binds a variable. The LF representation of the NP in (53) would be something like (54).

(54)   [$_{NP}$ 'the' 'senator' [$_{CP}$ O$_x$ [$_C$ [−Q] [$_{TP}$ 'she' [$_T$ 'will' [$_{VP}$ 'support' [$_{NP}$ x's 'proposal']]]]]]]

Take O$_x$ to be the logical operator that binds the variable x in the relative clause VP. Note also that the relative pronoun *whose*, like its interrogative counterpart, will be interpreted as referring to a person or persons. But unlike the variable bound by the quantificational interrogative pronoun, the variable bound by O$_x$ has a definite antecedent "senator."

The syntax of relative clauses allows for a certain range of variation that doesn't occur with interrogative clauses. Consider the following paradigm.

(55)   a.   a student who I met at the conference
        b.   a student that I met at the conference
        c.   a student I met at the conference
        d.   *a student who that I met at the conference

In (55a) the relative pronoun *who*, which is interpretively linked to *student*, is interpreted as the object of the verb *met*. The wh-movement analysis accounts for this interpretation. (55b) lacks an overt relative pronoun, but has instead a complementizer *that*, in contrast to the covert finite C in the relative clause in (55a). Nonetheless, *student* is still construed as the object of *met* in the relative clause. This construal is represented syntactically by positing a covert logical operator in place of the overt relative pronoun. The covert operator merges with the V *met* as its complement and then it is merged as the Spec-CP of the relative clause. This mirrors overt wh-movement. (55c) is just a variant where the relative operator and the complementizer are both covert. The only variant that is not viable is the one where both the relative pronoun and the complementizer are overt, which cannot be ruled out as a violation of Spec-head agreement.

The paradigm for a finite relative clause involving a variable in subject position (as opposed to object position in (55)) is more restricted.

(56)   a.   a student who met me at the conference
        b.   a student that met me at the conference
        c.   *a student met me at the conference
        d.   *a student who that met me at the conference

In addition to prohibiting a relative clause in which both the relative pronoun and the complementizer are overt, it also prohibits a relative clause in which neither is overt.[1] The differences in the two paradigms are considered evidence of a **subject/object asymmetry** in language.

With infinitival relative clauses the range of variation is even more restricted. First consider the finite relative clause in (57).

(57)   a book which you can read

(57) shows that the overt relative pronoun that takes *book* for an antecedent is *which*. In this case the relative pronoun is interpreted as the object of *read*. Converting the finite relative clause into an infinitival yields the following paradigm.

(58)   a.   *a book which you to read
        b.   a book for you to read

c.   *a book you to read
d.   *a book which for you to read

In contrast with the corresponding paradigm for the finite relative clause (55) where there are three possible variants, there is only one viable outcome in (58).

Exercise 8.8

a.   What is the syntactic derivation for (58b) – including both PF and LF?
b.   On the basis of your analysis for (58b), what would the syntactic analyses of the other examples be?
c.   What accounts for the deviance of the prohibited examples?

Hint: you may want to review some parts of the analysis of infinitivals in Chapter 6.

The paradigm in (58) involves an overt infinitival subject. However, an infinitival clause can also occur with a covert subject (i.e. PRO). The covert subject paradigm corresponding to (58) is given in (59).

(59)   a.   *a book which to read
          b.   *a book for to read
          c.   a book to read
          d.   *a book which for to read

Again there is only one viable outcome.
    Infinitival relative clauses have the following paradigm.

(60)   a.   *a student who to help me at the conference
          b.   *a student for to help me at the conference
          c.   a student to help me at the conference
          d.   *a student who for to help me at the conference

As with (59), there is only one viable outcome for this infinitival paradigm, the one in which both the relative pronoun and the complementizer are covert.

Exercise 8.9

a.   Give the syntactic analysis of (60c), including both the PF and LF representations.
b.   Of the remaining three examples, which two are deviant for the same reason and how do they differ from the one that remains?
c.   Compare the paradigm in (60) with the paradigm in (59). Discuss whether all the deviant examples in the latter are ruled out for the same reasons as the deviant examples in the former.

8.2   Syntactic islands and the Subjacency Condition

Given that there are two kinds of wh-phrase, one an interrogative and the other a relative, a question arises about whether a single clause can contain an instance of each. Can a relative clause involve an interrogative wh-phrase as part of its derivation? Consider first the simplest clause containing a relative clause.

(61)   The professor has just published a book which her students admire.

Turning the NP *her students* into a wh-phrase *whose students* yields (62), which is itself deviant.

(62)   *The professor has just published a book which whose students admire.

However, (62) cannot yield a legitimate direct wh-question as the deviance of (63) demonstrates.

(63)   *Whose students has the professor just published a book which admires?

At Spell-Out, (63) would have the syntactic structure (64).

(64) $[_{CP} [_{NP}$ whose students$] [_{C} [+Q] [_{TP} [_{NP}$ the professor$] [_{T}$ has $[_{VP}$ just $[_{V}$ published $[_{NP}$ a book $[_{CP}$ which $[_{C} [-Q] [_{TP} [_{NP}$ whose students$] [_{T}$ T $[_{VP}$ admire which$]]]]]]]]]]]]]]$

(64) involves two instances of wh-movement. The one that involves the relative pronoun *which* creates a nontrivial chain with single link. The two members of this link are separated by only one TP boundary. In contrast, the wh-movement involving the interrogative wh-phrase *whose students* creates a chain whose two members are separated by two TP boundaries. The chain violates the Subjacency Condition (65) (see Chapter 6, especially (94–95).

(65)   **The Subjacency Condition**: the two members of each link in a chain must be subjacent.

Recall that two syntactic objects are subjacent if and only if neither is contained in more than one clausal constituent (i.e. TP) that does not contain the other. In (64) *whose students* is contained in both the relative clause TP and the root clause TP, neither of which contain the copy of *whose students* in Spec-CP. Therefore this instance of wh-movement violates the Subjacency Condition. In effect, one cannot question out of a relative clause.

Exercise 8.10

The deviant example (63) involves an interrogative wh-phrase in subject position (Spec-TP) and a relative wh-phrase in the complement of VP (i.e. in the predicate phrase). If the positions of the relative and interrogative wh-phrase are reversed, a deviant construction still results. Consider the deviant construction (i), given that the interrogative wh-phrase *which of the books* is construed as the direct object of the V *read*.

   (i)   *Which of the books has the professor just met a student who read?

a.   What is the syntactic structure of (i) at Spell-Out?
b.   How does this structure violate the Subjacency Condition?
c.   Construct another deviant construction in which both the relative wh-phrase and the interrogative wh-phrase are construed as internal arguments (i.e. constituents of the VP of the relative clause).
d.   Provide the syntactic analysis of this example, showing how the deviance can be accounted for with the Subjacency Condition.

The deviance of examples like (63) demonstrates that relative clauses are syntactic constructions out of which wh-movement is not possible. Using the terminology of Ross 1967, such constructions are designated as **syntactic islands**, of which a relative clause is thus one instance. Under Ross's analysis, the islandhood of a relative clause is just a sub-case of a more general syntactic configuration that he designated as a **complex NP**. The islandhood of complex NPs followed from a more general **Complex NP Constraint** (CNPC), formulated by Ross as (66).

(66)   **The Complex NP Constraint:**
         No element contained in a sentence dominated by a noun phrase
         with a lexical head noun may be moved out of that noun phrase by a
         transformation. [his (4.20)]

In addition to wh-movement out of a relative clause, the CNPC also prohibits wh-movement out of a clause that functions as a complement of a N, as illustrated in (67).

(67)   a.   *Who did you believe the claim that Bill will dislike?
         b.   *The man who you believed the claim that Bill will dislike just
              arrived.

(67a) involves displacement of an interrogative pronoun; whereas (67b) involves a relative pronoun. While it is clear how the CNPC overlaps with the Subjacency Condition with respect to the islandhood of relative clauses, it not obvious how this overlap might extend to constructions like (67).

In the deviant (63), an interrogative wh-phrase is moving over a relative wh-phrase in Spec-CP. The same sort of deviance occurs when the relative wh-phrase moves over an interrogative wh-phrase in Spec-CP. (68) provides one example.

(68)   *The student who they asked Mary which book borrowed from the
         professor is arriving this afternoon.

In (68) it is the movement of the relative wh-phrase *who* that violates the Subjacency Condition, but not the CNPC.

Exercise 8.11

a.   Give the at Spell-Out syntactic analysis of the relative clause in (68).
b.   How exactly does the movement of the relative pronoun violate the Subjacency
     Condition?
c.   Why does it not violate the CNPC?

Nonetheless, the indirect question construction in (68) functions as a syntactic island. This kind of construction has been designated as a **wh-island**. A wh-island can be characterized as a TP that is the complement of a C whose Spec position contains a wh-phrase. Formulating a "wh-island constraint" along the lines of the CNPC won't be necessary here because the effects of such a constraint follow automatically from the Subjacency Condition, which is more general because it also blocks super-raising as discussed at the end of Chapter 6. Note, however, that under the characterization of wh-island, relative clauses are also wh-islands. In general certain clause constructions constitute syntactic islands for inter-clausal wh-movement.

One further case to consider involves a sentence that contains multiple interrogative wh-phrases, as illustrated in (69).

(69)   a.   Who read what?
          b.   John asked Mary who read what.
          c.   John asked Mary what Bill gave to whom.
          d.   What did Bill give to whom?

Inter-clausal wh-movement out of an indirect wh-question also results in deviance.

(70)   a.   *What did John ask Mary who read?
          b.   *To whom did John ask Mary what Bill gave?

Both examples in (70) can be analyzed as violations of the Subjacency Condition and as involving wh-islands based on the crucial assumption that *who* in (70a) moves to Spec-CP of the complement clause.

Exercise 8.12

a.   Give the syntactic representation of (70b) at Spell-Out.
b.   Explain how this violates the Subjacency Condition.
c.   What syntactic representation of (70a) results if only one wh-phrase moves?

So far, all of the cases of wh-islands are subsumed under the Subjacency Condition, and thus one of the two cases of complex NP islands is also. Whether inter-clausal movement out of the clausal complement of a noun can also be subsumed under Subjacency depends on how constructions like (67) are analyzed. Consider the derivation of (67a). At the point where the C *that* is merged, the clausal complement of *claim* will be a CP as analyzed in (71).

(71)   [$_{CP}$ that [$_{TP}$ Bill [$_T$ will [$_{VP}$ dislike who]]]]

If this CP is merged as the complement of the N *claim*, then wh-movement will only apply to the root Spec-CP in (67a) and the resulting chain will violate the Subjacency Condition. However, it cannot be assumed that this is what happens because it is also possible that the interrogative pronoun undergoes an intermediate covert movement to the Spec-CP of the clausal complement of *claim*. Then the resulting structure of the clausal complement of *claim* would be (72).

(72)   [$_{CP}$ who [$_C$ that [$_{TP}$ Bill [$_T$ will [$_{VP}$ dislike who]]]]]

The chain formed in (72) does not violate the Subjacency Condition. Moreover, the chain formed by the further movement of *who* to the root Spec-CP position will only cross one TP boundary, so the second created also does not violate

Subjacency. Under this analysis, the deviance of (67a) would not result from a Subjacency Condition violation.

The intermediate wh-movement has no visible effect and furthermore prevents us from using the Subjacency Condition to account for this second case of complex NP islands. So why assume it? The answer concerns the analysis of legitimate cases of inter-clausal wh-movement, as in (73).

(73)   Who did you believe they claimed that Bill will dislike?

(73) is minimally different from (67a) in that the noun *claim* has been changed to a verb (with the requisite subject added). If the derivation of (73) doesn't involve an intermediate movement represented in (72), it will produce a Subjacency violation – which is a false prediction. Therefore, the derivation of (73), which also contains (71), must involve an intermediate covert movement of the wh-phrase to Spec-CP, as given in (72).

(71) must be a point in the derivations of both (67a) and (73), but at this point – because of the bottom-up nature of Merge – the derivation contains no information about whether this construction will be merged with the N *claim* or the V *claim*. To know this would require a **look-ahead** property that would contribute significantly to the complexity of derivations. It is generally assumed that such derivational complexity is to be avoided. Instead, because wh-movement must be an option for the derivation of (73), it must also be an option for the derivation of (67a). Therefore, the deviance of (67a) must involve something beyond the Subjacency Condition as formulated.

The analysis of (73) involves three TP boundaries, indicated in (74).

(74)   a.   Who did [$_{TP}$ you believe [$_{CP}$ ç [$_{TP}$ they claimed [$_{CP}$ that [$_{TP}$ Bill will dislike]]]]]

         b.   Who did [$_{TP}$you believe [$_{TP}$(who) ç [$_{TP}$they claimed [$_{TP}$(who) that [$_{TP}$Bill will dislike (who)]]]]]

Interclausal wh-moment starting from the most deeply embedded TP requires three instances of wh-movement apply in the derivation, as illustrated in (74b). Otherwise, the wh-chain formed will have a link that violates the Subjacency Condition by crossing more than one TP boundary. The most deeply embedded link will involve the object position of *dislike* and the Spec-CP of the overt complementizer *that*. This link crosses only one TP. The next link must involve a copy of *who* in the Spec-CP position of a CP complement of *believe* and the Spec-CP of *that*, otherwise the connection between the overt *who* in the main clause and the Spec-CP position of the clausal complement of *claimed* will cross two TP boundaries. Each link of this nontrivial chain of four members (and three links) crosses only one TP; thus the chain satisfies the Subjacency Condition. In this way the Subjacency Condition enforces **successive cyclic** wh-movement in the same way it enforces successive cyclic NP movement. For wh-movement, each CP constitutes a cyclic domain (**a cycle**), in contrast to NP-movement, where TP is the relevant cyclic domain. Furthermore, the Subjacency analysis requires that a clausal complement without an overt complementizer must in some cases be a CP with a covert C.

Exercise 8.13

This analysis generalizes to infinitival complements. Consider the following example.

   i.   Which painting is John likely to buy.

a.   Give the syntactic representation of (i) at Spell-Out.
b.   Discuss how the nontrivial wh-chain satisfies the Subjacency Condition.
c.   What does (i) show with regard to NP movement out of a CP?

While English manifests no overt evidence for successive cyclic wh-movement, there are languages in which successive wh-movement has distinct PF effects. Consider the formation of wh-questions in Spanish. Like English, Spanish has SVO order in indicative root clauses, as illustrated in (75). The Spanish data that follows is from Torrego 1984.

(75)   a.   The journal had published my article.
          b.   La revista había publicado mi artículo.

Replacing the NP object of the verb *publicado* with an interrogative pronoun *qué* 'what' yields the wh-question (76a), which contrasts with the corresponding question in English (76b).

(76)   a.   ¿Qué había publicado la revista?
          b.   What had the journal published?

(76a) shows that wh-displacement to clause initial position also occurs in Spanish. Suppose that this is movement of a wh-phrase to Spec-CP as in English. However, the PF effects in the two languages differ. In Spanish the entire verbal string is pronounced before the subject, whereas in English, only the finite auxiliary verb is. (77), which corresponds in linear order to the English (76b), is deviant.

(77)   *¿Qué había la revista publicado?

If the LF representation of (76a) is identical to that of (76b) – the basic assumption – then the inversion of the verbal string and the subject in Spanish wh-questions is a PF effect that occurs after Spell-Out. However it is done on the PF side, the evidence suggests that it is triggered by wh-movement to a local Spec-CP.

    This PF inversion occurs in indirect wh-questions, as illustrated in (78).

(78)   No sabía qué había publicado la revista.
            Not I-knew what had published the journal
            "I didn't know what the journal had published"

Thus the syntactic structure of (76a) occurs as the clausal complement of the verb *sabía* "I-knew." Spanish contrasts with English, where the inversion of the subject and the finite verbal auxiliary is limited to root clauses.

    This PF inversion in Spanish wh-questions also occurs in clauses that do not show overt wh-movement – i.e., where no wh-phrase occurs in the Spec-CP of the clause in PF. This is demonstrated in the direct question (79), which contains two levels of clausal embedding.

(79)   ¿Qué pensaba Juan que le había dicho Pedro que había publicado la
         revista?
         What thought Juan that him had told Pedro that had published the journal
         "What did Juan think that Pedro had told him that the journal had published?"

In (79) each of the three clause subjects follows the verbal string of the clause (cf. (80) where the subjects are marked in boldface and the verbal strings are underlined. The clitic pronoun *le* "him" is assumed to be attached to the finite auxiliary *había* "had" and therefore is part of the verbal string.)

(80)   [$_{CP}$ Qué pensaba **Juan** [$_{CP}$ que le había dicho **Pedro** [$_{CP}$ que había
         publicado **la revista**]]]

Only the root clause shows overt wh-movement, but inversion has occurred in both embedded clauses. One way to account for this is by postulating an inversion operation that is triggered by the presence of a wh-phrase in Spec-CP prior to chain reduction, which deletes the unpronounced copies of the wh-phrase. The inversion operation would thus apply to the syntactic structure (81) before deletion applies to the three silent copies of *qué*.

(81)   [$_{CP}$ Qué [$_{C}$?? [$_{TP}$ Juan [$_{T}$ T [$_{VP}$ pensaba [$_{CP}$ qué [$_{C}$ que [$_{TP}$ Pedro
         [$_{T}$ le había [$_{VP}$ dicho [$_{CP}$ qué [$_{C}$ que [$_{TP}$ [$_{NP}$ la revista] [$_{T}$ había
         [$_{VP}$ publicado qué]]]]]]]]]]]]]]]

Not only can inversion apply in clauses that do not contain an overt wh-phrase in Spec-CP, but in direct questions like (79), such inversion is obligatory.

(82)   *Qué pensaba Juan que Pedro le había dicho que había publicado la
         revista?

In (82) inversion occurs in the root clause and the most deeply embedded CP. The deviance of (82) results from the failure of inversion in the CP complement of the main clause verb *pensaba*. This analysis of (82) also supports the claim that covert as well as overt wh-movement has an overt PF effect in Spanish. Thus (80) provides overt evidence for covert successive cyclic wh-movement.

   Irish is another language that manifests an overt PF effect which can be associated with wh-movement. This phenomenon involves the morphosyntax of Irish complementizers. Unlike English, which utilizes C *that* for both finite clause CP complements and relative clauses, Irish has two distinct forms (referred to in the literature as *go* and *aL*).[2] The former occurs in finite CP complements (e.g. (83a)), while the latter occurs in relative clause CPs (e.g. (83b)).

(83)   a.   Creidum gu-r inis sé bréag.
              I-believe go-PAST tell he lie
              "I believe that he told a lie"
         b.   an ghirseach a ghoid na síogaí
              the girl *aL* stole the fairies
              "the girl that the fairies stole away"

Each morphosyntactic form of the finite C is associated with a specific construction.

(84)   a.   *Creidum a inis sé bréag.
          b.   *an ghirseach go ghoid na síogaí

As (84) shows, these forms are not interchangeable.

Given our analysis of the relative clause, (83b) will have a LF representation in which the object of the verb *ghoid* "stole" is a variable bound by the logical operator O_x in Spec-CP, and moreover that this is derived via covert wh-movement of O_x to Spec-CP. The same C element shows up in direct wh-questions with overt wh-movement, as in (85).

(85)   Céacu ceann a dhíol tú?
          which one aL sold you
          "which one did you sell?"

In the syntactic analysis of (85), the wh-phrase *céacu ceann* "which one" is first merged as the complement of the verb *dhíol* and then the wh-phrase is merged as Spec-CP. What the relative clause (83b) and the direct wh-question (85) share in common is that both their derivations involve a form of wh-movement and that both CPs derived contain a *aL* C.

(83b) by itself provides evidence that covert wh-movement (hence without PF effects) determines the choice of *aL* rather than *go*. Given the two cases in (83b) and (85), it could be that this choice is only determined by a wh-phrase that is interpreted in Spec-CP. However a more complex construction whose derivation involves wh-movement to an intermediate Spec-CP position (e.g. (86)) shows that any instance of wh-movement triggers the choice of *aL* (putting aside the C *aN* associated with constructions containing a resumptive – see note 2). In (86) the C elements are marked in boldface.

(86)   an t-ainm **a** hinnseadh dúinn **a** bhí ar an áit
          the name aL was-told to-us aL was on the place
          "the name that we were told was on the place"

Details aside, (86) would have a syntactic representation along the lines of (87), which makes explicit how wh-movement applies in its derivation.

(87) $[_{NP}$ an t-ainm $[_{CP} O_x [_C$ **a** hinnseadh dúinn $[_{CP} O_x [_C$ **a** $[_{TP} O_x$ bhí ar an áit$]]]]]]$

The occurrence of C *aL* as the head of the CP complement of *hinnseadh* "told" in (87) demonstrates that even movement to a Spec-CP that plays no role in interpretation at either LF or PF still triggers the choice of the *aL* C.

Exercise 8.14

a.   Discuss to what extent this pattern follows from the Subjacency Condition.
b.   Discuss whether the insertion of Irish complementizers requires the derivation to be able to look ahead.
c.   How would a spec-head agreement analysis of Irish complementizers allow us to avoid relying on look-ahead?

Exercise 8.15

This analysis generalizes to more complicated structures with more levels of sentential embedding. (i), which involves an interrogative wh-phrase, contains one more level of clausal embedding than (87).

(i)   Céacu   fear **a** deir siad **a** chreideann siad **a** roghnófas   siad
which-of-two man aL say they aL believe they aL choose-FUT-WH they
"Which of the two men do they say that they think that they will choose?"

a.   What is the syntactic analysis of (i) in terms of CP/TP?
Notice that while the intermediate copy of O_x in (87) is neither pronounced not interpreted, it nonetheless occurs in the same clause (CP) where O_x is interpreted. With this in mind, consider the structure of (i).

b.   In what ways does (i) differ from (87)?

Given the evidence for successive cyclic wh-movement, it seems that wh-movement generally applies successive cyclically. Consequently the complex NP islands that are not also wh-islands (e.g. the direct question in (67a) and the relative clause in (67b)) cannot be subsumed under the Subjacency Condition as it is currently formulated. The qualification at the end of the previous sentence leaves open the possibility that Subjacency might be reformulated in a way that could subsume these additional cases. One way to do this is to include NP as a second bounding category for the Subjacency Condition in addition to TP (see Chomsky 1977).

Exercise 8.16

Discuss how this reformulation of the Subjacency Condition now accounts for all complex NP islands – i.e. especially constructions like (67).

Taking NP as well as TP to be bounding categories for the Subjacency Condition extends the coverage of the condition to other constructions that are clearly deviant. Wh-movement out of a Spec-TP that properly contains the wh-phrase is the clearest case. Consider for example the deviance of (88b–c), where (88c) involves the pied piping of the preposition along with the interrogative pronoun.

(88)   a.   Rumors about layoffs have been circulating in the office.
       b.   *What have rumors about been circulating in the office?
       c.   *About what have rumors been circulating in the office?

As the analyses of these deviant examples given in (89a–b) show, the chain link between the wh-phrase in Spec-CP and its copy in the NP Spec of TP crosses both an NP and a TP boundary, in violation of the Subjacency Condition.

(89)   a.   [$_{CP}$ what [$_C$ have [$_{TP}$ [$_{NP}$ rumors [$_{PP}$ about what]][$_T$ have [$_{VP}$ been [$_{VP}$ circulating in the office]]]]]]]
       b.   [$_{CP}$ [$_{PP}$ about what] [$_C$ have [$_{TP}$ [$_{NP}$ rumors [$_{PP}$ about what]][$_T$ have [$_{VP}$ been [$_{VP}$ circulating in the office]]]]]]]

The same effects occur when (88b–c) are reformulated as indirect wh- questions, as in (90).

(90)   a.   *Beatrice asked us what rumors about have been circulating in the office.
         b.   *Beatrice asked us about what rumors have been circulating in the office.

Note that (90a) could also be parsed so that *what rumors* is analyzed as a NP, in which case the P *about* does not fit into a viable syntactic structure, hence the deviance. However, the analysis of (90a) under consideration is parallel to the analysis of (91). A similar comment holds for (90b).

(91)   a.   *Beatrice asked us what topics rumors about have been circulating in the office.
         b.   *Beatrice asked us about what topics rumors have been circulating in the office.

Note also that making the wh-phrase in (91) more specific than the one in (90), from *what* to *what topics*, does not appear to affect the grammatical status of the construction.

Exercise 8.17

a.   Give the syntactic analysis for each of the following examples.

   (i)   a.   Photographs of several philosophers will appear in tomorrow's newspaper.
         b.   *Which philosophers will photographs of appear in tomorrow's newspaper?
   (ii) a.   Several complaints about a few doctors were never investigated.
         b.   *Which doctors were several complaints about never investigated?
         c.   *About which doctors were several complaints never investigated?

b.   Discuss the differences and the similarities between the syntactic structures of (i.a) and (ii.a).
c.   Show how the deviant examples violate the Subjacency Condition.

If the displacement of a wh-phrase that is properly contained in a subject NP results in deviance because the wh-movement involved violates the Subjacency Condition, then the corresponding wh-movement out of a non-subject position (e.g. direct object or object of a preposition) should also result in deviance. This is borne out in the following examples.

(92)   a.   The hospital destroyed Bill's complaints about several doctors.
         b.   *Which doctors did the hospital destroy Bill's complaints about?
         c.   *About which doctors did the hospital destroy Bill's complaints?
(93)   a.   The newspaper will be publishing Annie's photographs of several philosophers.
         b.   *Which philosophers will the newspaper be publishing Annie's photographs of?

c.   *Of which philosophers will the newspaper be publishing Annie's photographs?

The movement of *which doctors* in (92b) creates a chain link that crosses the NP boundary projected by *photographs* and the TP of the clause, as indicated in (94) where the bounding categories are indicated in boldface.

(94)   [$_{CP}$ [$_{NP}$ which doctors] did [$_{TP}$ the hospital destroy [$_{NP}$ Bill's complaints about [$_{NP}$ which doctors]]]]

Note that the same deviance occurs when the deviant wh-questions in (92–3) are embedded as indirect questions.

There is however a difference between the deviant constructions in (92–3) and those in (88) and (90). In the former, the NP that properly contains the wh-phrase also contains a possessive NP (e.g. *Bill's*) whereas the corresponding NP in the latter does not. Eliminating the possessive NPs in (92–3) yields the following examples.

(95)   a.   Which doctors did the hospital destroy complaints about?
           b.   About which doctors did the hospital destroy complaints?
(96)   a.   Which philosophers will the newspaper be publishing photographs of?
           b.   Of which philosophers will the newspaper be publishing photographs?

Some speakers of English find that in comparing (95a) with (92b), while they judge (92b) to be deviant, (95a) seems a lot better – for some, fully acceptable. This phenomenon shows that linguistic judgments are not always categorical (e.g. deviant vs. nondeviant), but rather gradient (involving a scale of values) – what is sometimes referred to as **relative grammaticality**. Note further that cases involving wh-movement out of a subject NP (whether or not it also contains a possessive NP) are comparatively more deviant than the cases of wh-movement illustrated in (95–6). This too constitutes an instance of a subject/object asymmetry.

The Subjacency account of these deviant cases of wh-movement out of a NP does not capture the kind of gradience exhibited in these examples. This suggests that the analysis of Subjacency should not be extended to NP as a bounding category. Instead, an explanation for the range of facts concerning wh-movement out of NPs must be sought elsewhere. At present this remains a desideratum for a theory of wh-movement.

The Subjacency analysis of wh-islands, in contrast, works without exception for English. However, in other languages, for example Italian, it appears that some TP complements of a C whose Spec contains a wh-phrase are not islands with respect to wh-movement. In (97), the relative clause, set off by commas, contains an embedded indirect wh-question. (The following Italian examples are from L. Rizzi 1982.)

(97)   Il mio primo libro, che credo che tu sappia a chi ho dedicato,
           me é sempre stato molto caro
           "My first book, that I believe that you know to whom I dedicated,
           has always been very dear to me"

As the analysis of this relative clause (given in (98)) shows, the nontrivial chain formed by the relative clause operator O_x contains two links, one of which crosses two TP boundaries (marked in boldface). The element *io* in parentheses represents the silent hence covert first-person singular subject of the predicates *credo* and *ho dedicato*.

(98)   a. $[_{CP} O_x [_C$ che $[_{TP} (io) [_T T [_{VP}$ credo $[_{CP} O_x [_C$ che $[_{\textbf{TP}}$ tu $[_T T [_{VP}$ sappia $[_{CP} [_{PP}$ a chi$] [_C C [_{\textbf{TP}} (io) [_T$ ho $[_{VP}$ dedicato $O_x [_{PP}$ a chi$]]]]]]]]]]]]]]]]]$
        b.   (see next page)

In Italian *che* functions as the finite clause complementizer corresponding to English *that*. In (98) the *che* that marks the relative clause is also C and not an overt relative pronoun. Note further that Italian is a null subject language, in which subject pronouns in finite clauses may not be pronounced (either deleted or not merged in the derivation—thus *io* in parentheses in (98)). Under the definition of wh-island above, the TP in the complement of *sappia* 'know' constitutes a wh-island. Nonetheless, (97) demonstrates that in Italian it is possible to extract the relative clause operator out of this construction via wh-movement. If Subjacency as formulated for English applies to the grammar of Italian, then (97) should be a Subjacency violation. Given the acceptability of (97), the Subjacency Condition as formulated for English cannot apply in Italian.

Nonetheless, wh-movement in Italian shows locality effects – i.e. there are syntactic distances that it cannot legitimately cross. Consider the following deviant example.

(99)   *Il mio primo libro, che so a chi credi che abbia dedicato, me é sempre stato molto caro.
        "My first book, that I know to whom you believe that I dedicated, has always been very dear to me"

(99) is identical to (98) with the exception of the relative clause. The difference between the two relative clauses is that the order of the two verbs "know"and "believe" in (98) is reversed in (99). The relative clause in (99) could have the analysis given in (100).

(100) $[_{CP} O_x [_C$ che $[_{\textbf{TP}} (io) [_T T [_{VP}$ so $[_{CP} [_{PP}$ a chi$] [_C C [_{\textbf{TP}} (tu) [_T T [_{VP}$ credi $[_{CP} [_{PP}$ a chi$] [_C C [_{\textbf{TP}} (io) [_T$ abbia $[_{VP}$ dedicato $O_x [_{PP}$ a chi$]]]]]]]]]]]]]]]]]$

Under this analysis, the wh-PP *a chi* has moved successive cyclically from the most deeply embedded clause to the Spec-CP where it is pronounced at PF. The relative clause operator has moved once across three TP boundaries (marked in boldface). However before considering the possibility that Subjacency in Italian is defined on three rather than two TP boundaries, it is useful to consider the other possible derivation for the relative clause in (99). This is given in (101).

(98b)

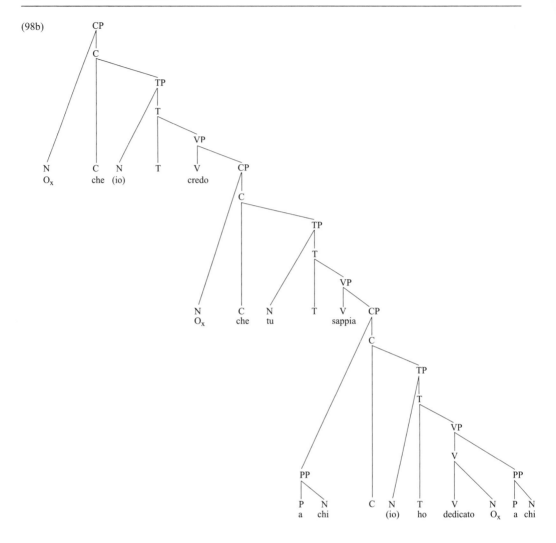

(101) $[_{CP}$ O$_x$ $[_C$ che $[_{TP}$ (*io*) $[_T$ T $[_{VP}$ so $[_{CP}$ $[_{PP}$ a chi] $[_C$ C $[_{TP}$ (*tu*) $[_T$ T $[_{VP}$ credi
             $[_{CP}$ O$_x$ $[_C$ C $[_{TP}$ (*io*) $[_T$ abbia $[_{VP}$ dedicato O$_x$ $[_{PP}$ a chi]]]]]]]]]]]]]]]]]

In (101) neither chain for O$_x$ or the wh-PP *a chi* contains a link that spans three
TP boundaries. The chain for *a chi* contains a single link that spans two TP boundaries. Thus the syntactic span of this link is the same as the widest link in (98),
which involves no Subjacency Condition violation, so it cannot be the source of
the deviance in (99). That leaves the single chain link for the relative operator O$_x$.
But here again, the link only spans a pair of TP boundaries, so it cannot account
for deviance of (99).

   A careful analysis of the deviant (99) in contrast to (98) shows that TP cannot be
a bounding category for Italian. Another obvious candidate for bounding category
is CP. In the analysis given in (100), the single link in the chain for O$_x$ spans two CP
boundaries (represented in (102) where the relevant CPs are rendered in boldface).

(102)   [$_{CP}$ O$_x$ [$_C$ che [$_{TP}$ (io) [$_T$ T [$_{VP}$ so [$_{CP}$ [$_{PP}$ a chi] [$_C$ C [$_{TP}$ (tu) [$_T$ T [$_{VP}$ credi
         [$_{CP}$ [$_{PP}$ a chi] [$_C$ C [$_{TP}$ (io) [$_T$ abbia [$_{VP}$ dedicato O$_x$ [$_{PP}$ a chi]]]]]]]]]]]]]]]]

The same chain in (101) also contains a link that spans two CP boundaries, as
indicated in (103), where the relevant CPs are rendered in boldface.

(103)   [$_{CP}$ O$_x$ [$_C$ che [$_{TP}$ (io) [$_T$ T [$_{VP}$ so [**$_{CP}$** [$_{PP}$ a chi] [$_C$ C [$_{TP}$ (tu) [$_T$ T [$_{VP}$ credi
         [**$_{CP}$** O$_x$ [$_C$ C [$_{TP}$ (io) [$_T$ abbia [$_{VP}$ dedicato O$_x$ [$_{PP}$ a chi]]]]]]]]]]]]]]]]

In contrast, neither link in the chain for O$_x$ in (98) spans more than one CP
boundary, even though one link spans two TP boundaries. Taking CP as a
bounding category for Italian allows us to retain the Subjacency Condition
as a locality principle for movement operations. The principle says that a
single movement operation cannot involve positions that are not subjacent.
The definition of subjacent is subject to some parametric variation across
languages (e.g. TP for English, but CP for Italian). Because Italian does not
allow multiple wh-phrase questions (in contrast to English), there are no
examples of wh-movement of an interrogative wh-phrase out of an indirect
wh-question.

Exercise 8.18

French also exhibits wh-movement of a relative wh-pronoun out of an indirect
wh-question. Consider the following nondeviant construction. The following data is
from Sportiche 1981.

    (i)   Voilà quelqu'un à qui je crois que je sais lequel j'offrirais.
           "Here is someone to whom I think that I know which one I will offer"

a.   Give the analysis of the relative clause in (i).
b.   Identify the two wh-chains of (i).
c.   Discuss the syntactic distance each link of each chain spans.
d.   How does this construction compare to a corresponding construction in English?
e.   In what way(s) is the syntactic structure of this example similar to Italian?

Now consider the deviant French construction in (ii).

    (ii)   *Voilà quelqu'un à qui je sais lequel je crois que j'offrirais.
           "Here is someone to whom I know which one I think that I will offer"

f.   What are the two possible derivations for the relative clause in (ii)?
g.   Identify the wh-chains in each derivation/syntactic representation.
h.   Discuss the syntactic distance of each link in each of the chains in both syntactic
     representations.
i.   Using your analyses of (i) and (ii), discuss whether TP could be a bounding
     category for French wh-movement.
j.   Discuss how CP could be a bounding category for French.
k.   How is wh-movement in the French examples different from the Italian data
     discussed above?

Exercise 8.19

In wh-questions in Spanish, wh-movement to Spec-CP is linked to an inversion of the subject and the verbal string – an overt effect at PF, as discussed above. As previously discussed this phenomenon can be correlated with successive cyclic wh-movement. With this in mind, consider the following paradigm. Data from Torrego 1984.

(i) a. ¿Qué pensaba Juan que le había dicho Pedro que había publicado la revista?

"What thought Juan that him had told Pedro that had published the journal"

   b. *¿Qué pensaba Juan que Pedro le había dicho que había publicado la revista?

   c. *¿Qué pensaba Juan que Pedro le había dicho que la revista había publicado?

   d. ¿Qué pensaba Juan que le había dicho Pedro que la revista había publicado?

a. Given that (i.a) is derived via successive cyclic wh-movement, what would be the derivation (or syntactic representation) of (i.b)?

b. What is the wh-chain in (i.b)?

c. Which link of that chain violates the Subjacency Condition? (and on which formulation(s)?

d. Answer questions (a–c) for (i.c).

e. Answer questions (a and b) for (i.d).

f. (i.d) is not deviant. What does this tell us about the formulation of the Subjacency Condition for Spanish wh-movement?

In Italian, wh-movement is somewhat less constrained than in English, but in Russian, it is significantly more constrained. Wh-movement to Spec-CP also occurs in Russian, as illustrated in (104).

(104)   a. Kogo ljubit Marija
              who-ACC loves Mary-NOM
              "who does Mary love?"

          b. Ja znaju, kogo Marija ljubit
              I know who-ACC Mary-NOM loves
              "I know who(m) Mary loves"

(104a) illustrates wh-movement in a root clause; (104b), in a subordinate clause. Both are cases of intra-clausal wh-movement. The word order in the indirect question in (104b) looks like a standard case of wh-movement of the sort investigated above. Russian, unlike English, French, and Italian, does not allow inter-clausal wh-movement. Thus (105) is deviant in Russian.

(105)   *Kogo govorit Ivan, cto Marija ljubit?
           who-ACC says Ivan that Mary-NOM loves
           "who does Ivan say that Mary loves?"

Suppose that (105) were derived via successive cyclic wh-movement. This would yield a syntactic structure (106), abstracting away from the PF position of the root clause subject *Ivan*.

(106)   [$_{CP}$ kogo [$_C$ C [$_{TP}$ Ivan [$_T$ T [$_{VP}$ govorit [$_{CP}$ kogo [$_C$ cto [$_{TP}$ Marija [$_T$ T [$_{VP}$ ljubit kogo]]]]]]]]]]]

The three member wh-chain in (106) contains two links, one which spans only a single TP boundary and the other which spans both a TP and a CP boundary. The absence of inter-clausal wh-movement in Russian can be accounted for by hypothesizing that both TP and CP constitute bounding categories for Russian. This gives a third parameter setting for the Subjacency principle.

8.3   Beyond the Subjacency Condition

The parameterized analysis of the locality of wh-movement via Subjacency raises a problem for the notion of syntactic island. In English, wh-movement out of wh-islands is prohibited generally. However, the characterization for a wh-island in English is not a syntactic island for wh-movement in Italian. Nonetheless, there is a locality constraint on wh-movement in Italian and thus constructions out of which wh-phrases may not be moved. Trying to characterize these constructions as "wh-islands" is questionable. And further, the prohibition on inter-clausal wh-movement in Russian cannot be characterized in any way as a "wh-island" effect. The notion of subjacency captures what is arguably an underlying generalization, whereas the notion of island is a descriptive metaphor at best. With this understanding, the term "island" in its intuitive descriptive sense is used in what follows because of its general currency.

The Subjacency Condition alone cannot account for locality constraints on wh-movement in English (and other languages). For example, wh-movement out of indirect yes/no questions also produces deviance.

(107)   a.   *Who did they remember whether Bill praised?
            b.   *Who did they wonder whether Bill praised?

Under an analysis of (107) where *whether* is a complementizer C, hence selected by the matrix verbs *remember* and *wonder*, nothing seems to prevent the successive cyclic wh-movement from applying in the derivation of these examples. The TP complement of *whether* might be described as an island – i.e. a *whether*-island, in which case the deviance of (107) constitutes an island violation. This is merely a description of the fact, with no account of what grammatical mechanisms might explain this deviance. Furthermore, when *whether*-island violations are compared to wh-island violations, speakers generally judge the deviance of the former to be significantly weaker (see Sprouse 2007). The same difference in strength of deviance seems to hold for indirect questions involving the C *if*, as illustrated in (108).

(108)   a.   *Who did they remember if Bill praised?
           b.   *Who did they wonder if Bill praised?

Given that *if* is an instance of C, the successive cyclic movement of *who* can apparently apply – in which case the deviant examples in (108) cannot be analyzed as Subjacency violations.

Wh-movement out of Spec-TP where TP is the complement of a *that* C is also prohibited. Consider the following deviant examples.

(109)   a.   *Who did Vera think that left on time?
           b.   Who did Vera think left on time?

Exercise 8.20

The same effect occurs with the verb *believe*. Consider the pair of examples in (i).

(i)   a.   *Who did Vera believe that left on time?
        b.   Who did Vera believe left on time?

(i.a) is deviant on the analysis that corresponds to the analysis of (109a). However there is another possible analysis of (i.a) that should not be deviant. Consider (ii).

(ii)   Who that left on time did Vera believe?

a.   Give the syntactic structure of (ii) at Spell-Out.
b.   How could the PF string (i.a) be derived using the derivation of (ii)?
c.   Why isn't this analysis possible for (109a)?

Given Subjacency, the legitimate (109b) must be derived via successive cyclic wh-movement. The presence of the overt C *that* in (109a) does not prevent the intermediate wh-movement to the Spec-CP of the complement of *think* because successive cyclic wh-movement must apply in the derivation of (110) as well, which also contains an overt *that* C. The comparison of (109a) with (110) shows another subject/object asymmetry with respect to wh-movement.

(110)   Who did Vera think that Bill would consult?

Therefore, (109a) cannot be analyzed as a Subjacency violation.

Exercise 8.21

(109a) involves the movement of an interrogative pronoun to form a direct question.

a.   Provide evidence that the deviance in (109a) generalizes to any interrogative wh-phrase in a direct question.
b.   Provide evidence that the deviance in (109a) generalizes to all indirect question constructions.
c.   Provide evidence that the deviance in (109a) generalizes to any wh-phrase (i.e. relative as well as interrogative AND covert as well as overt).

Wh-movement of the subject in a finite indirect yes/no question also results in deviance.

(111)   a.   *Who did they remember whether praised Bill?
          b.   *Who did they wonder whether praised Bill?

Like the wh-movement in (107), the movement of the interrogative pronoun in (111) is out of a *whether*-island. Yet on comparison, the examples in (111) seem more strongly deviant than those in (107). Under the assumption that deviance increases when more than one constraint is violated, this disparity would fall out if (111) violates a second grammatical constraint. In contrast, (107) is only a *whether*-island violation. An obvious candidate would be the constraint that accounts for the deviance of (109a), a filter on syntactic representations that prohibits an overt complementizer followed by a silent copy – as opposed to a covert subject PRO – (what is called the **that-trace filter**, but more likely generalizes to all complementizers).

   How such a filter would be formulated given Merge is not clear because at PF nontrivial chains (and the copies that create them) have been erased, so this analysis can only be used descriptively by referring to the deviance of (109a) as a complementizer-trace effect. If (111) is judged more strongly deviant than (109a), the stronger deviance of the examples in (111) could be described as resulting from the combination of a complementizer-trace effect and a *whether*-island effect. The underlying grammatical principles that account for these effects remain to be discovered.

Exercise 8.22

Discuss whether complementizer-trace effects exist for wh-questions involving infinitival CPs.

   The complementizer-trace effect does not hold for C *that* in a relative clause, as (112) shows.

(112)   a.   the professor that praised her students
          b.   [$_{NP}$ the professor [$_{CP}$ O$_x$ [$_C$ that [$_{TP}$ O$_x$ [$_T$ T [$_{VP}$ praised her students]]]]]]
          c.

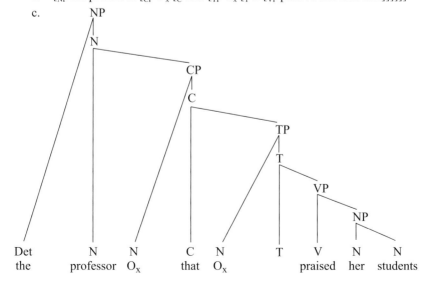

The relative clause operator O_x in Spec-TP constitutes a silent copy, but the *that*-trace construction in (112) does not create deviance. But as (113c–d) show – in contrast to (113a–b), the relative clause operator can induce a complementizer-trace effect.

(113)   a.   the professor that Fred thinks praised her students
          b.   the professor Fred thinks praised her students
          c.   *the professor that Fred thinks that praised her students
          d.   *the professor Fred thinks that praised her students

This is shown in the analysis of (113d) given in (114) where the complementizer *that* is followed by the silent relative clause operator.

(114) $[_{NP}$ the professor $[_{CP} O_x [_C C [_{TP}$ Fred $[_T T [_{VP}$ thinks $[_{CP} O_x [_C$ that $[_{TP} O_x [_T T [_{VP}$ praised her students]]]]]]]]]]]]]

This shows that complementizer-trace effects are not restricted to interrogative wh-phrases, but apply generally to wh-movement phenomena in general.

Exercise 8.23

Cleft constructions (mentioned briefly in Chapter 3), for example (i) and (ii), also exhibit properties of wh-movement constructions.

    (i)   a.   It was David who I met at the conference.
            b.   It was David who met me at the conference.
    (ii)   a.   It was David that I met at the conference.
            b.   It was David that met me at the conference.

a.   Give the syntactic structure of the subordinate CPs in (i) and (ii).
b.   How are these CPs similar to relative clauses and how are they different?

Consider the following examples.

    (iii)   a.   It was David who Vera thinks I met at the conference.
            b.   It was David who Vera thinks that I met at the conference.
    (iv)   a.   It was David that Vera thinks I met at the conference.
            b.   It was David that Vera thinks that I met at the conference.
    (v)   a.   *It was David who Vera thinks that met me at the conference.
            b.   *It was David that Vera thinks that met me at the conference.
            c.   *It was David Vera thinks that met me at the conference.
    (vi)   a.   It was David who Vera thinks met me at the conference.
            b.   It was David that Vera thinks met me at the conference.
            c.   It was David Vera thinks met me at the conference.

c.   Give the syntactic analysis of the largest subordinate CP in (iii) at Spell-Out.
d.   Why is there no syntactic difference between the two examples in (iii) at LF?
e.   What is the syntactic difference between (iii.a) and (iii.b) at PF?
f.   How does the syntactic analysis of (iv) compare to (iii)?
g.   Given your answer to (c), what is the syntactic analysis of (v.a) at Spell-Out?
h.   How does your answer to (g) compare to the corresponding analyses of (v.b–c)?

i.   What accounts for the deviance of (v)?
j.   How does the syntactic analysis of (vi.a) compare to the corresponding analysis of (v.a)?
k.   How does the syntactic analysis of (vi.a) compare to that of (vi.b–c)?
l.   Why aren't the examples in (vi) deviant?

Exercise 8.24

Consider the cleft construction in the following quote from Walter Mosley's *Fear Itself* (see note 1).

> "It was you came to me and asked for help. It was you that white man shot at us was lookin' for. It was you sent me lookin' for a man dead in his living room."

a.   Give a syntactic analysis at Spell-Out for each sentence.
b.   In what way(s) do these sentences diverge from "standard" English?
c.   Do they violate any principles of grammar that have been proposed?

There is one other constraint on wh-movement that does not follow from the Subjacency Condition, island effects, or the complementizer-trace effect. This concerns multiple wh-questions, as illustrated in (115).

(115)   a.   Who brought what?
         b.   Marjorie won't tell us who brought what.

Normally the answer to a direct question like (115b) would be a list of pairs linking bringers with things brought. The derivations of both the direct question in (115a) and the indirect question in (115b) will at one point contain the syntactic structure (116).

(116) $[_C$?? $[_{TP}$ who $[_T$ T $[_{VP}$ brought what]]]]

At this point, wh-movement could apply to either interrogative pronoun (i.e. wh-phrase), all things being equal. This is not the case, however, since wh-movement applied to *what* yields deviant results, as shown in (117).

(117)   a.   *What did who bring?
         b.   *Marjorie won't tell what who brought.

The wh-movement from object position intra-clausally is otherwise unexceptional, so the constraint on this application must be related to the presence of the wh-phrase in subject position.

This construction involves two potential targets for wh-movement where one asymmetrically c-commands the other. When a category A asymmetrically c-commands a category B, A is **superior** to B. The deviant constructions in (117) result from an application of wh-movement where Merge bypasses a superior candidate. This can be prohibited by a **Superiority Condition** on movement operations that restricts movement to the superior constituent.

(118)   **The Superiority Condition:**
Merge the superior target constituent in a structure.

In the case of wh-movement, the target constituent will be a wh-phrase; in the case of movement to Spec-TP, it will be a NP or CP. (117) violates the Superiority Condition.

One question about the Superiority Condition is whether it generalizes to other pairs of constituents that don't include Spec-TP. Consider for example the VP *talk with* X *about* Y and its alternative ordering *talk about* Y *with* X.

(119)   a.   Fred talked with Melanie about plans for the conference.
          b.   Fred talked about plans for the conference with Melanie.

Changing the two objects of the two prepositions to interrogative pronouns yields four potential outcomes. (119a) corresponds to the two results in (120).

(120)   a.   Who(m) did Fred talk with about what?
          b.   *What did Fred talk with who(m) about?

(119b) corresponds to the two results in (121).

(121)   a.   What did Fred talk about with who(m)?
          b.   *Who(m) did Fred talk about what with?

In the syntactic structures that binary Merge produces for the two examples in (119) neither interrogative pronoun will c-command the other and therefore the relation "superior" will not apply to them. The deviance of the b-examples in (120–121) therefore does not follow from the Superiority Condition.

Another problem for the Superiority analysis is that it makes the wrong prediction for wh-phrases other than bare interrogative pronouns. The following examples are not even marginal.

(122)   a.   Which books did which students borrow?
          b.   Whose books did which students borrow?
          c.   Which books did whose students borrow?
          d.   Whose books did whose students borrow?

Wh-phrases like *which books* and *whose students* can be distinguished from bare interrogative pronouns in that the former are linked to a discourse (**d-linked**) by the specific nouns (*books* and *students*) they contain, whereas the latter are not. However limiting the Superiority Condition to non d-linked wh-phrases undermines a potential for generality by restricting it to the two cases in (117).

Exercise 8.25

Consider the following two paradigms.

    (i)   a.   Which reviews of whose books did he read?
           b.   Which reviews did he read of whose books?
           c.   Whose books did he read which reviews of?
    (ii)   a.   Whose reviews of which books did he read?

> b.   Whose reviews did he read of which books?
> c.   *Which books did he read whose reviews of?

a.   What is the syntactic structure of (i.a) at Spell-Out?
b.   Why can't the PF representation of (i.b) be derived by wh-movement of *which books* by itself to Spec-CP?
c.   How is the PF representation of (i.b) derived?
d.   What are the two possible derivations for the PF representation of (i.c)?
e.   What is the syntactic structure of (ii.a) at Spell-Out?
f.   Why can't the PF representation of (ii.b) be derived by wh-movement of *whose books* by itself to Spec-CP?
g.   How is the PF representation of (ii.b) derived?
h.   How could (ii.c) be derived? Why is (ii.c) deviant?

Exercise 8.26

a.   Convert the direct questions in (122) into indirect questions.
b.   Discuss whether this affects the status of these constructions.
c.   Discuss in detail how the Superiority Condition as formulated in (118) would incorrectly prohibit (122).
d.   How might a structural formulation of the Superiority Condition distinguish between multiple wh-questions like (122) and (117)?
e.   Convert (120–121) into examples with d-linked wh-phrases (e.g. *which mathematicians* and *which problems*) and discuss how this affects the status of the resulting sentences and our analysis of them.

In spite of the problems posed by multiple wh-questions for a Superiority Condition, the notion of superiority as asymmetric c-command has other applications for a theory of movement. Wh-island effects are subsumed under Superiority as are some constraints on successive cyclic movement to Spec-TP. In fact, all of successive cyclic movement might be reducible to some sort of superiority effect by changing the focus from movement to attraction. Instead of a constituent moving to another position, movement could be conceptualized as the attraction of a constituent to a position, focusing instead on the element that attracts. Thus for wh-movement, the element in C would attract a wh-phrase – i.e. the closest wh-phrase. The relation "closest" should then involve some notion of "superior," thus implicating asymmetric c-command. Chomsky 1995b (p. 311) formulates a **Minimal Link Condition** (MLC) along these lines.

(123)   **Minimal Link Condition:**
        K attracts α only if there is no β, β closer to K than α, such that K attracts β.

The MLC will apply to a number of cases covered in this and previous chapters, depending on how "closer" is defined. Whether such a condition is preferable to the Subjacency analysis of movement remains an open question that is worth serious consideration.

Exercise 8.27

Consider again the deviance of Example (28) in Chapter 3, given here without any analysis.

> (i) *This book, it would have been to Mary that Bill gave.

Note that topicalization of either *Bill* or *to Mary* is possible with a non-cleft construction.

> (ii)   a.   This book, Bill gave to Mary.
>   b.   To Mary, Bill gave this book.

Note also that switching the positions of *this book* and *to Mary* in (i), yielding (iii) also yields a deviant construction.

> (iii)   *To Mary, it would have been this book that Bill gave.

a.   Assuming that cleft constructions involve wh-movement in the embedded CP, give the syntactic analysis of the following nondeviant examples.

> (iv)   a.   It was to Mary that Bill gave the book.
>   b.   It was the book that Bill gave to Mary.

(Notice that (iv.b) has two distinct possible interpretations, one involving a relative clause that modifies *book* – to be set aside for this exercise).

b.   Given your analysis in (a), discuss how the deviant examples in (i) and (iii) might be prohibited using the principles discussed in this chapter.

c.   What does your answer to (b) reveal about the analysis of topicalization (i.e. the syntactic analysis of the examples in (ii))?

8.4   Summary

The architecture of the system of grammar presented in this chapter is as follows:

a.   Mechanisms of the computational system:
   i.   Merge
   ii. Delete (chain reduction)

b.   Constraints on derivations and representations:
   i.   Subjacency Condition
   ii.   Complex NP Constraint
   iii. Wh-island Constraint
   iv.   Superiority Condition
   v.   Minimal Link Condition

c.   Parameters:
   i.   chain reduction
      1.   retain the head (English, French, German, Spanish, etc.)
      2.   retain the tail (Chinese, Japanese)
   ii. bounding categories for Subjacency
      1.   in English: TP
      2.   in Italian: CP instead of TP
      3.   in Russian: both CP and TP

Displacement of wh-phrases in direct and indirect wh-questions involves pro-nunciation in Spec-CP and interpretation in some argument position in TP. At LF, the wh-element functions as a quantifier that binds a variable. Therefore wh-displacement must occur prior to Spell-Out. In Chinese where there is no overt displacement of wh-phrases, wh-questions must still have the same LF represen-tations as their English counterparts. Therefore wh-movement to Spec-CP must apply prior to Spell-Out but chain reduction in Chinese applies to the front of a chain, leaving the tail in PF. Parametric variation again holds on the PF side. On the LF side in English, a complementary operation occurs for certain pied-piped wh-phrase (e.g. *whose proposal* in *whose proposal did she select?*) where the VP is interpreted as "selected x's proposal" and the displaced N *proposal* is not interpreted as part of the quantifier binding a variable. This analysis carries over to relative clauses, where the same phrase will modify a N rather than serve as the complement of a V. There is a range of variation in relative clauses on the PF side involving both finite and infinitival forms, but LF requires that all of them involve wh-movement whether or not it is overt.

As with movement to Spec-TP, the Subjacency Condition constrains the move-ment of wh-phrases to Spec-CP. The condition overlaps with some island con-straints, in particular the Complex NP Constraint (CNPC) and the wh-island constraint. In the case of the latter, the overlap is total. The Subjacency Condition enforces successive cyclic wh-movement, just as it enforces successive cyclic movement to Spec-TP. Empirical evidence for successive cyclic movement is provided by subject inversion phenomena in Spanish and the distribution of com-plementizers in Irish. The Subjacency Condition could subsume all the empirical effects of the CNPC if NP is considered a bounding category. This works for movement out of NPs that contain possessive subjects, but not for object NPs that do not. However, the notion of island, specifically wh-island, is suspect given that in Italian it is possible to extract a relative wh-phrase out of an indirect wh-question. This is accounted for under the Subjacency analysis by changing TP for CP as a bounding category. In Russian, there is no interclausal wh-displacement. This follows if in Russian the bounding categories for Subjacency are both TP and CP.

The Subjacency Condition cannot account for all constraints on wh-displace-ment. Indirect yes/no questions are also islands for interclausal wh-displacement (*whether*-islands). Furthermore, wh-displacement is blocked out of subject posi-tion in the presence of an overt complementizer (so-called *that*-trace violations). Also, when there are multiple wh-phrases in a clause and hence multiple targets for displacement, the one that asymmetrically c-commands the other must be selected (Superiority Condition). However this applies only in the case of bare interrogative pronouns and does not apply with *which*-phrases. Nonetheless, conditions like the Superiority Condition involve intervention effects which generalize to wh-islands (in English) and movement to Spec-TP. Changing the perspective from movement to attraction, a Minimal Link Condition can be for-mulated that can be construed as a condition on minimal computation. However, the problems mentioned remain.

Bibliographical notes

The literature on wh-displacement (aka wh-movement) in generative grammar is enormous. Chomsky 1977 is one of the classic papers. See Huang 1982 for the original discussion of covert wh-movement in Chinese; for a related discussion of Japanese with an alternative analysis to wh-in situ constructions, see Watanabe 1992. The discussion of relative clauses is based on the analysis of Chomsky and Lasnik 1977. See the bibliographical notes of Chapter 6 regarding the Subjacency Condition. See also Chen and Corver 2006 for a collection of articles taking Chomsky 1977 as a starting point and re-examining the issues it raised in light of recent developments in syntactic theory. The empirical evidence for successive cyclic wh-movement in Spanish is from Torrego 1984; the evidence from Irish is discussed in McCloskey 2002. The parametric analysis for Subjacency in Italian comes from Rizzi 1980. For discussion of *whether*-island violations compared to CNPC violations, see Sprouse 2007. On movement violation that involve "complementizer-trace" phenomena, see again Chomsky and Lasnik 1977 and also Pesetsky 1981. The original formulation of the Superiority Condition on transformations is given in Chomsky 1973, which uses a very different framework. See Chomsky 1995b for a formulation of the Minimal Link Condition that gives a precise characterization of the relation "closer" and the operation "attracts." Given the formulation of the MLC, a "closer" target constituent blocks the movement of other possible target constituents – what is often called an **intervention effect**. The MLC belongs to a group of proposals about intervention effects going back to at least the late 1970s, including Wilkins 1977, Koster 1978, and Rizzi 1990 among others.

9   Ellipsis: unpronounced syntax

Problems worthy
of attack
prove their worth
by hitting back.

Piet Hein, *Collected Grooks*, vol. 1.

In the syntactic theory developed over the last eight chapters, deletion is analyzed as a syntactic operation that applies after Spell-Out on the PF side of the derivation. By hypothesis, it erases all the remaining features of a syntactic constituent (i.e. its phonetic, morphological, and syntactic features). One fundamental function of deletion is chain reduction in PF representation, which is required by the Principle of Full Interpretation. Such deletions are thus obligatory. However, there are also instances of deletion that do not appear to involve nontrivial chains. One case that came up briefly at the end of Chapter 3 concerned the deletion of a single verb in the second clausal conjunct of a coordinate structure, which goes under the rubric of **gapping**. This is illustrated in (1b), where the main verb of the second clausal conjunct is deleted.

(1)   a.   Jonathan left yesterday and Mary left the day before.
        b.   Jonathan left yesterday and Mary ~~left~~ the day before.

Although the verb *left* is not pronounced in the second conjunct in (1b), it is nonetheless interpreted at LF as the main verb of that clausal conjunct. Obviously (1b) has the same LF representation as (1a). Gapping is one form of ellipsis in natural language, which allows a single LF representation to map onto two PF representations, one a reduced version of the other. Unlike chain reduction, ellipsis via deletion is an optional operation. Minimally, both ellipsis and chain reduction involve the erasure of phonetic features in a PF representation.

In contrast to the deletion of a single overt lexical item in (1b), phrasal constituents may also be optionally deleted. The pair of sentences in (2) illustrates that an entire TP is also subject to optional deletion.

(2)   a.   Adam will study an Asian language, but I don't know which Asian
             language ~~Adam will study~~.
        b.   Adam will study an Asian language, but I don't know which language
             Adam will study.

In (2), the complement of the verb *know* is analyzed as a CP with an interrogative wh-phrase *which language* in Spec-CP via wh-movement. This CP has the structure given in (3).

(3)   [$_{CP}$ [$_{NP}$ which Asian language] [$_C$?? [$_{TP}$ Adam [$_T$ will [$_{VP}$ study [$_{NP}$ which Asian language]]]]]]

The derivation of (2a) on the PF side involves the deletion of the TP in (3), an operation called **sluicing** (see Ross 1969 for the original discussion, though in a different framework). The derivation of (2a) on the LF side will be identical to the corresponding derivation of (2b). Thus (3) will occur as part of the second conjunct at Spell-Out in the derivation of (2a). Sluicing constructions involve a combination of wh-movement and deletion. Exactly how this interaction operates will be discussed in Section 9.3.

Intermediate between gapping and sluicing, there are ellipsis constructions in which only a VP deletes, as illustrated by the pair in (4).

(4)   a. Louise will eat oysters and Fred might eat oysters too.
         b. Louise will eat oysters and Fred might ~~eat oysters~~ too.

Given the synonymy of (4a) and (4b), they will have the same LF representation, whereas the derivation of the PF representation of (4b) involves the deletion of the VP in the second clausal conjunct. This operation is referred to as **VP ellipsis** (or alternatively **VP deletion**).

In gapping, sluicing, and VP ellipsis (henceforth VPE), the deleted syntactic construct matches a corresponding overt syntactic construct in the preceding conjunct. In the following discussion the overt matching construct is designated as the **antecedent** of the deleted construct, which is called the **ellipsis site**. One issue that arises for the deletion analysis of ellipsis is the exact nature of the match between the ellipsis site and its antecedent, the **matching property**. Another issue concerns the syntactic configuration in which the two constructs can occur, the **configurational property**. As illustrated below, the three types of ellipsis construction identified above manifest different configurational properties, though close to the same matching property.

The following analysis of ellipsis phenomena begins with VP deletion, then moves on to gapping, and concludes with an analysis of sluicing.

9.1   VP ellipsis

The first issue to determine in the analysis of VPE phenomena is the precise nature of the ellipsis site. In (4b) the deleted material obviously constitutes a V phrase, but is it the maximal VP in the second conjunct? The answer hinges on whether *too* is a constituent of the VP or not. If it is, then VPE in (4b) involves deletion of a non-maximal projection of V. This can be tested with other VP constructions in which the VPs in the two conjuncts contain contrasting material.

(5)   a. Louise won't eat oysters for lunch but Fred might eat oysters for dinner.
         b. Louise won't eat oysters for lunch but Fred might ~~eat oysters~~ for dinner.

The VP in the second conjunct of (5a) has the structural analysis given in (6).

(6)   [$_{VP}$ [$_V$ eat oysters] [$_{PP}$ for dinner]]

Thus the deletion of the phrase *eat oysters* in (5b) involves a non-maximal projection of V. (6) itself can become a target for VPE when it is embedded in a larger VP like (7).

(7)   [$_{VP}$ [$_V$ [$_V$ eat oysters] [$_{PP}$ for dinner]] tonight]

Consider the pair of examples in (8).

(8)   a.   Louise won't eat oysters for dinner tonight, but Fred might eat oysters
                 for dinner tomorrow.
           b.   Louise won't eat oysters for dinner tonight, but Fred might eat oysters
                 ~~for dinner~~ tomorrow.

Moreover, the entire VP in the second conjunct (i.e. (7)) can undergo VPE, as shown in (9).

(9)   Louise won't eat oysters for dinner tonight, but Fred might ~~eat oysters for dinner tonight~~.

Furthermore, the maximal VP undergoing VPE can be as small as a single verb. Consider for example, the following constructions.

(10)   a.   Louise won't eat oysters for dinner, but Fred might ~~eat oysters for dinner~~.
           b.   Louise won't eat oysters, but Fred might ~~eat oysters~~.
           c.   Louise won't eat, but Fred might ~~eat~~.

In each instance of VPE above, the ellipsis site is identical in syntactic structure and lexical content to its antecedent. If this generalizes to all other cases of VPE, then the matching property is identity of syntactic and phonetic structure.

   Under the analysis of clauses developed in the previous chapters, a nonfinite aspectual auxiliary (e.g. the tenseless forms of auxiliary *have* and *be*) will head a VP and take a VP as its complement. Consider the syntactic structure of (11) as given in (12).

(11)   Fred won't have studied for the entrance exam.
(12)   [$_{TP}$ Fred [$_T$ won't [$_{VP}$ have [$_{VP}$ studied [$_{PP}$ for [$_{NP}$ the entrance exam]]]]]]

Thus (11) contains the two VPs listed in (13), one contained in the other.

(13)   a.   studied for the entrance exam
           b.   have studied for the entrance exam

If VPE is a purely syntactic phenomenon whereby a VP is deleted under identity, then VPE should be possible in both sites. Now consider the following examples.

(14)   a.   Fred won't have studied for the entrance exam, but he should have
                 ~~studied for the entrance exam~~.
           b.   *Fred won't have studied for the entrance exam, but he should ~~have studied for the entrance exam~~.

(14a) is a perfectly acceptable variant of the sentence without the ellipsis. In contrast, (14b) is not. If the sentence corresponding to (14b) – i.e. (15a) – has an interpretation, then it would be something like (15b), where the perfective auxiliary has dropped out.

(15) a. Fred won't have studied for the entrance exam, but he should.
       b. Fred won't have studied for the entrance exam, but he should study for the entrance exam.

Nonetheless, (15a) strikes some speakers as odd and the interpretation (15b) seems somewhat forced. Note that even if (15b) were acceptable as a viable interpretation for (15a), there would still be the problem of explaining why (14b) is not a legitimate outcome of applying VPE to the clause *he should have studied for the entrance exam*. Thus it appears that VPE cannot apply to a VP whose head is the bare form of the perfective auxiliary.

EXERCISE 9.1

Consider a similar paradigm for cases involving the progressive auxiliary.

(i) a. Fred won't be studying for the entrance exam, but he should be ~~studying for the entrance exam~~.
      b. ?*Fred won't be studying for the entrance exam, but he should ~~be studying for the entrance exam~~.

a. Putting aside that (i.b) is marked as questionably deviant, do you actually find a difference in acceptability between the two examples? (And if so, how would you characterize that difference?)
b. How do the examples in (14) compare to those in (i)?
c. Based on your answers to (a) and (b), what would you conclude about constraints on VPE constructions?

The prohibition against the perfective auxiliary as the head of a VP ellipsis site can also be illustrated in another more complex case where the perfective auxiliary is sandwiched between a modal and a progressive auxiliary. Thus consider the clause structure of (16), given in (17).

(16)   Fred won't have been studying for the exam.
(17)   [$_{TP}$ Fred [$_T$ won't [$_{VP}$ have [$_{VP}$ been [$_{VP}$ studying for the exam]]]]]

In (17) there are three potential VPE targets, listed in (18).

(18) a. have been studying for the exam
       b. been studying for the exam
       c. studying for the exam

Using (16) as a first conjunct in a coordinate construction (19a) yields three potential VPE constructions in the second conjunct.

(19) a. Fred won't have been studying for the exam, but he could have been studying for the exam.
       b. Fred won't have been studying for the exam, but he could have been ~~studying for the exam~~.

c.   *Fred won't have been studying for the exam, but he could have ~~been studying for the exam~~.

d.   *Fred won't have been studying for the exam, but he could ~~have been studying for the exam~~.

Of the three (19b–d), only (19b) where the VP headed by the main verb has been deleted is unquestionably viable. (19d), in contrast, is unquestionably deviant, and (19c) also seems to be deviant.[1]

Although it is clear that some applications of VPE yield deviant results, complicating the formulation of the deletion operation to exclude the deviant cases is not the only way to account for the perceived deviance of examples like (19c–d). Under the simplest and most general formulation of VPE as "delete VP under syntactic and phonetic identity," any VP – including one that is headed by an aspectual auxiliary – would be subject to the grammatical operation. The perceived deviance of the starred examples could not be explained on the grounds that VPE could not produce such a result. Instead an explanation for this must be sought elsewhere. With this in mind, consider the discussion above of the deviant (14b)/(15a), where sentence processing yields the interpretation (15b). This sentence processing effect yields a different structure to the sentence, one which violates the matching property for VPE. In this way the perceived deviance would result from a combination of sentence processing effect and a grammatical constraint governing these constructions (i.e. matching). This is the normal situation for speaker judgments. The perceived deviance of an example could result from a problem with grammatical structure or processing (or a combination of the two factors, as in this case). Since introspection cannot reveal which factors are involved, the best that can be done is to formulate hypotheses, test them, and see what insights they might yield.

Keeping to the simplest and most general formulation of the computational system regarding VPE, the application of the operation will not exclude the deviant examples (14b) and (19c–d). The alternative would be to complicate the formulation of the grammatical mechanism in a way that leads to stipulating the facts. Thus, as long as the matching property is satisfied, VPE should be applicable. Note that this is just another instance where a construction made possible by the computational system turns out to be unusable (cf. the discussion of multiple center embedding of relative clauses in Chapter 1).

There is one case that appears to be a counterexample to formulating the matching property as syntactic and phonetic identity. This involves a mismatch of verb forms between the ellipsis site and its antecedent.

(20)   Harry lectured on the syntax of sluicing this morning and June will ~~lecture on the syntax of sluicing~~ again tomorrow.

Given (20) it looks like the ellipsis site contains the bare form of the verb *lecture* while its antecedent contains the finite inflected past tense form *lectured*. However, as discussed in Chapter 7, the finite form of a main verb is derived via affix-hopping. Prior to the application of this operation, the main verb will be the

bare form, so before the application of affix-hopping, the ellipsis site and its antecedent are in fact phonetically and syntactically identical in spite of appearances
to the contrary. If VPE applies to the second conjunct prior to affix-hopping in
the first conjunct, then the formulation of the matching property as phonetic and
syntactic identity can be maintained.

EXERCISE 9.2

Discuss whether (20) provides empirical evidence for the affix-hopping analysis.
One way to address this question is to consider how (20) must be analyzed if instead
of affix-hopping, finite main verbs were merged fully inflected from the lexicon.

There is another case of mismatching verb forms that is less easily resolved.
Thus consider the pair of sentences in (21).

(21)   a.   Harry will join us once June has joined us.
         b.   Harry will join us once June has ~~joined us~~.

Again it appears that the verb in the ellipsis site does not match the corresponding verb in the antecedent because the latter is in the bare form while the former
is a past participle. If matching occurs under identity, then the ellipsis site should
have the form (22) – i.e. with the bare form of the verb.

(22)   [$_{VP}$ join us]

If it does, then there would be a selectional violation with the perfective auxiliary
has, depending on how selectional violations are determined. Suppose that selectional violations involving the morphology of verbal elements are determined in
PF representations at the interface, then deletion – in this case VPE – eliminates
the violation. That is, deletion of the offending verb form "repairs" the structure
so that it no longer contains a selectional violation. If VPE does not apply, then
the resulting structure violates selection between the perfective auxiliary and the
overt head of its complement VP.

EXERCISE 9.3

Consider the following paradigm.

    (i) a.   Once June has joined us, Harry will join us.
        b.   Once June has joined us, Harry will.
        c.   *Once June has joined us, Harry will joined us.

a. Assuming that the matching property for VPE is syntactic and phonetic identity,
   why can't the structure of (i.a) be part of the derivation of (i.b)?
b. What then must be the derivation for (i.b) and how does this involve (i.c)?
c. What accounts for the deviance of (i.c)?
d. In what way(s) is the analysis of (i) the same as the analysis given for (19)? In
   what way (if any) is it different?

Notice that under our characterization of the ellipsis site, VPE seems to subsume gapping, where a single main verb inside a larger VP is deleted. The perception is misleading. Consider first that VPE can occur in subordinate clauses as well as conjuncts of coordinate clauses. (23) provides one illustration and (24), another.

(23)   a.   Adam bought a new computer when his brother bought a new computer.

              b.   Adam bought a new computer when his brother did ~~buy a new computer~~.

However, gapping can only occur in a conjunct of a coordinate structure, not in a subordinate clause. Thus gapping is impossible in (24).

(24)   a.   Adam bought a new computer when his brother bought a new refrigerator.

              b.   *Adam bought a new computer when his brother ~~bought~~ a new refrigerator.

The contrast between the legitimate (23b) and the deviant (24b) provides striking evidence that VPE and gapping must be distinct grammatical operations. Furthermore, (24b) shows that VPE applies to phrasal constituents, not to a head as a head. VPE only applies to an isolated head when it by itself constitutes its maximal projection and thus functions as a phrasal constituent.

The examples discussed so far show that a VP ellipsis site can occur in both a main clause conjunct of a coordinate construction (e.g. (20)) and a subordinate clause (e.g. the temporal adjunct clause in (23)). (25) shows that VPE can also occur in a clausal conjunct that is also a subordinate clause.

(25)   Marsha told us that Harry lectured on the syntax of sluicing this morning and (that) June will ~~lecture on the syntax of sluicing~~ again tomorrow.

In (25), (20) occurs as the clausal complement of *told*. In the coordinate constructions discussed above, the VP ellipsis site and its antecedent are on the same syntactic level. This is not necessary, as (26) shows.

(26)   Harry lectured on the syntax of sluicing this morning and we have heard that June will ~~lecture on the syntax of sluicing~~ again tomorrow.

The antecedent occurs in a root clause clausal conjunct, while the ellipsis site occurs in a subordinate clause of the other root clause conjunct. In terms of hierarchical structure, the antecedent in (26) is higher than the ellipsis site. In (27), the antecedent is lower than the ellipsis site.

(27)   We were promised that Harry would lecture on the syntax of sluicing, but he didn't ~~lecture on the syntax of sluicing~~.

The ellipsis site is in a root clause conjunct, while its antecedent occurs in a subordinate clause of the other root clause conjunct. These examples demonstrate that the configurational property for VPE is not affected by the relative height of the antecedent to the ellipsis site in a coordinate construction.

EXERCISE 9.4

Consider the analysis of the following sentences.

(i) a. Fred says that Mary will be praising every wine by the end of the evening and Susan says that Bill won't be.
   b. Fred says that Mary will be praising every wine by the end of the evening and Robert heard that Susan says that Bill won't be.
   c. Roberta heard that Fred is predicting that Mary will be praising every wine by the end of the evening, and Susan maintains that Bill won't be.

a. What is the syntactic structure of each example in (i)? (If you think that more than one structure can be assigned to any of these examples, give the additional structures.)
b. Identify the relationship between the ellipsis site and its antecedent in each case.
c. How do these examples confirm what has already been discovered about the configurational property for VPE?
d. What new information (if any) do they provide?

When the VP ellipsis site is in a subordinate clause, then its antecedent will be higher if that antecedent VP properly contains the ellipsis site, as in (23b) for example. And as (28) illustrates, the antecedent can be separated from the ellipsis site by multiple clause boundaries.

(28)   a. John will attend our meetings when Mary confirms that Sally will ~~attend our meetings~~ (too).
        b. John will attend our meetings when Susan has announced that Mary confirms that Sally will ~~attend our meetings~~ (too).

The syntactic distance between an ellipsis site in a subordinate clause and its antecedent does not appear to matter.

EXERCISE 9.5

Consider the following example:

(i) John said that he will attend our meetings when Mary confirmed that Sally will.

(i) is ambiguous; the ambiguity depends on which verb (*said* vs. *attend*) is construed as modified by the *when*-clause.

a. Give the two syntactic analyses that demonstrate this and the two distinct interpretations to their corresponding syntactic structures.
b. Which syntactic structure gives us a new piece of information about the configurational property of VPE and what is that information?

So far, we have been examining VPE only in finite clauses, but as (29) demonstrates, VPE also occurs in infinitival subordinate clauses.

(29)   a. Mary will leave early if she wants to ~~leave early~~.
        b. We think that Mary should leave early, because she said that she
            wanted to ~~leave early~~.

In (29a) the antecedent VP occurs in the root clause and the ellipsis site, in a
subordinate clause. In (29b) both the ellipsis site and its antecedent occur in
subordinate clauses.

EXERCISE 9.6

Because there are two ways to analyze the scope of the *because*-clause, (29b) is
apparently ambiguous, whereas (29a) is not.

a. Give the syntactic analysis for (29a).
b. Identify the two different possible syntactic analyses for (29b).
c. Discuss the configurational relationships between the ellipsis site and its
    antecedent for the syntactic structures you give for (29a) and (29b).
d. Consider the interpretations of the two syntactic structures for (b): are they in fact
    distinct?

VP complements of an infinitival *to* may also contain aspectual auxiliaries, as
shown in (30).

(30)   a. Mary wants Jeff to have tasted every wine we served for dinner.
        b. Jeff expects Mary to be meeting with every member of our committee.

Given that both the root clause verbs and the two subjects in (30) can be
exchanged, yielding (31), these examples can also combine into the compound
sentences (32).

(31)   a. Jeff expects Mary to have tasted every wine we served for dinner.
        b. Mary wants Jeff to be meeting with every member of our committee.
(32)   a. Mary wants Jeff to have tasted every wine we served for dinner and
            Jeff expects Mary to have tasted every wine we served for dinner.
        b. Jeff expects Mary to be meeting with every member of our committee
            and Mary wants Jeff to be meeting with every member of our
            committee.

These coordinate constructions in (32) make VPE derivations possible. With an
aspectual auxiliary in addition to the main verb in these infinitival complement
VPs, there are two potential VPE targets – in (32a) for example, (33).

(33)   a. tasted every wine we served for dinner
        b. have tasted every wine we served for dinner

The two potential results for a VPE derivation are given in (34).

(34)   a. Mary wants Jeff to have tasted every wine we served for dinner and
            he expects her to have ~~tasted every wine we served for dinner~~.
        b. *Mary wants Jeff to have tasted every wine we served for dinner and
            he expects her to ~~have tasted every wine we served for dinner~~.

Again VPE that applies to the VP headed by a main verb is preferable. This holds as well for VPE involving subordinate clauses.

(35)   a.   ?Mary wants to have tasted every wine we served for dinner because
                Jeff expects her to have ~~tasted every wine we served for dinner~~.
           b.   *Mary wants to have tasted every wine we served for dinner because
                Jeff expects her to ~~have tasted every wine we served for dinner~~.

In contrast, infinitivals without an aspectual auxiliary take VPE naturally.

(36)   a.   Mary wants Jeff to taste every wine we served for dinner and he
                expects her to ~~taste every wine we served for dinner~~.
           b.   Mary wants to taste every wine we served for dinner because Jeff
                expects her to ~~taste every wine we served for dinner~~.

In (36a) VPE involves a coordinate construction where the antecedent occurs in the first conjunct and the ellipsis site occurs in the second. In (36b) the ellipsis site and its antecedent occur in clauses that are subordinate to the root clause.

EXERCISE 9.7

The following example is ambiguous.

  (i) Mary wants to taste every wine we served for dinner because Jeff expects her to.

Putting aside the possible scope ambiguity involving the *because*-clause, one interpretation would be the one represented in (36b).

a. What is the other interpretation?
b. What is the syntactic structure of the ellipsis site under each interpretation?
c. Discuss whether the same ambiguity is possible with the PF representation for
    (36a).

EXERCISE 9.8

The VPE analysis given thus far has covered infinitival VPs containing a perfective auxiliary. What happens with infinitival VPs containing a progressive auxiliary?

a. Using (32b), what are the two potential antecedents and hence two potential
    ellipsis sites in the first conjunct?
b. Construct the example that results from choosing each antecedent.
c. Discuss the viability of each example and how they compare.
d. Recast the second conjunct of (32) as a subordinate clause to the first conjunct
    (but without any VPE, cf. (35)).
e. Give the two possible VPE constructions based on (d).
f. Discuss the viability of each example and how they compare.
g. Compare these examples with those involving perfective *have*.
h. Compare these examples with those in (36).

i. On the basis of what you have seen with the perfective auxiliary in an infinitival VP complement and your analysis of such VPs headed by the progressive auxiliary, what would you conclude about VPE in infinitivals?

In virtually all of the viable examples examined so far, the antecedent precedes the ellipsis site. If the two are switched in any of these examples, the result is deviant. (37a) gives an example involving a coordinate construction; (37b–c) involve a subordinate clause.

(37)   a.   *Harry did ~~lecture on the syntax of sluicing~~ this morning and June will lecture on the syntax of sluicing again tomorrow.
          b.   *John will ~~attend our meetings~~ when Sally will attend our meetings.
          c.   *John will ~~attend our meetings~~ when Sally attends our meetings.

The subordinate *when*-clause in (37c) can also occur in clause initial position as (38) illustrates.

(38)   When Sally attends our meetings, John will attend our meetings (too).

In this structure, antecedent precedence also holds.

(39)   a.   When Sally attends our meetings, John will ~~attend our meetings~~ (too).
          b.   *When Sally does ~~attend our meetings~~, John will attend our meetings (too).

If this precedence relation functions as a constraint on the application of VPE, then VPE must apply after the operation that places the subordinate clause in clause-initial position.

EXERCISE 9.9

If the subordinate clause in clause-initial position is a copy of this CP at the end of the clause, issues about the ordering of the application of operations arise. In this case there are three: VPE, Merge, and chain reduction.

a. Because one operation feeds the other, chain reduction and Merge are inherently ordered. Discuss.

This is not the case with VPE and Merge as it applies to the *when*-clause. Consider the derivation of (i).

(i) When Sally attends our meetings, John will.

b. What would happen in the derivation of (i) if VPE applies before Merge displaces the subordinate clause to clause-initial position?
c. What problem does this ordering create?
d. What would happen in this derivation if the operations apply in the reverse order?
e. Show what happens in the derivation of (i) if VPE applies before chain reduction.
f. Now show what happens in the derivation if the operations apply in the reverse order.
g. Discuss what your answers to (e) and (f) tell us about the ordering of VPE and chain reduction.

VPE in infinitivals is further constrained. For example, there cannot be an ellipsis site in a purpose clause infinitival even if antecedent precedence is satisfied.

(40)   a.   *John showed up to help us move and Bill showed up to ~~help us move~~
               too.
          b.   *Mary wants to leave early if Bill will wake up at 5 a.m. in order to
               ~~leave early~~.

In (40a), both the antecedent VP and the corresponding ellipsis site are in infinitival purpose clauses; whereas in (40b), while the ellipsis site is in a purpose clause, its antecedent is in the infinitival complement of a root clause verb. (41) shows that an ellipsis site in a infinitival complement can have an antecedent that occurs in a purpose clause.

(41)   a.   John showed up to read the children stories because he wanted to.
          b.   John showed up to read the children stories because he wanted to
               ~~show up to read the children stories~~.
          c.   John showed up to read the children stories because he wanted to
               ~~read the children stories~~.

The PF representation (41a) is ambiguous. Under the interpretation indicated in (41b), the antecedent is the root clause VP, but in the case of (41c) the antecedent VP is the VP of the purpose clause. Thus the prohibition regarding VPE and infinitival purpose clauses is restricted to the ellipsis site.

VPE in infinitivals is also prohibited when the ellipsis site occurs within certain wh-infinitival constructions, like the CP complement of (42).

(42)   a.   Mary will decide who to invite to the conference.
          b.   Mary will decide $[_{CP}$ who $[_{C}$ C $[_{TP}$ PRO $[_{T}$ to $[_{VP} [_{V}$ invite who$]$ $[_{PP}$ to the
               conference$]]]]]]$

This is demonstrated in (43).

(43)   *Mary will decide who to invite to the conference because John can't figure
               out who to.

The ellipsis site consists of the VP (44).

(44) $[_{VP} [_{V}$ invite who$][_{PP}$ to the conference$]]$

The deletion operation that produces (43) would eliminate the nontrivial chain for *who* in the *because*-clause, thereby preempting chain reduction. However, the result is deviant for VPE. In contrast, if the entire wh-infinitival is deleted, then the result is viable.

(45)   Mary will decide who to invite to the conference because John can't
               ~~decide who to invite to the conference~~.

The prohibition extends to other wh-infinitivals.

(46)   a.   *Mary can't decide where to go for a vacation, so Bill has to choose
               where to ~~go for a vacation~~.
          b.   *Fred never knows when to quit, so we always have to tell him when
               to ~~quit~~.

Moreover, it includes not only indirect wh-questions, but also indirect yes/no questions.

(47)   *Bill plans to take a vacation in August, but Mary can't decide whether to ~~take a vacation in August~~.

Note that (47) appears to be as deviant as the examples in (43) and (46). Given that *whether*-islands appear to be weaker than wh-islands (i.e. a clause with a wh-phrase in Spec-CP, in contrast to a wh-C), the source of the deviance for these ellipsis constructions cannot be accounted for by postulating that islands create barriers for deletion as well as movement.

Moreover, in more complicated constructions, VPE can apply to an infinitival VP inside a wh-CP (i.e. one with a wh-phrase in Spec-CP).

(48)   a.   John will leave the meeting when Mary tells him to ~~leave the meeting~~.
            b.   Mary had to tell John to enroll in the syntax course because he couldn't decide whether he wanted to ~~enroll in the syntax course~~.

While the syntactic analysis of (48b) is essentially straightforward, the analysis of (48a) is more complicated, in part because (48a) is ambiguous. Under one interpretation, John will leave the meeting the moment Mary asks him. Under the other, he will leave the meeting at the time Mary specifies, which need not be the moment her request is made. Under the former interpretation, *when* would be an adjunct of the VP headed by *tells*, which modifies *tells* (and therefore is not a constituent of the VP headed by *leave*). Under the latter interpretation, *when* would be an adjunct of the VP headed by *leave*, thus modifying *leave* and not *tells*. (48a) under either interpretation seems totally unexceptional compared to (49).

(49)   (?)*John will leave the meeting if Mary tells him when to ~~leave the meeting~~.

(49) also contrasts with (50), where the infinitival TP has been replaced with a finite clause.

(50)   John will leave the meeting if Mary tells him when he should ~~leave the meeting~~.

Like (48a), (50) is also ambiguous. On one interpretation, when it's time for John to leave the meeting, Mary tells him "leave the meeting." On this interpretation the *when*-clause functions as an adjunct modifying *tells*. On the other interpretation, Mary tells John the time he should leave, in which case the *when*-clause functions as a complement of *tells*. Regardless of this ambiguity, (50) demonstrates that VPE occurs naturally inside a finite wh-CP.

EXERCISE 9.10

While (50) is ambiguous, (i) is not.

(i) John will leave the meeting if Mary tells him when to leave.

a. Which of the two interpretations of (50) corresponds to the interpretation of (i)?

b. What is the syntactic analysis of (i)?

c. How does it compare to the analysis of (50)?

d. Discuss whether this comparison provides a basis for explaining why (i) is unambiguous in contrast to (50).

EXERCISE 9.11

So far only wh-CPs that allow VPE in infinitival clauses where Spec-CP contains *when* have been considered.

a. Construct examples similar to (48a) in acceptability where Spec-CP contains: *who*, *what*, *where*, and *why*.

b. How do the analyses of the examples you constructed compare with that of (48a)? For example, are any of them ambiguous in the same way that (48a) is?

c. With the same wh-words, construct examples that correspond to (49).

d. How do the analyses of the examples you constructed compare with that of (49) (e.g. in terms of acceptability)?

The contrast between (49) vs. (48a) and (50) suggests that the problem with the former is limited to CPs with the form (51).

(51) $[_{CP}$ wh-phrase $[_C$ C $[_{TP}$ PRO $[_T$ to ~~VP~~]]]]

Comparing the deviant (47) to the acceptable (48) demonstrates that CPs with the form (52) are also problematic.

(52) $[_{CP}$ whether $[_{TP}$ PRO $[_T$ to ~~VP~~]]]

Why both (51) and (52) are deviant remains to be explained. Whether they are subcases of the single violation is not obvious. Note that (52) is also similar to the prohibition against [*for to*] infinitivals, as in (53d).

(53)   a.   They want Fred to join us.
        b.   They want to join us.
        c.   They want very much for Fred to join us.
        d.   *They want very much for to join us.

The infinitival complement in (53d) is similar in structure to (52), as shown in (54).

(54) $[_{CP}$ for $[_{TP}$ PRO $[_T$ to VP]]]

Therefore, it is plausible that whatever prohibits (54) also prohibits (53). Whether this account can be extended to (51) remains to be determined.

Further restrictions on VPE occur with infinitivals that form constituents of NPs. Consider, for example, the sentence (55a) and its corresponding nominalization (55b).

(55)   a.   The university plans to create a linguistics department.
        b.   the university's plan to create a linguistics department

In both, the infinitival clause *to create a linguistics department* constitutes a complement – of the verb in (55a) and of the nominal in (55b). Suppose that when it comes to creating linguistic departments, there is also a decision to do so that might come before or after the plan to create one. This leads to sentences like (56).

(56)   The plan to create a linguistics department was formulated after the
            decision to create a linguistics department was made.

However the repetition of the VP in the complement of *decision* does not constitute a viable ellipsis site, as the deviance of (57) establishes.

(57)   *The plan to create a linguistics department was formulated after the
            decision to ~~create a linguistics department~~ was made.

In (57) both the ellipsis site and its antecedent are constituents of NPs. The deviance of (57) could be due to either the position of the antecedent or the position of the ellipsis, or possibly the combination of the two (i.e., when only the antecedent or else the ellipsis site is a constituent of a NP, then there is no deviance). The deviance of (58) shows that a VP inside a NP is not a viable antecedent.

(58)   a.   *The plan to create a linguistics department was formulated after the
             Board of Trustees decided to ~~create a linguistics department~~.
        b.   *The Dean formulated a plan to create a linguistics department after
             the Board of Trustees decided to ~~create a linguistics department~~.[2]

In (58a), the nominal containing the potential VP antecedent occurs in clausal subject position (Spec-TP), whereas in (58b), the corresponding nominal occurs in the object position of the root clause verb. The ellipsis site in both cases is in a clausal complement of the subordinate clause verb *decided to*. Now consider the case where the ellipsis site is inside a NP, but not the antecedent.

(59)   a.   *The Board of Trustees decided to create a linguistics department, after
             the Dean formulated a plan to ~~create a linguistics department~~.
        b.   *The Board of Trustees decided to create a linguistics department, after a
             plan to ~~create a linguistics department~~ had been formulated by the Dean.

It makes no difference whether the NP containing the ellipsis site is in a subject position (59b) or an object position (59a). (57–59) establish that if either the VP ellipsis site or its antecedent occurs in a NP, VPE is prohibited. These examples contrast with those in (60), where neither the ellipsis site nor its antecedent occur in a NP.

(60)   a.   The President planned to create a linguistics department before the
             Dean decided not to ~~create a linguistics department~~.
        b.   The President planned to create a linguistics department before the
             Dean could decide not to ~~create a linguistics department~~.
        c.   The Board of Trustees decided to endorse the creation of a linguistics
             department after the Dean announced that she was going to ~~endorse the~~
             ~~creation of a linguistics department~~.[3]

(60c) shows that both the ellipsis site and its antecedent may contain a nominalization, in contrast to (57–59) which demonstrate that they cannot be contained in one.

The prohibition against VPE involving infinitivals inside a NP carries over to infinitival relative clauses.

(61)   *Tom sent Dick a script to memorize and he sent Harry a song to ~~memorize~~.

(61) is deviant on all interpretations of *he* (i.e. with Tom, Dick, or someone else (excluding Harry) as the antecedent). Although it might appear that VPE could not apply to the relative clause modifying *song* because it is not identical to the one modifying *script* and therefore deletion would violate the identity constraint, this is not obviously correct. The analysis of *a script to memorize* would be (62).

(62) $[_{NP}$ a $[_N$ script $[_{CP}$ O$_x$ $[_C$ C $[_{TP}$ PRO $[_T$ to $[_{VP}$ memorize O$_x$]]]]]]]]

The fact that the copy of the logical operator O$_x$ that occurs as the object of *memorize* becomes a variable at LF linked to *script* does not register on the PF side. Therefore the infinitival relative clause that modifies *song*, given in (63), has the same syntactic and phonetic structure as (62).

(63) $[_{NP}$ a $[_N$ song $[_{CP}$ O$_x$ $[_C$ C $[_{TP}$ PRO $[_T$ to $[_{VP}$ memorize O$_x$]]]]]]]]

The identity requirement for VPE would be met, so the deviance of (61) must follow from some other prohibition. One possibility would be to generalize the prohibition against VPE involving infinitivals inside NP. In (61) both the ellipsis site and its antecedent are contained inside NPs.

EXERCISE 9.12

Consider the following deviant example.

(i) *Harry wants to memorize a song that Tom sent him to ~~memorize~~.

a. What is the syntactic analysis of (i).
b. Why is VPE prohibited in this structure?

The prohibition against VPE involving infinitival relative clauses does not generalize to finite relative clauses.

(64)   Martin refuses to chair the next meeting, but I can easily find someone who
         will ~~chair the next meeting~~.

Moreover, if *will* is changed to *won't*, another interpretation of the ellipsis site is possible.

(65)   Martin refuses to chair the next meeting, but I can easily find someone who
         won't ~~refuse to chair the next meeting~~.

And with a few minor changes in (64), including changing the main clause verb to *agreed*, two distinct interpretations can be derived, as represented in (66).

(66) a. Martin agreed to chair the next meeting, and I can also find someone
          else who will ~~chair the next meeting~~.
      b. Martin agreed to chair the next meeting, and I can also find someone
          else who will ~~agree to chair the next meeting~~.

Given that the main clause in (66) allows for two distinct antecedents, the main
clause in (64) should also on purely syntactic grounds. It would appear that one
of these potential interpretations is ruled out on semantic grounds. Notice that if
and is substituted for *but,* and *someone else* for *someone* in (64), the other interpretation becomes more plausible.

In (64–66) the ellipsis site is contained within a relative clause, hence inside
a NP, while the antecedent is either the main clause VP or the VP of the complement of the main clause verb. VPE is also possible when both the ellipsis site and
its antecedent are contained in separate finite relative clauses, as in (67).

(67) Martin mentioned someone who has agreed to chair the next meeting and I
      know someone else who has ~~agreed to chair the next meeting~~.

It is also possible for just the antecedent VP to occur in a finite relative clause.

(68) Martin mentioned someone who has agreed to chair the next meeting and I
      know that Martin himself has ~~agreed to chair the next meeting~~.

(64–68) demonstrate that with respect to finite relative clauses, all configurations
concerning the ellipsis site and its antecedent are possible.

EXERCISE 9.13

Consider the following constructions where VPE appears to fail.

(i)   a. John's claim that Marsha annoyed us annoyed us.
       b. *John's claim that Marsha annoyed us did ~~annoy us~~.

(ii)   a. That John claimed that Marsha annoyed us annoyed us.
       b. *That John claimed that Marsha annoyed us did ~~annoy us~~.

(iii) a. It annoyed us that John claimed that Marsha annoyed us.
       b. *It annoyed us that John claimed that Marsha did ~~annoy us~~.

a. Give the syntactic analyses of the a-examples in (i–iii).
b. Discuss whether the matching and configurational properties for VPE are satisfied
   in these structures.
c. How are these constructions different from those where VPE is viable?
d. Speculate on what might account for the failure of VPE in the b-examples. (Is
   there a general account that covers all three cases?)

EXERCISE 9.14

There is one other construction in which VPE applied to an infinitival fails. First
consider that certain predicate adjectives can take a bare infinitival (i.e. without an

overt subject) complement and because they assign only one θ-role, they occur with a pleonastic subject, as in (i.a).

(i)   a.   It could be dangerous to handle poisonous snakes.

       b.   To handle poisonous snakes could be dangerous.

As discussed in Chapter 6, such clausal complements can be displaced to subject position if no pleonastic element is merged as Spec-TP, an example of which is given as (i.b). Embedding these examples as subordinate clauses where the main clause repeats the complement VP creates a proper context for VPE.

(ii)   a.   You should not handle poisonous snakes because it could be dangerous to handle poisonous snakes.

       b.   You should not handle poisonous snakes because to handle poisonous snakes could be dangerous.

The repetition of the VPs in (ii) is awkward, but presumably not structurally unsound. Applying VPE to (ii) yields (iii).

(iii)   a.   You should not handle poisonous snakes because it could be dangerous to ~~handle poisonous snakes~~.

       b.   *You should not handle poisonous snakes because to ~~handle poisonous snakes~~ could be dangerous.

Now consider the following pair.

(iv)   a.   It would be self-defeating not to study for the exam.

       b.   Not to study for the exam would be self-defeating.

The sentences in (iv) can also be embedded as subordinate clauses.

(v)   a.   John should study for the exam because it would be self-defeating not to study for the exam.

       b.   John should study for the exam because not to study for the exam would be self-defeating.

Applying VPE to (v) yields (vi).

(vi)   a.   John should study for the exam because it would be self-defeating not to ~~study for the exam~~.

       b.   John should study for the exam because not to ~~study for the exam~~ would be self-defeating.

a.   Compare the derivations of the deviant (iii.b) and the viable (vi.b).

b.   In the derivation of (vi.b) can VPE apply before Merge?

c.   Construct other more complex sentences that show that VPE can apply to infinitivals in Spec-TP.

d.   Construct the full paradigm that shows how VPE applies to finite clause complements of predicate adjectives and discuss what this shows.

9.1.1   Antecedent contained deletion

In every viable case of VPE considered so far, the VP antecedent is in a linear relation with the ellipsis site – i.e., the former always precedes the latter. There is a class of VPE constructions where this relationship does not appear to hold. These involve VP ellipsis sites in relative clauses, as illustrated in (69).

(69)   a.   Mary doesn't like the authors that Bill does.
          b.   Mary doesn't like the authors Bill does.

Under the syntactic analysis of (69a) as (70), the ellipsis site (rendered as a VP in bold-face) is a constituent of the main clause VP, which is presumably its antecedent.

(70)   [$_{TP}$ Mary [$_T$ doesn't [$_{VP}$ like [$_{NP}$ the authors [$_{CP}$ O$_x$ [$_C$ that [$_{TP}$ Bill [$_T$ does
          VP]]]]]]]]]

The syntactic structure of (69b) would be identical to (70) except that the C head of the relative clause would be the phonetically null ç. Note that the relative clause operator O$_x$ in Spec-CP is a copy of the same operator that is in the ellipsis site **VP**, where it would be the object of V in the relative clause. If (70) is the correct analysis for (69) and the main clause VP is the antecedent of the ellipsis site, then the antecedent contains the ellipsis site, making (69) a case of **antecedent contained deletion** (ACD).

ACD constructions create a puzzle for the PF-deletion analysis of VPE if the VP in boldface in (70) must match its antecedent both phonetically and structurally. The problem is perhaps easier to grasp by first considering an alternative analysis where the ellipsis site is constructed as an empty VP, hence no deletion at PF, and is instead replaced at LF with a copy of its antecedent VP via an LF-copying operation. Under the LF-copying analysis, (69) would have a different syntactic analysis because the ellipsis site would be a single syntactic element without internal structure. Because of this, the relative clause operator would have no syntactic source and therefore would not occur in Spec-CP of the relative clause. Thus under the LF-copying analysis, (69) would have the syntactic structure (71).

(71)   [$_{TP}$ Mary [$_T$ doesn't [$_{VP}$ like [$_{NP}$ the authors [$_{CP}$ that [$_{TP}$ Bill [$_T$ does **VP**]]]]]]]]

(71) would presumably be expanded under the LF-copying analysis to provide a full LF representation of (69). Replacing **VP** with its putative antecedent yields (72).

(72)   [$_{TP}$ Mary [$_T$ doesn't [$_{VP}$ like [$_{NP}$ the authors [$_{CP}$ that [$_{TP}$ Bill [$_T$ does [$_{VP}$ like [$_{NP}$
          the authors [$_{CP}$ that [$_{TP}$ Bill [$_T$ does **VP**]]]]]]]]]]]]]]

The purpose of LF-copying is to provide an interpretation of the ellipsis site **VP**. However, LF-copying doesn't achieve this in ACD constructions because it produces another ellipsis site in the resulting representation that apparently requires further interpretation. Thus the procedure of LF-copying leads to an infinite regress. This is in addition to the problem of not representing the subordinate CP as a standard relative clause where there is an operator in Spec-CP that binds a variable in TP. And finally, an empty VP cannot be created by Merge and would almost certainly violate the Inclusiveness Condition.

The PF-deletion analysis of VPE runs into the same infinite regress if the ellipsis site **VP** in (70) is replaced by the main clause VP, which of course contains **VP**, as demonstrated in (73).

(73)   [TP Mary [T doesn't [VP like [NP the authors [CP Oₓ [C that [TP Bill [T does [VP like [NP the authors [CP Oₓ [C that [TP Bill [T does **VP**]]]]]]]]]]]]]]]

The problem for the deletion analysis is twofold. Like the LF-copying analysis there is the problem of specifying the LF representation of (69), and in addition, there is a problem with showing how the matching property is met, which is however satisfied trivially under LF-copying.

A first step in resolving these problems is to determine the analysis of the ellipsis site in the problematic ACD construction. This will involve the analysis of a related construction, the one in which the problematic relative clause has no ellipsis site. Thus compare the VPE construction (69) [repeated below as (74a)] with the standard relative clause in (74b).

(74)   a.   Mary doesn't like the authors (that) Bill does.
         b.   Mary doesn't like the authors (that) Bill likes.

The two sentences in (74) are virtually synonymous, which suggests that they ought to have the same LF representation. Moreover, they constitute a syntactic minimal pair. (74b) has the syntactic analysis (75).

(75)   a.   [TP Mary [T doesn't [VP like [NP the authors [CP Oₓ [C that/ç [TP Bill [T [−past, φ] [VP like Oₓ]]]]]]]]]]

         b.

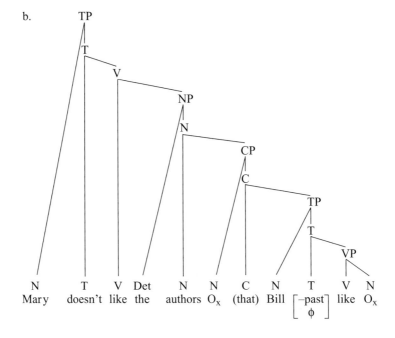

Given that O_x is the phonetically null equivalent of the relative pronoun *who*, the relative clause VP has the same syntactic structure as the main clause VP, i.e. $V - NP$. In LF representation, the relative clause operator in Spec-CP will bind a variable in VP, as with wh-movement involving an interrogative pronoun. If this is correct, then (75) should be the pre Spell-Out syntactic structure of (74a) as well. To derive the relative clause without ellipsis (74b), affix-hopping applies to the feature complex of the relative clause T in (75). To derive the relative clause with ellipsis, VPE applies to (75), deleting the VP (76).

(76)   [$_{VP}$ like O_x]

That leaves the tense and agreement feature complex in T stranded, so *do*-Support must apply to avoid a violation of the NFAC, as discussed in Chapter 7.

The syntactic derivations of the pair of sentences (74) are seemingly straightforward except for the application of VPE in the ACD construction. If the syntactic structure of the ellipsis site in (74a) is (76), then the characterization of the matching property for VPE has to be revised because this ellipsis site does not contain phonetic features identical to the proposed antecedent, hypothesized to be (77).

(77)   [$_{VP}$ like [$_{NP}$ the authors]]

Exactly how this structure, which does not exist in the syntactic analysis (75), can be derived is a question that will be answered below. Syntactically, (76) and (77) are identical, whereas phonetically they are different. However this difference does not involve disjointness in the two sets of phonetic features. That is, it is not the case that the antecedent contains phonetic features not contained in the ellipsis site (prior to deletion) *and also* that the ellipsis site contains features not contained in the antecedent. Rather, the antecedent contains phonetic features (e.g. *the authors*) that the ellipsis site does not. The ellipsis site thus contains only a subset of the phonetic features of the antecedent. In terms of phonetic features, the ellipsis site is nondistinct from its antecedent. If the matching property is revised from phonetic identity to phonetic nondistinctness, ACD constructions like (74a) can be accommodated straightforwardly.

This phonetic nondistinctness analysis suggests an explanation for the deviant status of VPE in a relative clause that contains an overt relative pronoun. Compare (74a), where there is no overt relative pronoun, with the corresponding sentence (78), whose relative clause contains the overt pronoun.

(78)   *Mary doesn't like the authors who Bill does.

As a further contrast, note that (79), which contains a relative clause without VPE is as acceptable as the examples in (74).

(79)   Mary doesn't like the authors who Bill likes.

(78) after Spell-Out would have the syntactic structure (80).

(80)   [$_{TP}$ Mary [$_T$ doesn't [$_{VP}$ like [$_{NP}$ the authors [$_{CP}$ who [$_C$ ç [$_{TP}$ Bill [$_T$ [−past, φ]
        [$_{VP}$ like who]]]]]]]]]]

Therefore the ellipsis site would be phonetically distinct from the antecedent (77). Deletion of the VP containing the relative pronoun should therefore be blocked.

This analysis imposes an ordering on VPE and chain reduction. If chain reduction could apply to (80) before VPE, then the ellipsis site and its antecedent would be phonetically nondistinct. Then chain reduction would create a context in which VPE could legitimately apply to (80) to produce the deviant (78). To exclude this derivational possibility, VPE must not apply to the output of chain reduction.

The syntactic part of the matching property for VPE would require no revision if the ellipsis site (76) has as its antecedent (77), making the two syntactically identical. The problem for the syntactic analysis of (74a) is deriving (77) from (75), where the string *like the authors* does not form a separate constituent because the relative clause is also a constituent of the NP headed by *authors*.

One solution is to drop the assumption that the ellipsis site and its antecedent must be identical constituents, and reformulate the syntactic matching property. Suppose instead this requirement is weakened as follows: the ellipsis site, which forms a single constituent, defines a syntactic string that has to match an antecedent. In the case of (74a), the ellipsis site (76) requires that there be an antecedent string consisting of a V followed by a NP (but not that these two syntactic objects form an independent constituent). This weakening of the syntactic matching property would accommodate the analysis of ACD constructions. Note that the phonetic nondistinctness constraint itself imposes a syntactic constraint on the matching of ellipsis site and antecedent because subsets of the ordered set of phonetic features are linked to syntactic category labels and these impose a certain syntactic structure on the whole. This may be sufficient to avoid problems that might arise if the syntactic matching constraint is weakened so that the antecedent needs only match the ellipsis site syntactically as a string rather than as a constituent. Given this analysis there is no phenomenon of ACD because the ellipsis site is no longer contained in its syntactic antecedent. It should be clear that for the non-ACD cases of VPE, where the stronger matching condition holds, this weaker matching condition also works.

Given that a relative pronoun can be merged in a subordinate clause contained in a relative clause, it should be the case – if all things are equal – that a VP ellipsis site can also be inside that subordinate clause. As an example, consider the pair of sentences in (81).

(81)   a.   Mary will not read a book (that) Jack wants her to read.
          b.   Mary will not read a book (that) Jack wants her to.

The relative clause in (81b) contains a VP ellipsis site, in contrast to the relative clause in (81a), which doesn't. Here again, the examples in (81) are virtually synonymous and therefore would (by hypothesis) have the same LF representation. (82) gives the syntactic structure of the relative clauses in (81a–b) at Spell-Out.

(82) $[_{CP} O_x [_C$ that $[_{TP}$ Jack $[_T [-$past, $\phi] [_{VP}$ want $[_{CP} O_x [_C C [_{TP}$ her $[_T$ to $[_{VP}$ read O_x]]]]]]]]]]$

The only difference between the two examples in (81) is that VPE applies to (82) in the derivation of (81b).

EXERCISE 9.15

Consider the corresponding examples to (81) that have overt relative pronouns.

(i) a.   Mary will not read a book which Jack wants her to read.
  b.   *Mary will not read a book which Jack wants her to.

a. What is the syntactic structure of both relative clauses in (i) at Spell-Out?
b. What is the PF representation of (i.a) and how is it derived from (a)?
c. What accounts for the deviance of (i.b)?

EXERCISE 9.16

In the following example the antecedent and the ellipsis site both occur in subordinate clauses.

(i) Mary is eager to read a book that Jack doesn't want her to.

a. Give the corresponding example where VPE has not applied in the relative clause.
b. Give the syntactic analysis of the relative clause at Spell-Out.
c. Discuss how VPE applies to (b) to derive (i).
d. Compare (i), (81b), and (74a) [perhaps changing the verb to *read*] in terms of acceptability. You can answer this based on just your own intuitions or you can collect additional information from other informants.

EXERCISE 9.17

Compare the following examples.

(i) a.   Mary will not take a class this semester that Jack refused to take last semester.
  b.   Mary will not take a class that Jack refused to take last semester this semester.

Assume that in (i.a) the relative clause modifying *class* has been extraposed and that therefore the syntactic structure for (i.b) must represent some point in the derivation of (i.a).

a. Give the syntactic structure for (i.b).
b. Give the syntactic structure for (i.a) and discuss how it is derived, assuming that the NTC is satisfied.
c. Give the two sentences that could be derived if VPE applies to the syntactic structures underlying (i).
d. Discuss the derivation of the VPE construction corresponding to (i.a).
e. Compare the examples in (i) to those from (c) in terms of acceptability.

The relative clause constructions in (81) (and the previous exercises) involve inter-clausal wh-movement. When there is no VPE in the relative clause, island effects will occur in the same way that inter-clausal wh-movement of interrogative phrases is subject to island effects. What happens in those same syntactic environments when VPE applies now becomes a crucial question. Compare, for example, the pair of sentences in (83).

(83)   a.   *Mary won't read a book that Jack cannot remember why Bill read.
         b.   *Mary won't read a book that Jack cannot remember why Bill did.

Both sentences seem to be equally deviant.[4] The syntactic structure of the relative clause at Spell-Out is given in (84).

(84) $[_{CP}$ O$_x$ $[_C$ that $[_{TP}$ Jack $[_T$ cannot $[_{VP}$ remember $[_{CP}$ why $[_C$ C $[_{TP}$ Bill $[_T$ [+past, φ] $[_{VP}$ $[_V$ read O$_x$] why]]]]]]]]]]]

The analysis (84) for the relative clause without VPE (i.e. (83a)) contains a nontrivial chain for the relative operator O$_x$ whose single link violates the Subjacency Condition by crossing two TP boundaries.

In the derivation of (83b) from (84), VPE would have to delete the V-phrase containing the verb and its covert object O$_x$. Under the criterion of phonetic nondistinctness this deletion ought to be legitimate; but it isn't. Nonetheless, applying VPE to (84) eliminates the nontrivial chain {O$_x$, O$_x$} and thus the Subjacency violation.

The analysis of (83b) raises an interesting question about how Subjacency violations are determined. Consider first the analysis of (83a), which involves wh-movement without the further complication of VPE. One way to register the Subjacency violation is on the PF side of a derivation.[5] Given that nontrivial chains are not legitimate syntactic objects at the PF interface, the Subjacency Condition would have to function as a condition that blocks the application of chain reduction. Under this analysis the resulting PF representation will contain a nontrivial chain in violation of Full Interpretation. This analysis will account for the deviance of (83b) as a Subjacency violation, but only if chain reduction applies prior to VPE. But this contradicts the conclusion reached previously regarding the analysis of (78), a construction in which VPE inside a relative clause is blocked when the relative clause contains an overt relative pronoun in Spec-CP.

At this point there are two ways to proceed. If the analysis that orders chain reduction before VPE is maintained, then another analysis of the deviance of (78) must be found. Alternatively, the proposed ordering can be rejected, in which case another way to account for the deviance of (83b) as a Subjacency violation will be required. The question is whether chain reduction can feed VPE – i.e. create an environment where VPE can apply when it couldn't apply without the prior application of chain reduction. So far no legitimate VPE construction whose derivation requires the application of chain reduction before VPE has appeared (but see Section 9.2 for discussion of such a construction).

EXERCISE 9.18

Apparently the same Subjacency effect can be found in coordinate structures (i.e. non-ACD constructions) that occurs in (83). Consider the analysis of the following pair of deviant examples (adapted from Merchant 2001).

(i) a. *They said that they would hire someone who speaks a Balkan language, but it remains unclear which Balkan language they said they would hire someone who speaks.

   b. *They said that they would hire someone who speaks a Balkan language, but it remains unclear which Balkan language they said they would ~~hire someone who speaks~~.

The second conjunct in (i.a) contains an indirect question (ii).

(ii) which Balkan language they said they would hire someone who speaks

a. What is the syntactic structure of (ii) at Spell-Out?
b. What is the syntactic structure of the second conjunct in (i.a)?
c. How does it constitute a Subjacency Condition violation?
d. In the first conjunct of (i.b), what would the antecedent to the ellipsis site of the second conjunct in (i.b) have to be if VPE applies?
e. How could the derivation of (i.b) yield a Subjacency violation?

   In (83) and (i) of the exercise above both wh-movement and VPE are prohibited in the same syntactic contexts. Turning now to contexts where wh-movement is allowed whereas VPE is prohibited, consider the paired examples in (85) (adapted from Fox and Lasnik 2003).

(85)   a. They read about a Balkan language, but I don't know which Balkan language they studied.
          b. *They read about a Balkan language, but I don't know which Balkan language they did.

In this pair, the derivation of the legitimate (85a) involves wh-movement but not VPE, while the derivation of the deviant (85b) involves both wh-movement and VPE. The second conjunct in (85a–b) contains an indirect question (86) with a syntactic structure (87).

(86)   which Balkan language they read about
(87) $[_{CP} [_{NP}$ which Balkan language$] [_C$ ç $[_{TP}$ they $[_T [$+past, $\phi] [_{VP}$ read $[_{PP}$ about $[_{NP}$ which Balkan language$]]]]]]]$

In (87), the movement of the wh-phrase *which Balkan language* is viable because the chain formed crosses only one bounding category (TP).[6] Thus there is no Subjacency violation in the derivation of either (85a) or (85b). If chain reduction applies to (87), yielding (88), then VPE could apply to derive the deviant (85b).

(88) $[_{CP} [_{NP}$ which Balkan language$] [_C$ ç $[_{TP}$ they $[_T [$+past, $\phi] [_{VP}$ read $[_{PP}$ about $[_{NP}$ ~~which Balkan language~~$]]]]]]]$

Under this analysis, why (85b) is deviant remains undetermined. But if VPE applies before chain reduction, then the ellipsis site in (85b) will have the syntactic structure (89), which is phonetically distinct from its putative antecedent (90).

(89)   [$_{VP}$ read [$_{PP}$ about [$_{NP}$ which Balkan language]]]
(90)   [$_{VP}$ read [$_{PP}$ about [$_{NP}$ a Balkan language]]]

The phonetic difference concerns just the opposition of the two determiners *a* vs. *which*. In this way, the deviance of (85b) has the same source as the deviant (78). The analysis of both examples requires that VPE apply before chain formation.

EXERCISE 9.19

One avenue that is worth considering is whether the wh-island constraint (see Chapter 8) could be utilized to block the application of VPE in the derivation of (85b).

a. How would this constraint have to be formulated to cover the application of VPE deletion?
b. Could it be used to account for the deviance of (78)? Why or why not?
c. Show how this analysis could generalize to (83b).
d. Identify the VPE constructions previously discussed that constitute empirical evidence against this hypothetical wh-island analysis.

Nonetheless the deviant (83b) remains a problem. If VPE precedes chain formation, then it can apply legitimately in the derivation of (83b) because the VP in the relative clause is nondistinct from the putative antecedent *read a book*. If VPE deletes the verb *read* and its covert complement the relative operator O$_x$, that will eliminate the nontrivial chain that violates the Subjacency Condition. However, if VPE applies only to the phonetic feature of the verb, leaving the copy of the relative operator behind, then VPE will not eliminate the nontrivial chain that violates Subjacency.

EXERCISE 9.20

There is a further distinction between VPE constructions and their relative clause counterparts. Consider the following pair of examples.

(i) a.   Jack visited a major city in every country that he had to visit.
    b.   Jack visited a major city in every country that he had to.

The relative clause without VPE (i.a) is ambiguous, whereas the one with VPE is not.

a. Identify the two interpretations of (i.a).
b. Give the unique syntactic structure that corresponds to each interpretation.
c. Which of the two interpretations of (i.a) is also the interpretation of (i.b)?
d. How is the syntactic structure of (i.b) derived from the syntactic structure of (i.a) under the same interpretation?
e. Do any of the constraints on VPE discussed above account for why (i.b) could not be derived from the syntactic structure for (i.a) under the interpretation that (i.b) does not have?

9.2   Gapping and pseudogapping

As noted above, a single verb can be deleted in various syntactic configurations. VPE usually involves deletion of a verb plus constituents of the phrase it heads. In contrast, gapping appears to be an operation that can delete just a finite V. Consider the sentences in (1) [repeated here as (91)].

(91)   a.   Jonathan left yesterday and Mary left the day before.
          b.   Jonathan left yesterday and Mary ~~left~~ the day before

The second conjunct in (91a) has the syntactic structure (92) at Spell-Out.

(92) $[_{TP}$ Mary $[_{T}$ [+past], $\phi]$ $[_{VP}$ leave the day before]]]

The derivation of the second conjunct in (91b) must involve the deletion of V and also the deletion of the tense and agreement features in T of (92). The deletion of V must be able to occur separately so that (93) can be derived.

(93)   Jonathan left yesterday and Mary did ~~leave~~ the day before.

The derivation of the second conjunct in (93) involves the deletion of the V *leave* in (92), an application of VPE followed by the application of *do*-Support to the feature complex of T, which is required to prevent the derivation from violating the NFAC. If the tense and agreement features of T in (92) were deleted before affix-hopping adjoins a copy to V, then the deviant (94) results.

(94)   *Jonathan left yesterday and Mary leave the day before.

However there is no reason to assume that T can delete independently of V. This is confirmed by derivations involving Ts containing phonetic features (e.g. modals), for example the paradigm given in (95).

(95)   a.   Jonathan will leave tomorrow and Mary will leave the day after.
          b.   Jonathan will leave tomorrow and Mary ~~will leave~~ the day after.
          c.   Jonathan will leave tomorrow and Mary will ~~leave~~ the day after.
          d.   *Jonathan will leave tomorrow and Mary ~~will~~ leave the day after.

(95d), where just the T *will* deletes, is deviant in contrast to (95b), where both T and V delete, and (95c), where just V deletes. The second conjunct in (95b) differs from the corresponding conjunct in (95c) in that only the latter can occur in a subordinate clause, as illustrated in (96).

(96)   a.   Jonathan will leave tomorrow because Mary will ~~leave~~ the day after.
          b.   *Jonathan will leave tomorrow because Mary ~~will leave~~ the day after.

The difference demonstrates how the operation that derives the second conjunct in (95b) is different from the one that derives (95c). The deletion of just V is a form of VPE. The operation that deletes T + V together in the derivation of the second conjunct in (95b) is called **gapping**. Because T + V do not form a constituent, gapping appears to apply to a string that is not also a constituent.

Like VPE, gapping involves an antecedent as well as an ellipsis site. The strongest formulation of the matching property for gapping would be phonetic as well as syntactic identity. Phonetic nondistinctness also works for gapping just because there isn't any syntactic variability in the target, as opposed to VP. The configurational property regarding linear order is that when the operation applies, the antecedent must precede the ellipsis site. When it does not, the result is deviant, as in (97).

(97)   *Jonathan ~~will leave~~ tomorrow and Mary will leave the day after.

However the configurational properties of the two operations differ with respect to ellipsis sites in subordinate clauses as noted above.

EXERCISE 9.21

Our examples of gapping show that it applies in coordinated root clauses and that it cannot apply in a subordinate clause, but to say that gapping cannot apply in all subordinate clauses would be incorrect as (i) illustrates.

   (i) Al said that Jonathan will leave tomorrow and Mary ~~will leave~~ the day after.

a. Formulate the correct restriction on the application of gapping.

(Hint: consider the syntactic relations between the ellipsis site and its antecedent.)

EXERCISE 9.22

If affix-hopping involves internal Merge (hence copies), there will be two derivational paths for (91b). One involves chain reduction and the other does not.

a. Give the two potential derivations for the second conjunct in (91a).
b. How does the principle of economy of derivations choose between the two possibilities?

EXERCISE 9.23

Consider what happens when there are two verbal auxiliaries, one in T and the other not. No judgments are marked on the following examples, so the absence of a * or a ? (or a combination of these) does not indicate that the examples are fully acceptable.

   (i) a. Fred has been reading mysteries and Jane has been reading science fiction.
      b. Fred has been reading mysteries and Jane has been ~~reading~~ science fiction.
      c. Fred has been reading mysteries and Jane has ~~been reading~~ science fiction.
      d. Fred has been reading mysteries and Jane ~~has been reading~~ science fiction.
      e. Fred has been reading mysteries and Jane ~~has~~ been reading science fiction.

a. Rank (i.b–i.e) in order of acceptability if you find one or more of these examples to be less acceptable than the others.

b.   Which of these examples could be generated via VPE? Discuss how the
     derivation would work.
c.   Which of these examples could not be generated via VPE? Why not?
d.   What problems arise for deriving the viable sentences or blocking the deviant
     ones (given your judgments of these sentences)?

In contrast to gapping and VPE there is an ellipsis phenomenon called **pseudogapping** that appears to involve discontinuous elements. Consider the paradigms in (98–99) – (99a) is from Lasnik 2003.

(98)   a.   The DA proved Smith guilty and the Assistant DA will prove Jones guilty.
          b.   The DA proved Smith guilty and the Assistant DA will ~~prove~~ Jones ~~guilty~~.
(99)   a.   Mary counted John a friend but John doesn't count Mary a friend.
          b.   Mary counted John a friend but John doesn't ~~count~~ Mary ~~a friend~~.

Note that in both constructions deleting just the verb is not an option.

(100)   a.   *The DA proved Smith guilty and the Assistant DA will ~~prove~~ Jones
               guilty.
          b.   *Mary counted John a friend but John doesn't ~~count~~ Mary a friend.

Thus it appears that in constructions where pseudogapping can apply, VPE is not
possible.

   Nonetheless, it appears that pseudogapping is similar to VPE in that the ellipsis site can occur in a subordinate clause when the antecedent does not.

(101)   a.   ?The DA proved Smith guilty after we predicted that the Assistant DA
               would ~~prove~~ Jones ~~guilty~~.
          b.   After the DA proved Smith guilty, we predicted that the Assistant DA
               will ~~prove~~ Jones ~~guilty~~.

Gapping is not possible in such configurations.

   Because both pseudogapping and VPE constructions can occur in subordinate
clauses, it is plausible to analyze the former as a species of VPE. Consider for
example the analysis of the second conjunct in (98), where the VP in the first
conjunct has the syntactic structure (102).

(102)   [$_{VP}$ prove [$_{\alpha}$ Smith guilty]]

The VP in (102) must serve as the antecedent for VPE in the second conjunct.
Consider *Smith guilty* to be some form of reduced clause along the lines of *Smith
to be guilty*; however the actual label of α is not important at this point. Because
the NP *Smith* is pronounced in PF, there appears to be a serious matching problem between the ellipsis site and its putative antecedent. So if VPE is the right
analysis for pseudogapping constructions, then two conditions must be met: one,
that the ellipsis site matches its antecedent; and two, that there must be a copy of
Smith that remains after VPE applies. This can be achieved by merging a copy
of that NP outside the VP of the second conjunct prior to the application of VPE.

Therefore the derivation for the second conjunct in (98b) would produce a syntactic structure along the lines of (103).

(103) $[_\beta [_{NP}$ Jones] $[_{VP}$ prove $[_\alpha$ Jones guilty]]]

The actual label that β represents is left open here. As it stands, the VP in (103) is distinct from its antecedent VP in (102). To make it nondistinct, the phonetic features of *Jones* in α would have to be eliminated. The most likely mechanism for this is deletion via chain reduction, which will remove the phonetic features of *Jones* in VP. Then the ellipsis site will be phonetically nondistinct from its antecedent in (98b) as required.[7] Chain reduction applied to (103) yields (104).

(104) $[_\beta [_{NP}$ Jones] $[_{VP}$ prove $[_\alpha$ ~~Jones~~ guilty]]]

Because the VP in (104) satisfies both the matching and configurational requirements of VPE, VPE can apply to (104), yielding the second conjunct in (98b) with the structure (105).

(105) $[_{TP}$ The Assistant DA $[_T$ will $[_\beta [_{NP}$ Jones] $[_{VP}$ ~~prove~~ $[_\alpha$ ~~Jones guilty~~]]]]]

(105) constitutes the PF representation of the second conjunct in (98b).

Notice that in this derivation an application of chain reduction feeds an application of VPE, contradicting the conclusion reached in the previous section. Prior to the application of chain reduction to (100), VPE could not apply to the VP because the ellipsis site and its antecedent are phonetically disjoint. This is the opposite ordering required to account for the deviance of (78) and (85b) as discussed above. It would appear that the ordering VPE before chain reduction cannot be used to explain the deviance of these examples. However, the pseudogapping analysis developed above is not without issues. The NP fronting application of Merge that must apply in pseudogapping constructions occurs independently from the application of VPE. But if object fronting occurs then VPE must also apply; otherwise the resulting construction will be deviant. VPE is normally optional, so the question remains as to what accounts for its obligatory application in pseudogapping constructions.

Another issue to keep in mind is that simple VPE where only the V is deleted is not possible in pseudogapping constructions. However, in simple VPE constructions where only the main V deletes, it is possible to give a pseudogapping derivation for the same sentence. Consider the paradigm in (106).

(106)   a.   Mary will cook the fish and Bill will cook the potatoes.
         b.   Mary will cook the fish and Bill will ~~cook~~ the potatoes.

The derivation of (106b) could involve the displacement of the NP object *the potatoes* out of VP yielding a structure (107).

(107) $[_\alpha [_{NP}$ the potatoes] $[_{VP}$ cook $[_{NP}$ ~~the potatoes~~]]]

If chain reduction applies to (107), then the ellipsis site (taken to be the entire VP) will be phonetically nondistinct from the antecedent VP *cook the fish* in (106b). Alternatively, VPE could affect just the V, which is phonetically identical to the antecedent V and then chain reduction would eliminate the NP copy in VP. So applying chain reduction first is not necessary in these cases. Furthermore, the pseudogapping derivation involves an extra step, the displacement of the object NP, and therefore such derivations for simple VPE constructions would be ruled out on the grounds of economy of derivations (fewest steps) all things being equal.

The VPE analysis of pseudogapping does raise a possibility that simple VPE (i.e. without NP displacement out of VP) may not handle. Consider a VP with several adjuncts in addition to an object. If VPE applies after chain reduction, then pseudogapping as VPE can apply to larger VP structures. Consider for example the VP (108), which contains two adjuncts in addition to an object NP.

(108)   cook the fish tomorrow for dinner

Recasting the examples in (106) using (108) and a corresponding VP for the second conjunct yields (109).

(109)   a.   Mary will cook the fish tomorrow for dinner and Bill will cook the
                  potatoes tomorrow for dinner.
           b.   ?*Mary will cook the fish tomorrow for dinner and Bill will cook the
                  potatoes tomorrow for dinner.

The derivation of (109a) involves no deletion. Although the VP in the second conjunct is almost entirely repetitious except for the object NP, (109a) is completely acceptable compared to its gapped counterpart in (109b). (109b) is somewhat degraded in spite of the fact that it eliminates some of the repetition that makes (109a) stylistically unappealing.[8] In contrast to the gapping construction (109b), the corresponding pseudogapping construction (110) eliminates all the repetition in the second conjunct with the exception of the modal *will*.

(110)   Mary will cook the fish tomorrow for dinner and Bill will the potatoes.

(110) is potentially synonymous with (109a), but not necessarily so. Notice that (111b) could be interpreted as synonymous with (111a) where no VPE occurs.

(111)   a.   Mary will cook the fish tomorrow for dinner and Bill will the potatoes
                  tomorrow for dinner.
           b.   Mary will cook the fish tomorrow for dinner and Bill will cook the
                  potatoes.

Presumably the potential synonymy between (109a) and (110) is not the result of VPE. Therefore, there is so far no reason to derive simple VPE constructions via pseudogapping. If so, then pseudogapping constructions will be quite limited.

9.3   Sluicing

In contrast to VPE, the derivation of sluicing constructions necessarily involves both wh-movement and deletion. In this regard, sluicing is like pseudogapping, which obligatorily involves a movement operation along with a deletion. But unlike either VPE or pseudogapping, sluicing is an ellipsis operation that involves the deletion of a larger constituent than VP, as illustrated in (2), repeated here as (112).

(112) a. Adam will study an Asian language, but I don't know which Asian language Adam will study.
       b. Adam will study an Asian language, but I don't know which Asian language ~~Adam will study~~.

In terms of overt material, the deletion in (112b) involves a TP.

Given that sluicing constructions are like other forms of ellipsis, it will involve an ellipsis site and an antecedent. The sluicing structure is itself a CP with a wh-phrase in the Spec position. In (112b) this construction has the syntactic analysis (113).

(113) [$_{CP}$ [$_{NP}$ which Asian language] [$_{C}$?? [$_{TP}$ Adam [$_{T}$ will [$_{VP}$ study [$_{NP}$ which Asian language]]]]]]

Sluicing occurs when the phonetic material in TP is deleted, yielding (114).

(114) [$_{CP}$ [$_{NP}$ which Asian language] [$_{C}$?? [$_{TP}$ ~~Adam~~ [$_{T}$ ~~will~~ [$_{VP}$ ~~study~~ [$_{NP}$ ~~which Asian language~~]]]]]]

Exactly how (114) is derived depends on what matching property holds for the sluicing operation, as will be discussed below.

Configurationally, the relation between the ellipsis site and its antecedent in sluicing has the same properties as in VPE. In (112b) the antecedent TP occurs in the first root conjunct, and the ellipsis site, in a subordinate clause of the second conjunct. In (115b) the ellipsis site is contained in a subordinate CP in the second conjunct while its antecedent occurs in a subordinate CP in the first conjunct.

(115) a. Eric told us that Adam will study an Asian language, but we don't remember which Asian language Adam will study.
       b. Eric told us that Adam will study an Asian language, but we don't remember which Asian language ~~Adam will study~~.

As might be expected, sluicing is also possible when either the ellipsis site or its antecedent is more deeply embedded.

(116) a. Joan insists that Eric told us that Adam will study an Asian language, but we don't remember which Asian language ~~Adam will study~~.
       b. Eric told us that Adam will study an Asian language, but he knows that we won't remember which Asian language ~~Adam will study~~.

In (116a) the antecedent in the first conjunct is contained in a clause subordinate to another subordinate clause, while the ellipsis site is contained in only a single subordinate clause. In (116b) the ellipsis site in the second conjunct is contained in a clause subordinate to another subordinate clause, while its antecedent is contained in a single subordinate clause. Now consider (117), which combines with slight modification the first conjunct of (116a) and the second conjunct of (116b).

(117)   Joan insists that Eric told us that Adam will study an Asian language, but
         she knows that we won't remember which Asian language ~~Adam will study~~.

(117) is as viable as (116a–b) and (112b), thereby demonstrating that depth of embedding of either the sluicing antecedent or ellipsis site does not affect acceptability.

Turning now to the matching property for sluicing, the first thing to notice is that at Spell-Out the antecedent TP and the ellipsis site TP are syntactically identical but phonetically distinct. Consider the derivation of (112b). At Spell-Out, the antecedent TP in the first conjunct has the syntactic structure (118a) while the ellipsis site TP has the syntactic structure (118b).

(118)   a. $[_{TP}$ Adam $[_T$ will $[_{VP}$ study $[_{NP}$ an Asian language]]]]
         b. $[_{TP}$ Adam $[_T$ will $[_{VP}$ study $[_{NP}$ which Asian language]]]]

The phonetic difference rests entirely on the contrast between the two determiners *an* and *which*. This problem can be resolved in exactly the same way a similar problem with pseudogapping was resolved. Suppose that chain reduction applies to the complement CP of the second conjunct before sluicing applies. Then the matching of antecedent and ellipsis site in (112b) is not between (118a) and (118b), but instead between (118a) and (119).

(119) $[_{TP}$ Adam $[_T$ will $[_{VP}$ study $[_{NP}$ ~~which Asian language~~]]]]

(119) is phonetically non-distinct with respect to (118a), so sluicing can apply because the matching property is satisfied. Here again the matching property determines that chain reduction must apply before an ellipsis operation, even though it might appear that the ellipsis operation itself could eliminate the non-trivial chain.

EXERCISE 9.24

Consider the example in (i).

(i) Fred told us that Adam wants to study an Asian language, but we don't
    remember which Asian language.

a. What is the syntactic structure of the second conjunct in (i) at Spell-Out?
b. Given this structure, identify the antecedent and the ellipsis site involved in
   derivation of the PF representation of the second conjunct.
c. Discuss the derivation of the second conjunct before Spell-Out.
d. Discuss how the PF representation of the second conjunct is derived after
   Spell-Out.
e. What is the LF representation of the second conjunct?
f. There is more than one candidate for the antecedent of the ellipsis site. Explain.
g. Discuss how a sluicing derivation based on this other antecedent leads to the same
   phonetic string, but a different LF representation.

EXERCISE 9.25

The following example is triply ambiguous.

> (i) Fred told us that Sarah believes Adam wants to study an Asian language, but we don't remember which Asian language.

a. If (i) is triply ambiguous, then there must be three distinct candidate antecedents possible for the ellipsis site. Identify the three possible antecedents in the first conjunct.
b. Using your answers to (a), what would the syntactic structures of the second conjunct be at Spell-Out?
c. Discuss how sluicing maps the syntactic structures from (b) onto the same phonetic string in PF representation.

EXERCISE 9.26

Notice that (i.a) and (i.b) have essentially the same intepretation.

> (i) a. Roberta knows that she can solve some of the problems, but she can't say which problems she can solve.
>   b. Roberta knows that she can solve some of the problems, but she can't say which problems it is that she can solve.

The syntactic structure of (i.a) at Spell-Out can be mapped onto (ii), which contains a sluicing construction in the second conjunct.

> (ii) Roberta knows that she can solve some of the problems, but she can't say which problems.

a. Identify the antecedent in the first conjunct of (i.a) and ellipsis site in the second conjunct of (i.a).
b. Given our analysis of sluicing, why can't (i.b) map onto (ii) as well?

However (ii) can map onto (iii) via a deletion operation.

> (iii) Roberta knows that she can solve some of the problems, but she can't say which problems it is.

c. Identify the ellipsis site and its antecedent and discuss how the ellipsis site satisfies matching and configurational properties for ellipsis.
d. How is this ellipsis operation different from sluicing? (Is there any way to reformulate either or both so that they become the same operation?)
e. Discuss how this derivation proceeds from Spell-Out to a PF representation.

One argument for a PF deletion analysis of sluicing constructions involves the analysis of the following pair (adapted from Ross 1969).

(120)   a. We are supposed to do some problems for tomorrow, but which problems isn't clear.
         b. *We are supposed to do some problems for tomorrow, but which problems aren't clear.

Under the deletion analysis, the ellipsis site is a TP constituent of a CP that occurs in the Spec-TP of the second conjunct. Agreement between T and a clause in Spec-TP is always in the singular. Thus the sentences corresponding to (120) without sluicing would be (121).

(121) a. We are supposed to do some problems for tomorrow, but which problems we are supposed to do isn't clear.

   b. *We are supposed to do some problems for tomorrow, but which problems we are supposed to do aren't clear.

If the syntactic structure of the sluicing conjuncts in (120) involved only a wh-phrase (in this case a NP) in Spec-TP, then the legitimate (120a) would violate Spec-head agreement while the deviant (120b) satisfied it.

 Further evidence in favor of a PF deletion analysis involves the syntactic relation between the wh-phrase in a sluicing construction and the syntactic structure of the ellipsis site. This is referred to as a **connectivity effect**. One such effect involves Case marking in language with rich morphological Case. Consider the following examples from German (from Ross 1969).

(122) a. Er will jemandem schmeicheln, aber sie wissen nicht, wem er
     he wants someone-DAT to-flatter but they know not who-DAT he
     schmeicheln will.
      to-flatter wants
     "he wants to flatter someone, but they don't know who he wants
     to flatter"

   b. *Er will jemandem schmeicheln, aber sie wissen nicht, wer er
                       who-NOM
     schmeicheln will.

   c. *Er will jemandem schmeicheln, aber sie wissen nicht, wen er
                        who-ACC
     schmeicheln will.

As illustrated in the first and second conjuncts of (122a), the verb *schmeicheln* takes an object in the lexical dative, rather than the configurational accusative. In the second conjunct, the dative object of the verb is a wh-phrase that is pronounced in Spec-CP. (122b–c) show that this wh-phrase cannot occur in the nominative or accusative. The same Case facts hold when the second conjunct contains a sluicing construction.

(123) a. Er will jemandem schmeicheln, aber sie wissen nicht, wem.
     he wants someone-DAT to-flatter but they know not who-DAT
     "he wants to flatter someone, but they don't know who"

   b. *Er will jemandem schmeicheln, aber sie wissen nicht, wer.
                       who-NOM

   c. *Er will jemandem schmeicheln, aber sie wissen nicht, wen.
                       who-ACC

A wh-movement plus deletion analysis accounts naturally for this connectivity effect. An LF-copying analysis of (123), in which an empty TP is filled by a copy of the antecedent in the first conjunct, would require additional machinery to explain why the wh-phrase in Spec-CP must match the morphological Case of the object of the verb in the first conjunct.

EXERCISE 9.27

Consider the following related examples.

(i) a. Er will jemanden loben, aber sie wissen nicht, wen er loben will.

   he wants someone-ACC to-praise, but they know not who-ACC he to-praise wants

   "he wants to praise someone, but they don't know who he wants to praise"

   b. *Er will jemanden loben, aber sie wissen nicht, wer er loben will.

   who-NOM

   c. *Er will jemanden loben, aber sie wissen nicht, wem er loben will.

   who-DAT

a. What is the difference between (i.a) and (122a) in the first conjunct?
b. What is the syntactic structure of the complement CP in the second conjunct at Spell-Out?
c. How does this structure account for the deviance of (i.b–c)?

Compare (i) to the corresponding paradigm (ii) where sluicing applies.

(ii) a. Er will jemanden loben, aber sie wissen nicht, wen.

   he wants someone-ACC to-praise, but they know not who-ACC

   "he want to praise someone, but they don't know who"

   b. *Er will jemanden loben, aber sie wissen nicht, wer.

   who-NOM

   c. *Er will jemanden loben, aber sie wissen nicht, wem.

   who-DAT

d. Discuss the derivation of the sluicing construction in the second conjunct of (ii.a) from Spell-Out to the PF representation.
e. Exactly how are the deviant examples (ii.b–c) prohibited?

Preposition stranding provides another connectivity effect for sluicing constructions. In English, wh-movement often allows for two options when the wh-phrase is the object of a preposition. Either the entire PP may be copied and merged as Spec-CP, in which case the preposition has been pied-piped along with the wh-phrase as in (124a), or just the wh-object itself is displaced as in (124b).

(124)   a. To whom has Mary spoken?
          b. Who has Mary spoken to?

In (124b) the preposition is characterized as "stranded." In many other languages, like Greek, preposition stranding is prohibited. Thus (125a), where the preposition and its wh-phrase object do not form an overt constituent in PF, is deviant in Greek (the following data are from Merchant 2001).

(125)   a. *Pjon milise me?
              who she-spoke with
              "who did she speak with?"
          b. Me pjon milise?
              with who she-spoke

When the preposition is pied-piped along with the wh-phrase, the resulting interrogative is legitimate. This same constraint holds for sluicing constructions in Greek.

(126)   a. I Anna milise me kapjon, alla dhe ksero me pjon.
              the Anna spoke with someone, but not I-know with who
              "Anna spoke with someone but I don't know with whom"
          b. *I Anna milise me kapjon, alla dhe ksero pjon.'

The clausal complement in the second conjunct of (126a) would have the syntactic structure (127) at Spell-Out.

(127)   [$_{CP}$ [$_{PP}$ me pjon] [$_C$?? [$_{TP}$ I Anna [$_T$ T [$_{VP}$ milise [$_{PP}$ me pjon]]]]]]

After Spell-Out, (127) undergoes chain reduction so that at least the phonetic features of the PP in VP are deleted, yielding (128).

(128)   [$_{CP}$ [$_{PP}$ me pjon] [$_C$?? [$_{TP}$ I Anna [$_T$ T [$_{VP}$ milise [$_{PP}$ ~~me pjon~~]]]]]]

At this point, the ellipsis site TP is phonetically nondistinct from the antecedent TP. Sluicing then deletes the remaining phonetic features of TP, yielding (129), the PF representation of the complement clause in the second conjunct of (126a).

(129)   [$_{CP}$ [$_{PP}$ me pjon] [$_C$?? [$_{TP}$ ~~I Anna~~ [$_T$ T [$_{VP}$ ~~milise~~ [$_{PP}$ ~~me pjon~~]]]]]]

However, if only the interrogative pronoun is displaced to Spec-CP, then at Spell-Out the representation of the complement clause in (126b) would be (130).

(130)   [$_{CP}$ [$_{NP}$ pjon] [$_C$?? [$_{TP}$ I Anna [$_T$ T [$_{VP}$ milise [$_{PP}$ me pjon]]]]]]

Chain-reduction would yield a stranded preposition *me*.

(131)   [$_{CP}$ [$_{NP}$ pjon] [$_C$?? [$_{TP}$ I Anna [$_T$ T [$_{VP}$ milise [$_{PP}$ me ~~pjon~~]]]]]]

Even though the resulting TP is now phonetically nondistinct from its potential antecedent in the first conjunct, deleting the TP under sluicing, which would yield (132), does not save the structure from being deviant.

(132) $[_{CP}$ $[_{NP}$ pjon] $[_C$?? $[_{TP}$ ~~I Anna~~ $[_T$ T $[_{VP}$ ~~milise~~ $[_{PP}$ ~~me pjon~~]]]]]]

The deviance of (126b) shows that even when the phonetic effects of the operation do not show up in PF, the derivation that produces this construction must
be blocked. The prohibition against preposition stranding thus appears to operate derivationally, possibly as a constraint on chain reduction. Why this is so and
exactly how this is captured in terms of the computational system are very much
open questions.[9]

In contrast to preposition stranding, the effects of other constraints on displacement (e.g. Ross's island constraints) appear to be mitigated under sluicing. Consider the following examples of wh-movement phenomena where the
Complex NP Constraint (see Chapter 8) and the Coordinate Structure Constraint
(see Chapter 2) are violated. (133b), in contrast to (133a), constitutes a CNPC
violation where *who* is interpreted as the object of *cheated* and thus extracted out
of a complex NP, the NP headed by *rumor*.

(133)   a.   Do we believe the rumor that Bill cheated someone?
             b.   *Who do we believe the rumor that Bill cheated?

(134b), in contrast to (134a), violates the CSC under the interpretation of the
interrogative pronoun as a conjunct of a coordinated structure *Mary and who*.

(134)   a.   Are Mary and someone collaborating on a project?
             b.   *Who are Mary and collaborating on a project?

Recasting (133a) as an indicative and (133b) as an indirect question, a coordinate
structure (135) can be constructed.

(135)   *We believe the rumor that Bill cheated someone, but Susan doesn't have
             any idea who we believe the rumor that Bill cheated.

(135) is deviant because, like (133b), wh-movement violates the CNPC.
(Wh-movement in the second conjunct can be analyzed as a Subjacency Condition
violation, as will be discussed below.) However, if the complement TP in the second conjunct undergoes sluicing, the result is no longer deviant.[10]

(136)   We believe the rumor that Bill cheated someone, but Susan doesn't have
             any idea who.

Under the analysis of sluicing as TP deletion, (136) has a simple and straightforward derivation from the structure underlying as (135). First chain reduction eliminates the copy of the interrogative pronoun *who* that was merged as
the object of *cheated* (137a) and then the matrix TP of the second conjunct is
deleted (137b).

(137)   a.   We believe the rumor that Bill cheated someone, but Susan doesn't
                   have any idea who we believe the rumor that Bill cheated ~~who~~.
             b. $[_{TP}$ We believe the rumor that Bill cheated someone], but Susan doesn't
                   have any idea who $[_{TP}$ ~~we believe the rumor that Bill cheated who~~].

Given this derivation, (136) should have an interpretation that is identical to the deviant (135). An assumption that (136) under this interpretation is significantly less deviant than (135) leads to the conclusion that the deviance of (135) is a PF rather than a LF phenomenon.

Given the analysis of sluicing as the deletion of TP, there is another possible source for (136) that does not involve a complex NP island. Thus consider (138).

(138)   We believe the rumor that Bill cheated someone, but Susan doesn't have any idea who Bill cheated.

Syntactically, the derivation from the structure underlying (138) to (136) ought to be possible. If so, then analysis where sluicing mitigates island effects rests on the interpretive facts – i.e., whether speakers interpret (136) as ambiguous.

EXERCISE 9.28

Note further that the same sort of ambiguity is found in sluicing examples where islands are not involved. Consider the pair of sentences in (i):

(i) a.   We believe that Bill cheated someone, but Susan doesn't have any idea who we believe Bill cheated.
    b.   We believe that Bill cheated someone, but Susan doesn't have any idea who Bill cheated.

a. Give the PF representations for the second conjunct in (i.a) and (i.b).
b. Show how sluicing can apply to the second conjunct of each example in (i).
c. Discuss in what way the PF representations derived via sluicing are identical.
d. Discuss what, if anything, this tells us about the analysis of (136).

A similar account could provide an alternative analysis for a sluicing construction that might otherwise involve a CSC violation. Thus compare (139a), which violates the CSC, with (139b), which doesn't.

(139)   a.   *Mary and someone are collaborating on a project, but we don't know who Mary and are collaborating on a project.
         b.   Mary and someone are collaborating on a project, but we don't know who.

This also works with more complex wh-phrases, e.g. *which student, which student from Princeton*, or *which student from Princeton that you met last semester*. So, for example, *some student* would contrast with *which student*.[11] Unlike the CNPC cases (e.g. (135)), there is no alternative derivation for (139b) that avoids the island violation for the wh-movement component.

In the literature on sluicing, the phenomenon exemplified by (139a) and (139b) are analyzed as showing how sluicing can "repair" island violations. To see exactly how this **island-repair** might work, consider the derivation of the clausal complement of the second conjunct, which contains the sluicing construction. Take (136) as an example. At Spell-Out, the CP that undergoes sluicing would have the syntactic structure (140) given successive cyclic wh-movement.

(140)   [CP who [C ?? [TP we [T [−past, φ] [VP believe [NP the rumor [CP who that [TP
               Bill [T [+past, φ] [VP cheated who]]]]]]]]]]]

The TP in the first conjunct is syntactically identical with the TP in (140) and almost phonetically identical with the exception of *someone* vs. *who*.[12] Chain reduction, which deletes the phonetic features of *who* in two positions within the embedded CP of the second conjunct, renders the two TPs phonetically nondistinct, yielding (141).

(141)   [CP who [C ?? [TP we [T [−past, φ] [VP believe [NP the rumor [CP ~~who~~ that [TP
               Bill [T [+past, φ] [VP cheated ~~who~~]]]]]]]]]]]

Without this application of chain reduction, the matching condition for sluicing would not be met. With the matching condition satisfied, sluicing can apply to the TP in (141), producing (140).

(142)   [CP who [C ?? [TP ~~we~~ [T [−past, φ] [VP ~~believe~~ [NP ~~the rumor~~ [CP ~~who that~~ [TP
               ~~Bill~~ [T ~~[+past, φ]~~ [VP ~~cheated who~~]]]]]]]]]]]

Given the relative nondeviance of (137b), the representation (142) does not register as a violation of the CNPC.

How the derivation of (136) from (137b) avoids an island violation depends on the syntactic structure of the ellipsis site at Spell-Out given in (140). As analyzed, the final link of the wh-movement chain for *who* crosses one NP and one TP. Suppose, for the sake of discussion, that this violates the Subjacency Condition (but cf. Section 8.2). This is illustrated in (143), where the relevant boundaries are highlighted in boldface.

(143)   [CP who [C ?? [**TP** we [T [−past, φ] [VP believe [**NP** the rumor [CP who that [TP
               Bill [T [+past, φ] [VP cheated who]]]]]]]]]]]

Given that island repair occurs in this example, Subjacency cannot be interpreted as a condition on either chain formation or chain reduction since neither would distinguish the viable (136) from the deviant (135). It appears that the deletion operation itself is what makes the difference. Suppose that the ellipsis operation "delete TP" eliminates not only phonetic and morphological features but also the syntactic structure of the ellipsis site itself. Then the PF representation of (140) would no longer represent a Subjacency violation because the highlighted TP and NP boundaries in (143) would be erased at PF. This analysis covers the CSC violation in (139a) as well, but does not extend to all CSC violations (see (19b–c) in Chapter 2). This result suggests that the Subjacency Condition, along with whatever else accounts for the full range of CSC violations, should be construed as conditions on PF representations.[13]

This implementation of the Subjacency Condition also explains why VPE does not repair island constructions. Consider the contrast between a viable sluicing construction and a corresponding VPE construction, which will be deviant.

(144)   a. Fred will be collaborating with Mary and someone else on a project,
              but he won't tell us who.
         b. *Fred will collaborate with Mary and someone else on a project, but he
              won't tell us who he will.

By hypothesis, the second conjunct is derived by deleting a VP that is phonetically nondistinct from the VP in the first conjunct (145).

(145)   [$_{VP}$ collaborate [$_{PP}$ with [$_{NP}$ Mary and someone else]] [$_{PP}$ on a project]]

The ellipsis site meets this condition after chain reduction applies as illustrated
in (146).

(146)   [$_{VP}$ collaborate [$_{PP}$ with [$_{NP}$ Mary and ~~who~~]] [$_{PP}$ on a project]]

Again by hypothesis, VPE will eliminate both the remaining phonetic and morphological material in (144) and its syntactic structure. What remains of the
second conjunct in PF representation will be (147).

(147)   [$_{CP}$ who [$_C$ C [$_{TP}$ he [$_T$ will ~~VP~~]]]]

Suppose for a moment that wh-movement in this construction has violated the
Subjacency Condition. If so, then the TP boundary would be one of the boundaries
involved in determining the violation. Suppose further that boundaries involved
in a Subjacency violation are marked during a derivation as in (143) above. Then
(147) would at PF contain a marked TP boundary, highlighted in (148).

(148)   [$_{CP}$ who [$_C$ C [**$_{TP}$** he [$_T$ will ~~VP~~]]]]

It would then be the survival of this single boundary in PF representation that
accounts for the deviance of this construction.[14] It couldn't be the nontrivial wh-
chain because that has been eliminated. It also cannot be the NP boundary of the
coordinate structure because that has also been erased from the representation.[15]

   The analysis under investigation raises a number of nontrivial issues. The
marking of certain constituent boundaries in PF representation is prima facie a
departure from the Inclusiveness Condition. This would mean that there can be
more to syntactic structure than what is given in the lexicon. It also locates the
basis for ellipsis on the PF side, anchoring the interpretation of ellipsis sites to
phonetic representation. On the other hand, ellipsis sites also involve specific
interpretations and so it may be that constraints on ellipsis should be formulated
in terms of parallel LF representations (see Merchant 2001 and Fox and Lasnik
2003 among others for discussion). There is also the question of the status of
island repair phenomena. And on this may rest how the computational system
handles locality in general and island violations in particular. The discussion
of ellipsis in this chapter, as the discussion in the previous chapters, is merely a
beginning, an introduction to how syntactic analysis provides essential tools for
pursuing a deeper understanding of linguistic structure and the language faculty
that determines it.

9.4   Summary

The architecture of the system of grammar presented in this chapter is as follows:

a.   Mechanisms of the computational system:

    i.   Merge
    ii. Delete

      1.   VPE (= delete VP)
      2.   Gapping (= delete T + V)
      3.   Sluicing (= delete TP)
      4.   chain reduction

b.   Constraints on derivations and representations:

    i.   phonetic identity condition on deletion
    ii. Subjacency Condition

Ellipsis is fundamentally a PF phenomenon involving the deletion of various pieces of syntactic structure that match other parts in the same sentence. The matching part is called the antecedent of the ellipsis site, the portion that deletes and is therefore not pronounced. The antecedent/ellipsis site pairs thus must meet a matching property and also a configurational property. Given three distinct types of ellipsis, VPE, gapping, and sluicing, there is a question whether they have the same matching property. They do not share the same configurational property. For example, gapping cannot occur in a subordinate clause where the antecedent is in the main clause, unlike VPE where this is possible. With VPE, deletion can affect as much as the maximal project or as little as the head, including projections in between. VPE in finite clauses allows a wide variety of configurations. Where the antecedent precedes the ellipsis site, it can be higher or lower in hierarchical structure. In infinitival clauses VPE can apply to VP headed by a main verb, but not to a VP headed by aspectual *have*. It also cannot apply to infinitival purpose clauses or VPs that take a PRO subject adjacent to a wh-phrase in Spec-CP. There are also constraints against VPE applying to the complements of infinitival *to* inside NP, including relative clauses. In contrast, VPE in finite relative clauses is fine. VPE can also apply inside finite relative clauses where the antecedent of the ellipsis site appears to include the relative clause itself, so-called antecedent contained deletion constructions. This analysis appears to create an infinite regress. One solution is to reformulate the matching constraint in terms of phonetic identity alone, dropping the requirement that the antecedent constitute a single constituent. Under this analysis, if VPE precedes chain reduction, then there is an explanation for why VPE in ACD constructions are deviant with an overt relative pronoun but not deviant otherwise. The derivation of gapping constructions, were T + V is deleted as a non-constituent, supports the phonetic nondistinctness formulation of the matching constraint. However, pseudogapping constructions require that chain reduction precedes VPE, as does sluicing constructions in which a TP that contains a silent wh-phrase is deleted. Moreover, sluicing constructions appear to mitigate island violations, unlike VPE. This suggests that a locality constraint like the Subjacency Condition should be interpreted as a constraint on PF.

Bibliographical notes

For further discussion of VPE phenomena, see Johnson 2001. For discussion of other solutions to the ACD puzzle see Fiengo and May 1994; Lasnik 1999 and 2003. An analysis of VPE based on LF-copying is given in Chung, Ladusaw, and McCloskey 1995; see also Williams 1977. On gapping see Johnson 2009; on pseudogapping, Lasnik 2003. See Ross 1969 and Merchant 2001, 2006 on sluicing. For discussions of island repair in sluicing, see Lasnik 2007, 2009 and Merchant 2008.

Notes

Chapter 1   The computational nature of human language

1 Note that the term **sentence** is being reserved for a free-standing clause, where a **simple** sentence contains no embedded clause as a subpart – be it subordinate to a main clause that contains it, yielding a **complex** sentence, or a coordinate of non-subordinate clauses, yielding a **compound** sentence.

2 Intonation does not seem to be enough to distinguish PF representations for all examples that involve some form of structural ambiguity however. Consider (i), where *flying* may be construed as an adjective modifying the noun *planes* or as a gerund, a nominal form of the corresponding verb (*fly*), which takes *planes* as an object.

(i)   Flying planes can be dangerous.

It seems that there is no clear difference in pronunciation that distinguishes one interpretation from the other.

Chapter 2   Knowledge of language as an object of inquiry

1 Because writing systems are primarily cultural artifacts and moreover not essential for language use, it could turn out to be a mistake to model the mental lexicon on how the particular writing system of English represents language. After all, being able to read and write does not change a speaker's fundamental knowledge of his/her language. Just consider preliterate children (or adults). Knowledge of a language does not require the ability to read and write the language.

Furthermore, not all writing systems are based on the correspondence between an orthographic character and a specific sound segment that forms an identifiable part of the PF of a lexical item, as in the alphabetic system of English. And as every literate English speaker knows, even in an alphabetic writing system the correspondence between letters and their pronunciation is not always one-to-one. Moreover, in some alphabetic systems, the same PF representation can correspond to several distinct orthographic representations, as in French.

(i)   Il   était   fort.
           He   was   strong
(ii)   Elle   était   forte.
           She   was   strong
(iii)   Elles   étaient   fortes.
           They   were   strong
(iv)   Ils   étaient   forts.
           They   were   strong

The imperfect forms of the French verb *être* ('to be') have the same PF (pronounced in (i–iv) as if they were written *étai*) for the third person whether singular or plural, masculine or feminine. Also the different forms of adjective for 'strong' have the same PF even though they are orthographically distinct. The form in (i) designates masculine singular; in (ii), feminine singular; and in (iii), feminine plural; and in (iv), masculine plural.

Some writing systems include single characters that designate lexical items in terms of their meaning rather than their sound – e.g. ideographs in Chinese and Japanese (kanji). This complete dissociation of orthographic character and PF demonstrates that the correspondences found in the writing systems of other languages are by no means necessary ones.

2   The qualification is necessary because there are lexical items that have no meaning – for example, pleonastic elements like English non-referential *it* in (i) (in contrast to the pronoun *it* in (ii)).

(i)   a.   It rains every day.
         b.   It is likely that it will rain tomorrow.
(ii)   John baked a tart and ate it.

Neither instance of *it* in (i) acts like a pronoun, standing in for some unexpressed antecedent nominal expression (e.g. *a tart* in (ii)). There are also syntactic elements that have a distinct interpretation, but no pronunciation.

(iii)   To memorize a Scarlatti sonata quickly is not always possible.

(iii) contains no overt nominal expression that is construed as the subject of *memorize*; nonetheless, the construal of the sentence includes a subject for *memorize* roughly equivalent to *one* or *someone*. The LF representation of this sentence contains a phonetically null subject, minimally a lexical item consisting of the syntactic category feature N (for noun) and the features third person and singular, the same features that *one* and *someone* share. Partial evidence for this claim comes from the observation that the memorizer is obligatorily identical to the individual for whom the possibility of memorizing is in question. Presumably no lexical item lacks both a sound and a meaning, in which case it could not be detected at either interface (PF or LF).

It is worth noting that in human languages, lexical items with sound but no meaning are unique to natural human language. This is also true of covert lexical items (i.e. those without a PF) that have a specific interpretation. Artificial languages (e.g. logic and the various computer programming languages) do not contain either.

3   English contains many such noun/verb pairs (e.g. also *reject* and *export*). Similar phenomena occur in other languages. For example in Norwegian, the word for the noun 'water' is *vannet* where *vann* is the noun stem and *-et* is the neuter singular definite affix. The corresponding Norwegian verb *vanne* consists of a verb stem *vann* and an infinitival suffix *-e*. The "t" is not pronounced, so the two words contain exactly the same phonetic segments. However there is a difference in pronunciation involving tone. The verb is pronounced with a falling tone on the first syllable and a rising tone on the second. The noun, in contrast, has a high tone on the first syllable and a falling tone on the second. Thanks to Tarald Taraldsen for this example.

4   More recently a fifth question about how knowledge of language came to be a property of the human species (i.e., how language evolved) has become a focus of inquiry. See Hauser, Chomsky, and Fitch 2002, reprinted in Larson, Déprez, and Yamakido 2010 along with fourteen papers that respond in various ways to the Hauser, Chomsky, and Fitch paper.

5   For example, compare the syntactic distribution of the English the verb *want* with its French counterpart *vouloir*.

(i)   a.   I want John to be happy.
         b.   *I want that John be/is happy.
(ii)   a.   *Je veux Jean être heureux.
              I want Jean to-be happy
         b.   Je veux que Jean soit heureux.
              I want that Jean be happy

In English *want* cannot occur with a finite clause as in (ib), whereas the French counterpart (iib) is fine. Conversely, French *vouloir* cannot occur with an infinitival construction as in (iia), whereas the English counterpart (ia) is fine. Granting that *want* and *vouloir* have the same meaning, these differences reflect idiosyncracies of lexical properties. The complementarity of syntactic contexts of these examples (finite vs. infinitival clause arguments) does not hold for other verbs in English, e.g. *believe*.

(iii)   a.   Ed believes that syntax is simple.
         b.   Ed believes syntax to be simple.

In contrast, French does not allow the counterpart to (iii.b).

(iv)   a.   Edouard croit que le syntaxe est simple.
              Edward believes that the syntax is simple
        b.   *Edouard croit le syntaxe être simple.
                            to-be

This suggests that the complementarity in (i-ii) is not significant.

6   "[Die Sprache] muss daher von endlichen Mitteln einen unendlichen Gerbauch machen" (Wilhelm von Humboldt, *Über die Verschiedenheit des Menschlichen Sprachbaues*, quoted in Chomsky 1964). See Chomsky 1964, 1965, and 2009 for references and discussion.

7   It worth noting that the notion of grammatical deviance under discussion is not based on some notion of comprehensibility. A linguistic expression that is completely comprehensible can nonetheless be deviant. Consider the following pair.

(i)   a.   John knows that he is intelligent.
       b.   *John knows that himself is intelligent.

(i.a) is ambiguous. It can be construed as a statement about one person, (*John*) or two people (*John* and some other male). (i.b) can only be construed as a statement about one person (*John*), identical to the corresponding interpretation of (i.a). However, in spite of its comprehensibility, (i.b) is deviant. The deviance of (i.b) falls under a theory of binding. See Freidin 1992, chapters 7 and 8 for discussion and references. See also note 2 in Chapter 3.

8   Whether there is more to a child's initial linguistic experience beyond PLD is controversial – for example, whether PLD contains meta-data (i.e. explicit instruction about the language that identifies deviance). In general children are not instructed about the language that they acquire – e.g. being told that some utterance they make is deviant, not part of the language. The utterances that constitute the PLD for each child are usually delivered within a social context (usually involving the child and a speaker of the language). It seems obvious that this context will contribute significant information that bears on the interpretation of these utterances – for example the speaker's facial expressions and other physical gestures, as well as the physical context in which the linguistic expression is uttered. The question remains, however, whether any of this bears directly on the core properties of the computational system acquired – and in particular, the covert structure of linguistic expressions. To the extent that these contexts are open to interpretation, hence ambiguous or vague, it seems unlikely that they could account for core computational properties of human language.

9   Not only can speakers of a language distinguish between deviant and nondeviant utterances, but they can also make systematic distinctions between deviant utterances where one deviant utterance is judged to be more deviant than another. Consider the following set of deviant examples.

(i)   a.   *what does he wonder whether Mary chose?
       b.   *what does he wonder who chose?
       c.   *who does he wonder what chose?

It appears that speakers of English systematically judge (i.c) to be more deviant than (i.b), and (i.b) to be more deviant than (i.a). See Sprouse 2007 for experimental evidence and discussion of this phenomenon.

10   That there is a unique language faculty distinct from other cognitive faculties is an empirical hypothesis – one that continues to be controversial. The issue is whether the content

of UG is specific to language or instead belongs to general cognitive resources of humans. The counter-proposal, which has been discussed in various forms by psychologists and philosophers, as well as linguists, is that all properties of language, covert as well as overt, can be accounted for by general cognitive machinery – i.e. mechanisms that apply across cognitive domains (e.g. vision and reasoning as well as language) and moreover are not inherently connected to any one of them (see Cowie 1999, Tomasello 2003, and Goldberg 2006). Such proposals characteristically rely on some form of inductive procedure applied to input data. However, no such proposal has been shown to account for a speaker's ability to distinguish between novel and deviant linguistic expressions, let alone speakers' systematic judgments about relative deviance (see the preceding footnote). Moreover, it is not clear that such proposals are even successful in general for other cognitive domains.

11 Chomsky 1986a designates this as "Descartes' Problem," after the French philosopher who first discussed it over 300 years ago: "if there were machines which bore a resemblance to our body and imitated our actions as far as it was morally possible to do so, we should always have two very certain tests by which to recognize that, for all that, they were not real men. The first is, that they could never use speech or other signs as we do when placing our thoughts on record for the benefit of others. For we can easily understand a machine's being constituted so that it can utter words, and even emit responses to action on it of a corporeal kind, which brings about a change in its organs; .... But it never happens that it arranges its speech in various ways, in order to reply appropriately to everything that may be said in its presence, as even the lowest type of man can do." R. Descartes, *Discourse on Method*, part V, first published in French in 1637 (quote from *The Philosophical Works of Descartes*, Volume I, translated by E. S. Haldane & G. R. T. Ross, Cambridge University Press, 1911, p. 116).

Chapter 3   Categories and constituents

1 This phonetic form when interpreted as a noun can further be differentiated as either singular or plural. The singular and plural should probably not be treated as separate lexical items for reasons involving the overall structure and organization of the lexicon, which will not be investigated here. In the case of the noun versus the verb it is assumed, as is standard in English dictionaries, that there are two distinct lexical items. The fact that both have the same PF is to some extent an accident of history. In other languages they do not, as in French where the noun is *poisson* whereas the verb is *pêcher*.

2 The c-command relation also plays a central role in the relations between an anaphor and its antecedent. Consider the following examples.

(i)   a.   Rembrandt's portrait of himself
         b.   *Rembrandt's mother's portrait of himself

The reflexive pronoun *himself* is an anaphoric expression that stands in for an antecedent (e.g. *Rembrandt* in (i.a)) in much the same way that a third person pronoun can stand in for a name, as in (ii) under the interpretation that (ii) is a statement about one person.

(ii)   John knows that he is clever.

With non-reflexive pronouns, this interpretation of antecedence is optional. (ii) could also be interpreted as a statement about two people, *John* and some other male. In contrast, with reflexive pronouns the antecedent relation is obligatory. (i.a) cannot be interpreted as a description involving two people, therefore *Rembrandt* must be interpreted as the antecedent of *himself*. Note also that (i.a) has at least a couple of possible interpretations: it could describe the portrait of Rembrandt that Rembrandt painted or alternatively the one he owns that was painted by someone else.

The deviance of (i.b) involves the syntactic structure of the two NPs in (i), *Rembrandt* and *himself*.

(iii)   a.   [NP Rembrandt's [N portrait [PP of himself]]]
           b.   [NP [NP Rembrandt's mother's][N portrait [PP of himself]]]

In (iii.a) the N *Rembrandt* c-commands the reflexive pronoun *himself*, whereas in (iii.b) the same N c-commands the N *mother*, but not the reflexive pronoun. The deviance of (i.b) is explained by the general constraint on the occurrence of reflexive pronouns stated in (iv).

(iv)   A reflexive pronoun must be c-commanded by an antecedent that agrees in number, gender, and person.

(iii.a) satisfies (iv), but (iii.b) does not. The NP that c-commands the reflexive pronoun in (iii.b) is headed by *mother*, which does not agree with the gender feature of the reflexive pronoun. This problem could be eliminated by substituting the N *father* for the N *mother*, as in (v).

(v)   Rembrandt's father's portrait of himself

However, (v) has only one interpretation for the antecedent of the reflexive pronoun – namely, the portrait of Rembrandt's father that Rembrandt's father owns (or that conceivably that he, the father, painted himself).

Chapter 4   Phrase structure theory

1   In effect, this rules out phrase structure representations where a single syntactic object is an immediate constituent of two or more distinct phrases, as in (i).

(i)   a.

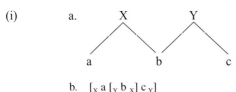

     b. $[_X \text{a} [_Y \text{b} _X] \text{c} _Y]$

Note that such "multi-dominance" structures would be possible if unconstrained Merge could group a syntactic object that has been already merged in a derivation with an independent syntactic object. Whether the phrase structure of human languages involves such representations is controversial. For some discussion see van Riemsdijk 2006.

2   Anaphora is a word/word relation – in contrast to reference, which is a word/world relation. In most discussions of anaphora in linguistics this distinction is blurred so that an anaphoric expression (e.g. a pronoun or reciprocal (e.g. *each other* in English)) is said to "refer" to or "be coreferential with" its antecedent. For detailed discussion, see Freidin 1986, 1992:chapters 7 and 8, and 1997; Lasnik 1989 and the works cited in these.

3   In English, Specifier-Head Agreement in NPs is restricted to the number feature. In French and Spanish the determiner counterparts to English singular definite article *the* split into two distinct forms that are distinguished in terms of grammatical gender (masculine vs. feminine):

	French	Spanish	
masculine singular	*le livre*	*el libro*	"the book"
feminine singular	*la bicyclette*	*la bicicleta*	"the bicycle"

In the plural however, only Spanish maintains this gender distinction with separate forms of the plural definite article.

	French	Spanish	
masculine plural	*les livres*	*los libros*	"the books"
feminine plural	*les bicyclettes*	*las bicicletas*	"the bicycles"

The French form *les* represents both the masculine and feminine plural in exactly the same way that the English determiner *the* represents both the singular and plural forms of the definite article.

4 Working out alternatives is an important part of syntactic analysis, even when they lead to dead ends and absurd conclusions. Only then do we thoroughly understand why these alternatives are not viable. And sometimes we are surprised to find that an alternative we at first glance were ready to dismiss may have some merit and may even turn out to be a better solution than the one we first assumed to be the right one.

Chapter 5   The structure of clauses

1 Whether VP contains a constituent that can be identified as a specifier in the same way that N does is not obvious. Given that specifiers generally occur to the left of their head – a property that appears to hold across languages regardless of other word order properties, the only candidate in VP appears to be an adverb phrase (AdvP), as in (i)

(i)   Mary very quietly left the room.

However as noted in the previous chapter, the fact that the AdvP can also occur at the right edge of VP, as in (ii), suggests that it is actually an adjunct.

(ii)   Mary left the room very quietly.

Furthermore there is no specifier-head agreement between V and Adv, which also might be taken as evidence against designating AdvP as the specifier of V – or at the very least, as a lack of evidence for this analysis.

2 Even though it is possible to leave internal arguments unexpressed in the physical signal (i.e. in PF), the sentences that do so have specific interpretations indicating that these arguments are nonetheless implicit rather than just absent. Thus the interpretation (8a) requires that Susan wrote a letter to someone. If *letter* changes to *poem*, the implication disappears. (8b–c) entail that Susan wrote something to John, and similarly for (8d). But in the case of (8e) there is no entailment that what was written was addressed to anyone. (8f–g) appear to involve implicit arguments.

3 On one analysis, modal verbs in English are marked for tense (i.e. present vs. past). Under this analysis, the pairs *will/would* and *can/could* are construed as present/past tense forms. The modals *may*, *might*, and *must* do not pair in this way, nor is it obvious that *shall/should* constitute a pair. There is a subtle argument due to Chomsky 1957 for considering the modal pairs as present vs. past tense concerning the sequence of tenses. Consider the interpretation of the following two examples.

(i)   a.   John says he owns a house.
           b.   John said he owned a house.

The interpretation of (i.a) entails that John said "I own a house." In contrast, (i.b) is ambiguous regarding what John said. He could have said "I own a house" where the verb is in the present tense, or alternatively, "I owned a house" where the verb is in the past tense and carries the implication that he no longer does. In (i.b) the past tense form *owned* can be interpreted as either present or past with respect to John's actual words. The same ambiguity occurs in (ii).

(ii)   a.   John says he will help.
           b.   John said he would help.

Both (ii.a) and (ii.b) can be interpreted as John saying "I will help," but (ii.b) can also be interpreted as John saying "I would help." Thus *will* correlates with the present tense (*owns*) and *would* with the past tense (*owned*). The same argument can be made with *can/could*.

4 The full paradigm for the English auxiliary system includes the passive auxiliary *be*, thus (i).

(i)   modal > perfective > progressive > passive > main verb

Sentences containing every auxiliary element tend to be unwieldy (cf. (ii)).

(ii)   The car could have been being fixed while we were at the concert.

Although the passive auxiliary will not be considered any further in this chapter, the analysis that follows will generalize to it as well. See the following chapter for further discussion of the passive auxiliary and passive constructions more generally.

5   Note that some caution about the characterization of this form is required. The form *having* does exist in English in constructions like (i).

(i)   Having finished her senior thesis at 3 a.m., Mary collapsed.

So it looks like perfective *have* can occur with the *-ing* suffix. However, this form of V+*ing* is different from the one in (37), which is in a selectional relationship with the progressive auxiliary *be*. In (i) there is no progressive auxiliary, nor can there be one.

(ii)   *Be/is/was having finished her thesis at 3 a.m., Mary collapsed.

Therefore the form *having* in (i) cannot be selected by some form of the progressive auxiliary. Nonetheless, it is clear that form is related to the perfective auxiliary because it takes a VP headed by a past participle form of the verb as a complement. The phrase headed by *having* also occurs in other contexts.

(iii)   a.   Mary collapsed, having finished her thesis at 3 a.m.
             b.   Mary, having finished her thesis at 3 a.m., collapsed.

In (iii.b) this phrase modifies the N *Mary* and thus functions like a relative clause. The phrase also shows up in NP contexts as illustrated by the comparison of (iv.a and iv.b).

(iv)   a.   Mary's accomplishment surprised no one.
             b.   Mary's having finished her thesis at 3 a.m. surprised no one.

This suggests that whatever form *having* is in these legitimate constructions, it is not a present participle.

6   The complementizer *for* should not be confused with the preposition *for*. The preposition assigns a benefactive role to its NP object, as in (i).

(i)   a topic for us

The benefactive interpretation can be separated from the interpretation as subject of *investigate*, as in (ii) and the somewhat less felicitous but still more acceptable than one might expect (iii).

(ii)   a topic for us that we should investigate
(iii)   a topic for us for us to investigate

Taken together these examples provide a basis for distinguishing the benefactive preposition *for* from the complementizer *for*.

Chapter 6   The syntax of Spec-TP

1   The raising adjectives *likely*, *unlikely*, and *certain* have nominalized forms (e.g. *likelihood*, *unlikelihood*, and *certainty*) that take finite clause complements, whereas there is no raising of infinitival clause complement subjects in NPs in which they are the head. Thus compare (i) to (ii).

(i)   a.   the likelihood that Mary will arrive on time
           b.   the unlikelihood that Mary will arrive on time
           c.   the certainty that Mary will arrive on time
(ii)   a.   *Mary's likelihood to arrive on time
           b.   *Mary's unlikelihood to arrive on time
           c.   *Mary's certainty to arrive on time

Moreover, it appears that these nominalizations cannot take infinitival clause complements of any form.

2 (25) abstracts away from the morphological affix *'s*. See below for a discussion of this affix in terms of Case.

3 This principle was originally formulated as an extension to an already existing principle (hence the name). However, this other principle has been dropped because of fundamental changes in the theory. The EPP however continues to be used and its name has not been changed. See Chomsky 1982 for the original proposal.

4 These constitute the author's judgments. The editors of *The American Heritage Dictionary of the English Language*, fourth edition, 2000 disagree. For them, *likely* and *probable* are synonyms on the first definition of *probable*. Such differences are not unexpected from the perspective of I-language (see Chapter 2), and in any case will not affect the syntactic analysis under discussion.

5 Examples (66–69) are from Lavine and Freidin 2002, which provides evidence and arguments that the clause initial ACC NP occupies the Spec-TP position.

Chapter 7   Head movement and the structure of root clauses

1 Note that this now solves the problem noted in Chapter 5 that the subordinating elements *that* and *for* in relative clauses were also not "complementizers" in the literal sense of the term.

2 The analysis of Russian is actually more complicated because other constituents aside from the finite verbal element can be attached to *li*.

(i)   a.   On li budet čitat' knigu.
             "is it he that will be reading the book?"
        b.   Čitat' li on budet knigu.
             "is it reading that he will be doing to the book?"
        c.   Knigu li on budet čitat'.
             "is it the book that he will be reading?"

However there is a crucial difference between the examples in (i) and those involving the fronted finite verbal element in (10). The fronted constituents in the examples in (i) have emphatic stress, in contrast to the fronted finite verbal element, which does not. Thus the fronted constituents in (i) are focused, thereby affecting interpretation, hence LF. The difference shows up in English when a simple indicative clause is compared to a corresponding cleft construction, (ii) and (iii) respectively.

(ii)   John left.
(iii)   It was John who left.

John is focused in (iii), which carries a presupposition that someone left, in contrast to (ii) under normal intonation, which does not.

   How the examples in (i) are analyzed raises interesting questions about their LF representations. For the present, assume that the displacement of the syntactic element preceding *li* occurs after Spell-Out, as with the non-focused examples and for the same reason.

3 It should be noted that in modern colloquial French yes/no interrogatives with a finite verbal element in C are rare. Instead, most speakers use the construction that begins with *est-ce que* followed by the indicative clause.

4 Assume that *did* in (49d) is not stressed. (49d) is marginal at best. When *did* is stressed, as indicated in (i) by the small capitals, the example is not deviant.

(i)   She DID quickly leave the room.

The interpretation of (i) is not identical to (49c). The pattern holds without the presence of the adverb.

(ii)   a.   *She did leave the room.
        b.   She DID leave the room.
        c.   She left the room.
        d.   She LEFT the room.

The interpretation of (ii.b) is not identical to (ii.c), nor is it the same as (ii.d). Furthermore, the interpretations of (ii.c) and (ii.d) are not identical.

5 If the VP-internal subject hypothesis is not merely an ad hoc proposal for handling word order facts in Celtic languages, then presumably it would apply generally across languages – i.e. including English. Consider this an open question. See Chapter 6 of Radford 2009 for an extended discussion of the VP internal subject hypothesis and references to work bearing on it.

Chapter 8   Wh-movement

1 Note that this holds for so-called "standard" English. Nonetheless, there are idiolects in which such relative clauses occur. Consider the following example from Walter Mosley's novel *Fear Itself*, Little, Brown and Co., Boston, 2003, p. 179. (See also (1a) in chapter 2.)

> "It was you came to me and asked for help. It was you that white man shot at us was lookin' for. It was you sent me lookin' for a man dead in his living room."

Each sentence in the quotation is a cleft construction (see below for more discussion). The second sentence also contains a relative clause with the property under discussion. The relative clause modifies the noun *man*.

2 There is actually a third complementizer designated as *aN* which occurs when a construction contains a resumptive pronoun, as in (i).

(i)   an ghirseach a-r ghoid na síogaí í
      the girl *aN*-PAST stole the fairies her
      lit.: "the girl that the fairies stole her away"
      " the girl that the fairies stole away"

In this case there is a resumptive pronoun occupying the position bound by the logical operator for relative clauses (see the analysis above). (i) and the Irish examples that follow are from McCloskey 2002.

Chapter 9   Ellipsis: unpronounced syntax

1 In (19) there appears to be no difference between the deletion of a VP headed by the perfective auxiliary and one headed by the progressive auxiliary. However, there appears to be a difference, as illustrated in the following examples.

(i)   a.   By the end of the evening, Mary will have praised every wine,
           but Bill won't have ~~praised every wine~~.
      b.   *By the end of the evening, Mary will have praised every wine,
           but Bill won't ~~have praised every wine~~.
(ii) a.   By the end of the evening, Mary will be praising every wine,
           but Bill won't be ~~praising every wine~~.
      b.   ?By the end of the evening, Mary will be praising every wine,
           but Bill won't ~~be praising every wine~~.

It remains to be explained why *be Ving* is more easily elided than *been Ving*. This may also involve perfective aspect to the extent that *been* is inflected as a past participle, which is associated with perfective aspect – in contrast to *be*, which is not.

2 The PF representation for (58b) actually has a viable interpretation, just not the one indicated in (58b). Consider (i).

(i)   The Dean formulated a plan to create a linguistics department after
          the Board of Trustees decided to.

(i) is viable under the interpretation rendered in (ii).

(ii)   The Dean formulated a plan to create a linguistics department after the Board of
          Trustees decided to ~~formulate a plan to create a linguistics department~~.

There is also the question of why (58a) has no corresponding viable analysis.
3 The PF representation of this example has another interpretation – namely (i).

(i)   The Board of Trustees decided to endorse the creation of a linguistics department
          after the Dean announced that she was going to ~~decide to endorse the creation of
          a linguistics department~~.

(60c) might be the more plausible interpretation, but (i) is nonetheless possible.
4 Speaker judgments may vary with these constructions. Lasnik 1999, for example, cites the
   following (p. 43, his (72) and (74)).

(i)   ?*Dulles suspected everyone Angleton wondered why Philby did.
(ii)   ??Who did Angleton wonder why Philby suspected?

The comparison is between movement of an overt interrogative pronoun in (ii) and a covert relative pronoun in (i). The minimal comparison would involve the relative clause in (i)
without VPE, hence (iii).

(iii)   *Dulles suspected everyone Angleton wondered why Philby suspected.

If (iii) is at least as deviant as (i) – the star reflects the author's judgment – then the island
effect for wh-movement holds for VPE.
5 The alternative is to register the Subjacency violation at the LF interface. See Merchant
   2001 for a treatment of some island conditions violations as LF phenomena.
6 Fox and Lasnik 2003 cite a slightly more complicated case (i).

(i)   They said they heard about a Balkan language, but I don't know which Balkan
          language they said they heard about.

In the derivation of (i), the wh-phrase would move successive cyclically through an intermediate Spec-CP, so the resulting nontrivial chain would satisfy the Subjacency Condition.
Their corresponding VPE construction (ii) is also deviant, just like (85b).

(ii)   *They said they heard about a Balkan language, but I don't know which Balkan
          language they did.

Given (i) there is another possibility for VPE involving only the most deeply embedded VP,
yielding (iii).

(iii)   *They said they heard about a Balkan language, but I don't know which Balkan
          language they said they did.

See Fox and Lasnik for a different analysis, one that concerns parallelism in LF
representations.
7 If chain reduction is just phonetic feature deletion, then the problem of nontrivial chains
   at PF could be explained on the grounds that an overt syntactic object (i.e. with phonetic
   features) can only be pronounced in one linear position. In effect, only trivial chains
   can be linearized in PF representation. See Nunes 2004; Fox and Pesetsky 2005 for
   discussion.
8 Even if the repetition in the second conjunct of (109b) is eliminated, the result still seems
   somewhat awkward.

(i)   ?Mary will cook the fish tomorrow for dinner and Bill ~~will cook~~ the potatoes next
          week for lunch.

(109b) seems worse than (i), so perhaps the repetition in the VP of the second conjunct is a
factor in ellipsis constructions.
9 See Almeida and Yoshida 2007 for discussion of these phenomena in Brazilian Portuguese.
   This article presents evidence that wh-movement can strand a preposition when it is then

deleted under sluicing, but not otherwise. One solution proposed is that for the grammar of Brazilian Portuguese, the constraint against preposition stranding operates as an output condition on PF rather than a derivational constraint. Note that there may be another related fact to be explained – namely that no language exists where overt preposition stranding is allowed, but sluicing of such constructions is blocked.

10 Ross 1969, the first syntactic analysis of these constructions, claims that they are nonetheless still marginal. Ross marks them with a ??. In most recent work on sluicing, researchers judge these constructions to be fully grammatical. See Merchant 2001 and Lasnik 2009.

11 (139) involves a coordinate structure in subject position. (i) shows that with respect to the CSC there is no distinction to be made between subjects and non-subjects (cf. subject-object asymmetries). Thus (i.a) where wh-movement is out of a non-subject position is as deviant as (139a) and the sluiced variant is equally acceptable.

(i)   a.   *Fred is collaborating with Mary and someone on a project, but
             we don't know who Fred is collaborating with Mary and on a project.
       b.   Fred is collaborating with Mary and someone on a project, but we don't know
             who.

It is worth noting here that in the literature on sluicing, an alternative syntactic source and hence the interpretation of examples like (i.b) has been discussed (cf. Merchant 2001). Thus (i.b) is essentially equivalent to (ii).

(ii)   Fred is collaborating with Mary and someone on a project, but we don't know
       who it is.

The assumption is that the TP that is sluiced is a single clause (iii).

(iii) [$_{TP}$ it is who]

This operation is called **pseudosluicing**. From the perspective of the analysis of ellipsis developed in this chapter, pseudosluicing would not meet the phonetic nondistinctness requirement for deletion. There is another potential problem. The TP (iii) contained in (ii) could itself result from sluicing, in which case (ii) would be derived from (iv).

(iv)   Fred is collaborating with Mary and someone on a project, but we don't know
       who it is that Fred is collaborating with Mary and on the project.

Thus (iv) raises the CSC issue of (i.b) and thus (ii) does not actually avoid it.

12 Note that if the interrogative pronoun *who* moves successive cyclically through the Spec-CP of the embedded CP in (140), then (140) would not be syntactically identical to TP in the first conjunct of (136), which has no element in Spec-CP. See Lasnik 2009 for additional discussion.

13 The conclusion is controversial. See Merchant 2001 for a somewhat different account where some island violations are registered at LF rather than PF.

14 This is essentially the proposal given in Chomsky 1972, where it is assumed that an island construction out of which a constituent has been moved will be marked # and further that if this marking is not deleted during the course of the derivation, the output containing it will be designated as deviant. Thus sluicing can delete #, whereas VPE does not.

15 For an alternative analysis, see Merchant 2008. Following suggestions in Merchant 2001 and Lasnik 2001, Merchant proposes a constraint MaxElide which enforces sluicing over VPE when both can apply to the same input. As formulated, MaxElide is limited to ellipsis sites containing a silent copy of a wh-phrase trace (i.e. a wh-trace). See also Merchant 2006 for additional discussion on sluicing.

Glossary

adjunct: a constituent of a phrasal projection of head that modifies that head (excluding determiners). Adjective phrases and adverb phrases are typical adjuncts, modifying nouns and verbs respectively. Prepositional phrases and CPs can also function as adjuncts as in *John slept for ten hours* and *John slept when he returned from his trip to China.*

Affix-hopping: a morphosyntactic operation by which tense and agreement features in T are attached to a main verb root that heads the VP complement of T.

anaphora: the phenomenon in which a linguistic expression (an anaphor) can stand in for another (usually more specific) expression (its antecedent). For example in *John thinks that he is clever* under the interpretation where this sentence concerns a single person, the pronoun *he* stands in for the name *John.*

antecedent contained deletion: deletion of a constituent whose antecedent syntactically contains it.

argument: (a) a NP, CP, or PP complement of V, predicate A, or nominalization related to a verb (e.g. *destruction*) or predicate adjective (e.g. *likelihood*); (b) a subject (Spec-TP or Spec-NP (e.g. *the student* in *the student's proof of the theorem*)) that is assigned a θ-role in that position. In general, arguments answer *who* and *what* questions, but never *why, how,* or *when* questions.

Argument Relatedness (θ-Relatedness): a condition on representations that each argument must be assigned an argument function/θ-role.

Argument Uniqueness (θ-Uniqueness): a condition on representations that no (nontrivial) chain can involve multiple argument functions/θ-roles. This constraint prohibits movement between two θ-positions.

Attract: an alternative formulation of internal Merge whereby the merger of a copy in a new position is motivated by a local attracting element (a probe) that targets an existing copy (a goal).

Case Filter: a condition on representations that marks a NP as deviant when it contains phonetic features and is not licensed for Case.

Case Uniqueness Constraint: a condition on representations that marks a NP-chain as deviant when it contains multiple members that are licensed for Case.

center embedded: a constituent, usually a clause, that is embedded inside another constituent of the same type which has lexical material to the left and the right of the embedded constituent.

chain: the set of copies of a constituent in a syntactic representation. If there is only one copy, then the chain is trivial. If there are multiple copies, then the chain is nontrivial.

chain link: a pair of linearly adjacent copies in a chain.

chain reduction: a species of deletion that eliminates the phonetic features of all but one of the copies in a nontrivial chain.

clause: a syntactic unit consisting of a subject and a predicate that is headed by a main V or predicate A. See also TP and CP.

complement: a constituent whose head enters into a selectional relation with the head it merges with. Thus verbs take NP, PP, and CP complements; prepositions take NP complements; predicate adjectives take PP and CP complements. In addition, C takes a TP complement and T takes a VP complement. Nonfinite auxiliary verbs also take VP as a complement. The complements of verbs and adjectives, and their corresponding nominalizations, are arguments and thus assigned a semantic function (θ-role) by the verb, adjective, or nominal.

complementizer: a subordinating particle labeled C that takes a TP as a complement and therefore selects T. There are two sorts of complementizer, interrogative and non-interrogative. Overt non-interrogative complementizers in English are either finite (*that*) or infinitival (*for*). The overt interrogative complementizers in English are *if* and *whether*.

complementizer phrase (CP): a phrase that has a C element (e.g. a subordinating particle, or a displaced verbal element in a direct yes/no question) as a head and takes TP as a complement.

Complex NP Constraint (CNPC): a constraint on the application of internal Merge that prohibits the movement of a constituent contained in a clause embedded in a NP to a position outside that NP.

computational system of human language (C_{HL}): the mechanisms, principles, and parameters that determine the syntactic structure of languages.

configurational property for ellipsis: the relation between an ellipsis site and its antecedent in terms of their syntactic relation.

conjunct: a constituent that is joined to another by a conjunction.

Constituency Constraint on Conjuncts: the requirement that a conjunct must form a single constituent.

constituent: a lexical item that forms a part of a linguistic expression, or a grouping of such parts.

constituent-command (c-command): the relation between two constituents such that A c-commands B if and only if B is the sister of A or B is a descendent of (dominated by) a sister of A.

coordinate construction: a constituent containing two or more subparts (conjuncts) that are joined together with a conjunction (e.g. *and* or *or*).

Coordinate Structure Constraint (CSC): a constraint on the application of internal Merge that prohibits the movement of a constituent out of a coordinate structure in which it functions as a subpart of one of the conjuncts.

creative aspect of language use: the characteristic properties of language use: being unbounded, innovative, stimulus-free, coherent, and appropriate to the situation. The first two follow from recursive Merge. The second connects to the problem of free will. The latter two constitute Descartes' Problem, which, when Descartes recognized they couldn't be explained in terms of mechanical models, led him to postulate "mind" as a second substance distinct from "body."

deletion: the process that eliminates phonetic features in a derivation.

derivation: the ordered set of steps from which the PF and LF of a linguistic expression are constructed.

determiner: essentially what in traditional grammar is called an article. This covers indefinites (e.g. *a* and *an*) and definites (e.g. *the* and the demonstratives *this*, *that*, *these*, and *those*).

displacement property: the linguistic property of human languages in which a constituent that is pronounced in one syntactic position (at PF) is interpreted in a different syntactic position (at LF).

dominance: the relation between a category label of a constituent and the category labels of the constituents it contains.

***do*-Support:** a morphosyntactic operation specific to English that adjoins a semantically empty auxiliary root *do* to stranded tense and agreement features when affix-hopping cannot apply. This operation prevents a derivation from violating the NFAC.

E-language: a characterization of a language that makes no direct reference to the mind of the speaker.

economy of derivation: the preference for derivations with fewest steps.

elementary operation: a basic operation that derives LF and PF representations: Merge and Delete.

ellipsis site: a deleted construct that is silent in PF but has the specific interpretation of its antecedent in LF.

endocentric: the property of a constituent that has a distinct head.

Exceptional Case Marking (ECM): a phenomenon where the overt Spec of an infinitival TP is licensed for (abstract) Case by some element outside that TP. In English there are two cases, one where the overt Spec-TP is adjacent to a verb (e.g. *They expect Mary to help them*) and another where the overt Spec-TP is adjacent to a *for* complementizer (e.g. *For Mary to have forgotten is unusual*).

exocentric: the property of a constituent that has no distinct head.

Extended Projection Principle (EPP): a requirement that every TP must have a Spec in its syntactic representation.

external Merge: the operation of Merge in a derivation that first groups constituents together.

First Miracle of Language Acquisition: the transformation of the continuous overt sound waves that constitute primary language data into structured linguistic representations (PF and LF) with their discrete parts, covert as well as overt.

Full Interpretation (FI): a constraint on the economy of representations that prohibits superfluous symbols in interface representations (e.g. phonetic features at LF and semantic features at PF). Thus FI requires Spell-Out.

gapping: a form of deletion that eliminates T+V in certain coordinate constructions under certain conditions.

generative grammar: any explicit formulation of the processes and principles of a grammar.

grammar: the computational system of human language plus a lexicon (see also I-language).

grammatical: the property of a linguistic expression that conforms to the principles and processes of the grammar.

grouping: one function of Merge that concatenates two or more constituents to form a single new constituent.

head: the lexical item that projects its label onto the constituent that contains it.

head movement: displacement involving two head positions.

Head Movement Constraint (HMC): a constraint on the movement of a head such that a head can only move to the closest c-commanding head position – i.e. the head that selects it.

head of a chain: the copy in a chain that c-commands the other copies. The tail of a chain is the copy that c-commands no other copies.

Head Parameter: a parameter that determines the linear order of a head and its complements. Most languages involve a single setting whereby all head-complement phrases are either head-initial or head-final.

hierarchical structure: the structure created by grouping a linear string of lexical items into constituents.

I-language: a computational system plus a lexicon (i.e. a grammar) in the mind of a speaker. "I" stands for internal and individual.

immediate dominance: a constituent A immediately dominates a constituent B if and only if B is dominated by A and not dominated by any other constituent that A dominates.

imperative sentence: a sentence which expresses a command, usually with a covert subject "you."

Inclusiveness Condition: a constraint that limits syntactic representations to elements that exist in the lexical entries of the lexicon.

indicative sentence: a sentence which expresses a statement.

interface levels: the levels of linguistic representation that interface with other cognitive components – i.e. PF and LF.

internal Merge: the operation of Merge in a derivation that creates an additional context for a constituent that already has a context via the operation of external Merge. Internal Merge creates copies, i.e. multiple contexts for a single constituent.

interrogative clause: a clause which expresses a question (either a yes/no question or a wh-question). Root (or main) clause interrogatives constitute direct questions. Embedded (hence subordinate) interrogatives constitute indirect questions.

label: the syntactic category that serves as the name of a constituent.

labeling: one function of Merge that projects the label of the head.

language faculty: the cognitive component of the human mind that is specific to language.

lexical ambiguity: the property of a linguistic expression in which the phonetic form of a single word can map onto two distinct interpretations. For example, *fish,* which can be interpreted as either a singular or plural noun or a verb (indicative or imperative).

lexical insertion: the process by which lexical items from the lexicon are introduced into derivations. This results from the application of Merge to lexical items.

lexical item: an individual entry in the mental lexicon of a speaker.

lexicon: the set of lexical items in the mind of the speaker.

LF-copying: an analysis of ellipsis constructions that does not involve deletion. Instead, the ellipsis site is posited as an empty maximal projection that is then filled in LF by a copy of its antecedent.

LF representation criterion: the hypothesis that two linguistic expressions that have the same interpretation but different phonetic representations will have the same LF.

linearization: the process by which constituents are assigned a single linear order in PF; one result of chain reduction.

Logical Form (LF): the linguistic representation that interfaces with the conceptual-intentional components of cognition, involving syntactic structure and semantic features (but not phonetic features).

matching property for ellipsis: the relation between an ellipsis site and its antecedent in terms of their phonetic content and syntactic structure.

maximal phrasal projection: the highest level of phrasal projection of a head.

Merge: the grammatical mechanism that creates constituent structure representations, consisting of two functions: grouping and labeling. Unconstrained, it is a recursive procedure that applies to its own output. It is the one and only structure-building grammatical process.

Minimal Link Condition (MLC): a constraint on internal Merge where a probe attracts only the closest goal and thereby creates the smallest links in nontrivial chains. See Attract.

morpheme: the identifiable subunits that compose words and which are associated with specific distinct interpretations. For example, the verb *walked* can be subdivided into two morphemes, the verbal root *walk* and the past tense affix *–ed*.

movement: the syntactic process in which Merge creates additional contexts for a single constituent resulting in multiple copies (see chain).

No Free Affix Condition (NFAC): a constraint on PF that prohibits an affix that is not attached to a stem.

No Tampering Condition (NTC): a constraint on the application of Merge that prevents Merge from altering the internal structure of the two syntactic objects it groups together.

nonrestrictive relative clause: a relative clause that provides information about the noun it modifies but applies to all such nouns. For example, in *bank presidents who live in mansions*, the nonrestrictive interpretation of the relative clause entails that all bank presidents live in mansions. The restrictive interpretation entails that there are bank presidents who do not live in mansions.

novel utterance: a linguistic expression recognized as legitimate that is new to the experience of the speaker.

order of Merge: a head merges first with its complements, then with its adjuncts, and finally with its specifier.

parameter: a limited set of choices for linguistic variation along a specific dimension. For example, V to T movement, which is not possible in English, is possible in French.

Phonetic Form (PF): the linguistic representation that interfaces with the sensory-motor components of cognition, involving syntactic structure and phonetic features (but not semantic features).

phrasal projection of a head: a phrasal constituent that bears the label of its head.

pied-piping: a phenomenon involving the displacement of a wh-phrase where non-wh elements syntactically linked to an interrogative element are also displaced. For example, in the question *how angry at them were you?* The string *angry at them* is pied-piped along with the interrogative *how*.

primary language data (PLD): the linguistic expressions that a child is exposed to prior to the acquisition of an I-language.

projection: the phenomenon where the category label of a constituent is projected as the category label of the constituent that contains it.

projection problem: the problem of projecting the finite and heterogeneous PLD onto the infinite and homogeneous I-language acquired.

pseudogapping: a variation of VP ellipsis where a direct object is displaced out of VP and then the remainder of the VP is deleted.

raising: the syntactic phenomenon in which a constituent is moved interclausally from a subordinate clause to a (matrix) clause that contains it.

recursion: the phenomenon in which a constituent can recur as a subpart of a larger constituent of the same type (with the same label). Also, the phenomenon where an operation applies to its own output.

recursive structure: a syntactic constituent that contains a constituent with the same label as a subpart.

reduced relative clause: a relative clause that lacks both a clause initial complementizer and a relative pronoun (e.g. the boldfaced relative clause in *books **he refuses to read***).

relative clause: a clause structure that functions as the modifier of a noun.

restrictive relative clause: a relative clause that limits the reference of the noun it modifies to the subset of such nouns it characterizes (e.g. the boldfaced relative clause in *bankers **that live in mansions***).

scope: the syntactic domain to which a modifier applies. Generally this domain can be defined as the one in which the modifier c-commands the element it modifies. (See c-command.)

selection: a head-to-head relation where the features of the head of a complement must satisfy the requirements of the head to which it is a complement. For example, the finite complementizer *that* selects finite T as the head of its TP complement.

Semantic Parallelism Constraint: the requirement that the conjuncts in a coordinate structure must perform the same semantic function.

sister: the relation between two constituents that are immediately dominated by the same constituent, thus the relation between two constituents that are directly joined together by Merge.

sluicing: deletion of TP in certain configurations and under certain conditions.

specifier: In NP, the determiner functions as the specifier and enters into a Spec-head relation with the head N it modifies and thus is merged last as a constituent of NP. In finite TP, the subject NP enters into a Spec-head relation with T and thus is merged last as a constituent of TP – i.e. as Spec-TP. This generalizes to nonfinite TP. In CP, a wh-phrase functions as a Spec-CP. In each case, the specifier (when it occurs) is an immediate constituent of the maximal phrasal projection of its head (N, T, or C).

Specifier-Head Agreement: the requirement that the features of a specifier must match the feature values of its head where they share the same features.

Spell-Out: the point in a derivation where phonetic and semantic features are segregated onto distinct derivational paths. Phonetic features are excluded from the derivation of LF and semantic features are excluded from the derivation of PF.

split-inflection analysis: an analysis of verbal morphology in which tense and agreement features constitute separate and independent heads of phrases (T and AGR).

structural ambiguity: the property of a linguistic expression for which a single phonetic representation maps onto two distinct LF representations in which the semantic interpretations of the individual lexical elements remain the same. For example, *the review of a book by three professors*.

subcategorization feature: a contextual feature of a head that specifies the syntactic categories of the complements that the head can occur with. For example, *mention* requires either a NP or clausal complement and may contain a PP complement. Therefore it has a subcategorization feature [+__ (PP) {NP, CP}].

Subjacency Condition: a constraint on chains such that the pair of members in each link of a nontrivial chain must be subjacent.

subjacent: a relation between two syntactic positions that does not cross more than one bounding category (e.g. TP in English).

subject/object asymmetry: any phenomenon in language where the constraints on subjects differ from the constraints on objects. For example, wh-displacement in

English from subject position in the presence of *that* complementizer is prohibited whereas the same displacement from object position in VP is not.

successive cyclic movement: movement that applies locally to successively larger domains to achieve a long distance movement result.

superior: a relation between constituents where one asymmetrically c-commands the other. The c-commanding constituent is superior with respect to the constituent it c-commands.

Superiority Condition: a constraint on the application of internal Merge that limits application to the superior constituent when two distinct target constituents are otherwise available.

syntactic island: a syntactic construction out of which movement is prohibited.

Syntactic Symmetry Constraint: the requirement that the conjuncts in a coordinate structure must bear the same syntactic label.

tense phrase (TP): a phrase that has a T element (e.g. infinitival *to*, finite auxiliary) as a head, takes VP as a complement and is itself a complement of C.

that-**trace filter:** a filter that prohibits a TP complement of C *that* which contains a silent copy of a wh-phrase in Spec-TP.

thematic relation/ θ-role: the semantic function that a predicate assigns to each of its arguments.

θ-Criterion: Every argument must be assigned one and only one θ-role; every θ-role of a predicate must be assigned to one and only one argument.

θ-position: the position to which an argument function is assigned by a predicate.

topicalization: a process in which a non-interrogative constituent is displaced to clause initial position in an indicative construction. Also, the construction that results from this process.

trace: a silent copy of a constituent. This term is used primarily in a framework where movement operations leave behind empty categories, which is not possible with Merge.

unacceptable: the property of a linguistic expression such that native speakers reject the expression as being a legitimate part of their language.

Unique Assignment of Argument Functions: Each argument function of a predicate can only be assigned once.

Universal Grammar (UG): the initial state of the language faculty; therefore the innate mental linguistic structure that every human is born with as part of human genetic endowment and thus is universal across the species. UG contains the processes and general principles that determine the structure of linguistic expressions.

VP ellipsis (VPE): deletion of VP in certain configurations and under certain conditions.

VP-internal subject hypothesis: an analysis in which the subject of a clause is first merged as a constituent of VP.

Wh-island: a TP complement of a C whose Spec contains a wh-phrase.

wh-movement: an application of internal Merge that produces nontrivial chains containing wh-phrases as members.

wh-phrase: a constituent (NP, PP, or AP) containing an interrogative element or relative pronoun that can undergo displacement to form a wh-question or relative clause.

wh-question: a direct or indirect question containing an interrogative wh-phrase in Spec-CP.

***whether*-island:** a TP complement of C *whether*.

References

Almeida, D. and M. Yoshida 2007. A problem for the Preposition Stranding Generalization. *Linguistic Inquiry*, 38, 349–362.

Baker, M. 2001. *Atoms of Language*, New York: Basic Books.

Boeckx, C. 2010. *Language in Cognition: Uncovering Mental Structures and the Rules Behind Them*, Chichester: Wiley-Blackwell.

Borsley, R., M. Tallerman, and D. Willis 2007. *The Syntax of Welsh*, Cambridge University Press.

Chomsky, N. 1957. *Syntactic Structures,* The Hague: Mouton.

    1964. *Current Issues in Linguistic Theory*, The Hague: Mouton.

    1965. *Aspects of the Theory of Syntax*, Cambridge, MA: MIT Press.

    1970. Remarks on nominalization. *In:* R. A. Jacobs and P. S. Rosenbaum (eds.) *Readings in English Transformational Grammar*. Waltham, MA: Ginn and Co.

    1972. Some empirical issues in the theory of transformational grammar. *In:* P. S. Peters (ed.) *Goals of linguistic theory*. Englewood Cliffs, NJ: Prentice-Hall Inc.

    1973. Conditions on transformations. *In:* S. Anderson and P. Kiparsky (eds.) *A festschrift for Morris Halle*. New York: Holt, Rinehart and Winston.

    1975. *The Logical Structure of Linguistic Theory*, New York: Plenum.

    1977. On *wh*-movement. *In:* P. Culicover, T. Wasow, and A. Akmajian (eds.) *Formal Syntax*. New York: Academic Press.

    1980. On binding. *Linguistic Inquiry*, 11, 1–46.

    1981a. Principles and parameters in syntactic theory. *In:* N. Hornstein and D. Lightfoot (eds.) *Explanation in Linguistics*. London: Routledge.

    1981b. *Lectures on Government and Binding*, Dordrecht: Foris.

    1982. *Some Concepts and Consequences of the Theory of Government and Binding*, Cambridge, MA: MIT Press.

    1986. *Knowledge of Language*, New York: Praeger.

    1988. *Language and problems of knowledge*, Cambridge, MA: MIT Press.

    1991. Some notes on economy of derivation and representation. *In:* R. Freidin (ed.) *Principles and Parameters in Comparative Grammar*. Cambridge, MA: MIT Press.

    1993. A minimalist program for linguistic theory. *In*: K. Hale and S.J. Keyser (eds.) *The View from Building 20: Essays in Linguistics in Honor of Sylvain Bromberger*. Cambridge, MA: MIT Press.

1995a. Bare phrase structure. *In:* H. Campos and P. Kempchinsky (eds.) *Evolution and Revolution in Linguistic Theory*. Washington, DC: Georgetown University Press.

1995b. *The Minimalist Program*, Cambridge, MA: MIT Press.

2000a. Minimalist inquiries: the framework. *In:* R. Martin, D. Michaels, and J. Uriagereka (eds.) *Step by Step: Essays on Minimalist Syntax in Honor of Howard Lasnik*. Cambridge, MA: MIT Press.

2000b. *New Horizons in the Study of Language and Mind*, Cambridge University Press.

2005. Three factors in language design. *Linguistic Inquiry*, 36, 1–22.

2006. *Language and Mind*, 3rd edition. Cambridge University Press.

2007. Approaching UG from below. *In:* U. Sauerland and H.-M. Gärtner (eds.) *Interfaces + Recursion = Language? Chomsky's Minimalism and the View from Syntax-Semantics*. Berlin: Mouton de Gruyter.

2008. On phases. *In:* R. Freidin, C. Otero, and M-L. Zubizarreta (eds.) *Foundational Issues in Linguistic Theory*. Cambridge, MA: MIT Press.

2009. *Cartesian Linguistics: A Chapter in the History of Rationalist Thought,* 3rd edition. Cambridge University Press.

Chomsky, N and H. Lasnik 1977. Filters and control. *Linguistic Inquiry*, 8, 425–504.

Chung, S., W. Ladusaw, and J. McCloskey 1995. Sluicing and Logical Form. *Natural Language Semantics*, 3, 1–44.

Collins, C. 2002. Eliminating labels. *In:* S. D. Epstein and D. Seely (eds.) *Derivation and Explanation in the Minimalist Program*. Oxford: Blackwell.

Cowie, F. 1999. *What's Within?: Nativism Reconsidered*, Oxford University Press.

Culicover, P. 1976. A constraint on coreferentiality. *Foundations of Language*, 14, 109–118.

Descartes, R. 1911. *The Philosophical Works of Descartes*, Cambridge University Press.

Fiengo, R. and R. May 1994. *Indices and Identity*, Cambridge, MA: MIT Press.

Fox, D. and H. Lasnik 2003. Successive cyclic movement and island repair: The difference between Sluicing and VP Ellipsis. *Linguistic Inquiry*, 34, 143–154.

Fox, D. and D. Pesetsky 2005. Cyclic linearization of syntactic structure. *Theoretical Linguistics*, 31, 1–46.

Freidin, R. 1975. The analysis of passives. *Language*, 51, 384–405.

1978. Cyclicity and the theory of grammar. *Linguistic Inquiry*, 9, 519–549.

1986. Fundamental issues in the theory of binding. *In:* B. Lust (ed.) *Studies in the Acquisition of Anaphora*. Dordrecht: Reidel.

1992. *Foundations of Generative Syntax*, Cambridge, MA: MIT Press.

1999. Cyclicity and minimalism. *In:* S. D. Epstein and N. Hornstein (eds.) *Working Minimalism*. Cambridge, MA: MIT Press.

2004. *Syntactic Structures* Redux. *Syntax*, 7, 100–126.

Fukui, N. 1986. A theory of category projection and its application. Doctoral dissertation, MIT. Revised version published as *Theory of Projection in Syntax*, Cambridge University Press and Stanford, CA: CSLI Publications, 1995.

Goldberg, A. 2006. *Constructions at Work: The Nature of Generalization in Language*, New York: Oxford University Press.

Greenberg, J. 1966. Some universals of grammar with particular reference to the order of meaningful elements. *In:* J. Greenberg (ed.) *Universals of Language*. Cambridge, MA: MIT Press.

Gruber, J. 1965. Studies in lexical relations. Doctoral dissertation, MIT.

Haegeman, L. and R. Zannutini 1991. Negative heads and the neg criterion. *The Linguistic Review*, 8, 233–251.

Hauser, M., N. Chomsky, and T. Fitch 2002. The faculty of language: what is it, who has it, and how did it evolve? *Science*, 298, 1569–1579.

Huang, C.-T. J. 1981. Move *wh* in a language without *wh*-movement. *The Linguistic Review*, 1, 369–416.

Jackendoff, R. 1969. Some rules of semantic interpretation for English. Doctoral dissertation, MIT.

　1972. *Semantic Interpretation in Generative Grammar*, Cambridge, MA: MIT Press.

　2010. *Meaning and the Lexicon: The Parallel Architecture 1975–2010*, Oxford University Press.

Johnson, K. 2001. What VP ellipsis can do and what it can't do but not why. *In:* C. Collins and M. Baltin (eds.) *The Handbook of Contemporary Syntactic Theory*. Oxford: Blackwell.

　2009. Gapping is not (VP) ellipsis. *Linguistic Inquiry*, 40, 289–328.

Kayne, R. 1984. *Connectedness and Binary Branching*, Dordrecht: Foris.

　1994. *The Antisymmetry of Syntax*, Cambridge, MA: MIT Press.

Klima, E. 1964. Negation in English. *In:* J. Fodor and J. Katz (eds.) *Readings in the Structure of Language*. Englewood Cliffs, NJ: Prentice-Hall.

Koizumi, M. 1995. Phrase structure in minimalist syntax. Doctoral dissertation, MIT.

　2006. The split VP hypothesis. *In:* R. Freidin and H. Lasnik (eds.) *Syntax: Critical concepts*, vol. I. London: Routledge [excerpt from Koizumi 1995].

Koster, J. 1978. *Locality Principles in Syntax*, Dordrecht: Foris.

Larson, R., V. Déprez, and H. Yamakido (eds.) 2010. *The Evolution of Human Language: Biolinguistic Perspectives*, Cambridge University Press.

Lasnik, H. 1981. Restricting the theory of transformations: A case study. *In:* N. Hornstein and D. Lightfoot (eds.) *Explanation in Linguistics*. London: Longmans.

　1989. *Essays on Anaphora*, Dordrecht: Kluwer.

　1999. *Minimalist Analysis*, Oxford: Blackwell.

　2000. *Syntactic Structures Revisited: Contemporary Lectures on Classic Transformational Theory*, Cambridge, MA: MIT Press.

　2001. A note on the EPP. *Linguistic Inquiry*, 32, 356–362.

　2003. Pseudogapping puzzles. *In:* H. Lasnik, *Minimalist Investigations in Linguistic Theory*. London: Routledge.

　2006. Conceptions of the Cycle. *In:* L. Chen and N. Corver (eds.) *Wh-Movement: Moving On*. Cambridge, MA: MIT Press.

2007. On ellipsis: the PF approach to missing constituents. *University of Maryland Working Papers in Linguistics*, 15, 146–157.

2008. On the development of Case theory: Triumphs and challenges. *In:* R. Freidin, C. Otero, M.-L. Zubizarreta (eds.) *Foundational Issues in Linguistic Theory.* Cambridge, MA: MIT Press.

2009. Island repair, non-repair and the organization of the grammar. *In:* K. Grohmann (ed.) *InterPhases: Phase-Theoretic Investigations of Linguistic Interfaces.* Oxford University Press.

Lavine, J. and R. Freidin 2002. The subject of defective T(ense) in Slavic. *Journal of Slavic Linguistics*, 10, 251–287.

Legate, J. 2007. Morphological and Abstract Case. *Linguistic Inquiry*, 39, 55–101.

Manzini, R. 1983. Restructuring and reanalysis. Doctoral dissertation, MIT.

Marantz, A., Y. Miyashita, W. O'Neil 2000. *Image, Language, Brain: Papers from the First Mind Articulation Project Symposium*, Cambridge, MA: MIT Press.

McCloskey, J. 2002. Resumption, successive cyclicity, and the locality of operations. *In:* S. D. Epstein and D. Seeley (eds.) *Derivation and Explanation in the Minimalist Program.* Oxford: Blackwell.

Merchant, J. 2001. *The Syntax of Silence: Sluicing, Islands, and the Theory of Ellipsis*, Oxford University Press.

2006. Sluicing. *In:* M. Everaert and H. van Riemsdijk (eds.) *The Blackwell Companion to Syntax.* Oxford: Blackwell.

2008. Variable island repair under ellipsis. *In:* K. Johnson (ed.) *Topics in Ellipsis.* Cambridge University Press.

Nunes, J. 2004. *Linearization of Chains and Sideward Movement*, Cambridge, MA: MIT Press.

Pesetsky, D. 1981. Complementizer-trace phenomena and the nominative island condition. *The Linguistic Review*, 1, 297–343.

Poeppel, D. and D. Embick 2005. Defining the relation between linguistics and neuroscience. *In:* A. Cutler (ed.) *Twenty-first Century Psycholinguistics: Four Cornerstones.* Mahwah, NJ: Lawrence Erlbaum Associates.

Poeppel, D. and G. Hickok 2004. Towards a new functional anatomy of language. *Cognition*, 92, 1–12.

Pollock, J.-Y. 1989. Verb movement, universal grammar, and the structure of IP. *Linguistic Inquiry*, 20, 365–424.

Quicoli, A. C. 1996. Inflection and parametric variation: Portuguese vs. Spanish. *In:* R. Freidin (ed.) *Current Issues in Comparative Grammar.* Dordrect: Kluwer.

Radford, A. 2009. *Analyzing English Sentences: A Minimalist Approach*, Cambridge University Press.

Reimsdijk, H. van 2006. Grafts follow from Merge. *In:* M. Frascarelli (ed.) *Phases of Interpretation.* Berlin: Mouton de Gruyter, 17–44.

Reinhart, T. 1976. The syntactic domain of anaphora. Doctoral dissertation, MIT.

Rizzi, L. 1980. Violations of the *wh*-island constraint and the Subjacency condition. *Journal of Italian Linguistics*, 5, 157–195.

1982. *Issues in Italian syntax*, Dordrecht: Foris.

1990. *Relativized Minimality*, Cambridge, MA: MIT Press.

Roberts, I. 1997. *Comparative Syntax*, London: Arnold.

2000. Head movement. *In:* C. Collins and M. Baltin (eds.) *Handbook of Contemporary Syntactic Theory*. Oxford: Blackwell.

2010. *Agreement and Head Movement*, MIT Press.

Ross, J. R. 1967. *Constraints on variables in syntax*. Doctoral dissertation, MIT.

1969. Guess who? *In:* R. I. Binnick, A. Davison, G. M. Green, and J. L. Morgan (eds.) Papers from the Fifth Regional Meeting of the Chicago Linguistic Society, 1969 Chicago, Ill.: Chicago Linguistic Society, University of Chicago, 252–286.

1984. *Infinite Syntax*, Norwood, NJ: ABLEX.

Speas, M. 1986. Adjunctions and projections in syntax. Doctoral dissertation, MIT.

Sportiche, D. 1981. Bounding nodes in French. *The Linguistic Review*, 1, 219–246.

Sprouse, J. 2007. A program for experimental syntax: finding the relationship between acceptability and grammatical knowledge. Doctoral dissertation, University of Maryland.

Stowell, T. 1978. What was there before there was there. *In:* D. Farkas, W. Jacobsen, and K. Todrys (eds.) Papers from the 14th Regional Meeting, Chicago Linguistic Society: 458–471. Reprinted in R. Freidin, and H. Lasnik (eds.) *Syntax: Critical Concepts*, vol. III. New York: Routledge, 2006.

Takano, Y. 1995. Predicate fronting and internal subjects. *Linguistic Inquiry*, 26, 327–340.

Tallerman, M. 2005. The Celtic languages. *In:* G. Cinque and R. Kayne (eds.) *Oxford Handbook of Comparative Syntax*, Chapter 19. Oxford University Press.

Tomasello, M. 2003. *Constructing a Language: A Usage-based Theory of Language Acquisition*, Cambridge, MA: Harvard University Press.

Torrego, E. 1984. On inversion in Spanish and some of its effects. *Linguistic Inquiry*, 15, 103–129.

Travis, L. 1984. Parameters and the effects of word order variation. Doctoral dissertation, MIT.

Vergnaud, J.-R. 1977/2008. Personal letter to Howard Lasnik and Noam Chomsky. *In:* R. Freidin, C. Otero, and M.-L. Zubizarreta (eds.) *Foundational Issues in Linguistic Theory*. Cambridge, MA: MIT Press.

Watanabe. A. 1992. Subjacency and S-structure movement of *WH*-in-situ. *Journal of East Asian Linguistics*, 1, 255–291.

Wilkins, W. 1977. The variable interpretation convention. Doctoral dissertation, UCLA.

Williams, E. 1977. Discourse and logical form. *Linguistic Inquiry*, 8, 101–139.

Yang, C. 2002. *Knowledge and Learning in Natural Language*, Oxford University Press.

2006. *The Infinite Gift : How Children Learn and Unlearn the Languages of the World*. New York: Scribner.

Index